Regionalism

in America

This Volume Is Published in Celebration of the
HUNDREDTH ANNIVERSARY
of the Founding of the University of Wisconsin

★ THE CONTRIBUTORS

Vernon Carstensen
John W. Caughey
Gordon R. Clapp
Merle Curti
John M. Gaus
William B. Hesseltine
Merrill Jensen
John Fabian Kienitz
Hans Kurath
Fulmer Mood
Rexford Newcomb
Howard W. Odum
Lancaster Pollard
E. P. Richardson
Walter A. Rowlands
Francis Butler Simkins
Benjamin T. Spencer
Elmer Starch
Rupert B. Vance
Louis Wirth

REGIONALISM

*IN AMERICA

Edited by MERRILL JENSEN
with a Foreword by Felix Frankfurter

Madison ★ 1952

The University of Wisconsin Press

COPYRIGHT 1951 BY
THE REGENTS OF THE UNIVERSITY OF WISCONSIN

SECOND PRINTING, 1952

PRINTED IN THE UNITED STATES OF AMERICA BY
THE WILLIAM BYRD PRESS, INC., RICHMOND, VIRGINIA

Editor's Preface

THE papers included in this volume were delivered at a symposium on American regionalism held at the University of Wisconsin April 14 and 15, 1949. This symposium was sponsored by the Committee on the Study of American Civilization, of the University of Wisconsin, a committee appointed to administer a grant of funds from the Rockefeller Foundation. The purpose of the grant was to encourage research and teaching in the field of American civilization, and the Committee undertook to make an intensive study of the "Wisconsin Region."

From the outset an obvious problem was to define the area within which to limit the work of the Committee. It was plain that the concept of "region" meant different things to different academic disciplines, to administrators of state and federal governments, and to executives of great industrial and financial organizations. In other words, the nature of a "region" varies with the needs, purposes, and standards of those using the concept.

Such being the case, we believed that it would be worth while to bring together men from various academic fields and from public life who had in common the fact that they were concerned with regionalism, either as a field of research or as a matter of practical administration. We did not expect to arrive at any common definition of a region, or even to agree upon a set of criteria by which a region could be described. We did, however, expect to show the great variety of approaches to regionalism and its utility both as a tool for research and as an approach to problems of public administration. The contents of this volume illustrate how our expectations were fulfilled.

Part I is an account of the development and use of the concept of regionalism from its historic beginnings in the eighteenth century down to the present day, both as a tool of research and as a practical force in the political and economic administration of national affairs.

Part II is an account of three of the historic regions of the United States. Obviously it would have been desirable to have a discussion of more regions, but time and space were limiting factors. Therefore we chose the oldest region, the Old South; one of the oldest and yet one of the newest, the Spanish Southwest; and the one truly new region of the United States, the Pacific Northwest. The contributors to this section were asked to consider as many factors as possible— geographic, economic, technological—and to discuss the relations of their regions with other regions and with the nation as a whole.

Part III deals with regionalism in American culture. When viewed from the vantage point of American literature, architecture, painting, and linguistics, regionalism takes on a breadth and depth which adds much to the approaches of historians and sociologists who have dominated most of the writing and thinking in the field of regional studies.

Part IV consists of contributions by men who have dealt with regionalism as a practical concept in the development and administration of government programs. We have here an account of a regional program in successful operation, the Tennessee Valley Authority; a study of a highly specialized regional problem, the Great Lakes cutover area; and an analysis of the background of a projected regional program, the Missouri Valley plan.

The volume concludes with the papers of two scholars who disagree on the value of the whole concept of regionalism as a tool for research, as a method of interpretation, and as a program of public administration.

It is plain from the papers in this volume that the regional concept is a complex one that cannot be reduced to simple formulas. On the other hand, its very complexity makes it a flexible tool for research in a great variety of areas and for the organization and administration of day-to-day public affairs. So far as this volume is a demonstration of this proposition, it should be of value to men in many fields of academic and public life.

The Committee is happy to acknowledge the grant of funds from the Wisconsin Centennial Commission which made it possible to bring scholars here from all over the United States. It is likewise grateful to the chairmen of the various sessions of the symposium who have written introductions and who assisted in preparing the papers for publication.

MERRILL JENSEN

Madison
April 16, 1951

Contents

Foreword

FOR a nonspecialist to praise the work of scholars implies a bit of impertinence. My justification for venturing to greet this collection of essays is that the Supreme Bench affords unparalleled opportunities for realizing that the contributors to this volume have cast illumination from their different angles upon our basic internal problem. For the concern underlying all these essays is how a country that is a continent can be governed by organs that fairly represent its disciplined will and at the same time adequately evoke the diverse civilized potentialities of its people.

With the exception of regionalism in architecture and in painting, all the phases of regionalism treated by these scholars as intellectual issues have made themselves felt in adjudications before the Supreme Court. To be sure, the social, economic, and cultural influences and needs comprised by regionalism usually do not appear in litigation with candid impact. But they are there, if at times only in the interstices of legal records. Through these too often dreary proceedings there emerge precisely those considerations of homogeneous diversities within the nation that do not correspond to the division between the Union and the forty-eight states. There are organic developments other than the nation and its constituent states that press for expression through various forms: through national legislation recognizing regional differences, through the constitutional device of compact among different combinations of states to meet different needs, through various informal arrangements among states, through legal uniformities of one sort or another, and through all the multiform recognitions of need for institutionalizing the harmonies and common interests and feelings within different regions.

The prescience of the founders of this country happily did not preclude the devising of these regional arrangements. They did not make the whole life of the people flow exclusively through national or through state organs. The vast and variegated resources of a nation lying between the Atlantic and the Pacific—above all, the rich resources within the people themselves—were not denied opportunities for resourcefulness in making a unity out of diversities apart from the Union of the states.

Not the least important lesson of these essays is that regionalism is not just another name for the political device of decentralization. It is not a delegation of authority from above. Regionalism is a recognition of the intractable diversities among men, diversities partly shaped by nature but no less derived from the different reactions of men to nature. And since man takes increasing liberties with nature, regionalism is not a fixed concept. No region, whether natural or cultural, is stable. At bottom, the problems of American regionalism are the problems of American civilization: the continuous process of bringing to fruition the best of which American men and women are capable.

It is because such is the concern of this book and because illuminating scholarship has been spent on it that I hope for it the wide attention its importance deserves.

FELIX FRANKFURTER

Washington
April 30, 1951

Part I

The Concept of Regionalism
Its History and Application

Introduction

Merrill Jensen

THE widespread use of the regional-sectional concept during the past few decades, especially by scholars and teachers in the social sciences, has tended to blind them to the fact that the concept had widespread use long before there was a generally accepted label for it. Consequently, the vast number of books and articles dealing with regional questions have often lacked a depth of perspective and hence a significance they might otherwise have had.

It is well, therefore, that a symposium on regionalism in America should begin with two papers which trace the development of the concept from the middle of the eighteenth century down to the present. As the first paper shows, the concept is rooted in the British colonies in the New World. Geography, economic life, and social traditions produced clearly recognizable regional groups such as the New England Colonies, the West Indian Colonies, and the Southern Colonies. These differences were recognized by administrators of the British Empire and by the colonists themselves, and they resulted in clashing interests and in differing legislation by Parliament and the colonial legislatures. Such regional differences and conflicts are a significant factor in the history of the United States from 1776 onwards. They are described by the "father of American geography," Jedidiah Morse, and by other geographers who followed him. As the United States grew, its government recognized the existence of regions or sections as a matter of course. In fact, it could not have avoided such recognition. Thus judicial and military districts were organized along regional lines. Census takers from 1790 onwards wrestled with the problem of organizing their data around regional-sectional concepts in order to give that data significance. By 1860 the term "section" was in common use. Meanwhile geographers worked to establish regional patterns. Eventually Frederick Jackson Turner adopted the concept and gave it wide currency in his studies of the process of American history.

The second paper shows how the regional concept has had ever widening use since 1900. Government agencies and bureaus organized on a regional basis have multiplied so rapidly that we have over a hundred regional schemes in use by various governmental groups. Businesses, ranging all the way from mail-order houses to vast oil companies, have set up regional organizations suited to their purposes. Scholars in the social sciences have divided and redivided the United States into a host of regions, the boundaries of which vary with the purposes and the criteria chosen. Scholars have continued to debate terminology without arriving at any general agreement on the precise content of the terms "regional" and "sectional," nor can they agree which of the two terms should be used, or whether they should be used interchangeably.

The problems involved in using the regional concept as a tool for research in the social sciences are set forth in the final paper of this section. Here there is sound advice and a warning to those who in their enthusiasm for a new idea seize upon the concept and use it without realizing the necessity for an adequate theoretical background, or without being aware of the complexities implicit in making a valid regional analysis.

The papers, taken together, give background for regional studies and provide sound guidance to those who undertake them. The subsequent papers in this volume may be related to this broad framework, to the profit of the reader.

Chapter 1

The Origin, Evolution, and Application of the Sectional Concept, 1750-1900

Fulmer Mood

An account of the concept of the section, viewed as a term in the American social sciences, may properly open with a rapid presentation of some definitions of the word itself, and of related words. Webster gives this definition of the word "section": "A distinct part of a country or people, community, class, or the like; a part of a territory separated by geographical lines, or of a people, considered as distinct." He gives as a secondary meaning: *"U.S. Region."* "Sectional," the adjectival form, is defined as "belonging to a distinct part of a larger body or territory; local, as *sectional* prejudices, interests." The verb "sectionalize," labeled *"Chiefly U.S.,"* is defined thus: "To make in, or divide into, sections. . . . To divide according to geographical sections or local interests." "Sectionalization" is listed but not defined. "Sectionary," as an adjective meaning sectional, and as a noun meaning a partisan, is considered to be rare.[1] Craigie, in *A Dictionary of American English,* lists "section," "sectional," "sectional feeling," "sectionalism," "sectionalist," "sectionalize," and "sectional party." Craigie gives for "section" the explanation: "A distinct part of the country; a territory set apart by geographical, economic, or cultural lines"; and for "sectional feeling": "A feeling aroused among people of a certain section through a consciousness of differences between their own interests and the interests of people in other sections."[2]

[1] *Webster's New International Dictionary of the English Language,* 2nd ed., unabridged (Springfield, Massachusetts, 1944), 2263.

[2] Sir William A. Craigie and James R. Hulbert (eds.), *A Dictionary of American English on Historical Principles* (4 vols., Chicago, 1938–44), IV, 2060–61.

One need not be bound by these dictionary definitions. But the conning over of the preceding array of terms affords help in at least two particular ways. It is clear, in the first place, that this complex of terms comprehends facts of various orders—geographical, political, economic, and psychological. And it is likewise clear that in thinking or writing about sections, or about a system of sections, one must necessarily take into consideration the existence of the all-embracing political, or geographic, or economic entity within which the several sections are comprehended. "Prairie Provinces" or "the Maritimes" implies the larger entity, Dominion of Canada. "The Middle Atlantic States," "the South," or "the Rocky Mountain States," implies the Union of American States.

A particular section, forming a part of a system of sections, comes into existence as the product of definite factors operating in time and place. Factors of geographic position, climate, soil types, local economy, populations, and ideas, imported or indigenously developed, provide differentiating elements. Given time, there arrives the moment when men in several sections, looking at each other, and at themselves, come to the realization that they are not as their fellows are, nor are their fellows as they are. Sectional self-consciousness has come to birth, and, therewith, consciousness of differences between kindred. One of the signs of the existence of a matured sectional self-consciousness is the coming into common use of individualizing terms which are applied to the particular section or to the several sections in a system of sections. When a nomenclature for sections is easily and frequently employed, when it forms part of the common parlance, then sections have come into being: then the spirit of sectionality has evolved.

Sections and systems of sections come into existence at this, that, or the other rate of historical speed. It is only after sections have attained existence as objective, contemporaneous realities that there first emerges the earliest phase of the concept of the section. In its earliest phase, this concept exists chiefly as a perception, so to speak, in a mind. Although the concept in this initial stage is as yet unformulated, it is an actuality. For the existence of the concept, at least in rudimentary form, is implicit in the practical application of the idea. In the second phase of its development, the concept, now partially and imperfectly formulated, attains verbal expression. It may manifest itself as a series of terms or names applied to members in a system of sections. The concept is still cloudy, but it is becoming gradually clearer because of the striving toward a full expression. The third phase in the history of the concept arrives when the concept receives explicit statement as an abstraction, conjoined with relevant illustrative data. Such formulations on the abstract level may be of varying grades of intellectual sophistication, as will later on appear.

To think sectionally does not necessarily imply the use of the word "section" and no other word. In the third quarter of the eighteenth century, for example, the terms most frequently used were "department," "part," and "quarter." Toward the end of the eighteenth century, "district," "division," and "subdivision" were used. The word "section" came into use in this sense at about the same time. During the period 1800–1860, "section" and "sectional" were the terms favored by congressmen and politicians, while inside narrow administrative circles in Washington, "district" and "department" enjoyed a continuing though limited usage. Meanwhile, through the circulation of books and manuals, "division," the virtually unanimous choice of American geographers, was gaining an immense currency. But by 1860 the term "section" bade fair to become the predominant usage. Bartlett (1860) gives it a place in his list and defines it thus: "A distinct part of a city, town, country, or people; a part of a territory separated by geographical lines, or of a people considered distinct. Thus we say, the Northern and Eastern *sections* of the United States, the Middle *section,* the Southern or Western *section.* Webster." Of the adjective "sectional" Bartlett says: "Relating to a section, having regard to the interests of a section, i.e., a division or part, of the country, as the North, South, East, or West. The word is often thus used by political speakers and writers in contradiction to *national.*"[3] Here the synonym "division" has been pressed into service to define a form of the rival term. After the Civil War the Congressional debaters continued to use the word "section," and thereafter the geographers, too, took up its use, now preferring it to "division." After 1870, "section" all but carried everything before it, and by 1900 it was supreme. Just before the end of the century, the term "region" was introduced by John W. Powell. This word has enjoyed wide currency in the years since 1920.

[3] John R. Bartlett, *Dictionary of Americanisms,* 3rd ed. (Boston, 1860), 391–92.

These preliminary considerations out of the way, one now comes to the main problem of this study: to set forth the origin of the concept of the section in the United States and to demonstrate how it was applied and how formulated as an abstraction. The discussion will range over the period from about 1750 to 1900, opening with a consideration of the old, far-flung system of sections within British America, as that geographical entity was understood in the years immediately following the Peace of Paris (1763). It will go on to show how the "British American" system of sections that existed down to the Revolution, having been destroyed by war and independence, was replaced after 1783 by a new and contracted "American" system of sections. The discussion will illustrate the emergence of a sectional nomenclature, first on the Atlantic seaboard in the period of the Revolution, and elsewhere, afterward; and will provide instances of the practical application of an implicit concept of sections to concrete political and administrative situations in American central and federal government. Moving forward from the year 1789, the discussion will then seek to elicit the relevant generalizations concerning the history of the concept of the section, by studies in several distinct though related types of problems. These problems involve data that may be sectionalized in their arrangement or administration.

The first type of problem to be considered is that presented by the works of several American geographers for the period 1789–1900. These books will be examined for the light they shed upon the origin, development, and application of a concept of American sections.

Next, the arrangement of the population data in the volumes of the United States *Census* (1790–1900) will be looked at. Inspection of these census volumes will show that this category of evidence will yield something of value for the present purposes.

Finally, the important paper by John Powell, "Physiographic Regions of the United States" (1895), will be considered in and for itself, as an expression of objective data capable of being given regionalized treatment.

Up to Powell's time more thought was devoted to the concept of the section than to its possible subdivisions—districts, regions, etc. Hence, the history of the sectional concept before 1895 tends to include the related history of the narrower term, region. When Powell's monograph came out, however, the foundation was laid for the consideration of regions apart from sections, and of subregions or districts apart from regions. Thus, only after the concept of the section was well established in American thinking, did the related concept of the region begin to find its own proper place in the scheme of things.

Powell's work will also be considered in relation to its effect upon the scholarship of the historian Frederick Jackson Turner, then of the University of Wisconsin. It was Turner who, late in the nineteenth century, called for the scientific study of sections, and himself did much to promote such studies in the special field of American history.

In 1763, British America—that is to say the complex of territories and possessions owing final allegiance to the Crown of Great Britain —consisted of an immense tract of land and islands ranging between the frigid and the tropic zones. In the far north lay "New Britain," otherwise known as the Hudson's Bay country, a vast fur-bearing area inhabited by native peoples and ruled over by a commercial corporation with head offices in London. The large island of Newfoundland was sparsely settled by a very few permanent residents; its offshore and its Grand Bank fisheries were worked largely by migrant fisherfolk coming out from England who seasonally plied their trade. The valley of the St. Lawrence was narrowly inhabited by a resident population relying on farming and fur trading for support. On the island of St. John's (now Prince Edward Island) a slender population grimly maintained itself. Cape Breton and Nova Scotia were distinct from the St. Lawrence country and were recognized as such; timber-working, agriculture, and fishing dominated their economic activities. Nova Scotia then embraced the additional district now known as New Brunswick. New England was a highly self-conscious section, busy with agriculture, trade, and the beginnings of manufacturing. After New England came the Middle Colonies, which comprised New York, New Jersey, Pennsylvania, and Delaware. Commerce, small manufactures, and much agricultural activity were the ruling pursuits in this section. As in New England, labor was free for the most part, and the owners of property were resident in the provinces. The line of the Potomac was taken by some contemporaries to cut off the Middle Colonies from the settlements to the south, as the southern climate became noticeable in the neighborhood of Maryland. Below the Potomac came a long, straggling line of settlements; it was a warm country, inhabited by whites and blacks and given over to the production of various staples. Virginia and Maryland produced tobacco and, after 1763, increasing amounts of wheat and corn. The Carolinas yielded naval stores, rice, and indigo. Georgia's products were on the order of the Carolinas'. Resident planters dominated the scene in this southern section. To it the Floridas had just been added. Beyond these staple-producing areas on the southern sector of the continent were the West Indies of the British Crown, still another distinct region. These were largely given over to sugar culture; the work force was black servile labor, and for the most part the ownership of the sugar plantations was lodged in absentee owners residing in England.

Here, then, was a system of sections characterized by local differences and variations in climate, soil, and society. From "New Britain" (Hudson's Bay) on the north to the British West Indies on the south one can add a total of eight sections, the several areas of which have just been enumerated. But this is not a complete count, for behind and above these tidewater settlements which ranged from Pennsylvania to Georgia lay the "back country," to the west of the fall line of the rivers. The majority of the population in most of these colonies lived in this "back country," and consisted of small farmers of diverse national origins and religious connections. This scattered population of pioneer farmers made clearings in the primeval forests, living in utter simplicity in the wilderness shades. Here was the "Old West." To the westward stretched the unbroken Indian country, where ranged the bands of natives, and the occasional fur traders who mingled with them. This "back country," and this "Indian country" beyond it, constituted still other sections in the system of sections that was being evolved in British America about 1765.

The British geographers and publicists of the time were quite aware that British America, as it was about 1765 and shortly thereafter, exhibited well-defined patterns of sectionalization. This truth was evident to Fenning and Collyer, authors of an extensive two-volume work, *A New System of Geography*. Forming a part of this general treatise is a long account of the British possessions in America. In the arrangement of their material, there is an implicit concept of the sectionalization of the British possessions. One chapter, opening a series of chapters devoted to the subject of American geography as a whole, bears this title: "Of the Northern Part of the British American Dominions, particularly of the Countries bordering on Hudson's-Bay; with the Islands of New-Foundland, Cape Breton, and St. John."[4] The areas discussed here are well characterized. The following chapter, "Of Nova Scotia, Canada, New England, New York, the Jerseys, Pennsylvania, and Maryland," deals with a section naturally bounded on the north by the St. Lawrence and on the south by the Potomac.[5] A third chapter recognizes another distinct section: "Of the Southern Part of the British Colonies on the Continent of America, particularly of Virginia, Carolina, Georgia, and Florida."[6] Thus far the authors have treated British America as though it consisted of three principal sections, characterized in the large by difference in situation, climate, economy, and society. But to these three sections they add a fourth—"Of the Country in the back Settlements on the Banks of the Mississippi, the Misauris, and the Ohio"[7]—recognizing the existence of a "West," of an "Indian Country," and of "back settlements." Their fifth section was described in a chapter entitled "Of the Bermudas, with a Description of the West Indian Islands; belonging to Great Britain."[8] Jamaica, Barbados, Grenada, Tobago, and other sugar islands are discussed therein, as well as the Bahamas and the Bermudan group, although the latter are far out in the Atlantic.

That the scheme of sectionalization here proposed happens to be a fivefold scheme of sections is of less moment than the fact that the authors actually are operating with an implicit concept of sections.

A somewhat different scheme of sections, and one that employs a liberal number of technical terms, too, is that embodied in a celebrated volume: *American Husbandry. Containing an Account of the Soil, Climate, Production and Agriculture, of the British Colonies in North-America and the West-Indies.* This comprehensive work was published anonymously, "By an American," in London in 1775. Husbandry being the anonymous author's alleged prime concern,

---

[4] Daniel Fenning and Joseph Collyer, *A New System of Geography* (2 vols., London, 1764–65), II, 627.

[5] *Ibid.*, 634.

[6] *Ibid.*, 659.

[7] *Ibid.*, 678.

[8] *Ibid.*, 680.

he largely ignored "New Britain's" frozen fur-bearing wastes, as well as Newfoundland's fisheries, and opened his book with accounts of Nova Scotia and its agriculture, fishing, and lumber, and Canada and its furs, wheat, and timber. Discussions of New England and New York are next introduced. Then follow in order accounts of New Jersey, Pennsylvania, Virginia and Maryland, the Ohio country, North Carolina, South Carolina, Georgia, East Florida, West Florida, and two other areas thus delineated: Eastern Louisiana ("the tract of country on the east side of the river Mississippi, from the boundary of West Florida to the forks of that river"); and the "Ilionois" country ("all that territory to the north-west of the Ohio, extending on both sides the river Ilionois quite to Lake Michigan and the river St. Joseph, the settlements made by the French on the river Myamis; but in particular the country east of the Mississippi, between the Ohio and Ilionois river, to the distance of about an hundred miles from the former").[9] Last comes a group of islands: Jamaica, Barbados, the Leeward Islands, the "Ceded Islands" (Dominica, St. Vincent, Grenada, and Tobago) gained by the Treaty of Paris, 1763, and finally the Bahama Islands. The author remarks, "In conducting the reader [on] the tour of all our colonies, I have laid before him every circumstance that was necessary for giving a complete idea of their agriculture; little has been said of their commerce or of their manufactures, because it was conceived, that it is upon the culture of their lands that the interest of this country in America chiefly depends; and because the channels through which my intelligence came, principally afforded communications relative to agriculture."[10]

The author's remarks on sections and on sectional nomenclature are of considerable interest. The Hudson's Bay country is conceived of as one section, and Newfoundland and its fishery as another. The settlements from Canada southward, to and including Pennsylvania, form still another section, of which the author observes: "As to the northern colonies, all to the north of the tobacco ones [i.e., Virginia and Maryland] may with propriety be classed together, since neither Pennsylvania, New Jersey, New England, Nova Scotia, nor Canada, have any staple product of agriculture; the consequence of which is their flying to all other employments; the culture of the soil is com-

---

[9] *American Husbandry* (2 vols., London, 1775), II, 62, 99.
[10] *Ibid.*, 208–209.

mon husbandry, like that of Britain herself; the employment of their towns, which are numerous and large, is manufactures, commerce, and fisheries."[11] To the south of these are Virginia and Maryland, "the tobacco colonies." "Tobacco is the grand staple of these settlements, a staple as proper as possible for a colony, and than which none is more valuable to this kingdom."[12] The middleness, or centrality, of Virginia, as to climate and situation, is commented upon: the climate "is the medium between the cold of the northern colonies, and the heat of the southern ones, as its situation is between both."[13] Occasionally the tobacco colonies are referred to as "these central colonies," the "central ones," and "the central country."[14] Next come "the southern continental colonies": North Carolina, South Carolina, Georgia, St. Augustine, and Pensacola.[15] "These produce rice, indigo, cotton, silk, wine, and other commodities which are of great value in a British market, and which Britain cannot produce herself."[16] The final group is the insular world of the Caribbean, the section comprising the British "sugar islands," or "sugar colonies."[17] Britain's "islands in the West Indies," says the anonymous author, "produce that great modern luxury, sugar, in larger quantities than she can consume; so that after satisfying her own consumption, there remains a surplus which is re-exported to other nations of Europe that have not sugar islands." On various grounds, he concludes, "we must decide that our West India islands are in every respect as valuable settlements as any the world can boast."[18]

This keen observer and student of British American climates, terrains, crops, and people well understood the differences between the tidewater and the interior areas. He clearly distinguishes between the Atlantic coastal settlements of Georgia and the Carolinas, on the one hand, and the "back country," those relatively remote and interior parts of the same provinces. The seacoasts, the "maritime lands," are described in detail as having a characteristic climate, physiography, soil, and way of life; and the "back country" as having

11 *Ibid.*, 235.
12 *Ibid.*, 227–28.
13 *Ibid.*, 291.
14 *Ibid.*, I, 50, 244, 313.
15 *Ibid.*, II, 223–24, 232.
16 *Ibid.*, 224.
17 *Ibid.*, 202, 219.
18 *Ibid.*, 216, 219–20.

its own climate, surface, soils, and products. East Florida, by contrast, is one extensive, swampy coastal area, having no elevated interior or back country. Virginia and Maryland also are differentiated into two main regions: the "maritime," coastal, or seaboard districts, which are flat, sandy, swampy, and hot; and the "back country," the districts where as the land rises, the temperature drops to a comfortable level. Pennsylvania, too, has a well-defined maritime region and a "back country," marked by the usual differences in climate and surface features. All along the seaboard, notes the author, the farmers and the planters are moving from the older coastal settlements "backwards," that is, into the "back parts" of the pioneer West. There are likewise in New York and New England, extensive "back countries," interior lands, vacant districts, or districts sparsely settled. Coastal New York and interior New York (on the upper Hudson and near Albany) form two distinct regions. The maritime parts of southern New England are thickly settled, but a little distance in from the coast are the districts inhabited by the "back-settlers," whence the vast forests extend northward into the trackless wilderness of Nova Scotia and Canada, and onward almost to the very edge of the St. Lawrence River valley. It is clear that this well-informed author was very much aware of the existence of the "Old West," that fringe of primitive, pioneering settlements which extended from interior New England on the north to interior Georgia on the south.

Three of this author's sections are thus subdivided into coastal and "back-country" districts. These three, to use his own terms, are the "northern colonies," the "central colonies," and the "southern continental colonies." The Hudson's Bay area and Newfoundland make up two more sections. The British West Indies bring the count up to six. And we must not leave out of the reckoning that transAllegheny area, the emergent section in the valley of the Ohio, the rich country of the future. Including this "Western country," we arrive at a total of seven sections comprising the system of sections of British America as it was in 1775. British America, then, extended from the Mississippi River valley to the Atlantic, and from the British West Indies and the Floridas to Hudson's Bay. Such is the anonymous author's understanding of the major complex and its sections. He has worked out a sevenfold system of sections; has shown that these are emergent and potentially developed or are well settled and mature;

and has demonstrated with a wealth of concrete data for three of them the internal differentiation between "back country" and coast country. This scheme of sections is obviously more differentiated, more sophisticated, than the one put forth ten years earlier by the British geographers Fenning and Collyer.

We may fairly assume, therefore, following the testimony of the writers cited above, that British America was thought of as being sectionalized by the opening of the third quarter of the eighteenth century. Was the fact of this sectionalization grasped by contemporary British administrators, and did they put it to use in the solution of their administrative problems? To these questions definite answers can be given. British officials of this period, when faced with particular British American problems, showed an awareness of the existence of sections within the King's dominions in North America, and some of these officials worked out solutions to their problems which were based upon the assumption of sectionalization. A few examples only will be cited. The reader should not expect to meet with the word "section" in the sources at this early date. He will come across various other terms, perhaps equally serviceable.

Thomas Pownall well illustrates the mind of the contemporary British administrator who could think sectionally in practice. After graduation from Cambridge in 1744, he spent three years in the office of the Board of Trade in London, where he learned the British side of colonial administration. In 1753 he went out to America as the private secretary to a royal governor. Afterward he traveled about British America, acquiring useful information and inciting others to compile it. He was quick to grasp the existence of sections in British America, and by 1755 he was able to recognize the significance of the then remote lands south of Lake Erie. In 1756, for example, he wrote the Duke of Cumberland, in a memorial drawn up for that peer's attention: "Were I to point out the natural division of these [American] tracts and interests, it would point out a new division of the governments of the colonies, which is not the purport of this paper." This passage shows that after but three years in North America, Pownall had learned to group the colonies according to a concept of "natural divisions."[19] He was already thinking sectionally. In 1757,

[19] Thomas Pownall, *The Administration of the Colonies*, 4th ed. (London, 1768), Appendix, 11.

Pownall became royal governor of Massachusetts, in which post he
further increased his knowledge of American conditions. Retiring to
London, he there published, in 1764, his influential work, *The Administration of the Colonies,* which went into five subsequent editions. Evidence is not wanting in this volume that Pownall could,
and did, think sectionally. He used such terms as "British West
Indies," "British Sugar Colonies," "Carolinas and other southern
Colonies," and "Northern British Colonies."[20] Embodied in this
treatise on American colonial administration one finds a proposal,
sectionally conceived, for judicial administration.

There was a need at this time, Pownall urged, for the establishment in British America of a system of circuit courts of appeal to hear
cases on a level above that of the provincial courts. Pownall drafted
a plan for such a judicial system. His higher court, he explained, was
to be a court "not confined to any one [colonial] government, but
circuiting through a certain district of governments; perhaps as follows; one to Nova Scotia and New England; one to New York, New
Jerseys [*sic*], Pensylvania, and Maryland—one to Virginia, the
Carolinas, and Georgia. It has been imagined, that this court should
be established by a commission issued to two or more persons for
each district, learned in the law. . . ."[21]

This tripartite judicial sectionalization of the Atlantic coast, as
proposed by Pownall, is not without a prophetic element, where the
future history of sections and of sectionalized administration on the
American seaboard is concerned. Pownall's scheme for judicial administration in the colonies remained in the proposal stage. But in
the sphere of Indian affairs and Indian administration a sectionalized
solution was worked out and applied.

During most of the Colonial period of American history, the
administration of Indian affairs was in the hands of the individual
colonies; no co-ordinated policy for the management of trade and
land-purchase had been worked out. At the opening of the great war
for the empire (1756–63), however, a step toward unified action was
taken. The entire area from Newfoundland to Georgia was, for
military purposes, brought under the British general and commander
in chief, Lord Loudoun. Since the problem of defense was closely

20 *Ibid.,* 6, 285, 286.
21 *Ibid.,* 113–14.

linked with the Indian problem, two departments of Indian affairs, each staffed by a superintendent, were now created. Sir William Johnson was commissioned for the Northern Department, in 1755, and Edmund Atkin for the Southern Department, not long afterward. Thus a sectionalized conception of the Indian country in the West was introduced into the British administration of Indian affairs. The southern superintendency had in its charge such tribes as the Creeks, Chickasaws, Choctaws, Catawbas, and Cherokees; the northern superintendency, the Iroquois confederacy of the Six Nations. Edmund Atkin, previous to his appointment, had drafted a "Plan of a General Direction and Management of the Indian Affairs throughout North America."[22] The Indian nations, according to this proposal, were to be divided into two districts. Over these districts were to be two imperial officers—superintendents or commissioners—who were to be independent of any particular governor, provincial authority, or British military chief. The line of the Tennessee River was to serve as the boundary between the northern and the southern superintendencies. The northern district was to comprise the tribes of the Six Nations, with their dependents; the southern district was to include particularly the Cherokees, Catawbas, Creeks, Chickasaws, and Choctaws.

The foregoing instances argue a recognition of the existence of sectionalism in British America in the third quarter of the eighteenth century. In the vast domain extending from the British West Indies to Hudson's Bay, the sectionalization pattern was presently complex, and potentially it was even more so. The adoption of the Declaration of Independence, in 1776, and the armed efforts to make that state paper good before all the world, naturally enough transformed the pre-1776 pattern into a pattern new and different.

During the third quarter of the eighteenth century, the term "British America" enjoyed currency not only among British writers but also among native-born residents of the colonies, who often even referred to themselves as "British Americans." Thus Oxenbridge Thacher of Massachusetts brought out a pamphlet in 1764 with the title of *The Sentiments of a British American*. James Otis, another

[22] John C. Parish, *The Persistence of the Westward Movement and Other Essays* (Berkeley, California, 1943), 151.

son of Massachusetts, wrote a tract for the times, *The Rights of the British Colonies asserted and proved* (1764). In this he made a promise that "the ministry [of Great Britain] . . . may rely on it, that British America will never prove undutiful till driven to it." And he made a further prediction: "The names of his present Majesty, and his royal Grandfather, will be ever dear to every loyal British American, for the protection they afforded us." John Adams about the same time confided to his Diary some thoughts relating to "the genius and guardian angel of Britain and British America."[23] In a letter written in June, 1774, Thomas Jefferson referred to "the dangers impending over British America."[24]

After the publication of the Declaration of Independence, the term "British American" lost its former utility. Those who were opposed to the principles of the Declaration, and who wished for the continuance of the British connection, came to be known as loyalists, or as Tories. Those who supported the Declaration were no longer known as British Americans; they were transformed into Americans, in the collective sense. In the localities, the problem was even more easily solved. The Virginian subjects of George III were now citizens of the republic of Virginia; Pennsylvanian subjects were now citizens of the republic of Pennsylvania. And so with other former subjects in other former colonies; they too became the citizens of independent republics, each republic or state having its own flag, its own great seal, and its own coat of arms.

The task of finding a substitute term for "British America" was not resolved with equal facility. It took some months before even a temporary and incomplete answer was found. The story of the search for a usable surrogate may be briefly told, as it unfolded during the period from September, 1774, to December, 1776.

In September, 1774, the delegates from "the Several Colonies and Provinces in North America" assembled at Philadelphia.[25] A month later, Congress, after a full discussion "by the Representatives of so great a part of America," adopted a memorial. For whom? For "the inhabitants of the British Colonies," who as yet had no collective

23 Craigie and Hulbert, *A Dictionary of American English*, I, 319.

24 Paul Leicester Ford (ed.), *The Writings of Thomas Jefferson* (10 vols., New York, 1892–99), I, 418.

25 Worthington C. Ford *et al.* (eds.), *Journals of the Continental Congress, 1774–1789* (34 vols., Washington, 1904–37), I, 13.

name for themselves and so were addressed, individually, thus: "To the inhabitants of the colonies of New-Hampshire, Massachusetts-Bay, Rhode-Island and Providence Plantations, Connecticut, New-York, New-Jersey, Pennsylvania, the counties of New-Castle, Kent and Sussex, on Delaware, Maryland, Virginia, North-Carolina and South-Carolina."[26] Congress ordered that this memorial "to the inhabitants of the British colonies" be printed, and further resolved, "That an Address be prepared to the people of Quebec [i.e., Canada], and letters to the colonies of St. John's, Nova Scotia, Georgia, East and West Florida, who have not deputies to represent them in this Congress."[27] As these official acts show, Congress at this moment was thinking in terms of a British America, slightly contracted, extending from the St. Lawrence along the Atlantic seaboard to the keys of Florida. In 1774, Congress showed no uniformity in the terminology with which it referred to itself, employing at one time or another variously "the American Continental Congress," "the Continental Congress," and "the Grand American Continental Congress." The preferred term, however, was "the American Continental Congress." This Congress thought of itself as representing "the several English Colonies," or "the Inhabitants of the American Colonies," or "the Inhabitants of the British American Colonies."[28] This last term was much in use in the official publications of Congress itself, beginning with the end of October, 1774.

The year 1775 brought some alterations in terminology. In official publications Congress employed new names—"the Twelve united English Colonies of North-America," "the Representatives of the United Colonies of North America, now met in General Congress at Philadelphia," "the Twelve United Colonies of North-America," and "the Twelve United English Colonies of North America"—as well as some of the terms previously cited for 1774.[29] From January until June, 1776, Congress seemingly chose short, spare forms. Its official publications now employed such terms as "the Continental Congress," "the Honorable Continental Congress," or the downright plain and curt style of "In Congress." For the colonies collectively taken, the preferred term at this period, as found in the *Journals* of

[26] *Ibid.*, 90.
[27] *Ibid.*, 101.
[28] *Ibid.*, 127–31 *passim*.
[29] *Ibid.*, III, 508, 510, 512.

Congress, seems to have been "United Colonies."[30] Now and then
even the colorless term "continent" was employed for collective use,
as (June 6, 1776), "The Marine Committee having recommended sun-
dry gentlemen . . . for the ships building or built for the continent,
the same was taken into consideration."[31]

On June 7, 1776, Congress had laid before it certain motions, the
first of which was: "Resolved, That these United Colonies are, and of
right ought to be, free and independent States, that they are absolved
from all allegiance to the British Crown, and that all political connection between them and the State of Great Britain is, and ought to
be, totally dissolved." The third resolution proposed "That a plan
of confederation be prepared and transmitted to the respective Colonies for their consideration and approbation."[32] In July the Congress adopted "The unanimous Declaration of the thirteen United
States of America."[33] On July 12, 1776, a printed text of the "Articles
of Confederation and Perpetual Union, Between the Colonies . . ."
was set up. This first draft used the term "colonies" by force of long-
standing custom, even though the "colonies" had now become states.
A month later the second draft came forth as a set of articles "Between
the States."[34] The Continental statesmen thus took a little time to
accustom themselves to their novel status and new style. The need
for uniformity was recognized by Congress itself, when on September
9, 1776, it made provision for an important change in official styling.
The end of an era was signaled in this new act: "Resolved, That in
all continental commissions, and other instruments, where, heretofore, the words 'United Colonies' have been used, the stile be altered, for the future, to the 'United States.'"[35] When the Declaration
came to be printed soon afterward, the heading chosen for the Philadelphia imprint was this: *In Congress, July 4, 1776. A Declaration
By the Representatives of the United States of America, In General
Congress assembled.*[36] Thus the former "British America" and "British Colonies in America" gave way to the official term, "United States

[30] *Ibid.*, VI, 1117, 1119–21; IV, 13.
[31] *Ibid.*, V, 422.
[32] *Ibid.*, 425.
[33] *Ibid.*, 510.
[34] *Ibid.*, VI, 1123, 1124.
[35] *Ibid.*, V, 747.
[36] *Ibid.*, VI, 1121.

of America." In the latter part of September, 1776, Congress had its printer publish a booklet containing the revised articles of war. This appeared as: *Rules and Articles for the better Government of the Troops Raised, or to be raised and kept in pay by and at the expence of the United States of America.*[37] And toward the close of the year 1776, Congress published an address to the people: "The Representatives of the United States of America, in Congress assembled, To the People in General, and particularly to the Inhabitants of Pennsylvania, and the adjacent States."[38] Thus "United States of America" came to be used as a collective or general term for the self-governing republics which succeeded the dependent colonies. But this term comprehended only a part of what formerly was implied by "British America." There remained the need for a general appellative for the combined territories occupied or possessed by these states, now united. Various names at one time or another were proposed—Columbia, Fredonia, Atlantic America, United America, etc.—but none met with any great degree of permanent favor. As late as 1791, the debate was going on. In the *Gazette of the United States* we read: *"America* is used very generally both by writers and public speakers, when they only intend the territory of the United States. . . . It may have first come into use as being much shorter to say *Americans,* than citizens of the United States: Some use Atlantic America for the United States—others United America—the last is the most proper."[39]

Although the former British Americans were now, after July 4, 1776, Americans, the people of this new nation for a while continued to cherish territorial ambitions that were demonstrably "old" British American rather than "new" American. For these new nationals the lands of the Old Thirteen were not enough; they had hopes of much more. At their general headquarters in Philadelphia, their shrewd leaders pondered the possibility of acquiring still other districts than those which had chosen to secede with them. The hold that this "old" British American outlook then had on the Continental Congress is shown quite clearly in the first draft of a treaty which Congress prepared to propose to France. It was drawn up in July, 1776. The eighth article in the first draft well exemplifies the large hopes of the future

---

[37] *Ibid.,* 1125.
[38] *Ibid.,* 1126.
[39] Craigie and Hulbert, *A Dictionary of American English,* I, 40.

that the Americans were then entertaining, in their freshest and greenest youth:

In Case of any War between the most Christian King and the King of Great Britain, the most Christian King, shall never invade, nor under any pretence attempt to possess himself of Labradore, New Britain, Nova Scotia, Accadia, Canada, Florida, nor any of the Countries, Cities, or Towns, on the Continent of North America, nor of the Islands of New-foundland, Cape Breton, St. John's, Anticosti, nor of any other Island lying near to the said Continent, in the Seas, or in any Gulph, Bay, or River, it being the true Intent and meaning of this Treaty, that the said united States, shall have the sole, exclusive, undivided and perpetual Possession of all the Countries, Cities, and Towns, on the said Continent, and of all Islands near to it, which now are, or lately were under the Jurisdiction of or Subject to the King or Crown of Great Britain, when-ever the [same can be invaded, and conquered by the said united States, or shall in any manner submit to or be] shall be united or confederated with the said united States.[40]

This eighth article of the proposed treaty registers an immense American ambition: nothing less than the wish to inherit the British dominions in North America, from Hudson's Bay on the north, to the Floridas and the Bahamas on the south, and even to the Bermudas far out at sea. These latter islands were enumerated because James Wilson, a delegate from Pennsylvania, specifically inserted them in the text of the draft. There can be doubt, however, whether the new-made Americans at this time were hoping to take over the British West Indies as well.

This attitude of expectant heirship kept up for some months longer. In September, 1776, Congress took up the proposed treaty with France; the carefully elaborated text of the treaty was now spread on the pages of the *Journals*. Article IX of this second draft stipulates that the King of France pledge himself never to invade, and never to attempt to gain possession of, "Labradore, New Britain, Nova Scotia, Acadia, Canada, Florida," or other lands on the conti-nent of North America, or Newfoundland, Cape Breton, St. John's, Anticosti, and other islands lying near to the continent, since it is the true intent of this treaty that the United States "shall have the sole, exclusive, undivided and perpetual Possession" of the districts, etc.,

---

[40] Ford *et al., Journals of the Continental Congress,* V, 579. The material enclosed in brackets formed part of the original text and was deleted from the draft by the Committee of Congress.

"which now are, or lately were under the Jurisdiction of or Subject to the King or Crown of Great Britain, whenever they shall be united or confederated with the said United States."[41]

By December, 1776, however, Congress was taking a less ambitious view of the restraints which the King of France was to be expected to impose upon himself. Congress now voted to instruct its commissioners at the court of France, that if a joint French and American armada should succeed in reducing Newfoundland and Cape Breton, and an American naval enterprise should reduce Nova Scotia, then the fishery should be enjoyed equally by the French and the Americans. Furthermore, half of the territory of Newfoundland should then become a French possession, provided that the remaining part of Newfoundland, as well as the province of Nova Scotia and Cape Breton Island, should "be annexed to the territory and government of the United States." If this bait should not prove sufficient to bring France to declare war on Great Britain, then the commissioners were to assure the court of France that all West India Islands that should fall to a joint Franco-American naval force should become possessions of the French king. Furthermore, the United States engaged to furnish supplies of provisions for carrying on such expeditions against these islands "and render any other assistance which may be in their power as becomes good allies."[42] Thus the erstwhile British Americans, as potential heirs to British America, were taking a markedly contracted view of their desired inheritance, within six months of the declaration. They now wrote off as lost to themselves the British West Indies; and now expressed themselves as being willing to give up to France half of Newfoundland and to share the fisheries with her, under certain conditions.

The treaty of 1783 between Great Britain and the United States put a temporary damper on the northern territorial ambitions of the new-fledged Americans. Hudson's Bay and Labrador, the St. Lawrence Valley and St. John's, Newfoundland and Cape Breton and the immense wilderness that in those days was Nova Scotia—all these they lost. They permanently lost, too, the Bermudas, the Bahamas, and the British West Indies. The Floridas, however, were but temporarily lost to them. Nevertheless, the American Confederation, how-

41 *Ibid.*, 770.
42 *Ibid.*, VI, 1056.

ever contracted or reduced its territories in comparison with those of old-time British America, was still extensive enough to be hailed by its friends at home and abroad as "a rising empire." On the Atlantic seaboard it ranged from Georgia on the south to the District of Maine, a possession of Massachusetts, on the north. Beyond the Alleghenies, the territory of this "rising empire" extended to the east bank of the Mississippi River, from Spanish Florida to the Great Lakes. The independent republic of Vermont and British possessions bounded the territories of the United States on the north; and on the west and south, Spain was the neighboring power.

Within this new Confederation, there had quietly come into being, even before the Revolution, still another pattern of a sectional system, and with it a fresh set of sectional terms. We may now pay a little attention to this second pattern of sections—a system that in its essence is less "British American" than "American."

That observant, self-taught geographer, Benjamin Franklin, writing in 1743, brought out "A Proposal for promoting Useful Knowledge among the British Plantations in America." Here he took occasion to point out that the English possessed a long tract of continent, from Nova Scotia to Georgia, extending north and south through different climates and different soils, producing different plants and minerals, and capable of different improvements, manufactures, and so on.

The central area on this long stretch of varied coast, Franklin asserted, was Pennsylvania; and the true meeting place of men coming from far off was its capital city—"Philadelphia, the city nearest the centre of the continent colonies, communicating with all of them northward and southward by post, and with all the islands by sea."[43] In 1747, Franklin expressed in a nutshell a sectional appreciation of the Atlantic coast system: *"Pennsylvania, . . .* situate in the Centre of the Colonies has hitherto enjoy'd profound Repose; and tho' our Nation is engag'd in a bloody War, yet, . . . defended, in a great Degree, from the *French* on the one Hand, by the Northern Provinces, and from the *Spaniards* on the other by the Southern, at no small Expence to each, our People have, till lately, slept securely in their Habitations."[44]

[43] Albert H. Smyth (ed.), *The Writings of Benjamin Franklin* (10 vols., New York, 1905–1907), II, 229.
[44] *Ibid.,* 337–38.

Franklin used easily such sectional terms as "Sugar Islands," "New England," and "Northern Colonies." "I made a long journey to the eastward," he wrote in a letter of 1753, "which consumed ten weeks; and two journeys to our western frontier." But always he came back to the centrality of his own section and city: "And as we are in the centre of the Colonies, a healthy place, . . . we suppose a good Academy here may draw numbers of youths for education from the neighbouring Colonies, and even from the West Indies."[45]

Lewis Evans, another Pennsylvanian, was thinking in 1755 in terms of an intermediate colonial zone; he preferred the word "middle" to "central" and used it in the title of his cartographical work: *Geographical, historical, political, philosophical essays. The first, containing an analysis of the middle British colonies in America. . . .* Not long afterward, Andrew Burnaby assisted in giving currency to the idea of an intermediate group of colonies. Burnaby visited the Middle Colonies on an extensive tour during 1759 and 1760. He chose for the title of a work first published in 1775, *Travels through the middle settlements in North-America, in the years 1759 and 1760.* Eastern Colonies, Middle Colonies, and so, by a natural extension, Southern Colonies, too. One example of the last term will suffice: Thomas Hutchinson used "Southern Colonies" in a private record in 1774.[46]

Thus, before the Revolution began, native-born Americans were recognizing the reality of a threefold system of sections, one that was "American" rather than "British American." When the Continental Congress convened, we find the delegates spontaneously using such terms as "Southern Colonies," "Middle Colonies," "Eastern Colonies," and "New England Colonies." The colonial leaders, when they were dominated by an "American" outlook, rather than by a "British American" outlook, could also use such phrases as "in all the colonies from Nova-Scotia to Georgia," or "from Falmouth in New England to Savannah in Georgia."[47]

It is worthy of note that by the era of the Revolution, referring to the Atlantic communities in a north-to-south order, as in the two phrases quoted above, had become a well-established custom. The history of this usage runs far back. In 1780, the historian Chalmers

---

45 *Ibid.*, III, 15, 68, 122, 163–64, 165, 192, 245.
46 Craigie and Hulbert, *A Dictionary of American English*, IV, 2180.
47 Ford *et al.*, *Journals of the Continental Congress*, I, 60 [1774]; II, 208 [1775].

commented on what is perhaps the origin of this habit: "Early historians, without much consideration, have given an account of the British empire in America, by beginning at the north and writing southwards; their successors have continued a similar mode without apparent reason."[48]

Americans were all but universally accustomed to enumerate the several colonies in this north-to-south order. Thus it naturally came about, when the Continental Congress convened at Philadelphia in September, 1774, that this well-established usage became the accepted order for making the roll call of the colonies. At the very first meeting of the Congress, on September 5, this order was adopted for roll call, without debate, and apparently as a matter of course. The order used in the roll call on this first occasion was New Hampshire, Massachusetts, Rhode Island, Connecticut—so ran the roster.

The adoption of this north-to-south roll call usage perhaps had an unforeseen consequence for the development of sectional thinking in Congressional circles. Since the colonies were listed in an order that corresponded to their several geographical situations on the seaboard, the announcing in Congress of that order, time and time again, served to remind delegates that three sections existed. First came the Eastern or New England Colonies; next the Middle Colonies; lastly the Southern Colonies. Enumerating the colonies in this geographical order must have reinforced the current consciousness of sectionalization. Enumerating them according to an alphabetical arrangement would not have had this consequence.

The widespread recognition of the threefold scheme of sections— Eastern, Middle, and Southern—by the American leaders in Congress is seen in the fact that certain administrative decisions made by Congress quite early in its career were based on sectional assumptions. Below are a few examples of these plans for sectional administration, drawn from the three spheres of Indian, naval, and military affairs.

The colonies in 1775 took their first steps toward common action on the Indian problem. In July of that year Congress resolved to establish three Indian "departments," one for the northern section of the country, one for the middle section, and one for the southern section. This tripartite plan may be contrasted with the prior British

---

[48] George Chalmers, *Political Annals of the present United Colonies from their Settlement to the Peace of 1763* (London, 1780), b, verso.

imperial subdivision into two departments. The Northern Department was to take in the Six Nations and the tribes to the northward; the Southern Department was to include the Cherokees and all the tribes residing to the south of them. The Middle Department was to have for its particular jurisdiction the tribes between the other two departments. Three commissioners were to have charge of the Northern Department, three more of the Middle Department, and five of the Southern Department. These commissioners reported to one or another of the Indian committees of the Congress. The last committee for Indian affairs was appointed in May, 1779.

Naval administration was likewise seen by Congress as a set of problems capable of a sectional solution. A Naval Committee was constituted by Congress, and began to function by the autumn of 1775. It laid the foundations of the American navy and then gave way to a new committee. The Marine Committee, its successor, began work in December, 1775. Afterward, two administrative boards were set up, both responsible to this committee of Congress: the Navy Board of the Eastern Department, or the Navy Board at Boston; and the Navy Board of the Middle Department, or the Navy Board at Philadelphia. The state navy of South Carolina was exceedingly active, and it often went to sea. This state navy was seemingly a substitute for a naval board of the Southern Department.

In military administration an understanding and an application of the realities of sectionalism early manifested themselves. In Richard Smith's diary for February 27, 1776—he was a delegate in the Congress from New Jersey—we read: "A Report from a Committee was confirmed which divides the Country into 3 Military Districts each to be commanded by some General Officers under the Commander in Chief viz. the 4 New England Colonies in the Eastern District, New York, New Jersey Pennsylvania Delaware and Maryland in the Middle District and the Colonies South in the Southern District and it is understood that Canada composes a 4th or Northern District. Some New England Delegates urged to have New York in their District sed non Allocatur."[49] The reference to Canada, that is, the valley of the St. Lawrence from Montreal to the gulf, as a potential fourth district was made at a time when the leaders in Congress were still cherishing

---

[49] E. C. Burnett (ed.), *Letters of Members of the Continental Congress* (8 vols., Washington, 1921–36), I, 366.

the hope that they were to inherit much, if not all, of King George's dominions in North America.

As other administrative problems arose, capable of being met on a sectional basis, Congress considered solutions. Such an instance occurred early in 1780. The matter of establishing a court of appeals had come up, and Congress was considering the report of the committee which had the matter in charge. On January 7, 1780, a motion was made and seconded that one judge of the proposed court of appeals should be an inhabitant of the state of Virginia, North Carolina, South Carolina, or Georgia; one an inhabitant of Maryland, Delaware, Pennsylvania, New Jersey, or New York; and one an inhabitant of Connecticut, Rhode Island, Massachusetts, or New Hampshire. This motion indicates a positive desire to have representation on the court from each of the three sections, and well illustrates the sectional assumptions underlying various legislative proposals that from time to time came up in the Congress of the United States.

Beyond the Alleghenies lay a forming section, and of this vast back country, "their unappropriated Western Territory," the Old Thirteen were quite conscious. Into various schemes and practical calculations "the Back Lands" entered as an important factor. One instance will serve to indicate how the existence of this potential section over the mountains was being reckoned with. In July, 1782, the superintendent of finance, Robert Morris, addressed a long memorandum to Congress on the current financial problems of the Confederation. Eventually he touched on "what are called the Back Lands." He foresaw that, under proper conditions, these lands would constitute an immense national property. Their value would be, he thought, in the nature of a future interest: "The Back Lands may afterwards be formed into a fund for opening new loans in Europe on a low Interest redeemable within a future period (for instance, twenty years) with a right reserved to the creditors of taking portions of those lands on the nonpayment of their Debts, at the expiration of that term."[50] Thus the influence of an emergent, a potential, section, the then straggling West, was manifesting itself, and in a very concrete way, in the minds of the delegates in Congress assembled.

Passing from the Confederation to the Constitutional Convention

[50] Ford *et al.*, *Journals of the Continental Congress*, XXII, 445–46.

of 1787, we note that the debates and discussions over the framing of the Constitution of 1787 abound with references which recognize the current sectional realities. A few instances only will be cited; they serve to show the presence of sectional self-consciousness at this time, and so, by implication, the existence of a concept of the section. Hamilton on one occasion remarked prophetically: "Distinctions of Eastern middle and Southern states will come into view."[51] As we have seen, these distinctions had already come into view in the administrative arrangements of the Confederation. George Mason, in a discussion of the proposed chief magistracy for the new government, declared: "If the Executive is vested in three persons, one chosen from the Northern, one from the Middle, and one from the Southern States, will it not contribute to quiet the minds of the people and convince them that there will be proper attention paid to their respective concerns?"[52] Williamson thought of a new, forming section; he "reminded the House of the prospect of new States to the Westward."[53] Mention was also made of "the Western States hereafter arising."[54] Contrasts between the Atlantic interest and the Western interest were indulged in by convention members. Besides the antithesis of the "Western world" versus the Atlantic world, Madison saw another sectional antithesis: "The great danger to our general government *is the great southern and northern interests of the continent, being opposed to each other. Look to the votes in congress, and most of them stand divided by the geography of the country, not according to the size of the states.*"[55] If ever the Union were to be broken asunder, would the Delaware be the line of cleavage? This query was brought out into the open. Gouverneur Morris essayed a glance into the future. "He looked forward also to that range of New States which wd. soon be formed in the west. He thought the rule of representation ought to be so fixed as to secure to the Atlantic States a prevalence in the National Councils. The new States will know less of the public interest than these, will have an interest in many

51 Max Farrand (ed.), *The Records of the Federal Convention of 1787* (3 vols., New Haven, 1911), I, 146.

52 *Ibid.*, 113.

53 *Ibid.*, 372.

54 *Ibid.*, 373.

55 *Ibid.*, 476.

respects different, in particular will be little scrupulous of involving the Community in wars the burdens & operations of which would fall chiefly on the maritime States."[56]

From the start of the new government under the Constitution, participants in the debates in Congress frequently exhibited a highly sensitive awareness of the existence of sections within the new Federal Union. The records of the debates in the Senate and in the House of Representatives are filled with references to sections and sectional realities. Such designations as "Southern States," "Middle States," "Eastern" and "Northern States," and "Western Territory" appear frequently. Some speakers, like Representative Lee, who spoke in July, 1790, were systematic in their approach to sectionalism. "Mr. Lee, after a few introductory observations, entered into a consideration of the relative interests of the Southern, Middle, and Northern States."[57] In the debates on public credit, which took up so much time in the spring of 1790, many observations were made on sectional peculiarities and sectional interests. The Congressional records give the gist of Mr. Wadsworth's remarks: "We hear much upon the subject of general duties, that they fall heaviest upon the Southern States; they are not manufacturers, and a great consumption of luxuries takes place among the people in those States. Mr. Wadsworth asserted that the consumption of luxuries is much the greatest in the Eastern and Northern States, and stated a variety of particulars to prove the assertion; he appealed to the Southern gentlemen who had travelled into the Middle and Northern States for its truth."[58]

The West also figured in the debates on public credit, in relation to a plan to pay a part of the Continental debt with government land. Representative Lee remarked: "It is well known to every gentleman on the floor, that the United States have extensive tracts of vacant and uncultivated lands." He asked "whether it would not be both prudent and politic to avail ourselves of this resource, and apply it to the immediate diminution of the public burdens?" "Let us," he continued, "use our extensive Western country, to repair the ruin which has taken place; draw from the impost, or any other source

---

[56] *Ibid.*, 533.

[57] *Annals of Congress, 1789–1824* (42 vols., Washington, 1834–56), 1 Cong., 2 sess., 1661.

[58] *Ibid.*, 1514.

of revenue, so much as can be obtained without distressing the community. . . ."[59] Representative White concurred, with this observation: "The equivalent in land is as favorable to the creditor as the circumstances of the country will admit. Twenty cents an acre for Western Territory is not too high; it is a very moderate valuation. Kentucky [lands] would sell for more than that, and ten years since the prospect there was not so favorable as that of the Western Territory."[60]

Washington's "Farewell Address" (1796) reveals in certain passages a consciousness of the existence of sections, and an awareness that sectional feelings, once out of control, boded ill for the Federal Union. Washington's famed state paper has added interest in the present connection because it shows the conclusions reached on the sectional problem in politics by the generation which grew to manhood as British Americans and then, as Americans, created an independent nation. In this address of the leading American of the day one may see that the President of the United States himself recognized the realities of sectionalism, employed a current sectional nomenclature, and used appropriate abstract terms ("Districts," "Sub divisions") when referring to sections as such.

Citizens by birth or choice, of a common country, that country has a right to concentrate your affections. The name of American, which belongs to you, in your national capacity, must always exalt the just pride of Patriotism, more than any appellation derived from local discriminations. . . .

The *North,* in an unrestrained intercourse with the *South,* protected by the equal Laws of a common government, finds in the productions of the latter, great additional resources of Maratime [sic] and commercial enterprise and precious materials of manufacturing industry. The *South* in the same Intercourse, benefitting by the Agency of the *North,* sees its agriculture grow and its commerce expand. Turning partly into its own channels the seamen of the *North,* it finds its particular navigation envigorated; and while it contributes, in different ways, to nourish and increase the general mass of the National navigation, it looks forward to the protection of a Maratime [sic] strength, to which itself is unequally adapted. The *East,* in a like intercourse with the *West,* already finds, and in the progressive improvement of interior communications, by land and water, will more and more find a valuable vent for the commodities which

[59] *Ibid.,* 1299–1300.
[60] *Ibid.,* 1425.

it brings from abroad, or manufactures at home. The *West* derives from the *East* supplies requisite to its growth and comfort, and what is perhaps of still greater consequence, it must of necessity owe the *secure* enjoyment of indispensable *outlets* for its own productions to the weight, influence, and the future Maritime strength of the Atlantic side of the Union, directed by an indissoluble community of Interest as *one Nation.* . . .

Is there a doubt, whether a common government can embrace so large a sphere? Let experience solve it. . . . We are authorized to hope that a proper organization of the whole, with the auxiliary agency of governments for the respective Sub divisions, will afford a happy issue to the experiment. . . .

In contemplating the causes wch. may disturb our Union, it occurs as matter of serious concern, that any ground should have been furnished for characterizing parties by *Geographical* discriminations: *Northern* and *Southern; Atlantic* and *Western;* whence designing men may endeavour to excite a belief that there is a real difference of local interests and views. One of the expedients of Party to acquire influence, within particular districts, is to misrepresent the opinions and aims of other Districts. You cannot shield yourselves too much against the jealousies and heart burnings which spring from these misrepresentations.[61]

The oncoming generations of legislators in Congress followed their predecessors in learning how to speak about sectional realities. A representative, speaking in December, 1803, asserted of five particular states: "They belong to the great subdivisions of the country, Eastern, Middle, Western, and Southern."[62] At about the same time, a senator spoke of "the greater divisions of our country, the Western, the Southern, the Middle, and the Eastern States."[63] These quotations are interesting, less because of the geographical terms they use, or the fourfold scheme of sections they reveal, than because of the general categorizing terms associated with them, such as "divisions" and "subdivisions." Josiah Quincy employed other terms, preferring "section" and "sectional." In April, 1806, on the floor of the House he stated an ominous truth: "But let a narrow, selfish, local, sectional policy, prevail, and struggles will commence, which will terminate, through irritations and animosities, in either a change of the system of government, or in its dissolution." Again, he warned: "Whenever any great section of the Union shall deem itself neglected, and the

[61] John C. Fitzpatrick (ed.), *The Writings of George Washington from the Original Manuscript Sources* (39 vols., Washington, 1931–44), XXXV, 219–23 *passim.*

[62] *Annals of Congress,* 8 Cong., 1 sess., 770.

[63] *Ibid.,* 7 Cong., 2 sess., 193.

opinion becomes general among the people that they are sacrificed or abandoned; that they have not any, or their just weight, in the national scale, a series of struggles must commence, which will terminate either in redress or in convulsions."[64]

Here the word "section" is used in its modern sense. It was still somewhat novel when Quincy employed it on this occasion, "division" being then the preferred term. On the novelty of the word "section" there is a reliable authority, contemporary with Quincy. John Pickering, in his handbook, *A Vocabulary, or Collection of Words and Phrases which have been supposed to be peculiar to the United States of America* (Boston, 1816), lists the word "section" and has this to say of it: "Since the French Revolution this word has been much used here instead of *part, quarter,* &c. Ex. 'in this *section* of the United States.' It is not thus used in England." Under "sectionary," Pickering comments: "Belonging to a *section* of a country; local. . . . I have never met with this uncommon word except in the following instance: 'This veneration arises not from a little and selfish spirit of *sectionary* attachment.' I have once also met with *sectional,* in the same sense."[65]

By degrees the men of Congress came to prefer to use the noun section, and the adjective sectional. At moments of great crisis and decision, the word came readily to a speaker's tongue. From the debates over the admission of Missouri to the Union a few examples may be taken to illustrate. In January, 1820, a senator observed: "Mr. President, it should be the pride of Congress to mete out to the inhabitants of the various sections of this vast Republic, equal and impartial justice. Let no one section have just cause of complaint."[66] Representative Holmes of Massachusetts recognized the realities, although he applied older terms to them: "The people of the United States can have but one interest. . . . There is a constant dependence of the parts, indispensable to the liberty, greatness, and glory of the whole. . . . A fear that a geographical division will receive more than its share of profit or power, will produce a corresponding jealousy, until every local or private act will become a matter of compromise and bargain. But an excitement which divides the United States in

[64] *Ibid.*, 9 Cong., 1 sess., 1042, 1038.
[65] John Pickering, *A Vocabulary, or Collection of Words and Phrases which have been supposed to be peculiar to the United States of America* (Boston, 1816), 170–71.
[66] *Annals of Congress*, 16 Cong., 1 sess., 172.

nearly equal halves is dangerous indeed."[67] Representative Tucker, speaking in 1822 on the apportionment bill which was based upon the lately completed census of 1820, stated: "If, by any particular, one State lost, it will universally be found that, by the same number, a neighboring State gained." The transcript of the speech goes on to explain: "He had compared the effect of different numbers [i.e., fractions or ratios] on different sections of the Union, and found that no number would make much difference between these great divisions."[68]

As one crisis after another shook the Union, "section" and "sectional" came more and more into legislative and then into popular usage. These words had long been in Noah Webster's dictionary, but now they were given a new application. Why they outdistanced their rivals—division, district, portion—is not clear; the fact is, however, that they did outstrip them. Bartlett (1860) also listed "sectional" and "sectionalism" and illustrated the meaning with a recent example from the debates in the House of Representatives, for January 26, 1859: "Mr. Miles, of South Carolina, said he was that bugbear a *sectional* man. He represented in part the South, which, being the weaker party, had to unite in order to protect herself, and was therefore *sectional*."[69] Worcester's dictionary expounded no definition that ran parallel with Webster's; however, Worcester did admit to his columns "sectional," of which he wrote: "Relating to, or embracing, a section or distinct part, as of a territory or country; partial." Worcester followed this with a disapproving comment enclosed in brackets: "[modern]." He did, however, list "division," and defined it: "The part separated from the rest; a portion; a section."[70] As an example he cited a phrase from Joseph Addison, who died in 1719.

The Civil War, as the greatest of all "sectional" conflicts on this continent, may have had something to do with the increased usage that the word "section" experienced after 1865. The language employed in Congress spread out to the people at large. It found a place in the editorials of newspapers, in the pages of books, and right down to 1900 it kept its hold. As will appear later, the geographers preferred the term "division" until the opening of the Civil War;

[67] *Ibid.*, 16 Cong., 1 sess., 988.
[68] *Ibid.*, 17 Cong., 1 sess., 836.
[69] Bartlett, *Dictionary of Americanisms*, 391.
[70] Joseph Worcester, *Dictionary of the English Language* (Boston, 1860), 1298, 430.

after the war they gave currency to "section." This change in allegiance on the part of the geographers is perhaps not without significance.

Just as statesmen in the halls of Congress were conscious of sectional terms and sectional differences, so votes in Congress were often sectional, too—the researches of the historian Frederick J. Turner and his students amply support this statement. And from time to time particular pieces of Congressional legislation, especially administrative measures that concerned all parts, all sections, of the Union, were frankly drafted on a sectional basis. The history of the circuit court judicial districts from 1789 to 1900 is a case in point; the record indicates that for more than a century this branch of federal administration continuously exhibited well-defined patterns of sectionalization. A rapid survey of some of the relevant statutes, with special attention to the geographical expansion of the circuit court system, will make this point clear.

By the Judiciary Act of September 24, 1789, the new Congress set up thirteen districts, with a federal district court in each; and three circuits, each with a federal circuit court. The eastern circuit consisted of the districts of New Hampshire, Massachusetts, Connecticut, and New York. Rhode Island was left out because she had not yet ratified the Constitution, and Vermont was still an independent republic. The middle circuit consisted of New Jersey, Pennsylvania, Delaware, Maryland, and Virginia; the southern circuit, of Georgia and South Carolina. North Carolina would be added to this circuit after she ratified. This pattern of a threefold sectionalization, together with the use of the familiar terms "eastern," "middle," and "southern," is one that has already been met with in the period of the Confederation. No provision was made in this law for a western circuit; it was a measure purely for the Atlantic seaboard.

Congress, by the act of February 13, 1801, set up a number of new districts, some of which were beyond the Alleghenies, and regrouped all districts into six circuits as follows: the first circuit, Maine, New Hampshire, Massachusetts, and Rhode Island; the second, Connecticut, Vermont, and Albany district and New York; the third, New Jersey, Pennsylvania, and Delaware; the fourth, Maryland and Virginia; the fifth, the two Carolinas and Georgia; and the sixth circuit, Tennessee, Kentucky, and Ohio. Thus the trans-Allegheny section, where circuit court business was presumed to be limited in amount, was given one circuit; while the Atlantic coast states, which had the bulk of such business, were very liberally provided for by the establishment of five circuits.

This statute did not long remain on the books. Repealed in March, 1802, it was replaced by the act of April 29, 1802. This latter act, supplemented by the act of February 24, 1807, established patterns of circuit court geography that endured for a full generation. New Hampshire, Massachusetts, and Rhode Island composed the first circuit; Connecticut, New York, and Vermont, the second; New Jersey and Pennsylvania, the third; Maryland and Delaware, the fourth; Virginia and North Carolina, the fifth; and South Carolina and Georgia, the sixth. There were now six circuits for Atlantic coast jurisdictions. The supplementary act of 1807 to some extent took care of the interests of the West of that day by establishing a seventh circuit, made up of Kentucky, Tennessee, and Ohio.

Although the country beyond the mountains grew rapidly and legal business multiplied accordingly, many years passed before Congress again legislated on the matter. At last the expansion of the western country forced the establishment of additional circuit court districts and the rearrangement of some old ones. The act of March 3, 1837, preserved untouched the existing patterns of judicial geography on the Atlantic coast, but made several changes in the patterns of the Mississippi Valley. The Northwestern states of Ohio, Michigan, Indiana, and Illinois now formed one circuit court district, and the Southwestern states of Alabama, Mississippi, Louisiana, and Arkansas formed a second. Kentucky, Tennessee, and Missouri made up a third and intermediate district.

Thus the legislation of 1837 retained the six circuits earlier set up on the Atlantic seaboard, and provided for three circuits in the Mississippi Valley. Here matters rested for some years. Then the discovery of gold in California led to a rapid growth of population in the Far West, and soon the volume of judicial business justified the establishment on the Pacific Coast of district and circuit courts. The act of March 2, 1855, set up a circuit court in and for California, which constituted the tenth circuit. In 1855, therefore, the pattern of sectionalization displayed one circuit for the Pacific Coast, three for the Mississippi Valley, and six for the Atlantic seaboard. By the act of March 3, 1863, Congress provided that Oregon should form a part of the tenth circuit and that the other circuits should remain as then constituted. After several minor alterations, there came in 1866 a major change in the circuit court districts.

The act of July 23, 1866, replaced the existing ten circuits by nine. The first and second circuits, composed of New England and New York, were maintained unchanged. The third circuit was composed of Pennsylvania, New Jersey, and Delaware; the fourth, of Maryland, Virginia, West Virginia, and the two Carolinas; and the fifth, of Georgia, Florida, Alabama, Mississippi, Louisiana, and Texas. The states of Ohio, Michigan, Kentucky, and Tennessee made up the sixth circuit; and Indiana, Illinois, and Wisconsin the seventh. The eighth circuit consisted of Minnesota, Iowa, Missouri, Kansas, and Arkansas; and the ninth and final circuit, of California, Oregon, and Nevada.

The Atlantic States had now four circuits instead of six. They had lost Georgia and Florida, which had been added to a new "Deep South" circuit extending from Texas on the west to Florida and Georgia on the east. The upper Mississippi Valley, east of the river, was served by two circuits—the sixth and seventh. West of the river lay the eighth circuit, which ran from Arkansas on the south to Minnesota on the north; to it Kansas belonged, as later on Nebraska and other states were also to belong. The high plains, the Rockies, and the interior plateaus had not yet been taken into the system, which at the moment was completed by the ninth, or Pacific Coast, circuit. It is evident that the patterns for the sectionalization of circuit court business, as set by the statute of 1866, differed markedly from those obtaining before the Civil War.

Omitting various interesting legislative details, we pass on to the end of the century. In 1900, the terminal year of this study, and nine years after the passage of the Circuit Court of Appeals Act, there were still nine circuit court judicial districts. These, from the first through the seventh, retained the bounds they had possessed in 1866. But the eighth circuit, which lay west of the Mississippi, had expanded enormously, and the ninth district—the Far West—quite considerably. The latter circuit now comprised Montana, Idaho, Nevada, Arizona, and the three Pacific seaboard states of Washington, Oregon, and California. The former circuit consisted of Wyoming,

Utah, Colorado, New Mexico, and all intervening jurisdictions east-ward to the Mississippi River, from Arkansas on the south to Minne-sota on the north. Thus the entire Union had been provided for by a ninefold system of circuit court judicial districts. The geography of these judicial districts, as they stood in 1900, more or less reveals sectional patterns modified by various limiting practical circum-stances.

During a century and more, then, Congressional legislation re-lating to circuit court judicial districts was framed by legislators who in a firsthand way understood the broad realities of the American sectionalisms of their times. Practical matters—such as the probable volume of litigation to come before the several courts, and the ease with which parties to litigation, and judges who were to hear it, could travel to the courts in the various circuits—were the concern of the pragmatic legislators who made these laws.

So it was that in dividing up the Union into a number of circuit court districts, to meet the needs of a special branch of legal adminis-tration, congressmen over the years gave continuing testimony to the proposition that as in the days of the Confederation, so in the time of the Federal Union, some particular problems of American federal administration had to be solved on a sectional basis if they were to be solved at all.[71]

Jedidiah Morse of Charlestown, Massachusetts, was a Congrega-tional pastor when he published, in 1789, *The American Geography; or, A View of the Present Situation of the United States of America.* This work was immediately received with great respect and en-thusiasm. A long series of revisions followed the original edition, and Morse was soon on the way to being recognized as "the father of Ameri-can geography." In the course of developing this series of scholarly tomes, Morse found occasion to formulate a statement of a system of American sections. His is therefore the credit for taking the now familiar threefold system of sections and treating it as an abstraction. He was the first American to give consideration to the implied con-cept of the section, and to undertake two tasks in relation thereto: first, to deal with the implied concept by making it explicit; and

[71] Felix Frankfurter and James M. Landis, *The Business of the Supreme Court; a study in the federal judicial system* (New York, 1927) provides a convenient key to the relevant legislation, and much else besides.

second, to use the explicit, now formulated concept as an organizing principle, as a principle of ordonnance, in his geographies.

We may look quickly at the route he traveled in originating, developing, and applying this abstraction. This scrutiny is justified: Morse is indeed the pioneer thinker in the history of the American concept of the section, and the first American to give serious thought to the problem.

His first book, a one-volume treatise published in 1789, opens with chapters entitled "Introduction," and "Geography." Next he offers a general description of the United States which is an effective combination of geography and history. This general account evidences that Morse was familiar with the sectional terms then current, and the current sectional differences. "Attempts are making," he writes, "to introduce a uniformity of pronunciation throughout the States, which for political, as well as other reasons, it is hoped will meet the approbation and encouragement of all literary and influential characters. . . . The time, however, is anticipated . . . when the language, manners, customs, political and religious sentiments of the mixed mass of the people who inhabit the United States, shall have become so assimilated, as that all nominal distinctions shall be lost in the general and honourable name of Americans."

From this generalized, preliminary account of the United States as a whole, Morse passes on to a description of New England. At the start he makes the point that these four states east of New York have "the general name of New England" and that they have "several things" in common. "Their religion, manners, customs, and character; their climate, soil, productions, natural history, &c. are in many respects similar. . . . These considerations," he concludes, "have led to the following general description of New England."[72] The general account on the section itself is twenty-one pages long, and is well organized under numerous specific headings. Morse follows this with concrete, detailed particular accounts of New Hampshire, Massachusetts (including the province of Maine), Rhode Island, and Connecticut.[73] He has given a carefully prepared, well-rounded description of

[72] Jedidiah Morse, *The American Geography; or, A View of the Present Situation of the United States of America* (Elizabethtown, New Jersey, 1789), 68, 140.

[73] The detailed treatment of Vermont, at this time an independent republic, is separated from the detailed treatment of the other parts of New England, but Morse clearly conceives of it as part of New England in his generalized discussion, *ibid.*, 140.

one section of the Union. However, he has not yet gone so far as explicitly to identify it as such. Not yet does he refer to it in the abstract as a section, or a division, although it seems plain that he is already conceiving of it in this very way.

His treatment of the remaining states in the Union offers a bold contrast to his implied sectionalized treatment of New England. These other states he describes and discusses separately without any sectional grouping or groupings. His method, after he leaves New England, is simply to enumerate and to discuss and describe, separately, in reasonable detail, New York, New Jersey, Pennsylvania, Delaware, Maryland, Virginia, Indiana ("a tract of land lying on the Ohio river, in the state of Virginia"), Kentucky ("belonging, at present, to the state of Virginia"), North Carolina, South Carolina, and Georgia. Here plainly he follows a north-to-south order, and when "Western" jurisdictions are related to parent states, he assigns these to their "natural" places in the sequence, as above. "The Western Territory" follows the discussion on Georgia. "Under this name is comprehended all that part of the United States which lies northwest of the Ohio."[74] The independent republic of Vermont is next described, and this account is followed by a compact discussion of the "British American dominions." Under this general heading Morse furnishes accounts of "New Britain," Labrador (termed North and South Wales), Canada, and Nova Scotia, which since 1784 had consisted of New Brunswick and Nova Scotia proper. As though to indicate that by now the new Americans had quite transcended the older British American outlook, Morse fits in a brief statement on the West India Islands, and to the tropic British islands adds, surprisingly, the northern islands of Newfoundland, Cape Breton, and St. John's. Here, of course, he is doing some injustice to the facts of geographical position.

In 1793, Morse published, under a slightly different title, a second edition, considerably revised and enlarged. Of some little interest for the present purpose is Morse's altered treatment of North America, which forms an improved introduction to his valuable work. After a short notice of Danish America and Greenland, he takes up "British America,"[75] under which term he now (1793) includes New

[74] *Ibid.*, 401, 402, 457.
[75] Jedidiah Morse, *The American Universal Geography* (2 vols., Boston, 1793), I, 130.

Britain, Upper and Lower Canada, Cape Breton Island, Nova Scotia and New Brunswick, the island of St. John's, and Newfoundland. Each of these areas is briefly discussed. Following the account of this now markedly contracted "British America," Morse gives a comprehensive and detailed general description of the United States, concluding his general discussion of the United States as a whole with the comforting observation that the first legislative and executive acts of the new Federal Union "open the fairest prospect of the peace, union and increasing respectability of the American States."[76]

Morse is now at the point where his next obligation to the reader of this volume is to introduce him to the geography of the several states of the new Union. And here the author takes, in the history of the concept of the section, a long step forward. He brings forth, at this juncture, a scheme which consists of a system of American sections comprehensive enough to cover all parts of the Union of that day. His purpose in making this conceptualized statement is to provide himself with a principle of arrangement, a canon of ordonnance, by the aid of which he can bring his myriad of particular parts into harmony and coherence. The abstraction formulated by Morse is the first of the kind in the history of the idea we are tracing. Hence it is presented in full, with the single preliminary comment that Morse does not use the term "sections," but a novel term of his own, "grand divisions." His abstraction or scheme of arrangement is indicated by a heading, in capitals—

GRAND DIVISIONS of the UNITED STATES.

Then begins a discussion which, since it contains a critical passage, must be given entire:

The American Republic, of which we have given a general account, consists of three grand divisions, denominated the *Northern,* or more properly *Eastern, Middle* and *Southern* States. The *first* division, (the Northern or Eastern States) comprehends Vermont, New Hampshire, District of Maine (belonging to Massachusetts), Massachusetts, Rhode Island, Connecticut. These are called the New England States, and comprehend that part of America, which, since the year 1614, has been known by the name of New England. The *second* division (the Middle States) comprehends New York, New Jersey, Pennsylvania, Delaware, Territory N. W. of Ohio. The *third* division (the Southern States) comprehends Maryland,

[76] *Ibid.,* 309.

Virginia, Kentucky, North Carolina, Territory S. of Ohio, South Carolina, Georgia. Of these we shall treat in their order.[77]

Morse gives no explanation of his reasons for making a sectionalization of the states described in his book. He simply recognizes the fact of sectionalization and makes use of it.

It is noticeable that he heads his list of states with Vermont, now a member of the Union, and continues on southward as before, inserting the Northwest Territory after Delaware; Kentucky after Virginia, its parent state; and the Territory South of the Ohio after North Carolina, its parent state. The lands on the "western waters" are thus brought into the historic pattern already worked out for the Atlantic coast, at the same time that the north-to-south order has been preserved. Morse has formulated a neat scheme. He was skillful enough, and sufficiently well informed, to apply it to the needs of his special geographical purposes. He supplies an excellent general account of the section of "New England, or Northern or Eastern States." This general description covers the situation of the division, its boundaries, climate, diseases, the face of the country, mountains, shrubs and plants, agricultural products, the population, its character and diversions, and the history of the section. Following this general discussion come accounts of the particular states within New England.

Then, after the sketch of Connecticut, the author announces "Middle States," and opens thus: "We now come to the Second Grand Division of the United States, comprehending New York, New Jersey, Pennsylvania, Delaware, Territory N. W. of Ohio."[78] This introduction is immediately followed by a general essay on the "Middle States." The account, founded on authoritative sources, is undeniably brief—but a page and a half long. The inference is allowable that Morse inserts this general account here for the sake of logical consistency. Having done that much for New England, he must do something like it—even if not quite so much—for the Middle States. But the length of the essay is not important; the principle exhibited is. The general sketch is followed by various particular accounts. New York is treated at length, New Jersey more briefly, then Pennsylvania and Delaware.

The "Territory N. W. of Ohio" having finally been discussed,

77 *Ibid.*, 309–10.
78 *Ibid.*, 416.

Morse proceeds to the "Southern States." "The Third, and much the largest Grand Division of the United States comprehends Maryland, Virginia, Kentucky, North Carolina, Territory South of Ohio, South Carolina, and Georgia."[79] The usual general essay on the division as a whole opens this part of the work. The account is less than a full page in length and, though brief, evidences some power in the ability to generalize. Morse picks on the salient characteristic of the division when he points out that it has thirteen-fourteenths of all the slaves in the United States. After this there follow sketches of the particular Southern states. The description of Virginia is the longest. Georgia is the last to be considered. An account of the Spanish dominions, opening with the two Floridas, follows these discussions of the Southern States.

This grouping of the states and territories into three "grand divisions" or sections; the preparation of the general accounts of the three sections, which involved synthesizing and generalizing upon numbers of facts, many of which had to be ascertained for the first time to carry out the general point of view in a systematic and uniform manner; and the composition of the particular sketches called for industry, insight, and scholarship. Morse, therefore, may justly be termed the father of the concept of the American section, even granting that his formulation is far from complex. However, he isolated the concept. His formulation was achieved less in abstract terms which head up into a definition than as a practical geographical scheme, comprehensible to the general readers of the time and applicable both broadly and precisely to the special data with which he was concerned. His applications were made with neatness, good sense, and authority.

Morse impressed this mode of discussing and writing sectionally upon other writers, both contemporaries and successors. Dr. Barton of Philadelphia prepared, in 1804, an account of United States geography for the American edition of a British work on modern geography. In the course of his preliminary remarks, Barton observes that the lands of this country have been classified "under three grand divisions," which he enumerates. He then adds, "But to this division there are many objections."[80] Barton objects to the threefold division,

---

79 *Ibid.*, 519.
80 John Pinkerton *et al.*, *Modern Geography* (2 vols., Philadelphia, 1804), II, 422.

not to the dividing up of the country into sections as such. Another compiler, Henry Moore of London, writing about 1812 on United States geography, referred to the "divisions" of the country and observed that modern American geographers divided the country into "grand divisions, according to their situation."[81]

Before taking leave of Morse's second edition, we note that after a discussion of South America, Morse gives consideration to the "West India Islands," provides a "general description of them," and then offers an account of the "British West Indies" and a few other British outlying possessions.[82] The distinct separation in this book between the descriptions of British America and the accounts of the British West Indies silently indicates that the Americans of 1793 were thinking, geographically, in new terms. The outlook of the third quarter of the century—the "old" British American outlook with its characteristic system of sections—was passing, or had already passed away.

The fifth edition of Morse's geography (Boston, 1805) presents the scheme of "Grand Divisions of the United States," with the appropriate additions and expansions necessitated by the growth of a "rising empire." New England remains unchanged, but the Middle States now comprise such additional new jurisdictions as Ohio and the territories of Indiana and Michigan. New jurisdictions in the Southern parts comprise Tennessee and the territory of Mississippi. "To which," Morse continues, "we may now add Louisiana."[83] The plan of organization followed in earlier editions (since 1793) is again followed. After the description of Mississippi Territory, Morse furnishes his account of Louisiana—an up-to-date piece of writing, and an extensive one, too. Louisiana, he declares, may be divided naturally into three divisions: Eastern, Lower, and Upper Louisiana. The chapter is replete with concrete and detailed information.

In this edition, Morse makes use of an acknowledged threefold system of sections, but actually assumes an unacknowledged fourth section, Louisiana. His scheme now stands on the verge of confusion, for some of the areas in his three divisions are Atlantic areas, and

81 Henry Moore, *A New and Comprehensive System of Universal Geography* (London, [1812?]), 1070.

82 Morse, *American Universal Geography* (1793 ed.), Table of Contents.

83 Jedidiah Morse, *The American Universal Geography*, 5th ed. (2 vols., Boston, 1805), I, 310.

others are "Western." Louisiana itself is wholly "Western." The scheme will soon need revision.

In the sixth edition (Boston, 1812), Morse replaces this threefold scheme by an acknowledged fourfold scheme. The fourth "division" of course is Louisiana, now divided into Orleans Territory and Louisiana Territory. The confusion noted above thus increases. Its root cause may be frankly recognized. The country was growing rapidly, new jurisdictions were being added, and these evidences of growth called for correspondingly frequent reconsiderations of the facts, and revisions, by Morse, of his scheme of "grand divisions."

Already a logical, simplified—perhaps oversimplified—scheme for a twofold system of sections had been worked out by Noah Webster in his *Elements of Useful Knowledge*. Webster seized on and made excellent use of the fact that the great chain of the Alleghenies divides the country into two large groups of states. The "Atlantic States," beginning with New Hampshire and Vermont and ending with Georgia, lay chiefly east of the mountain chain. The "Western States and Territories" lay beyond the mountains. This latter section comprised Kentucky, Ohio, Tennessee, the territory west of Georgia and south of Tennessee, Indiana Territory, Michigan Territory, and Louisiana.

In his seventh edition (Boston, 1819), Morse, perhaps taking a hint from Webster, replaced his own now awkward and illogical scheme of sections by a newly drafted fourfold scheme, which fused useful features drawn from the earlier Morse and perhaps from Webster, too. In this new scheme, the account of the first grand division— the Eastern States or New England—was followed by the discussion of the second division, the Middle States, all of which were on the Atlantic coast. The third grand division, the Southern States, was now composed of the jurisdictions from Virginia southward to and including Florida and Alabama. The fourth grand division consisted of the "Western States and Territories." Morse grappled thoroughly with the elements in this division and saw clearly that in constructing a scheme, position, and not civil status, was the prime consideration. Therefore he made no distinction between the states as such and the territories as such. Instead, he maintained only the positional distinctions. His fourth or Western division therefore consisted of two parts. East of the Mississippi River, and arranged from south to north, were Mississippi, Tennessee, Kentucky, Illinois, Indiana, Ohio, Michigan Territory, and the Northwest Territory. West of the great river were Missouri, "Arkansaw Territory," Louisiana, and the "Territories W. of these to the Pacific Ocean." [84]

This new scheme of sections is comprehensive, up to date, and logical. It does Morse much credit. The scheme forms part of his extended general account of the United States. This concluded, Morse provides a ten-page description and discussion of the "Eastern States; or New-England." Next follow the sketches of the particular states within the section, commencing with Vermont. After Connecticut, Morse announces: "Middle States." [85] But he does no more than enumerate these; he has deleted his general accounts of the three other sections. What stories lie behind this retrograde step? We do not know. In dealing with the country beyond the Mississippi, Morse took as great pains as he did elsewhere to provide reliable information. This is what he writes of the soon-to-be-aspersed plains far to the west of the river: "Nearly the whole of this wide spread country, is covered with a profusion of grass and plants, among which are a number of esculent, nutritious roots. The air is pure and dry, and the climate milder, than in the same parallels on the Atlantic. This district affords many advantages to settlers and is capable of yielding in abundance the necessaries of life." [86] Morse writes more sympathetically of these plains than those geographers who—soon after Long's expedition—were to follow the father of American geography.

The foregoing discussion has shown how Morse originated, formulated, and applied a simple concept of geographic sectionalism inherent in United States usages during his time. As the country expanded, he made various modifications in his scheme. His successors took over from him the concept of geographic sectionalization and applied it, with numerous modifications, during the next eighty years.

Between 1820 and 1900, many Americans compiled geographical handbooks and gazetteers. Those geographers who employed a con-

[84] Jedidiah Morse, *The American Universal Geography*, 7th ed. (2 vols., Boston, 1819), I, 209.

[85] *Ibid.*, II, 285, 382.

[86] *Ibid.*, I, 672.

cept of sections as a principle for organizing and arranging their data may be thought of as successors to Morse. A representative number of their works will be surveyed in order to indicate the main trends in the later development and application of the concept of the American section.

The convenience, for reference and for generalizing purposes, of an established system of American sectional terms is indicated by an excerpt from David B. Warden's description of the United States (1819). Warden, who was not a geographical writer but a general publicist, made this observation: "In a general point of view, the planters are the prevailing class in the southern states; the agricultural people in the western states; and the commercial in the eastern. In the middle states the agricultural and commercial classes are more equally balanced. The classes of mechanics and manufacturers are most numerous in the middle and eastern states."[87] This excerpt shows how a sectional analysis could be turned to good account in making fairly precise statements about a wide-spreading nation.

Joseph Worcester's handbook (1819) on general geography classified the sections into New England (which now begins with Maine), Middle States, Southern States, and Western States.[88] These last comprise Tennessee, Kentucky, Ohio, Indiana, Illinois, Michigan Territory, and Northwest Territory. In addition to these four sections, Worcester lists a fifth, Louisiana. Included under this rather indefinite term are Arkansas Territory; Missouri, then a territory but soon to be a state; the state of Louisiana; and the Louisiana country in the largest sense, stretching from the Mississippi River to the Pacific Ocean, and comprehending within its bounds the Rocky Mountains. Four divisions and "Louisiana" as constituted above, however, do not make a logical scheme of sections, since the fifth category includes some jurisdictions that could properly be assigned to the Southern States, and others that could be grouped with the Western States.

The proposition that the United States consists of four main divisions was accepted by Jacob A. Cummings (1821), who, after enumerating the divisions and the states and territories in each of them,

[87] David B. Warden, *A Statistical, Political, and Historical Account of the United States of North America; from the period of their first colonization to the present day* (3 vols., Edinburgh, 1819), I, xiv.

[88] Joseph E. Worcester, *Elements of Geography, Ancient and Modern* (Boston, 1819), *passim.*

provided discussions and characterizations for each.[89] Cummings included the Louisiana country under his heading of "Western States
and Territories," thus handling his scheme in neater fashion than
Worcester. Jacob Willetts' compendious little work (1822) listed
four main sections and the country of Louisiana.[90] This country—
actually a fifth main category—he divided into the states of Louisiana
and Missouri, the Arkansas Territory, and the uninhabited Indian
country, stretching to the Pacific Ocean. Florida, lately ceded by
Spain, was placed in the terminal position on his list, and hence outside its proper section.

The third volume of the American translation of Malte-Brun's
Géographie Universelle was published in 1827. This European work,
emended and altered by American hands in so far as the geography
of the United States is concerned, contains material relevant to the
development of a doctrine of sections. The author observes that at
present (1824) the American federation consists of twenty-four states;
three territories possessing civil governments; and three other territories, as yet unoccupied by a civilized population.

If we attend to the distinctions which exist among these various states
and territories, founded on their physical circumstances, or the pursuits
and character of the people, we may class them into four grand groups;
first, New England, embracing the Six States east of the Hudson, which
is the most thickly peopled, and the most commercial section of the
Union. Second, the Middle States, including New York, Pennsylvania,
New Jersey, Delaware, and Maryland, in which the agricultural character is united with, and qualified by the commercial. Thirdly, the Southern States, including Virginia and all the maritime country to the Mississippi, where the amount of commerce is comparatively small, where slaves
are numerous, and the husbandmen are generally planters. Fourth, the
Western States, in the basin of the Ohio, enjoying the best soil and climate
in the United States, where there are few slaves, and where the character
of the people is almost purely agricultural.[91]

The author then lists the Atlantic States from Maine to Georgia
and discusses each. He next considers Alabama, Mississippi, Louisi-

[89] Jacob A. Cummings, *An Introduction to Ancient and Modern Geography*, 8th ed.
(Boston, 1821), 11.

[90] Jacob Willetts, *A Compendious System of Geography; being a Description of the
Earth*, 2nd ed. (Poughkeepsie, 1822).

[91] M. Malte-Brun, *Universal Geography, or A Description of all the parts of the
World* (6 vols., Philadelphia, 1827–29), III, 214.

ana, Tennessee, Kentucky, and the states north of the Ohio River. The three relatively advanced territories—Florida, Michigan, and Arkansas—are next enumerated and described. Then come the three relatively uncivilized territorial areas—the "North West Territory," afterward Wisconsin; Missouri Territory (distinct from the state of Missouri),[92] the vast country east of the Rocky Mountains; and the "Western Territory," which includes the country watered by the Columbia and its numerous branches.

Malte-Brun's treatment of the American jurisdictions and sections illustrates a procedural error that the geographers were for long to persist in making. This was to distinguish between states and territories, setting up two distinct categories. Geographers refused for decades to see that in classifications of a positional or geographical kind, the nature of the civil status of a given area had no significance. From the areal point of view, the territories and the states occupying that area should have been considered together as forming one section. Florida, for example, should have been classed with the South, not left to trail along in a miscellaneous group of territories, separated by many lines of print from its "natural" place on the list, or in the "section." The geographers were slow to grasp this elementary fact, and because they were, they came more slowly than they might have, to soundly based schemes of sectional arrangements. These faults are demonstrated in the books written, among many others, by William Channing Woodbridge and Grenville Mellen.

The geography that Woodbridge issued (1831) was popular,[93] going through many editions. Woodbridge enumerates such usual groups as the Eastern, Middle, and Southern States. He counts as Western States Alabama, Mississippi, Louisiana, Ohio, Indiana, Illinois, Kentucky, Tennessee, and Missouri. After the four main groupings he gives a fifth—the territories of the United States. These he designates, in order, North-West Territory, Missouri Territory, Oregon or Western Territory, Arkansaw Territory, and Florida Territory. This fifth grouping is really composed of portions of the four preceding sections, and one or more other potential or unrecognized sections.

[92] *Ibid.*, 230.
[93] William Channing Woodbridge, *A System of Universal Geography, on the Principles of Comparison and Classification*, 4th ed. (Hartford, 1831).

Grenville Mellen (1836) observes that the states are familiarly classed under four divisions.[94] His Western section comprises Tennessee, Kentucky, Ohio, Indiana, Illinois, and Missouri. His territories are Florida, Michigan, Missouri, Arkansas, and Oregon.

Jesse Olney's handbook (1837) presents a skillful handling of the scheme of sectional arrangements. His twenty-fifth edition was happy in the date of its publication, since several former territories had now become states.[95] Olney's first and second sections extend from Maine to Delaware. The tract of land from Maryland to Louisiana, including the territory of Florida, constitutes his third section. His fourth or Western section straddles the Mississippi River; here are Tennessee, Kentucky, Ohio, Michigan, Indiana, Illinois, Missouri, and Arkansas, a new state. Under the heading of "Territories," Olney groups one east of the Mississippi, namely Wisconsin, and two west of that river, Missouri Territory and Oregon Territory. This is indeed a neat scheme.

In Samuel A. Mitchell's handbook (1838)[96] is found a simple, neat fourfold scheme of sections: Eastern States, Middle States, Southern States (including Florida Territory), and Western States and Territories. This last comprised the Ohio Valley, the Mississippi Valley, and the trans-Mississippi districts and regions west of Missouri and Arkansas. Mitchell's unification of the Western States and Territories under one heading is probably owing to the influence of Timothy Flint's geographical thinking. A few years earlier (1832) Flint had published a meritorious work, *The History and Geography of the Mississippi Valley*.[97] In this two-volume production the learned and accomplished author reversed the customary order followed by American geographers. Flint treated the West first, and at great length, and the Atlantic States afterward, in a comparatively brief manner. By undertaking to provide a systematic, detailed, and lengthy account of the geography of the Mississippi Valley, Flint put his contemporaries under great obligations. From the point of view of the development

[94] Grenville Mellen, *A Book of the United States, exhibiting its geography, divisions, constitution and government* (Hartford, 1836), 263.

[95] Jesse Olney, *A Practical System of Modern Geography*, 25th ed. (New York, 1837).

[96] Samuel A. Mitchell, *An Accompaniment to Mitchell's Map of the World* (Philadelphia, 1838).

[97] Timothy Flint, *The History and Geography of the Mississippi Valley*, 2nd ed. (2 vols., Cincinnati, 1832).

and application of the concept of sectionalization in geography, he registered an advance. The making of the clear-cut distinction between the Atlantic States and the Mississippi Valley, between East and West, is reinforced in positive fashion by his copious supply of facts and by his emphasis on the West in general—an emphasis which is confirmed by his inclusion in the book of passages bearing on western Pennsylvania and western Virginia, as well as on the North-West Territory, the Missouri Territory, and the Oregon Territory. The substance of this work on Western geography is arranged in an orderly manner and proceeds on a south-to-north basis as follows: Florida Territory, Alabama, Mississippi, Louisiana, Arkansas Territory, Missouri, Illinois, Tennessee, Kentucky, Indiana, Ohio, western Pennsylvania, western Virginia, Michigan, and North-West Territory, i.e. Wisconsin. The concluding two chapters are devoted to the Missouri and the Oregon territories.

Having made this logical and systematic description of the West of that day, with its outlying districts on the Atlantic (Florida), on the Pacific (Oregon), and in the intermediate basin of the Missouri, the author later on, in his second volume, disregards his own contribution—the definite, though broadly stated, sectionalization of the West as he has described it—and reintroduces the following illogical, contradictory scheme of sections. "The United States are divided either by physical landmarks, or by distinct climates and productions, into northern, middle and southern, and eastern and western states. The northern states include New England, or all the states east of Hudson River. The middle states include all the states between Hudson River on the east, and Potomac on the south and west; including, west of the Alleghany Mountains, Ohio, Kentucky, Indiana, Illinois, and Missouri. The southern states include the country south and west of these limits."[98] This statement manages to combine a threefold classification with a twofold classification, so that the two schemes are simultaneously uttered, but are not fused.

Charles Morrill (1840) used a fourfold classification scheme—Eastern, Middle, Southern, and Western States and Territories. In this last group he included Tennessee, Kentucky, Ohio, Maryland, Indiana, Illinois, Missouri, and Arkansas—eight states—and six terri-

[98] *Ibid.*, II, 4.

tories: Oregon, Missouri, Iowa, Wisconsin, Florida, and Indian Territory.[99]

In their *Complete Descriptive and Statistical Gazetteer of the United States of America* (1843), Haskel and Smith make several pertinent statements which point to one of the difficulties that the sectionalizers had to contend with. "All former gazetteers are rendered obsolete by the census [of 1840], which has but recently become available, and by the rapid changes which the country is undergoing, particularly in its newer portions," these authors point out. "Hundreds of new counties, towns, and post-offices, are described in this work, which are not to be found in any preceding gazetteer."[100] It was this prime fact that a continuously expanding country was always offering new areas for the geographers' consideration, that seemingly made their task of scheme-making somewhat trying. Yet the difficulty was apparent rather than real, as a University of Virginia professor, George Tucker, demonstrated in these very years.

The large territorial gains registered as a consequence of the Mexican War certainly made the task of the system-making geographers no easier than it had been, and probably made it more exacting.

The authors of geographical handbooks who wrote during the decade of the fifties made use of various schemes for organizing their facts according to sections. A few instances will show the trends. Jesse Olney (1851) offered a scheme[101] that included New England, the Middle States, the Southern States (from Maryland south to Florida and west to Texas), the Western States (which took in the states of the Mississippi Valley plus California), and, finally, a group of territories: Minnesota, Indian Territory, Nebraska, and Oregon. Olney provided attractive general descriptions of his several sections—a large point in his favor. After discussing the older territories, so to speak, he found he had to add discussions of California, a newly admitted state, and the territories of Utah and New Mexico. With territorial changes proceeding unexpectedly, he could not plan a logical,

---

[99] Charles Morrill, *A New System of Geography on the Classical Plan* (Concord, New Hampshire, 1840).

[100] Daniel Haskel and J. Calvin Smith, *A Complete Description and Statistical Gazetteer of the United States of America* (New York, 1843), 3, 4.

[101] Jesse Olney, *A Practical System of Modern Geography*, 68th ed. (New York, 1851).

comprehensive scheme. Roswell C. Smith (1853) tried to refine the current scheme in at least one detail.[102] He grouped his states under four headings, including as Western States, California and the states of the Mississippi Valley from Arkansas and Tennessee northward. Then came his innovation: he made a distinction between the organized and the unorganized territories. This distinction has only a slight bearing on the theme of sectionalization, but at the least it shows some thought.

Conventional in his use of a fourfold scheme was Francis McNally.[103] His elementary handbook (1855) presented a scheme of Eastern, Middle, Southern, and Western States, these last extending from Ohio on the east to California on the west. A fifth miscellaneous group was made up of eight territories, scattered from Washington and Oregon eastward to Minnesota, Kansas, and Nebraska.

Richard S. Fisher (1852) altered nomenclature to a slight extent, used a more than fivefold scheme, and seemed to be reaching for a continental view of the subject.[104] His groups in order are: the North-Eastern States, the Middle States (New York to Maryland), the Southern States (Virginia to Florida), the Western States (Ohio basin states, Wisconsin and Michigan, Iowa and Missouri), and the South-Western States (Tennessee, Alabama, Mississippi, Louisiana, Arkansas, and Texas). In the development of his remaining areas, Fisher exhibits a nascent feeling for sectional realities. In order, come discussions on the Indian Territory, Minnesota Territory, and the Western Territory, i.e., Nebraska. Next comes the country generally west of the Rockies, to which, with some feeling for a sectional approach, Fisher applies the general term "Pacific Country." This includes Oregon Territory, California, and Utah and New Mexico territories. New Mexico will be described under this heading, Fisher writes, "although not properly or altogether within the geographical limits of the country."[105] It certainly lies to Fisher's credit that in at least an informal way he has worked out a pattern of sectionalization that embraces three sections on the Atlantic coast, two in the eastern

[102] Roswell C. Smith, *A Concise and Practical System of Geography, for schools, academies, and families,* 28th ed. (New York, 1853).

[103] Francis McNally, *An Improved System of Geography designed for schools, academies and seminaries* (New York, 1855).

[104] Richard S. Fisher, *The Book of the World* (2 vols., New York, 1852).

[105] *Ibid.,* I, 318.

Mississippi Valley, one in the western Mississippi Valley, and one in the "Pacific Country," taking in New Mexico Territory. In a word, a sevenfold scheme in practice, even though not expressly avowed as such.

As the decade drew toward its close, sectional tensions mounted, intersectional rivalries intensified. The complex of sections that together made up the country underwent an ominous simplification. Men were now talking of North and South, of Free States and Slave States, as though but two sections existed. A reflection of this menacing oversimplification is to be seen in the then widely read and influential book by Hinton Rowan Helper, *The Impending Crisis of the South* (1857). The book opens with a chapter entitled "Comparison between the Free and the Slave States"[106] and then proceeds to bring out a long series of specific comparisons between North and South. The entire work is based upon an extensively developed comparison and antithesis between two main sections within the Republic. Sets of Southern statistics are matched for comparison with sets of Northern statistics; collections of Southern opinions are paired off and contrasted with collections of Northern opinions. The principle of sectionalization of data is given an ample application, and in a truly impressive manner. An implied concept of sections and an assumed view of a nation sectionalized provide the basis for the book.

Helper's contemporaries accustomed themselves to employing this oversimplified conception. A few days after Lincoln's election to the presidency, the editorial columns of the *Milwaukee Sentinel* carried the following opinion, a bold contrast between North and South: "That the North, with its twenty millions of 'persons', is inferior in resources or in any of the elements of wealth and strength, to the South, with its ten millions and its servile laborers, neither philosophy nor fact will establish, and if it is necessary for the North to subdue the South, or conquer the South, as a measure of self-defense, there is no occasion for discouragement in that direction."[107]

The secessions of the Southern States now occurred. These profoundly important events were soon reflected in the geographical handbooks. In 1862, John H. Rice published at Atlanta, Georgia, *A*

[106] Hinton Rowan Helper, *The Impending Crisis of the South: How to meet it* (New York, 1857), 11.

[107] *Milwaukee Sentinel*, November 16, 1861.

System of Modern Geography . . . for the Use of Schools and Academies in the Confederate States of America. This book reflects a transition accomplished from Southern sectionalism to Southern nationalism. The author claimed for the Confederacy all land lying between 25° and 40° north latitude, and included between the Atlantic Ocean and the Rocky Mountains. He opens his account of the several Confederate, formerly Southern, jurisdictions with Virginia. In order follow accounts of the two Carolinas, Georgia, Florida, Alabama, Mississippi, Louisiana, Texas, Arkansas, Missouri, Tennessee, Kentucky, the Indian Territory, and the territories of New Mexico and Arizona. Rice claimed Maryland also for the Confederacy, but in his list placed it after Arizona Territory, since, as he expressed it, Maryland, at the moment shackled by the bonds of federal despotism, was prevented from co-operating with the Confederacy.

Rice's book did not long maintain its usefulness. Appomattox took it out of currency. A geographer testified (1866), and on sectional grounds, too, that Providence had intended the country to be a united country: "The *Productive Plains of the Center and South,* the manufacturing region of the north-east, the broad plains and rich mines of the west, united by easy lines of communication and occupying positions perfectly adapted to each other—plainly show that Providence designed this nation to be One and Indivisible."[108]

The Union of American sections having been preserved by force of arms, the geographers were free to return to their books and bookmaking. S. A. Mitchell gave at least more than a passing thought to the old problem of sectional arrangement when he observed, in 1865, that "the usual division of the United States" had been into the New England or Eastern States, the Middle States, the Southern States (Virginia to Texas), and the Western States, or the remainder. He went on to point out, however, that there was another approach to the problem: "Some geographers have made but two divisions, viz.: according to climate and productions: thus, all the States lying north of 36° 30′ north latitude are called the Grain States, and those lying south of that line, the Cotton States." This twofold scheme recalls the oversimplified pattern of Helper. "Others again, make seven divisions, viz.: The Northeastern States, Middle States, Southern

108 James Monteith, *Monteith's physical and intermediate Geography; in two parts* (New York, 1866), 46.

States, Gulf States, Lake States, River States, and the Pacific States."
Mitchell then pointed out the objections to these schemes and presented his own plan. "As no one of these divisions is quite logical,
and as the admission of new States would constantly demand new
divisions, it has been thought best to enumerate the States according
to a systematic order, as they are arranged upon the map."[109] The
testimony as to the effect of the continuous stream of incoming states
upon the thinking of the American geographers is most interesting; so,
too, is the resolve to abandon a sectionalized treatment in favor of
simple enumeration. Mitchell, the reformer, as we may think of him,
began with Maine, New Hampshire, and Vermont and moved state
by state south and west to Kansas, California, Oregon, and Nevada.
He next enumerated the territories.

James Cruikshank (1867) did not give over an attempt to group
the states into a system of sections.[110] He set up four groups of states
and a group of territories. The Eastern States were followed by the
Northern States (extending from Kansas and Nebraska eastward to
New York and Pennsylvania), the Southern States (extending from
Arkansas and Texas eastward to the Carolinas, Virginia having been
grouped with the preceding complex), and the Pacific States (consisting of California, Oregon, and Nevada). The territories were
Indian Territory, New Mexico, "Dakotah," Montana, Idaho, Washington, Utah, and Arizona.

A small publication by D. M. Warren, *A New Primary Geography*
(1868), introduced a series of maps. Because of the requirements of
page size, these maps were not always logical in their presentation of
the sections. But at least the author was trying to think sectionally.
"With the aid of Maps, scholars should be required to name the
boundaries of each State, after each lesson on the Map of the section."[111] Noteworthy is the fact that Warren prefers the word "section" to the older word "division." His maps in the main are accurate
in the broad delineation of sections. They indicate that he thought
the concept of sectionalism had value in organizing a book intended
for young students.

A larger work (1870) by the same author accepts and again applies
the sectional scheme. "The States [politically speaking] are divided

[109] S. Augustus Mitchell, *A System of Modern Geography* (Philadelphia, 1865), 92.
[110] James Cruikshank, *A Primary Geography* (New York, 1867).
[111] D. M. Warren, *A New Primary Geography* (Philadelphia, 1868), 45.

into the Eastern, Middle, Southern, and Western."[112] Warren's Southern States range from Maryland to Texas; his Western States, from Ohio to California and Oregon. The territories consist of ten jurisdictions, including the new Wyoming and the old Indian territories. Five large, colored, well-delineated maps of the groups of states gave further emphasis to the sectional arrangement.

A considerable, indeed, a notable step in advance was made by two collaborators, A. von Steinwehr and Daniel G. Brinton. Together they copyrighted (1870) *An Intermediate Geography,* which ran to many editions. The authors gave further formulation to the sectionalization of the country, basing their advanced formulation on the leading facts of American physical geography. Discussing the surface of the land, they write: "The United States comprise three great *natural divisions*: (1) The Apalachian mountain system with the Atlantic coast plain, (2) the widest and most elevated portion of the Cordilleras . . . and (3) the Mississippi Valley with the Great Plains."[113] Each of these three "natural divisions" is then discussed briefly and well. The new sectional grouping is made on this large physiographic basis. "The states and territories may be conveniently classed under the following three groups, each of which includes one of the great physical regions of our country."[114]

The Eastern or Atlantic States include the Atlantic plain and the Appalachian Mountains. This group is divided into three sections: (1) New England States; (2) Middle States: New York to Virginia and West Virginia; and (3) Southeastern States: North Carolina to Florida.

The Central States occupy the Mississippi Valley and are divided into three sections: (1) North Central States east of the Mississippi; (2) North Central States west of the Missisippi; and (3) South Central States: Tennessee, Mississippi, Louisiana, Arkansas, Texas, and Indian Territory.

The Western States and Territories occupy the region of the Cordilleras and are divided into three sections: Rocky Mountain States, Plateau States, and Pacific States.

[112] D. M. Warren, *The Common-School Geography: An Elementary Treatise on Mathematical, Physical, and Political Geography,* rev. ed. (Philadelphia, 1870), 27.

[113] A. von Steinwehr and Daniel G. Brinton, *An Intermediate Geography, with lessons in map drawing* (New York, 1870), 20.

[114] *Ibid.,* 23.

The authors frequently employ the term "sections." Under the several sectional headings a uniform method of treating the facts pertaining to each section is worked out. The categories treated are position, surface, rivers and lakes, climate and vegetation, inhabitants and their occupations, and states and their cities. Under this final category the states are enumerated, along with the capitals and other cities. But plainly the main emphasis is on the sections themselves and on the sectionalization of the relevant information. The concept of the United States as a complex of sections has attained a clear, definite geographical statement. The authors have intelligently worked out and successfully applied in detail a ninefold scheme of sections—the most sophisticated thus far attempted by any American writers. They ignore the civil distinctions between state and territory, and seek the basis for their sectional scheme in the facts of physiography, considered in the large. They produced a reasonable intellectual product.

William Swinton (1875) followed these writers with regard to the three great "natural divisions" of the United States: the Atlantic slope, the Pacific slope, and the Mississippi Valley; but he refused to echo their view of nine sections. Instead, he asserted that the country could be "conveniently divided" into five sections: New England, the Middle States, the Southern States, the Western or Central States, and the Rocky Mountain or Pacific States.[115] He furnished general descriptions of the several sections. His information on the several states within each section was given treatment that subordinated it to the larger discussion of the section. Swinton introduced one or two remarks on nomenclature that must be noted. "The Western States," he wrote, "might better be called the Central States, for they are situated in the Mississippi Valley, which is the great central part of our country. . . . In fact, the name 'Western States' was given to this section at a time when it was really the farthest west that people had settled. But now that the Rocky Mountains and beyond to the Pacific Ocean contain great States, you can see that *Central* States is the proper name for this part of our broad country. . . . This section is so very large that the pupil must look long and often at the map of the United States so as to be able to form an idea of its vastness."[116]

[115] William Swinton, *Elementary Course in Geography: designed for primary and intermediate grades* (New York, 1875), 56, 57.
[116] *Ibid.*, 84.

Swinton's fifth section is made up of the "Pacific Highlands," which consist of Idaho, Montana, Nevada, Utah, Wyoming, Colorado, Arizona, and New Mexico. Then, perhaps as an afterthought, he writes: "There are two other Territories, lying east of the Rocky Mountains, which may as well be taken along with the Pacific Highlands. These are the Indian Territory and Dako'ta Territory."[117] This cavalier mode of assignment of "sectional position" clearly reveals that the geographers, as in Swinton's present case, were often operating quite subjectively; and that their sectionalizing procedures were not always based upon a clear, logically framed underlying concept as to what a "section" was.

In a larger, more advanced book (1880) Swinton revised his scheme of sections, and in the process considerably elaborated it.[118] The revised scheme is composed of the New England States; the Middle States (New York to Delaware and Maryland); the Southern States, Eastern Division (Virginia to Mississippi); the Southern States, Western Division (Louisiana, Arkansas, Texas, and Indian Territory); the Central States, Eastern Division (Ohio, Indiana, Illinois, Wisconsin, and Michigan); and the Central States, Western Division (Minnesota, Iowa, Missouri, Kansas, Nebraska, and Dakota Territory). Notable in this last category is the more reasonable position of Dakota. The new scheme is rounded out by his final section, that of the Pacific Highland States. This section consists of the Coast Division (California, Oregon, and Washington) and the Mountain and Plateau divisions. These last take in all the jurisdictions from Montana and Idaho territories on the north, to Arizona and New Mexico territories on the south. Accompanying his textual matter are an excellent physical map, a helpful commercial map, and seven maps of the sections in color. Swinton makes frequent use of the term "section": e.g., "How many and what states in this section [New England]?"[119] For each section and each division, he provides a general description under a convenient number of main headings; he then follows these with brief notes on the individual states comprising the section. "Supplementary Notes" bring out certain features that are peculiar to the several sections. On the whole, Swinton's

117 *Ibid.,* 91.

118 William Swinton, *Grammar-School Geography: Physical, Political, and Commercial* (New York, 1880).

119 *Ibid.,* 30.

books may be taken, for their day, as very good elementary treatments of geographical data ordered and arranged on a sectionalized basis.

Another title that must be considered in this series of geographical works is *Appleton's Higher Geography*. The anonymous author of this book (1881) makes use of a "classification of the States" which is plainly his own. The forty-four states may be arranged, he writes, "according to their situation and similarity of characteristics," in seven groups of states.[120] These he then enumerates. Incidentally, the author's employment of the useful term "Middle Atlantic States" to replace the older "Middle States," deserves recognition as a hard-won and tardily made gain in nomenclature. The author introduces a new distinction when he groups together Rocky Mountain and Pacific States and Territories into two divisions, thus: the Northern Division (Washington, Oregon, Idaho, Montana, and Wyoming) and the Southern Division (California, Nevada, Utah, Arizona, Colorado, and New Mexico). This gives a novel twist to the data. A list of "Regions distinguished for certain products" enumerates lumber, wheat, corn, hemp and tobacco, cotton, rice, pasture, and mineral regions.[121] These economic regions are also clearly indicated on his "Physical Map" of the United States.

Butler's Complete Geography (1887), by Jacques W. Redway, seems to indicate a desire on the author's part for a systematization in the use of sectionalized data.[122] He presents a scheme of "divisions," most of which are then subdivided into smaller "sections," thus: New England; Middle Atlantic States, northern and southern sections; South Atlantic and Gulf States, eastern section; Gulf States, western section; Central States, eastern and western sections; and Rocky Mountain and Pacific States and Territories, northern and southern sections. These several "sections" are indicated on appropriate, well-drawn maps, and the textual discussions are based on the maps. This well-arranged, systematic work assumes the existence of six main divisions, or nine divisions and subdivisions, in all. It represents a unified point of view given systematic presentation. A concept of sectionalism underlies its entire discussion of American geography and gives coherence and vitality to the contents.

[120] *Appleton's Higher Geography, embodying a comprehensive course with many original features* (New York, 1881), 29.

[121] *Ibid.*, 36.

[122] Jacques W. Redway, *Butler's Complete Geography* (Philadelphia, 1887).

Alexis Everett Frye published a *Complete Geography* (1895). His discussion of United States geography comprises a system of six "groups" of states.[123] This presentation is preceded by a series of short discussions devoted to various sectionalized economic activities and products, each discussion being illustrated by small sketch maps. Topics treated are cotton, wheat, corn, oats, tobacco, lumber, orchard products, hogs, beef cattle, etc.

Harper's School Geography (1894) contains a brief, interesting discussion of the rationale of sections. Such discussions being infrequently met with at best, it will be profitable to glance at the presentation, which is supported by a map in colors, bearing the legend "The United States subdivided into physical groups." In the essay, entitled "Divisions and Subdivisions of the United States," the authors state that "for convenience of study" the country may be divided into "sections and groups." This division

is based upon certain facts of the physical geography of the country. . . . *First,* One half of the country is "low," the other half "high." . . . *Second,* The lines of the coasts, mountains, plateaus, and of the Mississippi River, lie in a general north and south direction. These lines divide the country into seven nearly parallel physical belts; two of these belts are east of the Mississippi River, and five of them are west of it. *Third,* The Ohio River, the Potomac River, and the Chesapeake Bay form a well-marked line that divides the two eastern belts into groups of states which have widely different climatic, industrial, and social peculiarities. *Fourth,* The northern part of the most eastern belt is again divided by the line of the Hudson River and Lake Champlain.[124]

The application of those lines to the face of the country results in a scheme which may be stated thus: The "low half" of the United States comprises the Atlantic States (North Atlantic, Middle Atlantic, and South Atlantic) and the Central States (North Central, South Central, and West Central). The "high half" comprises the "Western or Highland States," consisting of the "States of the Plains," the "Rocky Mountain States," the "Basin States," and the "Pacific States." The authors' scheme of sections results in something rather highly developed and "logical"—a system of ten sections or subdivisions originating from two fundamentally different zones, the "low half" and the "high half." The scheme provides a principle of or-

---

123 Alexis Everett Frye, *Complete Geography* (Boston, 1895), 104.
124 *Harper's School Geography* (New York, 1894), 29.

ganization, which is used in accounts of the several subdivisions. It is illustrated by appropriate maps. The result as a whole is effective.

Jacques W. Redway and Russell Hinman, in their *Natural Advanced Geography* (1898), furnished a statement of principles after they had supplied, in a series of preliminary expositions, the concrete data—often illustrated by sketch maps—on which the "principles" rested. They therefore made something like a sustained effort to reach a theory of sections by a line of inductive reasoning. Their exposition is deserving of more attention than can here be permitted. Their conclusion, however, may be quoted:

Industrial Sections. We have seen that, owing largely to differences in surface structure, climate, and soil, the great productions of our country are confined more or less definitely to different regions. Hence the United States may be naturally separated into (1) the Northeastern, or cloth-manufacturing section; (2) the Northern, or food-, iron-, and coal-producing, and manufacturing section; (3) the Southern, or cotton-producing section; (4) the Plateau or grazing and gold- and silver-mining section; and (5) the Pacific, or Western food- and gold-producing section.[125]

If this scheme aimed at reducing the complexity of the pattern used in the Harper geography, it led to something altogether too broad and too simple. These authors have pushed their reaction against an overcomplicated sectional pattern too far.

The final geographical handbook to be considered in this long series of works of the kind is one by Ralph S. Tarr and Frank M. McMurry. This is their *North America* (1901). In this work the authors devoted considerable space to the physiographic basis. They aimed at presenting the physiographic facts relating to a given section or region and expounded the types of industries peculiar to the several sections. They set aside the state as the unit of study. "When the geography of the United States is studied by states, there is much repetition of the same kind of facts. . . . In order to avoid such waste of space and lack of perspective among the facts, the authors have proceeded by groups of states, rather than by individual states."[126] These authors were content with a system of five sections and deliberately refrained from providing an abstract discussion of the basis

[125] Jacques W. Redway and Russell Hinman, *Natural Advanced Geography* (New York, 1898), 61.

[126] Ralph S. Tarr and Frank M. McMurry, *North America, with an especially full treatment of the United States and its dependencies* (New York, 1901), viii–ix.

of their system, remarking merely, "In studying the different states it is convenient to group them into five sections and study each group by itself."[127] Their pattern of sections consists of New England, the Middle Atlantic States (New York to Virginia), the Southern States (everything from Oklahoma, Arkansas, Tennessee, and North Carolina southward), the Central States (from Ohio and Kentucky westward to the Dakotas and Kansas); and the Western States. Tarr and McMurry, also, show the emerging tendency to come forth with a relatively broad, simple scheme of sectionalization.

Before leaving these geographers—Jedidiah Morse and his successors—a few generalizations concerning their relationship to the concept of the section may be offered.

Morse, as we saw, from common parlance and common experience, took over the existing, implicit threefold system of sections and the nomenclature pertinent thereto. He made it explicit and definite and applied it as an organizing principle in his description of the geography of the United States. As the territory of the United States expanded, Morse revised and adapted his system of sections to fit the altered facts. He understood that behind his schemes of sectional classification there were the objective sectional differences themselves—phenomena of soils, physiography, situation, and climate; phenomena of agriculture, commerce, and manufacture; and phenomena of racial stocks, religious memberships, and political beliefs. He had learned these things from correspondents, from study, and from travel and firsthand observation.

Morse's successors who wrote geographies during the half-century from 1820 to 1870 borrowed from him the habit of using schemes of sectionalization. Sometimes with insight and skill, sometimes mechanically, they adapted these schemes as the country expanded and took over new sections. For the most part, they responded more to the need for convenience in arranging their data than to the calls of a strict logic. As a group they showed at least an elementary understanding of the fact that schemes of sections ultimately must rest upon a recognition of characteristic differences in soils, climates, crops, inhabitants, etc., as between the several areas of the country. Some of these writers showed but small power in generalizing about sectional characteristics and differences. On the other hand, a few

[127] *Ibid.*, 122.

writers, like Jesse Olney, Timothy Flint, Richard Fisher, and the American editors of Malte-Brun, displayed commendable ability in this field. No doubt exists that writers of their quality well understood that schemes for classifying sections were in the last analysis reasonable because of the existence of external "natural" differences between the sections.

The general geographers who published during the last thirty years of the nineteenth century raised their treatments onto a higher level. In the forefront of their understanding of sectionalization and sections in American geography was a quite clear comprehension of the real differences existing in America, and an equally clear recognition that these areal differences made, or brought about, the several characteristic sections. The richer the comprehension of the underlying objective features, the more highly developed the schemes of sectionalization to mirror these were likely to be. Knowledge of the details and varieties of American physiography, climates, and agricultures grew rapidly after 1870. Hence, after this date, there was a trend toward the production of progressively more complicated schemes. This is the movement of ideas underlying the developments from Steinwehr and Brinton through Swinton and Jacques W. Redway up to *Harper's School Geography,* as a culminating work, with its system of ten subdivisions. These books and others in the group provide a more richly articulated fusion of scheme with related concrete data than the books of the earlier period. These late nineteenth-century geographers made another advance in that they knew how to characterize the several sections tellingly with pertinent and abundant particular detail.

At the very end of the century a reaction set in. Adequate characterization of the several sections is preserved in the books that represent this new phase, but the schematic patterns of sectionalization were now comparatively simplified. Tarr and McMurry's *North America* (1901) illustrates the result of this countermovement: in this work an essential sectionality of geographical phenomena has been attained, which is based upon a recognition of consciously observed areal and positional features. At the same time, the wealth of data presented is patterned inside a simple fivefold scheme, which, in keeping with a trend dominant since about 1885, is erected upon a reliable physiographic basis.

The compilers of the published results of the decennial United States census were invariably presented with the problem of deciding upon the order in which to list the several states and territories of the Union, the populations of which had been enumerated by the census takers. In theory, the compilers of the published volumes could have listed the states in an alphabetical order or in a chronological order based upon date of ratification of the Constitution and admission into the Union. Without following further the various possible orders, we shall go on to see what orders they did in fact employ, during the period 1790–1900. This historical study of the literary ordonnance of an important administrative document issued as a series over more than a century will reveal that the compilers more often than not were striving to arrange their data according to a sectionalized plan or scheme. We shall see, too, that, before the nineteenth century had ended, the census officials were brought face to face with the urgent need for a soundly based scheme or system of sections, in accord with which they could classify and compare their statistics drawn from localities alike and unlike.

The returns of the First Census (1790) were arranged by census districts in the following order: Vermont, New-Hampshire, Maine and Massachusetts (these two were bracketed together), Rhode-Island, Connecticut, New-York, New-Jersey, Pennsylvania, Delaware, Maryland, Virginia and Kentucky (these two were bracketed together), North-Carolina, South-Carolina, and Georgia. Afterwards came "S. Western Territory" and then the "North Western Territory."

This order, it will be recalled, was that same north-to-south order used in the roll calls of the Confederation; it was the traditional order, and was the very plan one might have expected the compiler to use. The solitary surprise is in having Georgia followed by the "South Western Territory." Here the compiler may possibly have had the idea of pivoting, as it were, and so progressing according to a south-to-north direction in the Mississippi Valley—from the South Western Territory to the North Western Territory. The latter jurisdiction, incidentally, is without statistics, which may be another reason why it is given a terminal position.

The scheme employed in the Second Census (1800) used this order: New Hampshire, Massachusetts, Maine, Connecticut, Ver-

mont, Rhode Island, New York, New Jersey, Pennsylvania (two districts), Delaware, Maryland (including one part of the District of
Columbia), Virginia (three districts, including the remainder of the
District of Columbia), North Carolina, South Carolina, and Georgia.
Thus far the conventional north-to-south order has again been followed, for the Atlantic coast states. The remaining jurisdictions are
given in this order: Kentucky, "Territory N. W. of river Ohio," Indiana Territory, and Mississippi Territory. The return for Tennessee
was received late; hence its place comes after the listing of the territories. The compiler has separated the territories from the states and
has arranged them in the order of their establishment by law.

The order followed by the Third Census (1810) is by census districts thus: Maine, Massachusetts, New Hampshire, Vermont, Rhode
Island, Connecticut, New York, New Jersey, Pennsylvania, Delaware,
Maryland, Virginia, Ohio, Kentucky, North Carolina, Tennessee
(two districts), South Carolina, and Georgia. There then follow the
territories: Orleans, Mississippi, Louisiana, Indiana, Illinois, Michigan, and the District of Columbia. Perhaps one can see in this
scheme, in so far as the states proper are concerned, a desire on the
part of the compiler to establish a straight north-to-south order;
hence the inserted positions of Ohio and Kentucky after Virginia,
and of Tennessee after North Carolina. The compiler has evidently
wanted to draw up one unified list without making the distinction
between "Western" and "Atlantic" States. The states having been
grouped together in a unity, the compiler follows this with a consolidated group of territories.

The Fourth Census (1820) had a considerably enlarged territory
and several new jurisdictions to provide for. The compiler began
with Maine, passing thence to New Hampshire, Massachusetts, Rhode
Island, and Connecticut. Then he looped back to Vermont, went on
to New York (two districts), New Jersey, Pennsylvania (two districts),
Delaware, Maryland, the District of Columbia, Virginia (two districts), the two Carolinas, and Georgia. One sees in the scheme of
arrangement, up to this point, a desire to maintain in general a
north-to-south order. The compiler appears to have as a related desire, however, the desire to create a flowing sequence, without awkward gaps or lacunae. Hence his sequence of Connecticut, Vermont,
New York. After Georgia, this interest in a continuity of jurisdic-

tions is quite apparent. The order then becomes: Georgia, Alabama, Mississippi, Louisiana, Tennessee (two districts), Kentucky, Ohio, Indiana, Illinois, and Missouri. After this last state in the series, he lists the territory of Michigan and the territory of Arkansas. Thus, probably quite consciously, the compiler has worked out a south-to-north order for the "Western States," which keeps them together as a section, just as he has already taken over the customary north-to-south order for the "Atlantic States." The contrast between this pattern and that provided by the compiler of the census of 1810 is striking.

The Fifth Census (1830) follows an identical pattern. It opens with Maine and progresses southward to Georgia. Thence it moves successively through Alabama, Mississippi, and Louisiana and northward through the several states in the great valley to Illinois and then Missouri, the final state on the list. Again the Atlantic States have been kept together, and again the Western States, as a second broad section. After the states, the compiler lists the territories in this order: Michigan, Arkansas, and Florida. The District of Columbia has the terminal position. By 1830 an alphabetical arrangement, for the states at the least, would have been a boon for those who had to use this compilation frequently.

The Sixth Census (1840) presents the states in this order: Maine, New Hampshire, Massachusetts, Rhode Island, Connecticut, Vermont, New York (two districts), New Jersey, Pennsylvania (two districts), Delaware, Maryland, Virginia (two districts), North Carolina, South Carolina, Georgia, Alabama (two districts), Mississippi (two districts), Louisiana (two districts), Tennessee (three districts), Kentucky, Ohio, Indiana, Illinois, Missouri, Arkansas, and Michigan. Then follow the territories: Florida, "Wiskonsin," Iowa, and the District of Columbia.

The compiler, still following the patterns provided by his predecessors of 1830 and 1820, found himself in awkward case at the very end of his series, which reads, "Missouri, Arkansas, Michigan." This last state, plainly out of place, could easily have been inserted after Ohio, for the sake of maintaining the assumed principles of contiguity and continuity. However, he was more impressed by the principle of chronology: Arkansas became a state in 1836, Michigan in 1837. Thus he ends with an illogically formed list. The number of jurisdictions covered by this census is greater than the total in the census of 1830. Hence the reasonableness of an argument in favor of an alphabetical scheme was the greater.

The census publications by 1841 made up quite a shelf of valuable information and afforded the materials for the study, in time perspective, of many aspects of American life and activity. George Tucker, professor at the University of Virginia, decided to make a thorough analysis of the census from 1790 to 1840. He came to interesting conclusions on such subjects as the probabilities of life, proportion between the sexes, diversities between whites and Negroes, and progress of productive industry. He gave his results to the public in a short book, *Progress of the United States in Population and Wealth in fifty years* (1843). In order to institute comparisons between different areas within the country, Tucker had need of a scheme of sections— "divisions" he called them. He proceeded to formulate such a scheme, based on concrete details, and used it to group his statistics. His study of the elements and distribution of the American population brought him face to face with need for a scheme, and in these words he formulated his own: "As the States and Territories naturally arrange themselves into five divisions, which are separated not only by their geographical position, but also, with few exceptions, in their modes of industry and commercial interest, it is thought proper to compare the progress of population in these divisions, as may be seen in the following table."[128] Tucker then enumerates his five "natural" divisions: the New England States; the Middle States (New York, New Jersey, Pennsylvania, Delaware, and the District of Columbia); the Southern States (Virginia, North Carolina, South Carolina, Georgia, and Florida Territory); the Southwestern States (Alabama, Mississippi, Louisiana, Arkansas, and Tennessee); and the Northwestern States (Missouri, Kentucky, Ohio, Indiana, Illinois, Michigan, Wisconsin Territory, and Iowa Territory).

Tucker's fivefold scheme of sections was the most sophisticated sectional scheme yet devised. It was ingeniously framed for a comparative purpose and thus maintained a consistent point of view, including all jurisdictions that were contiguous to well-peopled areas, and all that presented enough population to warrant study. Tucker's

[128] George Tucker, *Progress of the United States in Population and Wealth in fifty years, as exhibited by the decennial Census* (New York, 1843), 57.

fivefold scheme reflects underlying economic and geographic realities; it has the great merit of calling attention not only to the three historic Atlantic coast sections but to the two forming Western sections, i.e., the upper Mississippi Valley and the lower Mississippi Valley. By leaving out of account the wilderness areas of Oregon and other remote trans-Missouri areas, and by treating states and territories together, geographically, without regard to the differences in their civil condition, Tucker contrived to bring forth this elegant structure.

His assumptions were that the states and territories "naturally arrange themselves" in five divisions; and that these divisions are owing, ultimately, to differences in "geographical position" and in "modes of industry and commercial interest."[129] This line of reasoning was originated when Tucker was studying the aggregate, general population of the United States. Further along in his book he felt obliged to consider "The Increase of the Atlantic and Western, Slaveholding and non-Slaveholding States, compared." Here again he had beforehand to lay down some sectional assumptions. The opening statements in his fourteenth chapter require to be quoted:

The several States and Territories have been differently divided, according to circumstances. Sometimes they are classed, as we have seen, under five divisions, as they severally agree in climate, products, and in the prevailing habits and pursuits of their people. Sometimes, again, they are divided into Atlantic and Western States; and lastly, according to the fact of their permitting slavery or not. By combining the last twofold divisions, they admit of a fourfold division, as the Atlantic slaveholding and non-slaveholding States, and the Western slaveholding and non-slaveholding States. These four divisions will now be compared as to their present numbers, density of population, and rate of increase.[130]

Tucker then furnishes three tabulations of statistics, one headed "Atlantic States," the second headed "Western States." The third is a comparative table.[131] The sectionalized treatment of the several categories of statistical data enabled Tucker to draw sharp and stimulating generalizations. A few of these will be quoted. "In the thirty years from 1810 to 1840," he writes, "the increase of the States without slaves has been as 100 to 258.8. That of the slaveholding States has

129 *Ibid.*
130 *Ibid.*, 119.
131 *Ibid.*, 119-20.

been as 100 to 210.7. . . . Increase of Atlantic States from 1830 to 1840, was as 100 to 173.4. That of the Western States from 1830 to 1840 was as 100 to 591.4."[132]

The skillful fusion of a well-clarified concept of sections with statistical data logically and relevantly related thereto, had now been accomplished. A powerful device had been fashioned by George Tucker wherewith well-grounded generalizations, comparisons, and contrasts relating to the different sections, and to the Union as a whole, could be reliably formulated. Tucker had shown how to make a significant step forward. He may be ranked with Morse as the second one to work importantly with the concept of the section. His contribution was not destined to fall upon stony ground.

Almost immediately, the influence of George Tucker made itself felt in the Seventh Census (1850) since in the pages of this census, for the first time, one meets with a discussion of the problems of sections and sectionalization. From the abstract of this census this key excerpt may be taken:

From the location, climate, productions, and the habits and pursuits of their inhabitants, the States of the Union may be properly arranged into the following groups: New England States, (6); Middle States, including Maryland, Delaware, and Ohio, (6); Coast planting States, including South Carolina, Georgia, Florida, Alabama, Mississippi, and Louisiana, (6); Central slave States, Virginia, North Carolina, Tennessee, Kentucky, Missouri, Arkansas, (6); Northwestern States, Indiana, Illinois, Michigan, Wisconsin, and Iowa, (5); Texas; and California.[133]

In support of this scheme of sectionalization, Superintendent J. C. G. Kennedy asserted that there were "points of agreement in the general characteristics of the States . . . which warrant the mode of arrangement adopted." He justified the classing of Maryland and Ohio "with the commercial and manufacturing section." He asserted likewise: "There seems to be a marked propriety for setting off the new agricultural States of the Northwest by themselves, as a preliminary to the comparison of their progress with other portions of the Union." Kennedy defended his distinction between the "Coast planting States" and "Central slave States" on several grounds. Texas,

132 *Ibid.*, 120–21.

133 *The Seventh Census, Report of the Superintendent of the Census for December 1, 1852; to which is appended the Report for December 1, 1851* (Washington, 1853), 135.

furthermore, he set off from the other "Coast planting States" because Texas had such a low density of population per square mile (0.89), whereas the Coast planting States had a much larger figure therefor (12.43). "For the same reason [of a small density of population per square mile (0.87)] and the additional one of the isolation of her position," he added, "California is considered distinct from other States."[134] Kennedy employed this scheme of sections in several discussions, and he used various sectional terms throughout his report.

Although Kennedy was conscious of the utility of a concept of sections, and used it, he continued to rely for the most part, in this abstract, upon an enumeration of the states in an order that was an extension of the inherited conventional order. By 1850, to be sure, the territory of the country had been much added to, over that of 1840, by reason of "annexation, conquest, and purchase."[135] The order used in considering the nativities of the aggregate general native-born population may be taken as an instance of the traditional order, now necessarily extended in view of the territorial growth of the country since 1840. Kennedy's list opens with Maine, and ranges southward down the coast to Florida. From Florida his sequence appears to try to maintain the principles of contiguity and continuity. The following is the order used: from Alabama, along the Gulf coast to Texas; then Arkansas, Tennessee, Kentucky, Ohio, Michigan, Indiana, Illinois, Missouri, Iowa, and Wisconsin. California is in the terminal position of the states. The territories are Minnesota, Oregon, Utah, and New Mexico, and they are listed in that order.

In 1853 the census of 1850, properly speaking, was published. This large work contains the bulk of the results of the enumeration; these results are arranged according to the traditional order. Superintendent J. D. B. DeBow was responsible for this publication. His order of arrangement is this: opening with Maine, he proceeds to Florida; then he ranges from Alabama westward along the Gulf to Texas; thence he ascends the great valley through Arkansas, Tennessee, Kentucky, Missouri, Illinois, Indiana, and Ohio. From Ohio he moves forward through Michigan and Wisconsin to Iowa. The continuity of this long sequence, ingeniously and laboriously established, is broken by isolated California, which occupies the terminal

134 *Ibid.*
135 *Ibid.*, 128.

position among the states. His list of territories follows: Minnesota, New Mexico, Oregon, and Utah.

This series of jurisdictions, counting the District of Columbia, numbers thirty-six political entities. That this long series could not be easily consulted, in the conventional order in which he stated them, was as obvious to DeBow as it is to us. Though bound by tradition, DeBow did bring himself to introduce one innovation: he prefaced the body of his work with an "Index to all of the subjects treated of in the state tables."[136] In this index the names of the states and territories are listed alphabetically, from Alabama and Arkansas, on to Virginia and Wisconsin.

DeBow did not lose sight of the advantages of a sectional classification of some special kinds of statistical data. Table XLIV, "Education Statistics of 1840," classifies the educational data of the states and territories into these five sections: New England, Middle States, Southern States, Southwestern States, and Northwestern States.[137] This fivefold scheme is identical with Tucker's; DeBow has silently jettisoned Kennedy's system in favor of one that is better based in theory. Table LII, "Occupations of the Free and Slave Population of the United States, of both sexes and of all ages, in 1840," makes use of the same fivefold grouping.[138] The third and last example of a sectional tabulation constructed by DeBow is Table LXII, "Ratio of the Increase of Population of the United States [1790–1850]."[139] In this table DeBow is obliged to introduce all thirty-six of the then existing jurisdictions into his columns for 1850, in order to make use of the then available, collected statistics. Thus he is led to the point where he must now draw up a sixfold scheme. Tucker's scheme of 1840 is too contracted for him. DeBow's sixth section—it has no name; neither do the other divisions in this group—is made up of California, Minnesota, New Mexico, Oregon, and Utah. If he had dropped Minnesota from this group and classed that territory with the preceding section (the Northwestern States and Territories, including Iowa), he would then have had a logically constructed

---

136 J. D. B. DeBow (comp.), *The Seventh Census of the United States: 1850. Embracing a statistical view of each of the states and territories, arranged by counties, towns, etc.* (Washington, 1853), *vii.*

137 *Ibid., lxi.*

138 *Ibid., lxxx.*

139 *Ibid., lxxxvii.*

"Northwest" and a logically constructed "Far West," i.e., Utah, New Mexico, Oregon, and California. Or, to view it differently, had he dropped Iowa from the Northwestern group and classed it with his sixth group, he would thus have created another logical class, which could have been known perhaps as the "Trans-Mississippi West." He did not, however, bother to think through this part of his work. Like many geographers of the day, and unlike Tucker, he felt no imperative need for a scheme that was rigorously logical.

In 1854, Superintendent DeBow published a *Statistical View of the United States . . . being a Compendium of the Seventh Census.* This four-hundred-page work is generously equipped with tabulations of a large variety of special kinds of figures; the tables are constructed upon a sectional basis. Some of the terms that DeBow uses in connection with these tables are "the several Geographical Divisions of the Union," "Geographical and Other Divisions," "the several sections of the Union," "different sections," "Section of the United States," and simply "Sections."[140] DeBow evidently, therefore, understood the value of a sectional study of particular kinds of statistical data, and took pains to cause a good number of such tables to be compiled.

About half of the space in this *Statistical View of the United States* is devoted to a presentation of the leading categories of statistical information as they relate to the several states and territories. The point must be made that, in this part of his work, DeBow abandoned the inherited conventional order (north-to-south on the Atlantic slope, etc.) and replaced it by one list in which states, territories, and the District of Columbia were filed in an alphabetical order. This alphabetical innovation in this minor census work pointed the way to a large development of the kind in the near future.

A volume entitled *Mortality Statistics of the Seventh Census of the United States,* also prepared by DeBow, was published at Washington in 1855. This work contains various sectional tables, and it has also various regional tables, or subdivisions within the states.

The Eighth Census (1860), prepared under the direction of Superintendent Kennedy, took over certain features which had first appeared in the preceding census. Kennedy made the now obviously

---

140 J. D. B. DeBow (comp.), *Statistical View of the United States . . . being a Compendium of the Seventh Census* (Washington, 1854), 41, 42, 67, 88, 115, 139.

reasonable decision to arrange his state tables of population according to the alphabetical principle. Kennedy also decided to list the territorial population statistics alphabetically by name of the territories. Thus the well-established convention of listing the states starting with the New England group—a convention which, as we have seen, went back to the middle eighteenth century—finally disappeared as a principle of ordonnance from the pages of the census publications.

Kennedy, in this Eighth Census, more than once introduced statistical tables based upon a sectional concept. For different purposes he used different schemes. In treating the distribution and density per square mile of the general population of 1860, he reverted to the scheme which he had earlier used, and DeBow had rejected. This was the sevenfold scheme ending with Texas and California as two separate divisions. In treating the absolute numbers and the percentages of blacks and mulattoes in the "Free States" and in the "Slave States," Kennedy made use of a twofold sectional system reminiscent of, though not of course originated by, Hinton R. Helper. In connection with his discussion of the statistics on mortality, Kennedy attempts some generalizations—to the extent of a little more than two pages—on the "relative mortality in the great natural divisions."[141] These are the "natural divisions" of the country as he defines them:

I. The Lowlands of the Atlantic Coast, comprising a general breadth of two counties along the Atlantic from Delaware to Florida inclusive.
II. The Lower Mississippi Valley, comprising Louisiana and a breadth of two counties along each bank of the river northward to Cape Girardeau, in Missouri.
III. The Allegheny Region, from Pennsylvania, through Virginia, Eastern Tennessee, &c., to Northern Alabama.
IV. The Intermediate Region, surrounding the Alleghenies, and extending to the lowlands of the Atlantic and to the Mississippi Valley.
V. The Pacific Coast, California, Oregon, and Washington.
VI. The Northeastern States, Maine, New Hampshire, and Vermont.
VII. The Northwestern States, Wisconsin, Iowa, and Minnesota.

All in all, the Eighth Census is quite generously supplied with sectional tabulations. A general reference to various examples of

[141] Joseph C. G. Kennedy (comp.), *Population of the United States in 1860; compiled from the original returns of the Eighth Census* (Washington, 1864), *xlii.*

statistical tables based upon a concept of sectionalization to be found in this census will be sufficient to close this part of the discussion.

The Ninth Census (1870) was prepared under the able direction of Superintendent Francis A. Walker. The principle of the arrangement of statistics alphabetically by states in one series and territories in another, or in one list of states and territories, is given thorough and frequent application in the three volumes of this census.

Walker provided no statistical tables of any kind based upon a concept of sectionalization. Thus the Ninth Census rejected a useful feature introduced by the Seventh Census, and applied and extended by the Eighth. But it is interesting to note that Walker introduced an innovation of his own which was to have important consequences in the further development and application of the concept of sections. Walker's striking innovation in the Ninth Census was to cause it to be illustrated by maps based upon the statistics contained in the census. This is the first United States census to be so illustrated.[142]

At this very time the new techniques of statistical cartography were being perfected in Europe; Walker imported these to the United States and exhibited their utility. The maps that were constructed by the application of these techniques to the statistical data of the Ninth Census often displayed an impressive sectionalization of the data concerned. Among the examples of statistical cartography that may appropriately be cited in this connection are the cotton-crop map, the hay-crop map, the tobacco-crop map, and the dairy-products map. Other maps that can be mentioned here are the maps showing the geographical distribution (1870) of the general foreign-born population, the distribution of illiterate persons, and the distribution of wealth. All these maps, and a large number of other ones, are solidly based on statistical foundations, and so reliably illustrate the facts of an objective sectionalization of the several interests studied.

Curiously enough, therefore, at the very time that the Superintendent of the Census gave thoroughgoing application of an alphabetical ordonnance to his statistical tables, completely rejecting the effective possibilities inherent in sectionally arranged tabulations, he also took on the responsibility of introducing into the census a novel

142 Fulmer Mood, "The Rise of Official Statistical Cartography in Austria, Prussia, and the United States, 1855–1872," *Agricultural History*, Vol. XX (October, 1946), 209–25.

feature—statistical cartography. From this innovation there were afterward to flow interesting sequelae for the study of sections. Armchair speculation on sectional areas and on the sectionalization of data was about to receive a powerful blow, and it was the modern techniques of statistical cartography which were to deliver the blow.

In 1874, Francis A. Walker, superintendent of the Ninth Census, published the *Statistical Atlas of the United States*. This pioneer work, though not a publication of the Census Office, was authorized by Congress, partly as a result of the deeply favorable impression which the maps accompanying the Ninth Census (1870) had made upon the public mind. The atlas contains some statistical tables which are arranged upon an alphabetical principle. Two examples are: "Area, Population, and Average Density of Settlement of Each State or Territory at Each Census," 1790–1870; and "Table Showing the Parcels of Territory Composing Each Political Division at Any Year from 1776 to 1874."[143]

The atlas also contains various monographic discussions by well-equipped scientific specialists, which bring out interesting generalizations on the sectionalization of particular kinds of data. A few instances of these may be cited. William H. Brewer announced a ninefold scheme of sections for the woodlands and forest systems of the United States: New England, Middle States, Southeastern region, Northwestern region, Southwestern region, the Plains, the Rocky Mountain region (Arizona, New Mexico, and the Great Basin), and the Pacific region. Brewer's map of the distribution of the woodlands illustrated his monograph in admirable fashion. Francis A. Walker contributed a series of maps covering the period 1790–1870; these exhibit the geographical distribution of the population at each census year, and simultaneously locate and define, for the first time, the several frontier lines of population.[144] Other maps based on markedly sectionalized data show the distribution of the Negro population, the general foreign-born population, the Irish-born, the German-born, etc.; the distribution of illiteracy among the aggregate population; the distribution of wealth, public indebtedness per

[143] Francis A. Walker (comp.), *Statistical Atlas of the United States based on the results of the Ninth Census 1870* (New York, 1874), Part II, "Areas and Political Divisions of the United States," 7, 8–9.

[144] Fulmer Mood, "The Concept of the Frontier, 1871–1898. Comments on a Select List of Source Documents," *Agricultural History*, Vol. XIX (January, 1945), 24–30.

capita, taxation per capita, various important crops (wheat, rice, to-bacco, hops, oats, cotton, hay, sugar, corn, dairy products), and improved land in farms. Also represented cartographically were predominating sex, birth rate, deaths from tuberculosis, and malarial diseases. In addition, maps were prepared which showed the distribution of blindness (the sectional scheme used was East, West, South, Pacific), deaf mutism, insanity, idiocy, etc.

As a result of the wealth of sectionalized data revealed in the maps which form part of the Ninth Census, and of this statistical atlas, Superintendent Walker came to see that, in addition to the alphabetical principle of arrangement, there was also a legitimate place for the principle of arrangement according to the several sections of the country. Maps had demonstrated that, objectively, sections did exist. Walker, having been appointed in 1879 to plan and direct the Eleventh Census, decided that he needed to have available for census administration purposes a well-considered, rational scheme of sections. He intended to group some of the census statistics according to the convenient alphabetical principle, state by state. And certain other data he expected to arrange by sections. To Henry Gannett, a member of his staff, he confided the task of working out a sound scheme for a system of sections. Gannett, whose title was Geographer of the Tenth Census, accordingly drew up a scheme. On November 1, 1881, Gannett wrote Walker a letter of transmittal, and submitted therewith "a plan for the subdivision of the States and Territories, for statistical purposes."[145]

Gannett's project had been purposefully decided upon. Substantively, it was an important and helpful accomplishment, partaking of the nature of a measure of reform and a measure of clarification. Gannett himself was not altogether displeased with his plan: "I believe [it] to be, in many respects, superior to the [plan] heretofore in use, as it seems to me to be more nearly in accordance with geographical conditions, the distribution of the elements of population, the different interests of the country, and the forms of local government."[146]

The content of Gannett's plan was embodied in *Census Bulletin No. 277*, dated at the Census Office, Department of the Interior, No-

---

[145] *Tenth Census. Census Bulletin No. 277* (Washington, November 1, 1881), 1.
[146] *Ibid.*

vember 1, 1881. As this *Census Bulletin* is quite unknown today and
not easily accessible to most readers, and, further, as it incorporates
a sophisticated rationalization of the concept of the section, its content will be considered carefully here.

Gannett opens by asserting that "the old subdivision of the states,
which appears to have originated in the early part of the century,
dividing the country into New England, Middle, Southern, and Western States," was suited to the country at that time "when nearly all
the population was upon the Atlantic slope." But today, he states,
it is "evidently a very curious arrangement which places New York,
New Jersey, and Pennsylvania among the 'Middle States,' and Ohio,
Indiana, and Illinois in the 'West.' "[147] Here Gannett is troubled by
small difficulties of nomenclature. "Middle Atlantic States" would
have corrected one of the "curious arrangements"; a term to replace
"West" would have corrected the other. But there is more than this
to the criticism that Gannett offers: "The sections are vastly dispro-
portionate under this scheme. The West includes a much greater
area than the sum of the other three sections, while it disregards, to
a great extent, geographical, social, and climatic, conditions."[148] Gannett then offers his constructive proposal, and illustrates it by a map.
The nomenclature as proposed is not fundamental to his scheme:
"The names to be given to the several divisions are matters of slight
moment, and might perhaps be changed to advantage."[149] Gannett's
suggested distribution is a fivefold one: North Atlantic division, nine
states, from Maine to Pennsylvania; South Atlantic division, nine
states, from Delaware to Florida, and including West Virginia; Northern Central division, eleven states and territories, from Ohio to Dakota, Nebraska, and Kansas; Southern Central division, eight states
and territories, from Kentucky, Tennessee, and Alabama on the east,
to Texas, Indian Territory, and Arkansas on the west; Western division, eleven states and territories, from the Pacific Coast eastward
to Montana, Wyoming, Colorado, and New Mexico.

The reasoning behind this scheme is now set forth.

As will be noticed, the country is divided primarily into three great
divisions: the Atlantic region, the region of the Great Valley, and the

---

147 *Ibid.*
148 *Ibid.*
149 *Ibid.*

Western or Cordilleran region, corresponding to the three primary topographical divisions of the country. Each of the two eastern divisions is divided by a line approximately east and west. This line between the two sections of the Atlantic division follows Mason and Dixon's line; that between the two sections of the Great Valley follows the Ohio river and the south boundary of Missouri.

This east and west line separates districts that are very sharply distinguished from one another by population, social conditions, and interests, as well as climate. The different conditions of rainfall and temperature upon the two sides of this line are too well known to require explanation.

From a historical point of view the divisions are characteristically different. The two Atlantic sections comprise the original thirteen states, with those formed from them, viz, Maine, Vermont and West Virginia, with the single addition of Florida. They were settled during the colonial period, and may be said to represent that stage of our progress. The two divisions of the Great Valley have been settled almost entirely since the country became independent of Great Britain, and may properly be regarded as representing the stage of our progress from the time of our independence up to the present day; while the West is still, as far as development is concerned, in its infancy, and may properly represent the development of the future.

The North Atlantic and Northern Central sections are sharply distinguished from the two southern sections by the character of the population. The two former contain not less than 85.8 per cent. of the foreign population, while, on the other hand, the two latter contain 90.5 per cent. of the negro element.

In regard to material interests, similar marked differences exist. The North Atlantic section comprises, as its primary interest, a large proportion of the manufactures of the country. The Northern Central section, although also comprising a considerable portion of the manufactures, especially in its eastern part, still is dependent upon agriculture as its primary interest; and, among the various branches of agriculture, mainly upon the culture of cereals, not less than 71 per cent. of the cereals of the country being produced in this section. The two southern sections are almost purely agricultural, and of the various branches of agriculture, 99.6 per cent. of the cotton, and all the sugar-cane and rice produced in the country are grown here. In the distribution of urban and rural population similar marked differences are to be observed. In the North Atlantic section the urban population forms a very large and powerful class, and evidently soon will be the governing element. In the Northern Central section, while the urban population still forms a considerable proportion, it is by no means a controlling element; and in the two southern sections the controlling interests are almost entirely those of the rural population. Out of a total number of 580 cities and towns of 4,000 population and over in the United States, comprising 12,936,110 population, 266, comprising 6,960,776 population, are found in the North Atlantic section, and 213, comprising 3,663,843 population, in the Northern Central section, while in the two southern sections combined there are but 78 cities and towns, comprising only 1,825,832 population.

In respect to civil organization, there are also very decided differences between the two northern and the two southern sections. In the two northern sections the township system of government obtains, with the exception of the state of Nebraska, and a few counties in southern Illinois, while in the two southern sections, without an exception, the county system of government is the one in use. The Western section is distinguished from the others by its topography, comprising as it does, the great western plateau, with the accompanying arid climate, light rainfall, and great extremes of temperature, by its present sparse settlement, and by the occupations of the inhabitants, which are mainly confined to mining and stockraising.

This scheme is susceptible of still further subdivision, as may be required for various purposes. New England will undoubtedly remain a distinct subdivision, while at the same time regarded as a portion of the North Atlantic section. The Northern and Southern Central divisions might properly be separated along the line of the Mississippi river. On some accounts a subdivision of the West is advisable, separating it perhaps into what might be denominated the Rocky Mountain region, the Plateau region, the Great Basin region, and the region of the Pacific.[150]

This is a thoughtful discussion, and the scheme it proposes is, "for statistical purposes," a sound and convenient one. One criticism that can be brought against it is the undue simplification of the sectionalization of the Atlantic coast, which Gannett breaks into the North Atlantic and the South Atlantic divisions, thus destroying, or ignoring, a historically self-conscious section, the Middle Atlantic States. Eventually the census authorities modified this element in Gannett's scheme and recognized (1913) the existence of the historic section mediate between the South Atlantic States and New England. The possible expansions and subdivisions hinted at by Gannett in his last paragraph were afterwards accepted by the Thirteenth Census, which recognized nine geographic sections. Thus his scheme commended itself to Walker and also to Walker's successors, and so has had a continuing vitality to the present day.

Gannett's new scheme of a system of American sections was given frequent application in various volumes of the Tenth Census (1880).

150 *Ibid.*, 1–2.

The increasing use, by census administrations in 1880, 1890, and 1900, of tables arranged according to a sectional plan does not preclude the continued use of statistical tables alphabetically arranged according to the names of states and territories. For the general purpose of the census, the alphabetical ordonnance proved suitable and convenient, in perhaps a majority of the tables published. For particular purposes, however, sectionally arranged tables were incorporated, and their popularity grew, decade by decade, from 1880 to 1900.

The census of 1880, as originally planned, was to be rounded off and completed by a copiously illustrated statistical atlas, somewhat on the order of Walker's *Statistical Atlas* of 1874, only larger. But the cost of producing the census volumes proper exhausted the appropriation and left no money for the proposed atlas. The copy that had been prepared was accepted for publication by a commercial publishing house in New York, Scribner's. Under the joint editorship of Henry Gannett and Fletcher Hewes, it was published at New York City in 1883 under the title of *Scribner's Statistical Atlas of the United States.*

This atlas served as a great conduit for carrying and diffusing throughout the country the concept of sectionalism. Its numerous illustrations showed how, in many specific ways, that concept could be applied to concrete data. Gannett condensed the statement of his sectional plan from *Census Bulletin No. 277* and incorporated it in an essay, complete with map, entitled "Natural Grouping of the States." His statement begins: "In the discussion of the subjects embraced in this work, it has been found necessary to adopt some characteristic mode of grouping the states and territories. . . . The grouping adopted in this work is that proposed by the Census office and used in its publications. It is illustrated in the accompanying map."[151] He then proceeds with an explanation of his scheme of 1881. In various tables and maps which form part of this atlas, Gannett's scheme was given practical application. Thus his plan was given wide circulation the country over, and reached many persons who never knew of his *Census Bulletin* or never saw the census tables constructed according to his scheme.

[151] Henry Gannett and Fletcher W. Hewes (eds.), *Scribner's Statistical Atlas of the United States, showing by graphic methods their present condition and their political, social and industrial development* (New York, 1883), *xxiii.*

Scribner's Statistical Atlas of 1883 met with an excellent reception; this welcome induced the publishers to bring out, in 1890, *Scribner's Historical Atlas of American Progress, showing by graphic methods, the territorial, industrial and political development and resources of the United States.* This new work, which was based on the data of the census of 1880, was almost entirely an abridgment of the earlier atlas, although it had various additions and explanatory notes. This work gave fresh circulation to Gannett's essay on "Natural Grouping of the States," and it again offered the rich abundance of economic maps showing the geographic distribution of various products and commodities. It also favored historians by providing two large maps showing the popular vote for President, by counties, in the elections of 1884 and 1888. *Scribner's Historical Atlas,* therefore, in several ways, gave renewed currency to sectional patterns, to the sectional concept, and to various applications of that concept to concrete data.

The Eleventh Census (1890) took over and gave further application to Gannett's unmodified scheme, in various statistical tables. The Twelfth Census (1900) followed in the same path, affording many other examples of the application of this scheme.

Gannett, as a private venture of his own, brought out *The Building of a Nation* (1895). In this work he took realistic account of the sectional features of the country, gave a brief but fairly detailed account of the topographic relief, and indicated the regionalism of temperature, rainfall, and forest cover. He presented a table of the total population of the country, by sectional groups and individual states, as of 1890, of course making use of the fivefold scheme of North Atlantic, South Atlantic, North Central, South Central, and Western divisions. There were various other tables, also arranged on a sectional basis. The book was well supplied with colored maps which demonstrated many patterns of sectionalization. This volume was based almost entirely upon the data of the census of 1890, and it brought data sectionally arranged, in the form of tables and maps, to general readers to whom the census volumes would not have appealed.

By 1900, therefore, as the result of the long and slowly worked out process which we have traced—a process in which such thinkers as George Tucker, Kennedy, DeBow, Walker, and Henry Gannett had each had a hand—the census authorities had come to recognize the practical utility of arranging certain census statistics according to an applied concept of a system of American sections. The sectional approach, for purposes of comparison, contrast, and generalization, had been accepted and frequently applied by these census administrators, who never thereafter abandoned it. From 1881 onward, Henry Gannett's is the example and influence that did the most to popularize this way of treating large masses of census data, and extracting from them valuable general views.

Gannett had sufficient faith in his *Census Bulletin* containing the scheme of sections to be willing to promote its use outside his own agency. We find him, in January, 1882, writing a letter to Major John Powell, the head of the United States Geological Survey: "Recognizing the fact that the old subdivision of the country into New England, Middle, Southern and Western States, resembles our first pair of trousers being now long outgrown, I beg to suggest to you a scheme for the classification of the states which in my opinion, suits the present condition of the country as well as any that could be devised, and to request you, in case you should approve of it and have occasion to use such a scheme, to assist in its introduction."[152] Gannett then submitted a condensed statement of his scheme, which he supplemented with a manuscript map.

Whether Powell was persuaded to give currency to Gannett's scheme is a circumstance not ascertained. But some few years later, Powell himself brought out a classification. His intent was to classify not statistical, but physiographic, data. "Physiography," he asserted, "is a description of the surface features of the earth, as bodies of air, water, and land."[153] In 1895, Powell published his monograph, "Physiographic Regions of the United States." In this he defined, first, the great slopes of the United States, then the main physiographic regions, and finally the several districts into which these regions in turn were divided. "Gradually," he explained, "as the new science of physiography has grown, physiographic regions have come

[152] Henry Gannett to John W. Powell, Washington, January 7, 1882, No. 34 in Letters Received, 1882, pp. 1–284, Department of the Interior, U. S. Geological Survey, in the National Archives, Washington.

[153] John W. Powell, "Physiographic Processes," in National Geographic Society, *The Physiography of the United States* (New York, 1896), 1.

to be recognized; and an attempt is here made, by map and verbal description, to define the principal regions of the United States, exclusive of Alaska."[154] Powell thought of these regions as "natural divisions, because in every case the several parts are involved in a common history by which the present physiographic features have been developed. They have been characterized by the more prominent features used in the name."[155] Gannett, like the geographers before him, had drawn the lines of his boundaries sharply and clearly. Powell, however, approaching the problem of making a scheme for the classification of sections and regions from the point of view of their prior earth history, was not taken in by a desire for rigid boundaries. "In dividing the United States into a few great physiographic regions," he said, "it is not found possible always to draw the lines with exactness. Often one region blends with another, the transformation in general characteristics being marked by a general change. There are some lines of division clearly drawn by nature within narrow limits; other divisions are imperfectly marked by slow gradation from one to the other."[156]

Powell counted four main slopes: Atlantic, Great Lakes, Gulf, and Pacific. These four grand divisions afford interesting comparisons and contrasts, chiefly owing to inequalities of rainfall, which produce, as a consequence, deserts, prairies, and forests. Without following his discussion into details, it will be sufficient to list the several regions which he derives, scientifically, from the four major slopes. In Powell's text each is well characterized by a succinct description: Atlantic plains, Piedmont plateaus, Appalachian ranges, Allegheny plateaus, New England plateaus, Lake plains, Prairie plains, Gulf plains, Ozark mountains, Great plains (plateaus), Stony mountains, Park mountains, Columbia plateaus, Colorado plateaus, Basin ranges, and Pacific mountains. The text is accompanied by a map in colors which sets forth in clear manner these sixteen "Physiographic Regions of the United States."

This monograph supplies a scientific foundation for the sectionalization of related data. It is a scheme based upon facts, rather than one which shapes facts (perhaps warping and twisting them in the process) to the framework provided. Not long after publication, Powell's

---

[154] John W. Powell, "Physiographic Regions of the United States," in *ibid.*, 65.
[155] *Ibid.*, 65–66.
[156] *Ibid.*, 66.

monograph came to the attention of the historian Frederick J. Turner, of the University of Wisconsin. An historical thinker already committed to the importance of a sectional approach in the study of American economic and political life, Turner heartily welcomed this monograph. He consistently used it for many years in his teaching and research work, and through his pupils the influence of this paper spread far and wide. It put the study of social data capable of a sectionalized treatment upon a new foundation. So Turner thought, as we shall see. How it was that certain American historians, Turner among them, undertook to study American history in terms of a sectional analysis, is the topic that next claims our attention. The development now to be chronicled is intimately associated with historians connected with the Department of History in the University of Wisconsin during the years 1867 to 1900.

The scientific study of American history in terms of the several sections that make up the Federal Union was well established at the University of Wisconsin before the year 1900. By that time there had already been offered, in the history department, lecture courses on sectionalism in American history, on the history of the South, and on the history of the West. Plans had been drafted to offer still other courses in the history of the South and also lectures on the history of New England. Various examples of historical research based upon a recognition of the existence of sectionalism in previous periods of history had already been published by Allen, Desmond, Turner, Libby, and others.

The true founder of historical studies in Wisconsin was William Francis Allen, a trained historian who had studied as an undergraduate at Harvard (Class of 1851), and later at Berlin and Göttingen. Allen was born in 1830 and died in 1889. Thus the mature years of his life span covered the heated political discussions of the fifties and the stern military struggles of the sixties. The men of his generation were especially sensitive to the existence of sectional realities. Allen was a native of New England, but he knew other sections of the country at first hand. Twice he resided for intervals in the Middle Atlantic section; and in the South Atlantic and South Central States—South Carolina and Arkansas—also. After 1867 his home was at Madison, Wisconsin, so that he came to know at first hand something of the Old Northwest, too. To him, therefore, such terms as South and West and Middle States and New England were not cold abstractions, but vital symbols charged with particular and differentiated meanings. He well knew that objective differences lay behind these much-used words.

A sectional or a regional approach was a natural approach for him to adopt when dealing with phenomena of a social or cultural character. His willingness to view some kinds of data from this point of view manifests itself in an early publication based upon his war-time experiences in the Southern States. From November, 1863, to July, 1864, Allen was in the employ of the Freedmen's Aid Commission, and lived on St. Helena Island, off the coast of South Carolina. Then, from September, 1864, until February, 1865, he served as an agent of the Sanitary Commission at Helena, Arkansas. While thus engaged in the South in these duties, he and two others gathered and recorded the music and the words of the songs sung by the freedmen, and published them in book form in 1867.

Allen's compilation, *Slave Songs of the United States,* consists of 136 pieces. The collectors arranged these songs according to a classification which is almost strictly geographical. This is their scheme: Part I, songs of the South-Eastern Slave States, including South Carolina, Georgia, and the Sea Islands; Part II, songs of the Northern Seaboard Slave States, including Delaware, Maryland, Virginia, and North Carolina; Part III, songs of the Inland Slave States, including Tennessee, Arkansas, and the Mississippi. Part IV, Miscellaneous, was added to the original plan, because the songs included therein were received too late to be included in the three original divisions.

In 1867, Allen became a professor in the University of Wisconsin, where he taught Latin and history. Gradually he gave more and more attention to the latter subject, which, under his hand, came to include European and American history. He wrote many notices of new history books for the New York *Nation.* An examination of some of these reviews establishes that this historian was thinking sectionally, and was watching other historians think sectionally, as he wrote of their books. His treatment of Von Holst's *History of the United States* bears out this statement. His syllabus of lectures on American history, *History Topics for the Use of High Schools and Colleges* (1883), shows an appreciation of the sectional character of our history; and his historical essay, "The Place of the Northwest in

General History" (1888), stands as an instance of a sectional topic broadly stated and interpreted. Allen directed the attention of his advanced students to topics relating to the history of the Northwest, especially Wisconsin. Frederick Jackson Turner was one of Allen's students—in fact, his leading student. As an undergraduate, Turner studied with Allen, before his graduation from Wisconsin in 1884. Four years later, under Allen's direction, he completed a master's thesis on the fur trade in early Wisconsin history. From Allen's teaching, Turner carried away an understanding of the importance of sectionalism in American history. This he afterward developed in an impressive and influential way. Turner's famous essay, "The Significance of the Frontier in American History" (1893), is not only a plea for the study of the West; it is also, though to a smaller extent, a plea for the study of the other three historic sections that had grown up on the Atlantic coast.

Of high interest in the present connection is a paper delivered on December 28, 1888, before the Wisconsin Academy of Sciences, Arts and Letters. Humphrey J. Desmond, with Allen in the chair, read an essay entitled "The Sectional Feature in American Politics." Desmond asserted that thus far the controlling fact in American politics was the fact of sectionalism. He cited numerous illustrations to support this proposition, and offered many generalizations that are striking to a degree. This paper furnishes one tabulation of "Electoral Apportionment by Sections from 1790 to 1890," and another of "Sectional Divisions in Ten Leading Political Contests, 1796–1884."[157] In both tables the data are grouped by sections (New England, Middle States, Western States, and Southern States) and arranged chronologically. The essay abounds with novel insights and well-considered opinions. "A federal government attempting to do a great many things in a great many directions is sure to arouse warring interests and clashing influences. And in a country which reaches from the Atlantic to the Pacific and touches the tropics, and stretches out to the land of the midnight sun, all such interests and influences are more or less geographical and sectional."[158] Desmond

---

[157] Humphrey J. Desmond, "The Sectional Feature in American Politics," *Transactions of the Wisconsin Academy of Sciences, Arts and Letters* (Madison, 1888–91), VIII, 7.

[158] *Ibid.*, 10.

casually threw off the remark that the Constitution, though a compact between the states, was essentially "a treaty of alliance between
two great sections having opposite civilizations and diverse interests."[159]

Desmond's paper is so suggestive that we would gladly know
more of its background. All we do know is that the author was a
graduate of the University of Wisconsin (1880), studied law, engaged
in politics, and for years practiced journalism in Milwaukee. This
paper—by no means the sole piece of historical writing from Desmond's pen—may reflect Allen's scholarly influence upon another
receptive pupil.

Turner it was, however, who brought about a widespread recognition of the importance of the sectional approach in American
historical studies. In census volumes and in atlases he had reliable
foundations for his work. While still an undergraduate, he had made
the acquaintance of *Scribner's Statistical Atlas* (1883) not long after
it was published. He studied its maps and discussions and thus early
gained clear impressions of the leading sections of American economic
and political life. Gannett's fund of data came to form a kind of
substrate in his historical thinking, and Gannett's work quietly ex-
ercised an influence of a kind on Turner for many years.

In several syllabi on American history published between 1891
and 1895, Turner made fundamental and effective use of the concept of the section as an instrument for teaching facts and interpretations of American history. His syllabus *The Colonization of
North America from the Earliest Times to 1763*, published in 1893,
has three chapters that are parallel with each other: the colonization
of the South, the colonization of the Middle region, and the colonization of New England. This treatment, quite obviously sectionalized,
is made even more pointed by one of his entries under the heading
"Sample topics for review": "evolution of sections."[160]

The syllabus of 1895 has for a title *American Development, 1789–
1829,* and it contains several indications of Turner's application of
the concept of the section to the interpretation of American historical
phenomena. *"Introduction.* Importance of the following processes
in American history: the evolution of the complex industrial organ-

159 *Ibid.,* 1.
160 Frederick Jackson Turner, *The Colonization of North America from the Earliest
Times to 1763* (Madison, 1893), 28.

ization; the movement away from Europe; the movement westward; the rise of democracy; the abolition of slavery; the triumph of nationalism over State sovereignty and sectionalism. All are interrelated." On the same page another reference to "sectionalism" may be found. The compiler further on refers to the South, to the Middle States, New England, the West, and to "The migration of the sections, and their antagonisms. Political balance of the sections." Under the heading "Jackson's Presidency," Turner writes: "Significance of the election of 1828; the democracy of the West and the middle region."[161]

From courses on general United States history which Turner taught during the years 1889–90 and afterward, there emerged a novel course in 1895–96 bearing this description: "Course 7. History of the West. Particular attention is paid to the advance of settlement across the continent, and to the results of this movement."[162] Thus the first course on the history of an American section came into being. This course on Western history was paired off, for one year, with a course on Southern history, offered by W. P. Trent, a Southern visitor to the Madison campus. To orient his students in the study of the history of a section, Turner prepared a paper, "The West as a Field for Historical Study."[163] He had not long before published a double article on "Western State-Making in the Revolutionary Era."[164] He encouraged his student, Orin G. Libby, to go forward with stimulating and important researches on the relationships between the physiographic and economic differences among the sections, and the expression of these differences in votes on legislation before Congress. Libby read a paper, "A Plea for the Study of Votes in Congress," at a meeting of the Historical Association, in December, 1896. "To study Congressional action, then, especially that of the Lower House, is to study a great plexus of forces, partly harmonious and partly antagonistic, whose outcome is national policy and national development."[165] Libby worked out a method for bringing to light the underlying sectional areas whose interests are expressed and

---

[161] Frederick Jackson Turner, *American Development, 1789–1829* (Madison, 1895), 3, 11, 12.

[162] *Catalogue of the University of Wisconsin for 1895–96* (Madison, 1896), 140.

[163] *Annual Report of the American Historical Association for the Year 1896* (Washington, 1897), I, 281–87.

[164] *American Historical Review*, Vol. I (October, 1895; January, 1896), 70–87, 251–69.

[165] *Annual Report of the American Historical Association for the Year 1896*, I, 323.

made manifest by the votes of the Congressional district spokesmen. This essay was a positive gain in the methodology of sectional studies. In 1897–98, Libby offered a course entirely devoted to this fundamental matter of American sectionalism. The course, described as "a study of the geographical distribution of political parties with especial reference to votes in Congress and in state legislatures," bore the title "American Sectionalism."[166]

Not long before, in 1894, Libby had made his mark with a dissertation written under Turner's direction. This was *The Geographical Distribution of the Vote of the Thirteen States on the Federal Constitution, 1787–8*. In the Editor's Note prefacing the work, Turner wrote that, from the point of view of the rise and growth of sectionalism and of nationalism, it was important to note the existence of great social and economic areas, independent of state lines, which have acted as units in political history, and have changed their political attitude as they changed their economic organization. Libby showed that the opposition to the Constitution was confined to those interior or sparsely settled districts which were the last to be populated and whose interests were agricultural rather than commercial, rural as opposed to urban. It was a study in the opinion, political and economic, of the Atlantic coast "back country" in 1787 and 1788. As such, it constituted a pioneer study of a region within a section, or of a group of regions within a group of sections. This valuable study was illustrated by a map which showed the votes of interior New England and coastal New England, of the interior and coastal regions of the Middle States, and of the interior and coastal regions of the Southern States.

Libby's course, as we saw, had American sectionalism for its theme and a study of votes in Congress and state legislatures for its technique. But Turner, as the philosophical thinker on the concept of sectionalism and the section, was already plunging far on in advance of his pupil. The depth and the novelty of his ideas appear in the course of a correspondence that he had with Horace E. Scudder and Walter Hines Page, the editors of the *Atlantic Monthly*. This correspondence belongs to the year 1896, and is now disclosed for the first time.[167]

---

[166] *Catalogue of the University of Wisconsin for 1897–98* (Madison, 1898), 146.
[167] These Scudder-Page-Turner letters are in the Harvard College Library. Permis-

In February, 1896, Scudder invited Turner to review a group
of books for the *Atlantic*. He praised Turner's contribution when
it was received, and thus a connection of importance was established.
Walter Hines Page soon after wrote Turner, proposing that he contribute an article to the periodical. He suggested that Turner try
his hand on the theme of the sectional differences between the East
and the West. Turner consented to write such an article. Then came
the Chicago convention, which gave the presidential nomination to
a Western Democrat, William Jennings Bryan. On July 14, Page
wrote Turner from Boston:

> The action taken by the Democratic Convention at Chicago has made
> immensely more timely the paper that you were good enough to promise
> some time ago should reach us in July, if possible. I understand of course
> that you do not wish to make any discussion of the political situation in
> a direct sense . . . but if I read the course of current events rightly the
> study that you have in mind of the actual relations between the east and
> west really gives the philosophical key to this political situation. In fact
> such a philosophic and economic study as you have made is necessary
> for an understanding of these recent political phenomena. For this reason
> I am doubly anxious that if it be possible we should have your paper
> for the September number.

The September *Atlantic* carried as its leading article Turner's
piece, "The Problem of the West." Not long after it was received,
Page again wrote Turner on August 22, 1896. This letter, and Turner's reply to it, will be given entire. The two letters, taken together,
reveal that Page made a suggestion that struck fire in Turner's prepared mind, and that Turner himself was well along in his thinking
concerning the theoretical and technical problems of sectionalism
as a force in American historical interpretation and in American life.
Page's letter was dated from Boston on August 22, 1896.

DEAR MR. TURNER:

I think that I wrote you the other day that I should trouble you with
another matter very soon—following your capital article that is now
published. It is a matter that the present paper naturally leads up to—is,
indeed, directly an introduction to.

We wish in the *Atlantic* next winter to "report civilization" in the
three characteristic parts of the country—the Middle West, the South,

---

sion to quote from them has been granted by Arthur Page, Esq., and by Mrs. Frederick
Jackson Turner.

and New England; and perhaps we shall add the trans-Rocky-Mountain region as a fourth. By "reporting civilization" I mean a continuation into somewhat greater detail of the very thing that you have done in this paper for the Septr. *Atlantic.* A man who knows life and character and characteristics and institutions in Georgia and in Minnesota, and in Vermont knows very well that they are different—as different as three individuals. To *tell* the differences is another matter. But that is the task.

Of course I do not mean to suggest that comparisons be made, but that the characteristic features of the life and character and tendencies of each section be seized and described, set in one order and arranged in proper proportion.

(It occurs to me to send you a copy of a letter that I have just written to Mr. Trent, who will probably do the Southern end of this task. In that I have tried to say what I mean.)

My general notion is that we might have 6 [*sic*] papers—3 Southern, 3 Western, 3 New England. But I am unwilling to fix any rigid mechanical limitations to the scheme. The thing to be desired above all things is the natural unfolding of the plan.

I confess that I am very enthusiastic about it. What Trent writes and what people tell me here, with whom I have talked, indicates that the plan has a real *raison d' être,* and, *as a plan,* provokes enthusiasm. And, while I have had more plans than one that looked well and did not work out well, I cannot help believing that this will lead to a notable contribution towards a formulation of who we are, and at what stage of development.

Will you not write me (I pray first that you will do the papers)—a sort of working schedule?

Who could write say *one* paper on the Pacific slope?

The newspapers here are at once taking up your article for discussion —very favorably.

Sincerely yours,

Walter H. Page

On August 30, 1896, Turner replied at length, from Madison, Wisconsin.

Dear Mr. Page:

The subject which you proposed in your last letter is so important that I have taken several days to reflect on it, before reply. I thoroughly agree that a series of papers on civilization in the United States of today would be of the highest importance. There has been a good deal done upon *resources* of different states or cities, but of the *spirit* of various sections, nothing of importance has been said, so far as I am aware. The time is ripe for some such survey, if my view that we have reached a turning point in our national life,—with the exhaustion of the supply of free land—is correct. The question is, What *is* this United States,—at the end of the movement of colonization—the colonization of the interior, with all the forces of city making, railroad building, immigration, sectional expansion, etc., involved in the movement. I know of no better man for the South than my friend Trent, whose ability I greatly admire. For New England it ought to be possible to find a good man with ease. Both New England and the South have a distinctive flavor. Of course they need analysis into regions—particularly the South—but they have a real self-consciousness.

The task is not so easy for the West. There is less distinctive flavor about the West. Western ideals, in a general way I have suggested already. But how to treat in detail so vast a region, with such varied types of industry and social traits, is hard to see.

The same difficulty would exist in regard to the middle region,—New York and Pennsylvania, as the types. You did not include them on your list; perhaps from an unconscious appreciation of the same difficulty which I see in the West. But the middle region is nearest like the West. The West, as a whole, is, after a fashion, an expansion of the Middle Region—with its complex, confused types; its fluctuations; its lack of unity.

I don't know when I have had a more difficult question put to me, than yours. I should like to have a part in the work you propose, and yet it will interrupt some historical work promised a year or two ago to publishers; and it requires a wider acquaintance with the different parts of the West than I can claim.

I confess I do not know of any one who quite fills my idea of the man rightly equipped for the task. In many respects I am as well prepared as any one I *know* of.

My opinion shapes itself like this: If you *can find some* one else for the West, I shall be well content to enjoy his work. There certainly ought to be some one better equipped than I am. If you cannot secure some one else, and can put my papers *last in order of publication,* I am willing to do my best in the matter. The project is one of profound significance, I think, and ought to reflect great credit on *The Atlantic* for undertaking it; but no mistake should be made in carrying it out, and you should look fully over the field before finally choosing your writers. I assure you that my interest in the plan is such that you will have my hearty acquiescence in whatever choice you finally make.

On the Pacific States, I would suggest Professor Bernard Moses, University of California; or Professor Frank Blackmar, of Univ. of Kansas (he formerly lived in California), or Professor H. H. Powers of Leland Stanford Univ.—he recently came there, but is observant and an incisive writer; or, perhaps, best of all, Mr. Shinn, formerly a J.H.U. man, and editor of *Overland Mo.*

Why do you not have some one for the Middle States—as Dr. Lever-more, for instance,—who is at work on New York governors; or some Columbia College man? The Middle States are very important in our history.

With regard to a schedule, I am bothered by the fact that the subject would have to be sounded more than I have, to determine the best plan. You suggest three papers, on the Middle West. "Middle West" is variously used: perhaps most accurately to describe the tiers of States included between the Rockies and the Mississippi; but sometimes including also the Old Northwest; and, sometimes, in place of the Old Northwest. Assuming that you mean to include the Old Northwest with the Middle West, what is to be done with Missouri, Arkansas, Texas, and other southwestern states? Do you intend the writer on the Middle West to deal with Kansas and Nebraska, Iowa and the Dakotas?

There would seem to be the following group of states in what is today reckoned as West.

1. The Old Northwest: closely connected—via Ohio—with the Middle Region
   Minnesota and Iowa form a transition between the above and
2. The Prairie States: The Dakotas, Nebraska, and Kansas
3. The Rocky Mountain States
4. Pacific Slope
5. Southwest

Each of these groups could be treated separately. Their history, economic basis, sources of their population, etc., give a certain unity to each group. Possibly two groups could be handled in one paper. I do not feel at all competent to do southwestern states; I know little directly of Kansas, Missouri, and Arkansas. Professor Blackmar, for instance could do that group, I suspect, better than I could, though I could work out my thesis of frontier origins very well in Kansas and Nebraska and the Dakotas.

Perhaps a more scientific method, would be to ignore state lines. My work in American history is based on natural physiographic divisions, as outlined by Powell in his *Physiographic Regions of the United States* (Am. Book Co.—pamphlet—National Geographic Society Monographs). I find it revolutionizes the study, and I hope sometime to work out a work along those lines.

According to this map, the *Old Northwest* is divided physiographically into three divisions:

1. Alleghany Plateaus, which include the strip along the Ohio—(and run back to the Appalachian Ranges)
2. Prairie Plains, which include the middle of Ohio, nearly all of Indiana, Illinois, and western Wisconsin,—running also to the Great

Plains on the West, and so including western Minnesota, eastern Dakotas, Iowa, northern Missouri, and eastern Nebraska and Kansas
3. Lake Plains, including Michigan, eastern and northern Wisconsin,
and northeastern Minnesota

The *Middle West* is divided between Prairie Plains and Great Plains,
with the Ozark Mt. region (in southern Missouri, northwestern Arkansas
and eastern Indian Ty) breaking the area.

The line between prairies and Great Plains is the line of the arid
lands, cutting through the middle of the Dakotas Nebraska and Kansas.
This line explains very much in modern western ideas, as you will see by
consulting the files of the "Irrigation Age." The pioneer came into this
region and vainly tried to follow old individual methods. His failure
helps explain why the Kansan farmer is raising less corn and more
H——l! to use the language of her prophets. The social structure that
shall arise in these arid lands, (capable of use only by irrigation, whether
by government or by corporations monopolizing water supply) will be
radically unlike the old individualistic Western society. It may even result in rearrangement of State lines in West.

The line of the Great Plains on the West is the mountains cutting
through the midst of states like Montana, Wyoming, Colorado.

These suggestions show why within a state diverse ideas of political
policy frequently take sectional groupings, and why portions of several
adjoining states have a political, economic, and social unity.

I think the ideal mode of treating the West would be to apply a combination of *modes of analysis to it,* and determine, if possible, the natural,
non-State, areas. Thus this *physiographic analysis would be one test.* The
crop areas, manufacture areas, etc., would be another. One might ascertain how business houses in the great centers divided up the "territory"
of their commercial agents. Analysis of votes in Congress, would indicate
how the representatives grouped themselves, and analysis of sectionalism
in politics as shown in State elections would check and aid this method.
Enquiry of the chairmen of national campaign committees as to their
divisions, would also help. Add a study of typical newspapers, literary
output, immigration maps, and historical basis, and the combined tests
would enable a man to divide the West into its proper regions and describe the spirit of each. I have thus outlined the task, and taxed your
patience, to let you see just how I am looking at the problem.

By taking only the Old Northwest the task would be simpler, and yet
here the question of arrangement would be difficult. Is it better to treat
separate sections of the Old Northwest in separate papers? If so, then is
it best to take groups of *States,* or *natural* economic-social-political groups?
and show their relation to the remoter East, and West, and South. Or, is it
best to handle *topics,* as Politics in the Northwest; Education and Letters
in the Northwest; the Economic Basis of Civilization in the Northwest?
etc.

Pardon me for writing so long a treatise. Your suggestion of noting the ideas prevalent in the period of Greeley's influence as a base line for work, is an excellent one, full of suggestion.

I will send you tomorrow a copy of an editorial in *Chicago Tribune,* perhaps the leading Chicago daily, giving a Western version of my *Atlantic* paper. You may be interested in the spirit of reciprocity exhibited by the writer of the enclosed clipping from one of our local dailies—*Madison Journal.* It has some significance, perhaps, as indicating western appreciation of the *Atlantic.*

Very truly yours,

FREDERICK J. TURNER

This letter eloquently speaks for itself in regard to Turner's grasp of the problems connected with the concept of sectionalism and the application of that concept as a tool in American social science research. It is as fundamental, as profound, today as when it was first dashed off, out of a full mind, and sent on to the *Atlantic* editor in his Boston sanctum. Better than any commentary, or summary, is this statement by the master himself, rich with insights and suggestions. This statement is, there is little doubt, the high-water mark for the nineteenth century, of serious thinking on the nature and utility of the concept of the section in American history. Under Turner's guidance in the next quarter-century, the application of this concept to historical problems was to lead to an immense harvest in creative scholarship.

The task of tracing the history of the sectional concept to the end of the nineteenth century has now been accomplished. This somewhat elusive concept has behind it a long and respectable history. To lay bare this history, it has been necessary to make an acquaintance with large numbers of unfamiliar or out-of-the-way facts. It is clear, in retrospect, that as nature makes sections, so man recognizes and names them. Eventually he reaches the point where he can think of sections in the abstract. Then he is ready to embody the concept in an institution or to use it in other practical ways.

By the middle of the eighteenth century, British America was composed of a congeries of varied, differing sections. New United America, seceding from the old colonial matrix, began as a simple system of three coastal sections, each with its related "back country." Even before 1776, men were using such terms as the South, the Middle region, and New England or the Eastern Colonies. They also recognized the existence of the "back country," and the Indian country beyond this. As decade after decade the country expanded westward to the Pacific, it took in section after section, and coined appropriate names for these new accessions.

The consciousness of the persisting realities of sections is reflected by the sectional nomenclatures used in Congress, and in the several institutional and administrative arrangements fashioned by the American Congresses and their successors under the Constitution. Thus common parlance and governmental institutions founded on sectional bases combine to bear witness to the existence of sections, and to the implied concept of the section itself.

The geographer Jedidiah Morse first made the concept of the section explicit. Abstracting it from the realm of observed, practical facts, he gave it generalized expression, in 1793, as a threefold scheme for ordering and arranging the details of American geography. The interest that Morse had in this threefold scheme of sections lay in the possibilities he saw therein of applying it in his descriptions of the United States. In his hands the original concept was skillfully applied. As the country grew, Morse altered and modified his applications of the concept to fit the changing facts. His own experience with it proved that this abstraction had high usefulness as a principle of ordonnance in writing books on American geography, and that it contained within itself the potentialities of growth.

Various geographers succeeded Morse. They followed him in continuing to use schemes of sections, which they drafted or redrafted in accord with the territorial expansion of the country and the enlargement of American geographical knowledge.

The compilers of the census reports show, during the period 1790–1900, a trend from an initial acceptance of a sectionalized arrangement of their data to a later acceptance of an alphabetical arrangement by states, coupled with some use of statistical tables constructed upon a sectional basis. Two writers of significance are associated with attempts to utilize census statistics in relation to a concept of sections. Both these writers formulated schemes of sections that had influence. In 1843, George Tucker produced two such schemes. Within these sectionalized frameworks, Tucker grouped the several categories of his statistics and then compared and contrasted them section by section. Thus he forged a powerful instrument with which to measure and to study sections in an objective, reliable way.

In 1881, Henry Gannett, of the Census Office, produced another notable scheme for classifying American sections. Gannett's purpose, like Tucker's, was to fashion a framework which could serve scholars in the production of significant statistical work. Thus the concept of sections, exemplified and given frequent application in various statistical tables in census publications and in commercially published works as well, tended more and more to make its influence felt as a practical tool for the analysis, comparison, and contrast of masses of statistical data.

Gannett's scheme of sections bore some crude relation to the underlying topography of the United States. John Powell's acquaintance with this plan led in course of time to a still more sophisticated scheme— a classification of American physiographic regions, giving a general view of the facts based upon an expert's scientific knowledge of the geology and geography of the areas described. Powell's discriminating, factual, and objective description of American sections (he himself preferred the term "regions") laid the foundations for oncoming historians to prepare sectional interpretations of American history grounded upon reliable geographical and physiographic bases.

Meantime the historians were manifesting an interest in the sectional concept and its utility in historical investigations. William F. Allen had an appreciation of the historical role of sections in American history. He passed this interest on to his pupil, Frederick J. Turner, who conducted studies of the sort himself and promoted them among his own disciples. Turner's opinion was that the monograph by Powell revolutionized the subject. A systematic attack on the problem of sectionalism in American history was well under way at the University of Wisconsin by 1900, and various contributions of the sort had already appeared before that year. Turner's own thinking on sections as historical phenomena represents the apex of development in the field during the time covered by this study. From Turner's classroom at Madison the study of sectionalism, historically considered, now spread outward by degrees, so that more and more its influence came to be felt in the study of history and the social sciences generally. But the greatest triumphs of sectional and regional studies were to be won after 1900.

Chapter 2

The Development and Application of Regional-Sectional Concepts, 1900-1950

Vernon Carstensen

I⊤ IS not practicable in the discussion of the development and application of regional and sectional concepts since 1900 to trace the story as fully and with such rich detail as has been done in the preceding paper. It must be noted at the outset, however, that with the mounting complexity of government, business, and scholarship in the twentieth century, the use of regional and sectional schemes has increased tremendously. This paper will attempt primarily to give examples of widening twentieth-century use of regional concepts and schemes as employed by the several governmental agencies and bureaus, by business and other organizations, and by scholars and writers.

The general political framework of the United States had been marked out by 1900; only three states were still to be admitted to the Union. Nevertheless, in the years after the turn of the century, the human patterns upon the land were to change extensively, gradually in some cases, drastically and rapidly in others. These internal changes in the composition and character of American society were to be brought on by a variety of interrelated causes—the exhaustion of old and the discovery or development of new resources, the various technological developments, internal migrations, political and economic leadership, and a host of other factors—and were to alter the nature and the extent of older patterns upon the land. Indeed, in March, 1949, *Time* published a story which indicated that California had, at least technically, entered the Cotton Kingdom as the third largest producer among the states of the United States.

Of all the governmental agencies which have had to be concerned with regional schemes for organizing data, the Census Bureau is of course the most experienced. For the census of 1900 the Bureau employed a fivefold system as it had in the two previous censuses. The divisions recognized were the North Atlantic, the South Atlantic, the North Central, the South Central, and the Western. In 1910, however, the Census Bureau divided the states into nine divisions, offering the following explanation:

Because . . . of the large number of states, it is extremely difficult to exhibit the broad geographical conditions regarding the population . . . by means of the statistics for individual states. In addition, therefore, to the presentation by states, this volume gives statistics for nine groups of states which are designated as geographic divisions. The states which constitute the respective divisions can be easily ascertained by reference to any of the general tables. . . .

This plan reduces the comparisons necessary to a general understanding of the geographic differences in conditions which can be readily grasped. The states within each of these divisions are for the most part fairly homogeneous in physical characteristics, as well as in the characteristics of their population and their social and economic conditions, while on the other hand each division differs more or less sharply from most others in these respects. . . . In forming these groups of states the lines have been based partly on present and partly on historical conditions. [These nine geographic divisions, it might be added, are sometimes grouped in the text tables in three great sections—the North, which includes the New England, Middle Atlantic, East North Central, and West North Central divisions; the South, which includes the South Atlantic, East South Central, and West South Central divisions; and the West, which includes the Mountain and Pacific divisions.]

The grouping of the states in geographic divisions has facilitated a geographical rather than an alphabetical order in the tables which present the results for individual states. The advantage of this geographical order lies in the greater ease with which conditions in contiguous states can be compared.[1]

Under this arrangement the six New England States comprised the first division. New York, New Jersey, and Pennsylvania comprised the Middle Atlantic division; Ohio, Indiana, Illinois, Michigan, and Wisconsin, the East North Central division (the old Northwest Territory except for a small part of Minnesota); Minnesota, Iowa, Missouri, North and South Dakota, Nebraska, and Kansas, the

---

[1] *Thirteenth Census of the United States, Population* (Washington, 1913), I, 18.

West North Central division; and Delaware, Maryland, the District of Columbia, Virginia, West Virginia, North and South Carolina, Georgia, and Florida, the South Atlantic division. Kentucky, Tennessee, Alabama, and Mississippi made up the East South Central division; Arkansas, Louisiana, Oklahoma, and Texas, the West South Central. Finally came the Mountain division, comprising Montana, Idaho, Wyoming, Colorado, New Mexico, Arizona, Utah, and Nevada; and the Pacific division—Washington, Oregon, and California.

This divisional arrangement has continued to be used by the Census Bureau and has, of course, been widely followed by students and others who have wanted to use the data so collected. The Roper Poll, for example, has employed this breakdown in reporting regional political intentions, and the Bureau of Agricultural Economics uses it in its periodical, *The Farm Income Situation.* On the other hand, when *Fortune,* in February, 1940, presented its description and analysis of the economic potentialities of the United States, a sevenfold arrangement of regions was employed: the Northeast, which included the New England States and New York, Pennsylvania, New Jersey, Delaware, Maryland, and West Virginia; the Southeast, which included the states from Virginia south to Florida, all those lying east of the Mississippi and south of the Ohio River, plus Arkansas and Louisiana; the Middle States, which included the five states of the old Northwest Territory in addition to Minnesota, Iowa, and Missouri; the Southwest, which included Texas, Oklahoma, New Mexico, and Arizona; the Mountain and Great Plains States, which included Kansas, Colorado, Utah, Wyoming, Nebraska, the Dakotas, and Montana; the Pacific Northwest, which included Idaho, Washington, and Oregon; and the Far West, which included California and Nevada.[2]

In the establishment of regional areas and offices for the various federal departments, bureaus, and agencies charged with inspection, regulation, law enforcement, and judicial and other federal functions, the Census Bureau divisions of the United States seem to have had little influence. Some of the federal regional arrangements have been provided for by law; some have been created and changed by the agencies themselves. The Federal Reserve districts provide an

2 *Fortune,* Vol. XXI (February, 1940), 148–49.

example of a regional arrangement established by direction of Congress. For purposes of the Federal Reserve Act (1913), the country was divided into twelve Federal Reserve districts, a number of which divided states. This act, Harold U. Faulkner has remarked, gave "tacit recognition that the nation was fundamentally a group of economic sections rather than an agglomeration of states."[3] On the other hand, the War Department has had a large measure of authority in determining its own regional organization. At the end of the nineteenth century it still possessed a regional organization which had been determined largely by the fact that one of the principal occupations of the Army in the years after the Civil War had been to hold the Indians in check. The Army was organized into eight departments for the performance of various administrative and service functions, and of these, seven were west of the Mississippi River.[4] There were several reorganizations during the next years—a department was added during the first years of the Alaska gold rush—and during World War I the country was at one time divided into thirteen supply zones. After the war, the War Department established nine corps areas, an arrangement which stood until World War II.

But whether created by acts of Congress or by executive fiat, the number of administrative governmental regions has increased rapidly during this century—most rapidly, of course, since 1933. In 1935, the National Resources Committee directed a survey to determine the facts about the number and nature of regional administrative schemes developed and employed by federal agencies of bureau status or higher. It was found that 74 agencies had such schemes "(1) to facilitate federal administration; (2) for planning and program making; and (3) for decentralizing control." Some of the agencies carried on more than one type of work. Hence, a total of 108 separate regional arrangements were in use by the federal government. The number of regions or sections into which the United States was divided ranged up to 307, but over half used less than 10 regions. Nevertheless, few of the schemes were identical. The committee reported:

State lines, physiographic features, politics, the localization of the objects

[3] Harold U. Faulkner, *American Economic History* (New York, 1943), 558.

[4] The changes in the administrative divisions of the country can be traced through the *Annual Reports* of the War Department. Raphael P. Thian's *Notes Illustrating the Military Geography of the United States, 1813–1880* (Washington, 1881) will be useful to anyone seeking information on military regions in the nineteenth century.

of administration, transportation convenience, and the desire to equalize the burden of work among the regions have all at one time or another played their part. The least frequent influences of those enumerated are probably politics and physiographic features. The other four factors are considered in the establishment of practically all regional schemes, but which ones actually do or should carry the greatest weight is not readily ascertainable.[5]

Just as the departments and agencies of the federal government have had to develop what Howard Odum calls "service regions," so business organizations and various educational, athletic, fraternal, and other organizations have had to form regional schemes. Business firms which operate over large areas of the country generally employ regional systems. Indeed, in some instances, the government has directed such action. The best-known case of this kind is that of the old Standard Oil Company of New Jersey. In compliance with a directive of the Supreme Court, the corporation was dissolved, and there emerged from the dissolution four regional companies: Standard of New Jersey, Standard of Indiana, Standard of New York, and Standard of California. But even before this directed breakup of the company, a somewhat similar regional arrangement had existed. Another example of what might be called government participation in the regionalization of business is to be found in the Public Utilities Act of 1935, which among other things directed that as soon as practicable after 1938 the public-utility holding companies must limit their operations to a "single integrated public utility" system. This was generally accepted to mean that a company must restrict itself to a contiguous area. Business use of regions is also exemplified in the mail-order houses, at least two of which publish catalogues to accommodate the different regional needs and tastes. Montgomery Ward and Company, for example, has mail-order houses at Chicago, Baltimore, Albany, St. Paul, Denver, Kansas City, Portland (Oregon), Oakland, and Fort Worth, each serving its assigned region. The area served by the Chicago office includes the following states: Illinois, Wisconsin, Michigan, Indiana, Ohio, Kentucky, Tennessee, Mississippi, Alabama, and fragments of Louisiana, Georgia, Missouri, Iowa, and Minnesota—a curious but apparently workable region.

[5] National Resources Committee, *Regional Factors in National Planning and Development* (Washington, 1935), 71–72. Outline maps of the federal regions are given, pp. 206–23.

In the last fifty years, numerous regional high school and college accrediting associations, athletic associations, and religious organizations have been formed. Most national membership organizations likewise employ some system of regional organization for election of officers and other purposes. There are Rhodes scholarship and Harvard scholarship districts. In short, in the workaday world of government and business, of religious, educational, fraternal, professional, and other organizations there exists a host of regional divisions of the United States, each established to serve its specific purpose or purposes. They have multiplied almost endlessly, in keeping, no doubt, with the variety and complexity of our society.

Scholars, too, have made increasing use of regional divisions for the purpose of collecting, arranging, analyzing, evaluating, and presenting various kinds of data about the United States. At the University of Wisconsin, for example, under the leadership of Frederick Jackson Turner, provision was made shortly after the turn of the century to offer courses in the history of the West, the South, and New England, in addition to the other topical and period courses on the history of the United States. In fact, the course in the history of the West, which Turner himself taught, had been inaugurated in the eighteen-nineties. In this course, according to the *Catalogue* of 1903–1904, "Particular attention is paid to the conditions of westward migration and to the economic, political, and social aspects of the occupation of the various physiographic provinces of the United States, together with the results upon the national development." The history of the South was taught by U. B. Phillips. It was described as follows: "The course deals with the period since the Revolution and especial attention is given to the economic and social forces involved in the plantation system, slavery, and the occupation of the Gulf Plains, as a basis for understanding the political history of the South and its place in the national history." The history of New England, offered by Carl Russell Fish, received less explanation: "Special attention will be paid to the colonial period and to New England expansion."[6]

Such a division of the study of American history was both a product of work already done by historians and a promise that sectional or regional histories would be written, or at least that the sectional and regional variations would be emphasized in general writing on

[6] *Catalogue of the University of Wisconsin, 1903–1904*, p. 97.

the history of the United States. Turner himself in *The Rise of the New West* (1906), a volume in the "American Nation Series," divided the country into New England, the Middle region, the South, the West, and the Far West to discuss the period from 1815 to 1830. In *The United States, 1830–1850; The Nation and Its Sections,* which appeared in 1935, he found a further regrouping necessary. He used a sixfold scheme of classification: New England, the Middle Atlantic States, the South Atlantic States, the South Central States, the North Central States, and Texas and the Far West. Meanwhile other historians wrote regional or sectional histories. U. B. Phillips' *Life and Labor of the Old South* was followed by a spate of others. At present a new ten-volume history of the South, a collective work, is under way. Although other regions or sections have not perhaps been as fully treated as the South, historians have used regions or sections both as fields of interest in themselves and as one means of studying the history of the United States. Besides the state historical society magazines, a number of publications of regional rather than state or local interest have developed: the *Journal of Southern History,* the *Mississippi Valley Historical Review,* the *Pacific Historical Review,* and the *Southwestern Historical Quarterly,* to name only a few. The editor of the *Guide to Historical Literature* (1936) was apparently unable to decide between the use of the terms "region" and "section" and so used both. A part of the *Guide* is devoted to "Histories of special periods, regions, or topics" of the United States. Under this appears a subhead, "Histories of sections," but no classification of such sectional histories is attempted beyond that of New England, the South, the West, and the Pacific Coast.

The *American Historical Review* regularly devotes several pages to brief reviews of lesser publications in United States history, divided into three parts as follows: New England and the Middle Colonies and States, the Southern Colonies and States, and the Western Territories and States. For the most part, historians have come to accept regional or sectional schemes, although there is little evidence of uniformity or agreement in their use.

The geographers, as their discipline has expanded, have continued to multiply the number of divisions or sections needed for purposes of study. In 1914, Wolfgang L. G. Joerg published a paper under the title "The Subdivision of North America into Natural

Regions: A Preliminary Inquiry."[7] "With the recognition of regional geography," he declared, "as the ultimate goal and highest expression of geographic research, which has come with the modern development of our science," there has been a marked increase in the attention devoted to this branch of investigation. "Economy of presentation and sound geographical reasoning both demand that such units be as homogeneous as possible." He then surveyed the natural regions of North America to show what had been done. A natural region he defined as "any portion of the earth's surface whose physical conditions are homogeneous." Three elements he considered of primary importance in determining a natural region: structure and relief, climate, and vegetation. In selecting natural regions, all elements should be taken into account; but where one predominated, that would be the determining factor. Thus structure would predominate in mountainous areas, climate in plains. The evaluation, he acknowledged, was in the end subjective. In marking out a region, he suggested, the problem was not whether it was right or wrong, but only whether it was expedient. Joerg presented a series of maps prepared by geographers between 1893 and 1912—twenty-one in all, showing various regions of the United States and North America based on structural, climatic, vegetational, zoographic, and other factors. The number of regions marked out on these maps ranged widely. The author's own map, the twenty-second in the list, divided the continent into fourteen "natural regions."[8]

The same year and in the same publication, Nevin M. Fenneman presented a paper on the physiographic boundaries within the United States. He lamented the confused and inconsistent usages which had developed but conceded that "no one set of subdivisions of a continent can be made to serve in all discussions. The scheme of subdivisions must vary according to the thing discussed." Thus, to a certain extent he differed with Joerg, who sought to harmonize the earlier divisions into a systematic scheme. Fenneman wanted a physiographic map to be physiographic and nothing more. He found two reasons for dividing the United States into provinces: (1) "for discussion and explanation of the physical features of the country" and (2) "as a basis for the plotting and discussion of social, industrial, historical, and other data of distinctly human concern." In his de-

[7] *Annals of the Association of American Geographers,* Vol. IV (1914), 55–83.
[8] *Ibid.,* 62–83.

scription of regions he used a criterion of "unity or similarity of physiographic history." In this paper he identified and described some twenty-one provinces within the United States.[9]

These papers gave impetus to the holding of a conference of geographers on the problem of delineating and more or less officially establishing the physiographic provinces of the United States. It was quickly found that physiographic maps would not satisfy regional geographers. Hence, the conference recommended concentrating first on that type of map, and, in 1916, Fenneman published a paper on the "Physiographic Divisions of the United States." The scheme there presented, Fenneman declared, rested upon physiographic data and the recognition that surface forms were determined by structure, process, and stage. He divided North America into eight "strongly characterized parts," all of which were represented in the United States. The term "region" was not used. Instead, he employed the term "major division." A major division was subdivided into provinces, sections, and districts. The major divisions, as outlined, comprised: Laurentian upland, Atlantic plain, Appalachian highlands, Interior plains, Interior highlands, Rocky Mountain system, Intermontane plateaus, and Pacific mountain system.[10] This arrangement was enlarged and revised somewhat in 1928.[11]

Other geographers, of course, drew their own maps for their own purposes, and regional schemes continued to multiply in scholarship as they had in government, in business, and in other organizations and fields of interest. In 1933, and again in 1934, the American geographers devoted full sessions of their annual meetings to the presentation and discussion of regional geography.[12] At the meeting in 1934, considerable discussion took place on the drawing of the boundary lines. Ellsworth Huntington and others agreed that the boundary of a region must be selected according to the purpose to be served, and Huntington declared that there were hundreds of different purposes and, therefore, systems. The *Atlas of American Agriculture*, published in 1936, contained regional maps based upon rural land use, climate, soils, and natural vegetation. Seven regions were marked out, for example, on a basis of rural land use alone.

9 *Ibid.*, 84–134.

10 *Ibid.*, Vol. VI (1916), 19–98.

11 *Ibid.*, Vol. XVIII (1928), 264–353.

12 *Ibid.*, Vol. XXIV (1934), 77–122; Vol. XXV (1935), 121–74.

The historical geographer Ralph H. Brown, in *Historical Geography of the United States* (1948), treated his subject by sections as follows: the Atlantic seaboard, the Ohio River valley and Great Lakes region, the new Northwest, the Great Plains and bordering regions, and the Mountain States together with the Pacific Coast.

The sociologists, too, have devised and employed various regional arrangements in making their studies. Howard Odum and Harry Estill Moore, in their *American Regionalism* (1938), brought together a vast and rich collection of data dealing with what they described as natural, cultural, and service regions. They presented a sixfold arrangement of the regions of the United States. Recognizing that no perfect arrangement exists and that it is impossible to devise one which would be satisfactory to even a majority of students, they nevertheless sought to designate areas which could be called "major societal regions." "Such a region to be definitive," they asserted, "must approximate the largest degree of homogeneity for the largest number of purposes."[13] In establishing the sixfold system of regions, they were governed by three criteria. The first was that the number of regions must not be too large. The second was "the measures of physiographic homogeneities, historical development, folk culture, and institutions, the origin and character of its people, and of special features commonly accepted as characteristic." The third consisted of "statistical indices of a socio-economic nature compiled from an inventory of physical, technological, economic, and social facts."[14] The six major regions as thus established consisted of the Northeast, the Southeast, the Northwest, the Southwest, the Middle States, and the Far West. The Northeast region included the New England States and New York, New Jersey, Pennsylvania, Delaware, Maryland, West Virginia, and the District of Columbia. The Southeast region included Virginia, North and South Carolina, Georgia, Florida, Alabama, Mississippi, Louisiana, Arkansas, Tennessee, and Kentucky. The Southwest region consisted of Texas, Oklahoma, New Mexico, and Arizona; while the Middle States comprised Ohio, Indiana, Illinois, Michigan, Wisconsin, Minnesota, Iowa, and Missouri. The Northwest region included North and South Dakota, Nebraska, Kansas, Montana, Idaho, Wyoming, Colorado, and Utah. The Far

[13] Howard W. Odum and Harry Estill Moore, *American Regionalism: A Cultural-Historical Approach to National Integration* (New York, 1938), 435, 437.
[14] *Ibid.*, 437.

West region included Washington, Oregon, California, and Nevada.[15]

In 1940, Arthur R. Magnus brought out *Rural Regions of the United States.* The regions are defined as those in which social and economic conditions are relatively uniform and among which there are significant differences. It was posited that "these subdivisions of the United States should be of value to administrators concerned with planning programs to fit specific areas and situations and with laying out the territory for decentralizing administrative functions." Such regions, Magnus argued, could be used as a basis for the administration of relief and unemployment, and for analyzing social conditions. He declared that "regionalization" based solely upon a type of farming was inadequate. Hence, the thirty-two rural farm regions and thirty-four rural regions in his scheme were based upon such elements as type of farming, population increase, standard of living, land value, tenancy, and race. "Large numbers of factors," Magnus explained, "are difficult to treat statistically, however, in a manner to yield regions and subregions."[16]

Regionalism in art and literature has been the concern of many artists and writers, critics, and literary historians. Much is said about this subject in the papers that follow, but it should be noted here that literary regionalism has stemmed in part from the desire to use local materials; in part it has represented, as the nineteenth-century French regionalist movement did, a revolt against the real or imputed despotism of the capital. In the late nineteen-twenties and thirties the subject of literary regionalism was agitated in the columns of the literary magazines, notably the *Saturday Review of Literature;* self-consciously regional literary magazines were established, and even some universities encouraged the trend by establishing schools of regional creative writing. Theodore Blegen has pronounced a most sensible judgment on this phase of regionalism. He quotes with approval a statement made by James Gray that a given region may contain "the meaning of everything that America has been and the knowledge of what it may become." "Regionalism," Blegen then wrote, "is not cultural separatism. It is not the doctrine of every region for itself. Its essence—and I think it is fundamentally a matter of attitude and not of subject matter—is a creative concern with the development of the region to its maximum for the cultural strength

[15] *Ibid.,* 435–36.
[16] Arthur R. Magnus, *Rural Regions of the United States* (Washington, 1940), 79.

of the nation."[17] Meanwhile, literary historians had for a long time been treating literary history at least in part on a regional basis. The recently published *Literary History of the United States* (1948), by Robert E. Spiller and others, yields perceptibly to the regionalists by including chapters on the writers of the South, New England, the Middle Colonies, the Middle States, and the Old South, and on the writers of western records and romance.

During the last three and a half decades there have been numerous attempts on the part of scholars to find general agreement on regions, natural or otherwise. In view of the origins of regional concepts and the use of these schemes by government, business firms, various organizations, and scholars, it is not surprising that these attempts have not been fruitful, particularly among scholars. As in the old Indian fable of the four blind men who were brought to examine the elephant, each has reached a different, yet for himself a valid, conclusion about the nature and outline of the object being examined.

Geographers have made many attempts to reach an agreement, first following the papers published by Joerg and Fenneman in 1914, and again at meetings in 1933 and 1934. The only general agreement reached was that the different branches of the science required different regional schemes. In 1937, John Leighly, in an article "Some Comments on Contemporary Geographic Method," directly attacked regional geography as unscientific. "There is no prospect," he wrote, "of our finding a theory so penetrating that it will bring into rational order all or a large fraction of the heterogeneous elements of the landscape. There is no prospect of our finding such a theory, that is to say, unless it is of a mystical kind and so outside the pale of science." Later in the same article he declared: "Our regionalists have apparently taken their stand on the possibility that by asserting the existence of a field not pre-empted or a point of view not occupied by the practitioners of other disciplines, they have laid the foundation for a fruitful and satisfying scholarly activity." He argued that it was impossible to synthesize "arbitrarily selected heterogeneous facts." This was the work of the artist, not the scientist. "Systematic regional description has its uses," he concluded, "uses similar to those of lexicography."[18]

[17] Theodore Blegen, *Grass Roots History* (Minneapolis, 1947), 8, 12.
[18] *Annals of the Association of American Geographers*, Vol. XXVII (1937), 125–41.

Two years later, V. C. Finch devoted the major part of his paper, "Geographical Science and Social Philosophy," to the subject of regionalism. Answering some of the criticisms made by Leighly, he argued that regions were recognizable although the region was also "an areal convenience delimited for a purpose." Commenting on the difficulty of setting regional boundaries, he declared that the "characteristics of a region should be most pronounced in its interior, and a logical description of it should . . . proceed not from the center to the circumference, but from the circumference to the center. Regions end in transition, seldom in definite boundaries."[19]

Although historians have been less disturbed by the problem of finding agreement on the term, the question was clearly raised in Fred Albert Shannon's appraisal of Webb's *The Great Plains* and was discussed without clear-cut conclusion by a committee.

The National Resources Committee, after identifying the 108 regional schemes used by federal bureaus, asked whether the numerous regional schemes ought not to be supplanted by a single set of divisions serving the whole federal government. Was such a standardization of administrative regions desirable and was it possible? The committee felt that much good might come out of such an arrangement. It asserted that "many administrative regional schemes are certainly inexpertly constructed, but the great majority of them have been so drawn as to secure a fairly good field administration of the particular function to be performed. The aggregate result, as will impress anyone comparing the maps, appears to be a chaos superficially unjustifiable, but in reality it is a chaos resulting simply from the fact that each agency has attempted to carry on its own activities upon a pattern scheme of regions designed by itself and supposedly best adapted to its needs." The committee felt that the question of the desirability of standard regions for federal administration could be answered only after thorough inquiry had been made. As to whether such standardization would be possible, the committee was equivocal although it declared that "it would be relatively easy if all bureaus and special agencies were classified into general functional groups: e.g., those which are engaged in administering a land program, a transportation program, or a program of social and economic regulation. Standardization within each group might easily reduce

19 *Ibid.,* Vol. XXIX (1939), 1–28.

the number of regional schemes to a dozen or less." [20] The committee inclined to the belief that this would be a good thing, although to a distinterested reader it seems that their own evidence argued to the contrary.

Is anything really gained by attempting to combine a number of such administrative regions for the purpose of attaining a harmony which at its best may be no more than synthetic? Such a combining of administrative regions might perhaps bring about a seeming harmony; but the chances are that this would have little more than a paper existence, since the specific tasks to be performed would still require the existence of an internal organizational structure adequate for the specific task to be done, and not necessarily in keeping with the regional structure requisite for carrying on some other specific functions, often related to it only by virtue of its being another of the functions of the federal government. Certainly if regional administrative schemes are set up to accomplish specific tasks, they ought to be permitted to do so without suffering from imported confusions.

Some difficulty has been experienced in the definition of the terms "region" and "section," although there is general agreement that the section embraces the regions rather than the reverse. Often the terms have been used interchangeably. Some regionalists, notably Odum and Moore, have found in the term "sectionalism" a content not generally ascribed to it.

By regionalism we mean a new American social economy and social determinism. Such regionalism is also opposed to the traditional literary localism. Indeed, perhaps the first distinction between the new realistic regionalism and the older sectionalism is that regionalism assumes first, last, and always a totality composed of the several areal and cultural units, a great national unity and integrated culture in which each region exists as a region solely as a component unit of the whole. Sectionalism, on the other hand, always assumes isolated, segregated areal divisions with potential completeness in themselves and looked upon as separate entities. This was the magnificent picture of Frederick Jackson Turner's sectionalism in American life. This was James Truslow Adams' *America's Tragedy.*

.   .   .   .

Herein lies the essential quality of sectionalism; inherent in it is the idea of separatism and isolation; of separate units with separate interests. It must be clear that, since the very definition of regionalism implies a unifying function, it must be different from sectionalism as everywhere

[20] National Resources Committee, *Regional Factors in National Planning,* 81–82.

defined by the historians. Here the distinctions are clear between the divisive power of self-seeking *sections* and the integrating power of coordinate *regions* fabricated into a united whole.

.   .   .   .

Regionalism is organic, basic to the evolution of all culture. Sectionalism is mechanical and is basic to specialized and temporary ends.[21]

Others have followed Odum and Moore in making this distinction. Thus Donald Davidson has observed, "Turner's words *section* and *sectionalism* have a schismatic and contentious look which the social scientist does not relish. The words *region* and *regionalism* serve his purpose better." Regionalism, says Davidson, suggests to the social scientist "the possibility of compromise between political action and natural law." He observes further that "regionalism in the view of the trained social scientist is neither a reversion to a primitive and simple economy, nor an attempt to revive sectionalism 'under a less offensive name,' but it is a necessary organic feature of an advanced and well ordered national civilization."[22]

In general, insistence on the strict differentiation between regions and sections will perhaps be useful, provided it is not necessarily assumed that regions possessing homogeneous elements are also areas in which there is no conflict. On this point William B. Hesseltine has been positive and clear: "The nation was born in the region and the region remained as the dominant force in the nation." He observed further that the contests between groups for the control of their region have been the dynamic force in American history. "It is the imperialism of the dominant groups that has given rise to the phenomenon of sectionalism in American history."[23]

Turner often used the terms "section" and "region" interchangeably. In his essay "The Significance of the Section in American History," he declared:

There is a sense in which sectionalism is inevitable and desirable. There is and always has been a sectional geography in America based fundamentally upon geographic regions. There is a geography of political habit, a geography of opinion, of material interests, of racial stocks, of

[21] Odum and Moore, *American Regionalism*, 18, 39, 43.

[22] Donald Davidson, "Regionalism as Social Science," *Southern Review*, Vol. III (1937–38), 209–24.

[23] William B. Hesseltine, "Regions, Classes, and Sections in American History," *Journal of Land and Public Utility Economics*, Vol. XX (1944), 36, 42.

physical fitness, of social traits, of literature, of the distribution of men of ability, even of religious denominations. Professor Josiah Royce defined a "province" or section, in the sense in which I am using the word, as "any one part of a national domain which is geographically and socially suffi- ciently unified to have a true consciousness of its own ideals and customs and to possess a sense of its distinction from other parts of the coun- try."[24]

Turner was keenly aware of the differences and conflicts within the regions and sections he described, as is revealed in the maps he so painstakingly prepared. Only four years before his death, he wrote to Charles O. Paullin, who was about to launch a study of sections in the United States. These hitherto unpublished words, resting on forty years of thinking and research on the subject, are richly sug- gestive.

Thank you for letting me see your plan for an investigation of Sec- tionalism in the United States.

I have been interested in the subject ever since I began historical re- search on the United States and have been collecting on the theme, draw- ing political, economic, and cultural maps for testing out the hypothesis, and working the historical sources. When I became Professor Emeritus at Harvard I gave the course of Dowse lectures at Cambridge (United States) on the subject, illustrated by a considerable portion of these maps on lantern slides, and I attempted to sketch an interpretation for the different periods somewhat on the lines you present, but with somewhat different periods and inclusion of some aspects not mentioned in your plan.

Here I am completing a book on the period 1830 to 1850, attempting to exhibit the sectional and regional (in distinction from sectional) as- pects of our history in those years, first outlining each section's geography and development, economically, socially, and politically in the period, and then showing the interplay in Congressional debates and votes and in the attitude of the leaders of the various sections. I am more and more aware of the difficulty of the task and am getting very humble.

I mention these personal matters in order to say that my own work has convinced me of several things. One of them is that when one tries to deal with the sections statistically he is practically forced by the group- ings in the Census either to use its Divisions (New England, Middle At- lantic, South Atlantic, etc.) or to attempt a rearrangement by *counties* or *precincts,* which involves work that some future group of investigators may undertake for the whole of our history, but which is too big a job

[24] Frederick Jackson Turner, *The Significance of Sections in American History* (New York, 1932), 45.

for one man. On the whole, I think the Census Divisions are wisely made and not misleading. The naming of sections as "Southeast," "Southwest," "Middle West," etc., has the difficulty that the meanings of these terms change with the periods of our development and that, even in the same period, they connote different state groups in the writings of different authors, and to the reader. At least a very definite statement of states included in whatever term is used is important, as I am sure you realize.

I am finding that I have to distinguish *regions,* within a section or across several sections, from *sections* as groups of states. Both have important influences. Second, I am finding also that the period of twenty years on which I am working at present involves much more knowledge and research into the economic, political, social, and cultural aspects and their mutual relations than I had thought when I began the study.

I am more impressed than you seem to be with the number of studies of particular states, or topics, that have already been produced concerning regionalism in the separate states. There is quite a long list of them, including the work of geographers. Sectionalism in the larger sense has not been adequately treated. Formerly it was conceived of as North against South, or less often East against West, but these big sections mislead the reader. Their complexity, as you know, is even more important in shaping the historical outcome.

Therefore, it seems to me that you are setting forth on a long journey, if as a piece of scientific research into all the sectional phases of American life (including such important aspects as the literature and church organizations, for example), you take the whole of United States history on the lines of your plan. A reconnaissance or suggestive sketch of the field is not impossible, and if my working days permit I may myself also try some such thing, on the basis of my previous studies.

Your fine work on the Atlas is an important preparation. But if I may suggest, I should (for correlation and interpretation of the forces behind maps) take a special period, rather than essay the whole course of our history. But you are younger than I am, and the courage of youth is a big factor in success. Apart from the consideration above outlined, the scheme is sound, I think, and important. God speed you, whatever choice you make![25]

BIBLIOGRAPHIC NOTE

In addition to the books and other materials cited in the footnotes of Chapters 1 and 2, the following items are listed for their general value

---

[25] I am indebted to Fulmer Mood for calling my attention to this letter and for giving me permission to quote it in this paper.

and suggestiveness. No attempt has been made to provide a comprehensive bibliography since anything of the kind would necessarily run to great length.

The history of the terms "section," "division," and "region" can be found in the following dictionaries: Sir James A. H. Murray, *A New English Dictionary on Historical Principles* (Oxford, 1888–1923), I–X; Sir William A. Craigie and James R. Hulbert (eds.), *A Dictionary of American English on Historical Principles* (4 vols., Chicago, 1938–44); John Pickering, *A Vocabulary, or Collection of Words and Phrases which have been supposed to be peculiar to the United States of America* (Boston, 1816); Noah Webster, *An American Dictionary of the English Language* (2 vols., New York, 1828); Joseph Worcester, *A Dictionary of the English Language* (Boston, 1860); John Russell Bartlett, *A Glossary of Words and Phrases usually regarded as peculiar to the United States*, 3rd ed. (Boston, 1860); and Noah Webster, *An American Dictionary of the English Language* (Springfield, Massachusetts, 1863).

The application to government of the sectional-regional concept during the period of the Old Congress and the early Republic can be traced in such special studies as the following: Stanley M. Pargellis, *Lord Loudoun in North America* (New Haven, 1933); Walter H. Mohr, *Federal Indian Relations, 1774–1788* (Philadelphia, 1933); Charles O. Paullin, *The Navy of the American Revolution* (Cleveland, 1906); *Journals of the Continental Congress, 1774–1789* (34 vols., Washington, 1904–37); E. C. Burnett (ed.), *Letters of Members of the Continental Congress* (8 vols., Washington, 1921–36); Max Farrand (ed.), *The Records of the Federal Convention of 1787* (3 vols., New Haven, 1911); and *Annals of the Congress of the United States, 1789–1824* (42 vols., Washington, 1834–56). Revolutionary and early national periods contain numerous references to sectional terms and sectional realities. Contemporary pamphlets such as Lewis Evans, *Geographical, Historical, Political, Philosophical and Mechanical Essays* (Philadelphia, 1755); Andrew Burnaby, *Travels through the Middle Settlements in North-America, in the Years 1759 and 1760* (London, 1775); Tench Coxe, *A View of the United States of America* (Philadelphia, 1794); Mathew Carey, *The Olive Branch; or, Faults on Both Sides, Federal and Democratic*, 6th ed. (Philadelphia, 1815); and Carey, *The New Olive Branch; or, An Attempt to establish an Identity of interest between agriculture, manufacture, and commerce* (Philadelphia, 1820) are also sources of early sectional data. These are but a few type specimens from a large pamphlet literature.

As indicated in Chapter 1, the early census reports are of basic importance to this study. From 1790 through 1840, the official returns comprise the following: *Return of the Whole Number of Persons within the Several Districts of the United States* (Philadelphia, 1791); *Return of the Whole Number of Persons within the Several Districts of the United States* [1801]; *Aggregate Amount of each Description of Persons within the United States of America and the Territories thereof* (Washington, 1811); *Census for 1820, Published by authority of an Act of Congress* (Washington, 1821); *Fifth Census; or, Enumeration of the Inhabitants of the United States* (Washington, 1832); and *Sixth Census; or, Enumeration of the Inhabitants of the United States* (Washington, 1841).

The historical geography of the United States Circuit Court districts, as outlined in Chapter 1, is based upon the legislation recorded in *Public Statutes at Large of the United States of America,* I–XVII (Boston, 1848–73); XVIII–XXVI (Washington, 1875–91). The geography of these districts since 1891 can be found in the *Official Congressional Directory,* 51 Cong., 1 sess., 1st ed. (Washington, 1889); 56 Cong., 2nd ed. (Washington, 1901); 81 Cong., 1 sess., 1st ed. (Washington, 1949). The key to much of this legislation is Felix Frankfurter and James M. Landis, *The Business of the Supreme Court; A Study in the Federal Judicial System* (New York, 1927). Statements about what should constitute workable districts in the Federal Reserve System are scattered through the testimony taken in *Hearings before the Committee on Banking and Currency, United States Senate,* 63 Cong. (3 vols., Washington, 1913). Objections of banking and business groups to the boundary lines of the original Federal Reserve districts and modifications of the boundaries to overcome some of the objections are shown in the first and second *Annual Report of the Federal Reserve Board* (Washington, 1914, 1915).

John W. Powell, *Physiographic Regions of the United States* (New York, 1896) was extremely influential and is still historically important. Nevin M. Fenneman, *Physiography of Eastern United States* (New York, 1938) and *Physiography of Western United States* (New York, 1931) are recent, valuable, and more detailed treatments. Ralph H. Brown, *Historical Geography of the United States* (New York, 1948) is a competent historical treatment.

Any reader interested in American regionalism will want to become acquainted with these two extremely useful collections of maps: Charles O. Paullin, *Atlas of the Historical Geography of the United States,* edited by John K. Wright (Washington and New York, 1932) and *Atlas of American Agriculture. Physical basis including land relief, climate, soils, and natural vegetation of the United States* (6 vols. in 1, Washington, 1936). In addition to these, the many maps in the several statistical atlases based upon the census reports from the Ninth to the Fourteenth Census are of prime importance.

Before the year 1900, the following writers, all but one of whom were historians, had demonstrated that the sectional-regional approach to the study of historical and social data was a fruitful one: William F. Allen and others (eds.), *Slave Songs of the United States* (New York, 1867); Henry Gannett, *The Building of a Nation: The Growth, Present Condition, and Resources of the United States* (New York, 1895); Frederick Jackson Turner, "The West as a Field for Historical Study," *Annual Report of the American Historical Association for 1896* (Washington, 1897), I, 281–87; and O. G. Libby, "A Plea for the Study of Votes in Congress," *Annual Report of the American Historical Association for the Year 1896* (Washington, 1897), I, 323–34. W. P. Trent also belongs to this group of writers, and his contributions to sectional studies are many: "Notes on the Outlook for Historical Studies in the South," *Papers of the American Historical Association* (New York, 1890), IV, 383–91; "The Study of Southern History," in Vanderbilt Southern History Society's *Publication No. 1* (Nashville, 1895); *Southern Statesmen of the Old Régime* (New York, 1897); "Dominant Forces in Southern Life and Character," *Atlantic*

Monthly, Vol. LXXIX (February, 1897), 42–53; "Tendencies of Higher Life in the South," *Atlantic Monthly*, Vol. LXXIX (June, 1897), 766–78; and *Progress of the United States in the Nineteenth Century* (Toronto, 1901). Woodrow Wilson, "Mr. Goldwin Smith's 'Views' on Our Political History," *The Forum*, Vol. XVI (December, 1893), 489–99, includes by way of refutation of Smith a sectional interpretation of American history, based on Turner. Woodrow Wilson, "The Proper Perspective of American History," *The Forum*, Vol. XIX (June, 1895), 544–59, includes a sectional interpretation of American history, partly derived from Turner, partly original with Wilson. Woodrow Wilson, "The Making of the Nation," *Atlantic Monthly*, Vol. LXXX (July, 1897), 1–14, is a sectional interpretation that refers to Turner by name.

Chapter 3

The Regional Concept
as a Tool for Social Research

Rupert B. Vance

IT IS a paradox that the development of regional analysis has paralleled the growth of world-wide communication and trade, the emergence of cosmopolitan culture, and the ideology of One World. The paradox has its explanation in the fact that the regional approach to social analysis has an integrative rather than a divisive function. Any practicing member of the social science fraternity who undertakes to use the regional concept as a tool for research will soon find, in Howard W. Odum's felicitious phrase, that the choice he has made is not that of regionalism *or* but regionalism *and*. The missing term is nation or world, for the region gains its significance only from its relation to a total structure. The relation that regionalism presumes to study is that of parts to wholes.

Without committing ourselves to either mechanistic or organic models, we must realize that the concept of a structure the elements of which are themselves smaller structures, is neither unfamiliar nor new. In philosophy Lucretius anticipated the atomic theory of physical structure, and Leibniz's treatment of the living organism as a plenum of organisms was an anticipation of cellular theory. In political science, federations from Ancient Greece to Modern Switzerland have given us examples of social structure whose component parts are similar structures.[1] No region can be defined except in relation to the total structure of which it is a component part. No more can the reciprocal relation of function to structure be grasped apart from this theme of unity in diversity, familiar to Americans in the motto of their Federal Union, *e pluribus unum*.

[1] Norbert Weiner, *Cybernetics: or Control and Communication in the Animal and the Machine* (New York, 1948), 181.

Regionalism is thus a concept that cuts across many lines. Recent developments testify to the interest such ideas have aroused in the teaching and research programs of the social sciences. There have emerged a whole series of new programs, variously termed "American Studies" and "American Civilization," in which several disciplines, notably English and history, have converged to explore the literature and civilization of the United States and its different regions.[2] Richard H. Shyrock sees these programs as an attempt to repair the effects of specialization and the fragmentation of fields "which threatened understanding." The effort "to re-establish synthesis," he writes, "has taken various forms—from a return to the certitudes of the Middle Ages to the integration of our own complex scholarship. The study of American Civilization is one form of the latter process."[3]

The area studies developed during the war as a military necessity have been carried forward in the study of major world areas.[4] "All the social sciences, along with the functional study of languages, are brought together in area studies to promote a comprehensive understanding of a particular region, country, nation or civilization as a 'highly individual social and historical configuration in which all sorts of facts and events stand related in intricate and peculiar ways.' "[5]

Studies in both these fields are largely in the descriptive stage, and

[2] Tremaine McDowell, *American Studies* (Minneapolis, 1948). The American Council of Learned Societies has a committee which brings together representatives of the disciplines concerned to consider mutual problems of research. The first issue of a new journal in this field, *American Quarterly,* published by the University of Minnesota, appeared in March, 1949.

[3] Richard H. Shyrock, "The Nature and Implications of Programs in American Civilization," *The American Heritage* (April, 1949). See also David F. Bowers, *The Princeton Conference on American Civilization: A Description and an Appraisal* (Princeton, 1944).

[4] Robert B. Hall, *Area Studies: With Special Reference to Their Implications for Social Science* (New York, Social Science Research Council, 1947). The Social Science Research Council has formed a committee on world-area research and has sponsored a large-scale conference on the problems involved. See Charles Wagley, *Area Research and Training: A Conference Report on the Study of World Areas* (New York, Social Science Research Council, 1948). The world areas here involved were Latin America, Europe, Soviet Russia, the Near East, Southern Asia, and the Far East. See especially Julian H. Steward, *Area Research: Theory and Practice* (New York, Social Science Research Council, 1950).

[5] Werner J. Cahnman, "Outline of a Theory of Area Studies," *Annals of the Association of American Geographers,* Vol. XXXVIII (December, 1948), 243.

their theoretical and conceptual organization remains relatively un-developed. Accordingly, it is not yet apparent how their attempts at synthesis are related to regionalism, although it is clear that both de-pend on areal and cultural concepts already developed in the con-tributions of geography and anthropology to regional analysis.

In the social science field one may note that the latest survey of American life, *Recent Social Trends* (New York, 1936), "took little notice of regional characteristics although its pages were full of data which invited a regional interpretation." On the other hand, there is a notable project in which specialists in the language, collaborating with specialists in social structure and geography, set out to develop a *Linguistic Atlas of the United States*.[6] Moreover, the work selected by specialists as the most noteworthy example of recent historical re-search was not conventional history at all but a regional monograph, showing in historical depth the development of civilization in a major area—the Great Plains.[7]

In 1936 the unilateral treatment of *Recent Social Trends* was cor-rected by one of its achitects in a full-scale analysis which developed six major composite regions of the United States and documented the complex character of one, the Southeast.[8] "The Southeastern program is noteworthy," writes Julian H. Steward, "because of the concep-tualization of the regional unit, and because it calls for a focus upon a particular problem for interdisciplinary collaboration."[9] The re-gional point of view was given official statement by the National Re-sources Planning Board in *Regional Factors in National Planning and Development* (1935) and reinforced by some baker's dozen of re-gional planning reports, all pointing to the close association of regional research and the planning movement. Few of these projects have developed complete and coherent regional theory, but all have served to show the contemporary interest in regionalism as a tool for research.

---

6 Hans Kurath, *The Linguistic Atlas of the United States and Canada* (Providence, 1936).

7 Walter Prescott Webb, *The Great Plains* (Boston, 1931). See Fred A. Shannon's drastic critique, *An Appraisal of Walter Prescott Webb's "The Great Plains"* (New York, Social Science Research Council, 1940).

8 Howard W. Odum, *Southern Regions of the United States* (Chapel Hill, 1936).

9 Steward, *Area Research*, 66.

It is evident that we have many disciplines making use of regional units as a means of analyzing and understanding the phenomena with which they have to deal. Most of these uses of the regional concept have distinct value for social science research, and it is the purpose of this paper to glance at (1) the kinds of questions they undertake to answer, (2) the techniques used, (3) the basic logic common to this approach, and (4) the different levels of conceptual integration involved.·

Several major questions arise: How is the concept of regionalism to furnish orientation for research in social science? What is a region? What frame of reference does regionalism employ? What point of view does it advance, and how does this point of view fit into the general background of social theory? What techniques are at its command, and what is the logic to be followed as the method of regional analysis is applied at various levels of explanation and interpretation? Consideration of these questions may well be preceded by a warning that standardization has not yet occurred in this field. Indeed it is doubtful that standardization is desirable at the present stage of regional analysis and theory. There can be no denial, however, that each specialist needs to know more about the developments made by his colleagues in the social sciences.

In political science the problem of relating parts to wholes is clarified by the fact that political entities have legal boundaries. In much of our social science analysis we deal with natural areas whose boundaries must be determined by research into the characteristics and functions of the regions under consideration. Given this advantage, history and political science have been able to specialize in the analysis of international and interregional relation in terms of formal structures and formal functions. By the same token, the social sciences are now proceeding to the analysis of cultural and economic phenomena where the basis has not been laid in formal political structures. "In both international and national affairs," Charles E. Martin has said, "regionalism has an office and a function. As a basis of consolidation and centralization, it integrates units within itself, and as a basis of decentralization, it forms units within the larger systems of administration and control." [10] Accordingly those who use regionalism

[10] Charles E. Martin, "Regionalism as Illustrated by the Western Hemisphere," *Social Forces,* Vol. XXI (March, 1943), 272.

as a guiding concept in research should never forget that when dealing with smaller units it has an integrating function. When considering relations to the universal system of which the area is a part, regionalism has a decentralizing function.

Once we abandon the formal boundaries set by political allegiance and the needs of internal administration, we are met with the question: What is a region?

What is a region? Geographers have variously defined the region as "any portion of the earth's surface whose physical conditions are similar"; as "distinguished by the use to which it is put"; and as defined by "an *ensemble de rapports* between man and the natural milieu." Sociologists have seen the region "as comprised of a constellation of communities"; as characterized by "a homogeneity of economic and social structure"; as a culture area, "an area whose people are bound together by mutual dependencies arising from common interests"; as "an area of which the inhabitants instinctively feel themselves a part." A Hindu sociologist, Radhakamal Mukerjee, points to the region as a psychological complex: "The region," he writes, "is a common and coordinate set of stimuli, eliciting a similarity of responses, habits and feelings which are reinforced by gregariousness and which are moulded and stabilized into a characteristic mental type and pattern of living."[11]

Manifestly, many definitions of the region reinforce each other. Points of view will vary by disciplines, but it is possible to have a general definition of the region as a unit of areal and cultural differentiation. Each region must differ from neighboring regions but must approximate a mode of homogeneous characteristics if it is to possess identity. As an objective entity and as a heuristic device for research, the ideal region will always be the composite region in which economic, political, and cultural identity is evident. Since part of this will inhere in the nature of the data and part will inhere in the purpose of the investigator, we are likely to have continued controversies about the structure and functions of specific regions.

In policy and planning, both practical considerations and the knowledge of people's attitudes will often determine the size and type of regions selected. Odum and Moore have suggested that in some such way as the astronomer's region is the space that can be

[11] Radhakamal Mukerjee, *Social Ecology* (New York, 1945).

explored with existing telescopes, so an administrative region must assure reasonable maximum distance for travel, organization, study, and administration. Obviously the choice and delimitation of regions is a function of the research to be undertaken or the public policy to be administered. Obviously, also, there are regions that will remain true regions regardless of whether any research is ever done or any administrative agencies ever set up with reference to their needs and functions.

Regionalism is thus a concept of many facets. Few areas of social science research have escaped its rays. To show its dynamic aspects and to relate it to history and social change, the region must be interpreted both as structure and as function, as process and product. It is not our commission to attempt a conceptual integration of the social science field. It would seem futile, however, to explore the logic of this approach except against the broad background of social theory.

Social research has on its agenda unfinished business—the task of providing an understanding of the society and the world in which we live. This, I fear, is a never-ending business, for society is forever changing beneath our feet and around our heads. No sooner does one generation lay claim to the understanding of its economic order, its political order, or its social order than the next generation reports that it has a new order—the old order has dissolved and resolved so that a new equilibrium and a new balance prevail.

Each generation of scholars is faced accordingly with the task of commanding its social life and its economic and political processes to stand still, as it were, so that they may be dissected and their structure and their organization presented in cross section. The social scientist today has come to realize the dilemma faced by the biologist of yesterday. The biologist found that the only still specimen was a dead specimen. The cross sections of his specimens gave him the structure of the animal, the icy perfection of anatomy; but when he wanted to determine the function, the physiology, he had on his hands for analysis "a living, breathing, pulsating riot." Society is no less dynamic. Certainly it took more than the dissection of cadavers to give us a knowledge of process; and yet how would Sir William Harvey have understood the circulation of the blood or the army surgeon William Beaumont the digestive processes of his half-breed, had they not known structure?[12]

The student of social theory accordingly can do no better, it would seem to me, than continually to remind himself that society exists both as process and as product. In the ongoing trend of society, the process is one of social change, but the end product is the development of social order. The energies of men are merged and channeled in a hundred different processes to result in a hundred different products. Structure is the product of ongoing processes, but structure itself becomes process as it goes over into function.

Regionalism as a research key is not to be understood apart from considerations of process, structure, and function. Regional structure is capable of analysis both as spatial pattern and as a facet of social organization. Its boundaries are both physical and cultural, and it is fortunate for the regionalist that, as Louis Wirth has said, the physical, economic, and cultural contours of the region usually coincide. It is characterized by "homogeneity of economic and social structure," for its order and organization have come out of the processes converging within the area.

This is also true for the structure of the larger unit. The nation is a fabric of regions, and it is the functioning of these interrelated structures that gives us the national life with its phenomena of regional-national balance and integration. Odum and Moore have developed the terminology for this interrelated regional structure. The term "region" denotes a composite major area which in America is a group of states corresponding both to a historic section and to a culture area. New England and the Midwest represent this type of composite societal region in American culture. For the minor area the term "subregion" is used. "Both of these are clearly differentiated from single purpose, isolated and specialized areas such as organizational or administrative units including districts, provinces, centers, zones, and the like." For subdivisions such as administrative areas the term "district" is suggested, while "zone" is also available.[13] Finally,

12 *See* Talcott Parsons, *Essays in Sociological Theory: Pure and Applied* (Glencoe, Illinois, 1949), especially Chapters 1 and 2. Parsons also makes the point that, in analogy with biology, the structural approach is needed to insure completeness of the system—a point that fits in well with the regional-national approach.

13 Howard W. Odum and Harry Estill Moore, *American Regionalism: A Cultural-Historical Approach to National Integration* (New York, 1938), 30–32.

it should be pointed out that studies of decentralization and of concentration, of international and national federation, of regional blocs and federations, are all studies of changing structure and function.

It is the contention of this paper that the potential role of regionalism as a conceptual tool for research has not been adequately understood in social science mainly for two reasons: First, its potential contributions have not been visualized against the background of general theory—an undertaking that must precede as well as follow the unfolding of regional analysis and theory.

In the second place, we have the problem of method and the logic of regional analysis. Regional analysis involves not one but several levels of attack developed along an ascending scale of complexity. It proceeds from the application, at an initial level, of simple techniques, to the development of complex theory at the highest level of integration. The remainder of the paper will discuss these four levels of analysis involved in regionalism as follows: (1) the delimitation of one-factor regions in the case of phenomena involving one variable, (2) the delimitation of complex regions, (3) the regional monograph involving the analysis and integration of the forces and processes acting in a complex region, and (4) the analysis of interregional relations.

The choice of single-factor regions follows logically from the choice of the problem to be studied. This method is valuable when one variable is involved and the main problem is to delimit component areas and show their relation to the whole. The analysis of such a universe in terms of a fabric of regions is simply an example of the convenience of studying the parts in order to understand the whole. This, I take it, is the only problem developed by those pragmatic specialists, the sales managers, in the following title which I lift verbatim from the December, 1937, issue of *Western Advertising:* "Regionalism Can Mean More Efficient Sales Volume, If Its Principles Are Rightly Applied."

We can begin with an illustration of what we call the first level of complexity in regional analysis. As an aid to understanding folk culture, anthropologists and sociologists might well note the country's distribution of rural house types as constructed by folk carpenters untrained in architecture.[14] Division of the nation into regions on the basis of one such trait or factor is a simple technique that represents the first use of the regional concept. In the same fashion, sales areas delimited by the United States Department of Commerce give the structure of wholesale and retail markets in the United States;[15] an account of the process involved in their relations would show how wholesale and retail trade function.

The second level of integration involves the regionalization of a universe on the basis of several variables or characteristics. The delimitation of complex regions may proceed by one of two methods, each having its own logic. One may (1) attempt to reconstruct the process by which a region has been built up out of its component parts, or one may (2) use statistical measurement to delimit areas homogeneous in certain economic, social, and cultural characters. The first method has been used in economics and ecology; the second has been developed as a cultural-statistical method.

How does this technique build up the subregion from its component units? An answer has been ventured at the theoretical level in economics by August Losch, whose *Die räumliche Ordnung der Wirtschaft* is promised an early English translation. Beginning with self-sufficing farmsteads equally distributed on a level plain of equal fertility, Losch follows the process as selected farmers, benefiting from the economics of large-scale production, make and distribute a product once made by hand on each of the self-sufficing units. As the product—bread, beer, or what you wish—is marketed to neighboring farmsteads, there appears the familiar scheme of hexagonal areas, each with a radius determined by the increasing cost of transportation. Losch here found three main types of economic areas that build up into regional constructs: (1) simple market areas, (2) nets of such areas, and (3) systems of nets. Such a subregion then is a system of nets; it integrates a complex of products and is thus a functioning organization rather than simply an areal structure. Finally, since in practice no such regions are themselves self-sufficing, their exchange with other regions will be mediated through central or port cities.

[14] This has been done by Fred B. Kniffen at Louisiana State University in a series of articles.

[15] See the series of maps in Robert A. Dier, *Natural Areas of Trade in the United States* (Washington, Office of NRA, Division of Review, February, 1936).

Losch also tried to test his theoretical construct against actual situation in a fairly uniform area and selected Iowa for this analysis.[16]

In something of the same fashion, Walter Chrystaller developed his central-place theory of the growth of communities and their integration in regional organization. He applied his hypothesis to an area in South Germany and arrived at a hierarchy of subregions by communities of different size.[17] The astronomical perfection of this approach to the constellation of communities has repelled many students who feel that actual situations do not yield social geometry of such symmetrical proportions.

It was at the University of Wisconsin that Charles J. Galpin's pioneer study of Walworth County developed the concept of the "rururban" community with its constellation of farmsteads integrated around the trade and service centers.[18] Carried forward by J. H. Kolb and others, this method has not only served to delimit the farmer's community but has enabled us to understand how communities build up in cumulative fashion into subregions.

The integration of smaller regions into the structure of the large metropolitan region was largely the work of R. D. McKenzie and others. Again the process is largely economic in its ordering and function. C. A. Dawson has summarized the impact of these studies as follows:

In each physiographic region a major or gateway city emerges. The expanse of territory tributary to each city depends on transportation advantages, the resources of its hinterland and the stage reached in its development. Its life cycle of development links it in increasing intensity with a widening hinterland. If such a city has certain natural advantages in location and means of transportation it tends to become the center of a metropolitan region which extends beyond its original physiographic area. Meanwhile, the central city becomes increasingly the point of dominance about which its tributary hinterland develops its natural organization. Each of the region's subsidiary cities, towns, and village communities finds a more or less specialized place and functions competitively in the intra-regional division of labor. The most active agents in differentiating the function of subsidiary communities and integrating them with the

[16] August Losch, "The Nature of Economic Regions," *Southern Economic Journal,* Vol. V (July, 1938), 71–78.

[17] Walter Chrystaller, *Die zentralen Orte in Suedendeutschland* (Jena, 1935).

[18] Charles J. Galpin, "The Social Anatomy of an Agricultural Community," *Bulletin 34,* Agricultural Experiment Station, University of Wisconsin (Madison, May, 1915).

center of dominance are the highly specialized institutions to be found in the latter. In the main all this takes place tentatively and selectively by means of the play of natural forces.

These metropolitan regions in turn compete with each other with regard to position and function. In such a struggle between giants the destinies of a region's subsidiary cities are involved. The region here competes as a unit through its gateway cities. In this fashion the whole of North America is in the process of being organized into a constellation of metropolitan regions. In the United States, New York and Chicago have come to play the role of super-centers of domination, integrating about them in a natural organization all outlying regions.[19]

In many instances, measures of common modes of life are taken to determine the structure of the region. This corresponds to the anthropologist's interest in the cultural areas of primitive societies. The logic here is fairly clear. "The fabric of modern society is composed," as C. L. Gregory writes, "of variable traits that are correlated among themselves." The approach to cultural areas thus is in terms of the culture complex, and the homogeneity of the region as contrasted with others is one of degree rather than of kind. Gregory has said that if no cultural trait were related to any other, a region would have to be determined by a single trait and thus would have no meaning except in terms of that trait.[20]

Regions are delineated in terms of statistical indices of important cultural, economic, or social conditions. Since these figures are gathered on the basis of administrative areas, such as enumeration districts, urban census tracts, minor civil divisions, and counties, the process is one of building up small political units into homogeneous subregions. We have discussed subregions organized and dominated by cities; it is fortunate that we can now draw examples from rural regions. Here the first important analysis divided the country into areas according to major types of farming.[21]

How important indices are selected and how they serve to delimit areas has been demonstrated with a rigorous statistical technique by Margaret Jarman Hagood and associates.[22] By applying correlation

[19] C. A. Dawson, in *Essays in Society* (Toronto, 1940), 30–31, commenting on R. D. McKenzie's *Metropolitan Community* (New York, 1933).

[20] C. L. Gregory, "Advanced Techniques in the Delineation of Rural Regions," *Rural Sociology*, Vol. XIV (March, 1949), 59–63.

[21] Foster F. Elliott, *Types of Farming in the United States* (Washington, Bureau of the Census, 1933).

[22] Margaret Jarman Hagood, Nadia Danilevsky, and Corlin O. Beum, "An Examina-

analysis to 83 measures of social and economic variation among Ohio counties, C. E. Lively and R. B. Almack had reduced the number successively to 32, to 16, and finally to 3 indices to which the 16 measures were related with correlation coefficients of .60 or above. The three indices were measures of rural fertility, average gross income per farm, and an index of the rural plane of living.[23] Hagood then applied the method of principal components (factor analysis) to develop homogeneous subregions on the basis of the selected characteristics. So that the counties of the subregions would be contiguous, latitude and longitude were introduced as two additional characteristics. The first-factor loadings were computed for the final series of measures on the 88 counties from a matrix of their intercorrelations. A composite index of subregionalization was formed by weighting each series with its first-factor loading. Counties grouped by class intervals of their values on this index then fell into contiguous subregions, with the exception of some six or seven counties containing large cities.

Arthur R. Mangus has made use of the technique developed by Lively and Almack to delimit two types of rural areas and subareas for the whole country. On the basis of farm indices he divided the country into 218 agricultural subregions and 32 general regions. When indices of industry and urban centers were admitted, Mangus found 106 strictly agricultural subregions and 158 agricultural-industrial subregions, which coalesce in 34 major areas. The general boundaries of the 32 major farm regions and 34 rural regions coincide with few exceptions.[24]

In a later paper Hagood applied this method of principal components to a test of the delimitation of groups-of-states regions in the United States as developed by Howard W. Odum. The results (shown in the accompanying map) can be interpreted as follows: Index values (numbers shown in circles) representing a composite of agricultural and population characteristics were developed for the states.

---

tion of the Use of Factor Analysis in the Problem of Subregional Delineation," *Rural Sociology,* Vol. VI (September, 1941), 216–33.

[23] C. E. Lively and R. B. Almack, *A Method of Determining Rural Social Subareas with Application to Ohio,* Mimeograph *Bulletin No. 106,* Ohio Agricultural Extension Station (Columbus, January, 1938).

[24] Arthur R. Mangus, *Rural Regions of the United States* (Washington, 1940). See maps, p. 4.

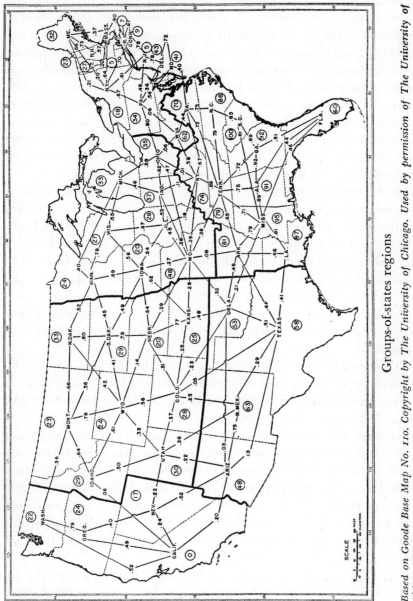

Based on Goode Base Map No. 110. Copyright by The University of Chicago. Used by permission of The University of Chicago Press.

Groups-of-states regions

Then, in order to group states into regions, a correlation analysis was made, showing the similarity of each state to its neighbors. (On the map, the coefficient of correlation between a state and each of its neighbors is shown by the small numeral in the break of the line radiating from the center of the state.) Florida is far from resembling any neighboring state on these measures; but since this plan admits of no one-state regions, Florida by necessity falls in the Southeast. Missouri offers something of a problem but shows its closest resemblance to Illinois. West Virginia is found to have its closest attachment to the Southeast on the basis of agriculture and population. If we desire to separate the Northeast into two areas, the homogeneity of the New England States is clearly demonstrated by this method.[25]

It is fortunate that the regionalist has this rigorous technique at his command if for no other reason than to demonstrate that regions are not to be determined on the basis of whim and personal predilections. This is not to say that regional analysis is all statistics, or that only measured and counted phenomena fall into the picture. In the case of West Virginia, for example, the historical fact that the area "seceded from secession" during the Civil War was given sufficient cultural importance in Howard W. Odum's analysis to outweigh certain other characteristics for which statistical indices were at hand.

To show that statistics is not everything, let us turn aside for the moment to ask a question about local history. Why is it that local history, with its infinite attention to detail, has proved so deadly dull and so lacking in general significance? Shall we say that the local historian often fails to delimit a significant area and, lacking a subregion of determinate characteristics and problems, has no principle by which to integrate his treatment or to relate his local area to other areas? Discursive and unpruned as it is, a book like Archer Butler Hulbert's *Soil: Its Influence on American History*[26] suggests how local historians, by combining several of their beloved counties into a natural subregion, might write history of distinctive value to social science.

[25] Margaret Jarman Hagood, "Statistical Methods for Delineation of Regions Applied to Data on Agriculture and Population," *Social Forces*, Vol. XXI (March, 1943), 287–97.

[26] The complete subtitle continues: *With Special Reference to Migration and the Scientific Study of Local History* (New Haven, 1930).

The next level of complexity in research involves the analysis and integration of forces and processes acting within a region. The delimitation of regions may solve certain scientific problems, but often it is to be regarded as preliminary to this portrayal of a complex region in process. To be functional and dynamic, regional analysis must transcend the limitations of the traditional survey, regional or social. In the choice of data this research task is closely related to that of the preceding level. The interplay and interaction of phenomena that create the regional *Gestalt*—the concurrence of forces—should logically find representation in the same indices that were used to delimit the area. The point at issue is simple: Whatever factors are found to fuse together to give us the regional economy, the regional culture, and the region's consensus of opinion—these, obviously, are the factors which in the beginning should be selected for use in drawing boundaries between regions. If this is regarded as close reasoning, it may be given illustration. A market analyst might be satisfied to delimit a network of trade areas in order to explain market phenomena. To delimit an economic region, however, would demand the use of multiple indices—indices representing the interplay of economic forces. Once the analyst has determined the economic forces whose integration he hopes to depict in a regional monograph—for example, the organization of physical production, of transportation, of distribution, and of finance—he has also selected the indices to be used in dividing his universe, in this case the national economy, into its component regional units.

Early geographers sought to determine and catalogue the geographic relationships and influences existing in a region. If enough could be catalogued, a satisfactory regional report could be prepared.[27] Contemporary regional analysis seeks to show the region as a totality. This point of view is well set forth in the eloquent statement of Vidal de la Blache:

A country is a reserve of energies whose origin lies in nature but whose development depends upon man. It is man who, by moulding the land to his own purposes, brings out its individuality. He establishes a connection between its separate features. He substitutes for its incoherent effects of local circumstances, a systematic concourse of forces. It is thus that a

[27] K. C. McMurry, in Stuart A. Rice (ed.), *Methods in Social Science: A Case Book* (Chicago, 1931), 234.

country defines and differentiates itself and finally becomes, as it were, a medal struck off in the effigy of a people.[28]

To present an integrated account of a region requires a dynamic rather than a static approach and necessarily cuts across the traditional frontiers drawn by our academic disciplines.

Preoccupation with regional structure and the task of defining regional boundaries on the map tends too much to the impression that the region is a fixed and static thing. This misapprehension is to be corrected in the present level of regional study. Here the task of research is dynamic; it aims at understanding the direction and redirection of a continual flow of forces. In the transition to the demographic and industrial region, inert resources, for example, become a flow of goods. With the emergence of equilibrium in flow and interflow, the regional balance of population, regional balance of trade, and regional hierarchy of resources testify that the cultural and economic region has arrived. This flow may come from the hands of nature, but it leaves the region man-made. Streams and water power, men and communities, goods and transportation, trade and the regional balance of exports, population and migration—the region maintains its economic equilibrium and its social consensus by a continual flow and reflow of goods, people, services, and ideas.

Finally, the regional approach stands in contrast to the prevailing academic tradition. It brings phenomena into juxtaposition simply because they converge in a given spatial area or *Gestalt,* and from this juxtaposition it develops the relationships that aim at depicting the "integrated social system of an area."

Regional research, it must be remembered, became the core and culmination of geographic study simply by unifying phenomena around this principle. "It is the original role of geography," wrote Lespagnol, "to put in contact the facts which other sciences study in isolation." "Western science," writes Rudolf Heberle, "has been developed by specialization along lines of problem complexes or by abstraction and isolation of certain meaningful aspects of the chaotic reality. The social sciences are no exception to this principle. The aim is always the establishment of general principles, not the comprehensive knowledge of a concrete regional society."[29]

28 Paul Vidal de la Blache, *Tableau de la géographie de la France,* 8.

29 Rudolf Heberle, "Regionalism: Some Critical Observations," *Social Forces,* Vol. XXI (March, 1943), 281–82.

Disciplines are thus logical systems by which we focus our attention upon one complex of phenomena to the exclusion of others. But new and different relationships are seen in regional analysis. As Heberle says, "A certain familiarity with details in various fields of observation which can be achieved only for a limited regional area enables one to see connections, causal and others, which may escape the less initiated specialist who is accustomed to think within the framework of his particular discipline."[30]

With these considerations in mind, it is not surprising to find that few of our major regions have received adequate analysis. If the University of Chicago holds out, we bid fair to learn more about its city than was ever known of any other metropolitan region. I am tempted to say the same thing of Howard W. Odum and the Southeast. Certainly the complex regional case study is one of the highest products of the regional method. It does not, however, complete the ambitious task of regionalism.

Finally we come to the highest level of integration—the use of regionalism as the areal-cultural frame of reference for the comparative study of society. Here it is not enough to have specialized knowledge of single regions. This fourth level of complexity, therefore, embodies the goal to which, I take it, all our disciplines aspire—the creation of valid and significant theory of society and human behavior. This is the area of interregional relations. The task of constructing a social science on which we can stand is not going to be as simple as men thought a generation ago. Regionalism will contribute to the achievement, but at the moment it promises to increase rather than lessen the complexity of the task.

The emphasis falls on interregional relations—the comparative study of problems common to many regions, regional-national balance, and the processes of interregional adjustment and equilibrium. Regionalism can be advanced to this level of complexity only on the assumption that in the field of learning there is still a place for historical and theoretical scholarship. The goal is, therefore, to contribute to the development of a universal and general science of society and human behavior. The most useful theoretical model would seem to be the idea of a structure, the elements of which are themselves similar, if smaller, structures. The assumption is that such

[30] *Ibid.*

theory may be approached by the analysis of society's component units, the relations of functioning parts and wholes.

If one theory could be made to fit all conceivable areas and situations, there would exist no need for the comparative theory that regionalism promises at this level. But, fortunately or not, regionalism in one form or another seems destined to review—if not to undermine—all those theories that speculate about some sort of abstract man, abstract culture, or abstract economy. Theories developed in one culture area or in one stage must be tested against those developed about other areas or stages. In a slightly different context, John Maynard Keynes has sharply drawn the issue for economics: "The characteristics of the special case assumed by the classical theory happen not to be those of the economic society in which we actually live with the result that its teaching is misleading and disastrous if we attempt to apply it to the facts of experience."[31]

Interregional comparisons have made necessary new beginnings, and as these new departures are integrated and interpreted, they will lead to new levels of theory. It has been the contribution of world-area studies to force us to the realization that many of our universal generalizations apply only to Western culture. The comparison of different world areas means the comparative study of economic, cultural, and legal systems. In anthropology the results of a comparative approach to the study of cultural units are clearly evident. We have on the one hand those studies in which each separate culture is presented as an integrated pattern, a totality in which the significance of each trait and complex is determined by its relations to a functional whole. On another level we find that anthropology has solved for the time being the baffling question of intercultural relationships on the basis of cultural relativity—a neutral solution in terms of mores and ethics, displeasing to some but justified if the analyst himself is to escape the charge of ethnocentrism.

For the moment we must leave to the future the task of exploring the application of this point of view to international relations. In the study of our national life, it was the task of Frederick Jackson Turner to demonstrate the historical depths of this concept. This he did by showing the accumulated experience left in our cultural tradition

---

[31] John Maynard Keynes, *The General Theory of Employment, Interest and Money* (New York, 1936), 3.

by those two great complexes, the frontier and the section. Both the frontier and the section can be characterized as an area, an economy, and a type of culture.

In his studies of interprovincial relations, Turner, as Merle Curti points out, interpreted American political history in terms of a contest between economic and social sections:

Below the surface of politics sectional groupings disclosed the lines on which new party issues were forming: rival sections made alliances, ententes, for no section could by itself determine national policy to suit its needs. . . . The existence of sub-sections within the larger sections complicated these interprovincial relations, often restrained sectional leaders and sometimes accounted for political straddling. National parties had their sectional wings, and party organization, also tended to diminish sectional antagonisms.[32]

Regional balance, as it is developed, will come out of the maturing of America's own political and economic experience with the frontier and the sections. The transition from an unsettled country marks the gradual change from the frontier process to social control. The intermediate stage in the transition is sectionalism; the ultimate stage may well be regionalism and regional-national planning. Under extreme laissez faire the frontier process carved human-use regions out of the differentiated area of newly settled territories. The frontier was a region in flux. The flow of population and the appropriation of regional resources proceeded apace in a process of extreme individualism, and the region did not appear until a degree of equilibrium was attained. In the self-contained economy of the frontier, the flow of population in a measure substituted for the flow of goods.

With the emergence of interregional trade and comparative advantage, and the coalescence of the economic interests of class groups now in possession of the region's resources of land, mineral rights, and industrial opportunities, the "sustentation region," in Giddings' phrase, becomes the section, conscious of the clash of economic interests within the nation. The section was a region smarting under economic penalties established in the national policy. The logic of sectionalism consisted in calculating the economic value of union and led more than once to overt separatist movements. Only once,

[32] Merle E. Curti, in McMurry, *Methods in Social Science*, 363.

however, has a sectional interest refused to accept peacefully its defeat at the polls.

Social control, hardly possible in the frontier flux, thus appears attainable when the flow and interchange of regional forces approaches equilibrium. Yet there is the danger that a frontier may remain a region in the raw material stage—contributing to national wealth and receiving little in return. The nationalization of business so vividly described by Ida M. Tarbell and others meant the localization of its returns in a few dominant areas. The historical acceptance of the income tax and the redistribution of these gains in the interest of national welfare marked the beginning of a shift toward regional-national balance.

What of the danger of sectional bias in the regional approach? It is customary to warn young scholars entering regional study of this danger, and it may be well to close this paper with a glance at the question. No doubt the problem has yet to be put in correct perspective, but I do not see that it differs essentially from the perennial problem of bias inherent in all social science research. To write of conflict and of war itself is not to advocate conflict. The historian of sectional conflict is not a participant; he is rather a recorder. We all live in regions as well as nations; for the scientist in the field, the problem is every whit as big as, but no bigger than, the problem of nationalistic bias in writing history. Some historians have passed the test; some have not. Can the reading public tell the difference between these attitudes, and does it respect objective history and reject chauvinism? Similarly with the analysis of class phenomena.

Then finally there is the saving honesty of the analyst who admits his value premises and yet refrains from a partisan presentation. The historian of a labor union can admit his sympathy with its aims and yet write honest, factual history. The critical faculty of the historian in treating the problem of sectionalism in his own area has been beautifully demonstrated, I feel, in Charles S. Sydnor's *Development of Southern Sectionalism, 1819–1848*.[33] Similarly a regional monograph will of necessity be organized around the problems of a region if the work is to have unity and point. The author can show, if he

[33] This is Vol. V of *The History of the South* (Baton Rouge, 1948), forthcoming in ten volumes.

likes, how much the realization of regional goals would affect other areas and other interests.

There exists one tendency to sectionalism, hardly on the level of social science, which has sometimes been allowed to flourish by default. This bias is more often shown in the treatment of the national economy, the national culture, and the arts than in analysis of the political process, where divergent interests are usually accepted for what they are—a basis of conflict. This point of view is found in the assumption that the designs, goals, and rewards of a dominant section are those of the nation itself. It is more subtle if it goes unstated; it grates harshly if the outlying provinces are explicitly called provincial. In the arts, for example, the artistic tastes or the artistic treasures peculiar to the metropolis are assumed to be those of the nation or for the good of the nation. This, of course, is precisely the point that should be argued, not assumed. The point of view is most sectional when it glosses over sectionalism or berates it.

In economics it is the bland view (so well exposed in Woodrow Wilson's *New Freedom,* 1913) which upholds monopoly under the guise of a theory of private enterprise—a theory which would stifle all private enterprise except that of monopolists. This type of sectionalism is sometimes accepted by good Americans who would recognize as sheer chauvinism its international counterpart—the assumption that the good of America is the good of all the world, whether the world wants that good or no.

It is no answer to this problem of sectional interest in sheep's clothing to state it in the familiar terms of the provinces against the metropolis. Ruralism against metropolitanism is not exactly the regional issue. We mediate our lives, our economy, and much of our cultural and artistic productivity today through cities. It is not a rural-urban issue, simply because each great region must finally develop its own regional centers and subcenters. Such regional capitals may well be artistic, literary, and cultural centers, as well as major livestock markets, cotton markets, and grain markets for the areas' economic production. An example of the danger to be avoided can be found in France. The extent to which Paris dominates the nation's artistic and intellectual life has reduced French provincial cities to cultural monotony. French travelers often remark on the economic and cultural rank of our regional cities as compared to those of France. Regional capitals need not be provincial. They should be regional, which to me means functional in relation both to the region and to the nation. The New York–Chicago axis will, I suspect, continue for some time to dominate, with occasional help from Hollywood, the financial, artistic, and cultural trends of our national life. As our great major areas pass from frontier, to sections, to regions, as they fill out their complex structure, they too will develop metropolitan centers and subcenters—centers which will realize their function and thus relieve the megalopolis of its centralizing tendency, thereby preventing "apoplexy at the center and paralysis at the extremities."

Part II

*Some Historic Regions
of the United States*

Introduction

William B. Hesseltine

Writers of American history sometimes—either for the sake of euphony or to avoid wounding supersensitive Southern feelings—refer to the Civil War as the War Between the States. Actually, of course, it was a "War Against the States"—ending in an unprecedented concentration of power in the hands of the national government and the weakening of the political power and influence of the several states. Other developments during and after the war—the rise of big business, technological improvements, and the concentration of money and credit in a few hands—contributed to a growing nationalism which drew attention away from local interests and concerns. Historians, following the trend toward political, economic, and cultural nationalism, have devoted a major part of their attention to national developments. They have seen politics from the perspective of the national government, surveyed cultural life from the offices of New York publishers, and viewed economics from the vantage point of Wall Street.

In so doing, they have ignored the infinite variations of American life. The United States is not—despite the centripetal forces of nationalism—a unified, coherent entity. It is, instead, a congeries of regions, a conglomeration of communities, a congregation of diverse districts. The nation's problems have been, in the last analysis, local problems; its policies have been largely posited upon local needs. For the most part, nationalism itself served primarily to advance the ends of controlling groups in urban districts of the Northeastern region.

In recent years, however, there has been a returning realization that American development can be understood only by a careful study of regional history. The three participants in this section of this symposium have attempted, each in his own way, to call attention to the problems of three historic regions of the United States. The differences in their approaches, their material, and their conclusions give added emphasis to the diversities of American regions and to the necessity for careful studies of regional history.

In the first paper, Francis B. Simkins makes no effort to define the Southern region, either as a historical or as a contemporary entity. He does not differentiate between upper and lower South, between mountain areas and Black Belt, or between the Cotton Kingdom and the provinces of rice, sugar, and tobacco. His concern is with attitudes: of the North toward the South, of whites toward Negroes, of liberals toward conservatives. Throughout, he argues for the right of the South to be left alone to foster its own institutions, wrestle with its own problems, and save its own soul. He protests against the twin perversions of ignorant outside critics and internal soreheads.

While Simkins deals with an area noted for its self-consciousness, John W. Caughey treats a region where local pride is sometimes intense, even belligerent, but where there is no overt consciousness of regional unity. In fact, Caughey resorts to history even for a definition of the Southwest—and finds the only common denominator of one-fourth of the nation's geography the one-time possession of the region by Spain. Yet the Spanish inheritance is, over much of the region, limited to place names and a few pseudoantique tourist attractions.

On the other hand, Lancaster Pollard traces the growth and decline of regional cohesion in the Pacific Northwest. Ingeniously defining a region as a kinship-area—a fruitful concept which might well be further explored—he suggests that the Pacific Northwest first developed a regional consciousness which was subjected to severe strains by extraregional group loyalties.

Taken together, these papers suggest that several considerations warrant further attention and analysis. First, if they have not ignored, the writers have at least chosen not to emphasize, the contest between groups within their regions. Historically, the regions of the United States have been the homes of contending groups, struggling for the control of each region's economic and cultural life. Then, implicit in these papers, is a factor of regional imperialism. In the three regions here discussed, the writers have placed emphasis upon "colonial" exploitation, complaining that their respective regions are colonies from which other regions extract wealth. But the obverse of colonialism is imperialism, and if there is colonial exploitation there must be imperial exploiters. Further study is clearly needed into the nature and methods of regional imperialism. Finally, these papers suggest that the regions here defined are too large for adequate study. In American history, regions—whether considered as areas of economic exploitation, cultural cohesion, or even of "area-kinship"— have not been static, their boundaries fixed and immutable. Regions have, instead, grown or shrunk, changing in size and importance from decade to decade. The study of smaller areas, which sociologists prefer to call subregions or districts, might be more fruitful than the study of regions considered as groups of states.

Chapter 4

The South

Francis Butler Simkins

THE European influence is the principal factor in American greatness. But this greatness could not be realized without a modification of this influence to meet the hardships and opportunities of a new land. Settlers in the North partly solved this problem by establishing themselves in American climates like those from which they came. Settlers in the South, on the other hand, were forced to face the problems of a semitropical climate. Because of this, the sufferings of the early Southerners were great. "The low and marshy ground, the hot sun, the unwholesome drinking water," says a historian of Virginia, "combined to produce an unending epidemic of dysentery and malaria."[1]

Adjustments to the climate of the South have enabled people of the North European race to live and multiply there for three hundred years. "Not elsewhere the world over," writes a geographer, "have Englishmen dwelt continuously in large numbers under semi-tropical conditions for so much as three generations."[2] Southerners did this, maintaining the English way of life to as great a degree as any group of Americans.

The Southerners' problem of modifying European habits to fit the New World was followed by another problem of like nature. It was to adopt benefits derived from the booming civilization of the northern half of the United States without abandoning progress in

[1] Thomas J. Wertenbaker, *The Planters of Colonial Virginia* (New York, 1937), 30–40.

[2] E. N. Vallandigham, "Our Men of the Midi," *Atlantic Monthly*, Vol. XCIX (June, 1907), 848.

making adjustments to the Southern environment. While winning its cultural and social independence from England, the region below the Potomac had to struggle against the tendency to become a colonial dependency of the North. Northern customs were in many respects more alluring than those of the mother country. England represented past glories; the region above the Potomac represented progress—a level of material wealth and democratic idealism greater than anywhere in Europe. The South achieved much progress through imitating the North. It learned to use Northern machines, Northern literature, art, and education, and Northern political reforms. But the pull forward of the Yankee spirit was no more successful in destroying the Southern qualities than the pull backward of the mother country in preventing Southern qualities from developing. There is, said Donald Davidson in 1938, the reality of regionalism acknowledged in the vocabulary of the people if not in the solemn documentations of statesmen.

The American devotion to centralization has not, Davidson adds, "stirred the Rockies from their base, or unchannelled the Mississippi, or removed the plains, the lakes, the climate itself."[3] The geographical diversity which these factors create divides America into a variety of sections, of which the South is the most distinct. There the winter is neither long nor very cold; in summer for fifty afternoons the temperature climbs to ninety degrees in the shade; throughout the year there is greater humidity, more sunshine, and less wind than elsewhere in the United States. At certain seasons there are torrential rains, and along the Gulf of Mexico the growing season lasts nine months.

These "imprints of sun, rain and wind" exert gross as well as subtle influences.[4] Long, hot seasons favored the creation of the kingdoms of tobacco, rice, sugar, and cotton, slowed the tempo of living and of speech, promoted outdoor life, modified architecture to make indoor living cooler, and encouraged the employment of Negroes on the land. The poorer soils, eroded and leached by heavy rains, gave white and black alike excuse for poverty and leisure.

Geography, coupled with the complications of social development, makes possible the recognition of distinctive features in Southern civilization. The doctrine of white supremacy, asserts the historian

[3] Donald Davidson, *The Attack on Leviathan* (Chapel Hill, 1938), 4, 5, 351.
[4] Rupert B. Vance, *Human Geography of the South* (Chapel Hill, 1932), 351.

Ulrich B. Phillips, is "the central theme" of Southern history.[5] In the presence of large masses of blacks, the white people developed a superior and unique attitude toward the other race. This attitude, according to Phillips, is the essence of Southernism. To white supremacy, Avery O. Craven adds another explanation—the prevalence of the country-gentleman ideal, a pattern of society borrowed from the English, justified by the physiocratic philosophy of the French, and taking root naturally in the agricultural South. The poet John Crowe Ransom regards Southernism as the creation, by the men of the Old South, of the ideal of a conservative civilization which "put the surplus energy in the free life of the mind" and which gave scope to the refinements of settled life in rural comfort.[6] By others, Southernism has been variously attributed to the fundamental piety of the people, their emphasis on home life, the peculiarities of their food, the survival of rural ways even in growing cities, a powerful nativism largely untouched within the past 175 years by immigration, and the survival of the Southern type of lady and gentleman, who are declared to be "the only types of 'complete souls' that the United States has yet produced."[7]

All observers admit that Southernism is a reality too elusive to be explained in objective terms. It is something like a song or an emotion, more easily felt than recorded. "Poets have done better in expressing the oneness of the South," remarks James G. Randall, "than historians in explaining it."[8] One of the characters in George W. Cable's *John March, Southerner* speaks of "a certain ungeographical South-within-the-South—as portable and intangible as the souls in our bodies."[9] In exile in the iron New England dark, Quinton Compson is asked, "Why do you hate the South?" "I don't hate it," replies this character in William Faulkner's *Absalom, Absalom!* "I don't hate it," he repeats. *I don't hate it,* he thinks; *I don't! I don't hate it! I don't hate it!*[10]

[5] Ulrich B. Phillips, *The Course of the South to Secession* (New York, 1939), 152.

[6] John Crowe Ransom, "The South Defends Its Heritage," *Harper's Magazine*, Vol. CLIX (June, 1929), 108–18.

[7] Count Hermann Keyserling, "The South—America's Hope," *Atlantic Monthly*, Vol. CXLIV (November, 1939), 607–608.

[8] James G. Randall, *The Civil War and Reconstruction* (Boston, 1937), 3–4.

[9] George W. Cable, *John March, Southerner* (New York, 1897), 327.

[10] Cited by Malcolm Cowley, "William Faulkner's Legend of the South," in Allen Tate (ed.), *A Southern Vanguard* (New York, 1947), 16–17.

A wealth of imaginative literature and factual scholarship have described the Old South as contrasted with the Old North. There is the difference between the land of the Cavalier and of the Puritan, of slavery and of freedom, of agriculture and of industry, of planter and of small farmer, of static contentment and of progressive aspiration. Contemporaries were so aware of the sectional differences that they spoke of two nations as distinct as the French and the English, with a Congress at Washington, not to discuss common interests, but to proclaim mutual grievances.[11]

Beginning in the eighteen-twenties, Southerners recognized the realities of sectional divergences by developing a social and political philosophy. Slavery, the region's most distinctive institution, once regarded as an embarrassing necessity, was interpreted as conferring positive benefits on all elements of Southern society. It was justified by arguments drawn from the Bible, from Aristotle, and from science. The relation between master and servant was explained as a bond made in heaven along with the bond of the human family. The pro-slavery argument was so cunningly combined with American ideals that servitude appeared the very condition of democracy. Since the Negro was made for manual labor, white skin protected the individual who was not a slave against social degradation. The ideal state was that of the slave master and his lady, who found a mirror of their lives in the chivalric society of the Middle Ages.

The North was adjudged guilty of attempting, through the tyranny of the majority, to impose unbearable hardships upon the minority section. These hardships were the protective tariff, the building of means of transportation at federal expense, the adoption of commercial strategies through which Southern wealth went into Northern pockets, the weakening of slavery through the harboring of fugitives, the keeping of slaves out of the Western territories, and agitations for the ultimate abolition of slavery. To protect themselves against these acts of aggression, the Southerners evolved the doctrine of states' rights. This took at first the form of threatened or actual nullification by the states of acts of the federal government, and the suggestion of a system of concurrent majorities through which the weaker section might veto the acts of the stronger. When these devices

[11] *Charleston Mercury*, cited in Avery O. Craven, *The Repressible Conflict* (Baton Rouge, 1939), 28.

failed, the Southerners asserted the right to withdraw from the Federal Union.

The distinctiveness of the Old South is perhaps best illustrated by its religion. Historic Protestantism was reduced to the consistencies of the Southern environment without sacrificing inherent fundamentals. Religious revivals lifted the common people out of frontier indifference to religion. The discipline of church schools held Southerners of both races in the Christian communions. The Southern mind, which at the beginning of the nineteenth century had been under the influence of liberal deists, was captured for the orthodoxies by an aggressive group of theologians. Both church- and state-controlled colleges were dedicated to the "old-time religion." These changes prepared the way for the complete reconciliation between slavery and the Southern churches, for the breaking of ties with the antislavery churches of the North, and for the use among the Negroes of the bondage of the soul as a means of making more secure the bondage of the body. On Biblical grounds, the Ethiopian was declared to be the descendant of Ham, fated to be the hewer of wood and the drawer of water. He solaced himself with the development of sacred songs proclaiming the joys of heaven as compensation for the tribulations of slavery.

Historians, in their efforts to explain the coming of the Civil War, emphasize the differences between the Old South and the Old North. They forget that conflicts can be as easily explained in terms of likenesses as of differences. Perhaps the American war between the sections was another example of Greek meeting Greek, of Anglo-Saxon quarreling with Anglo-Saxon with the same ideals and ambitions. The fight began in Kansas, where two groups of Americans used the controversy over slavery as an excuse for struggle to possess the land. Both sides, with Anglo-Saxon shrewdness, whipped out Bibles and guns to justify their desires.

The society of the Old South, like that of the Old North, was given to expansion both horizontal and perpendicular. Horizontal expansion for the Southerner meant frequent migration westward; even the slave was not a peasant tied to the soil. Perpendicular expansion meant that humble men could rise to the top. It was possible, says a historian of the Old South, for men to mount "from log cabin to plantation mansion on a stairway of cotton bales, accumulating slaves as they climbed."[12] This process was easy because of an expanding society and because of the relative absence of class lines. The dominance of all white men over the Negro created a sense of brotherhood not unlike the Greek concept of democracy. Universal white manhood suffrage was established in all Southern states. In the persons of John Randolph, William L. Yancey, and Albert G. Brown, the Dixie demagogue was almost as important as he was destined to be in the days of Ben Tillman and Theodore G. Bilbo. Education for all white children was progressively applied; to the Prussian purpose of using the school to promote skills and discipline, was added, without reluctance, the American notion of the school as an instrument for ironing out social distinctions.[13]

Abraham Lincoln was correct in assuming that no impassable barrier could be erected between the sections. The Old South did not have the will or the resources for national self-expression. It had no political, economic, or cultural capital. It was dependent upon the North for manufactured articles, cloth made from its cotton, styles for women's clothes, the books and the magazines it read, and the textbooks and many of the teachers of its schools. Bitterly did Southern writers like James D. B. De Bow complain of the high prices the North was able to charge for its goods; but the commercial and cultural conventions of the eighteen-fifties for the purpose of creating regional autonomy had scant success. The fact that a national soul did not survive the defeat of 1865 makes one wonder if such a soul ever existed.

The Old South of the differences and contrasts enumerated, was defeated at Appomattox. In its place was created a New South, in which slavery was abolished and in which industrialization and sectional reconciliation became aspirations. The South's central problem was to adjust its standards to those of the victorious North. As the result of war and reconstruction, it recognized the supremacy of the Union, free Negro labor, and the equality of all men before the law. Later the national ideals of business success and industrial advance won victories over the agrarian tradition; and the New South demonstrated in practice the New England concept of universal edu-

12 Charles S. Sydnor, *Development of Southern Sectionalism, 1819–1848* (Baton Rouge, 1948), 14.

13 Clement C. Eaton, *Freedom of Thought in the Old South* (Durham, North Carolina, 1932), 76.

cation. Imported views on religion and science were accepted by college-bred leaders; imported class alignments and recreations altered social life; in deference to the critical standards of metropolitan areas, the South created a literature that affronted its romantic pride; despite a painful sensitivity, it allowed the Negro to progress along lines consistent with Northern concepts of uplift; and with unrestrained patriotism, Southerners participated in the battles of three national wars and in the councils of three national administrations. Because of these concessions to Northern standards, there was basis for the conclusion that by 1930 the states of the former Confederacy had so far receded from the sectionalism of 1861 that they were about to become a mere segment of a unified republic.

To justify this progression out of an unhappy past, there arose a group of publicists known as the Southern Liberals. In the name of a liberal tradition said to be as inherently Southern as Thomas Jefferson, the Southern Liberals assaulted religious orthodoxy, puritanism, demagoguery, rural conservatism, and other aspects of the Southern scene. They were modern enough to advocate state action in social and economic fields quite beyond the Jeffersonian concept of an agrarian society. They advocated libraries, good roads, hospitals, school expansion, and other such material comforts as the common people in all progressive societies demand of their rulers.

The capital blunder of the leaders of the Old South was their emphasis upon slavery as an explanation of the sectional variations. This accent upon a despised institution brought upon the region the charge of blood guilt and led its enemies to compel the tragic exorcism of 1865. The leaders of the New South, once the conquerors had relented sufficiently to allow the restoration of white supremacy, did not pursue a policy which brought upon them a second civil war. They did not try to restore the old order. Under their direction the truly forgotten men of Southern history became Thomas R. Dew and the other writers who proclaimed the inequality of man as the prime justification of slavery. The Jeffersonian dream of the equality of all men became a Southern axiom. About this declaration was much unreality. Leaders of the New South such as Henry W. Grady and Charles B. Aycock pressed for the disfranchisement of the blacks and at the same time preached "glittering generalities" about progress and democracy. Nevertheless, they were not sweepingly reactionary toward the Negro. They allowed him schools, religious freedom, and the right to own property and to move away. This was because, as Gunnar Myrdal sapiently observes, the Southern white man had learned to adhere so deeply to the American creed of democracy that his conscience did not permit extreme actions against the Negro or the denial to him of hope of more equalities in the future.[14]

So much emphasis has been placed on the willingness of the South to move out of its past that a legend of greatest practical importance has been created. It is believed that the region is in a constant state of change which will ultimately result in the annihilation of the sectional differences in order that it may embrace all the benefits of the national life. "Everywhere," said two competent chroniclers of the national annals in 1932,[15] "the South gave way before the onrush of the North. . . . It would not be stretching too much to say that before the nineteenth century closed the South had become a mere appendage of New York or the Ohio Valley." This great change has been implemented by the bulldozing of much of the Southern landscape out of its original shape to make clearings for Northern-owned industries. Its reality has been accepted so thoroughly by the spokesmen of the South that a Harvard scholar is able to use their words as the basis of a book detailing the growth of sectional amity.[16]

The legend of the changing South has been, from time to time, the basis for optimistic thinkers to assume the actual or imminent solution of the problems which make the section different. It was possible for Frederick Douglass to assume as early as 1879 that conditions in the Southern States were so steadily improving "that the colored man will ultimately realize the fullest measure of liberty and equality accorded and secured in any section of our common country."[17] An eminent student of Southern history asserted in 1914 that the time had come for the section "to emancipate herself from the deadly one-party system" because the question of Negro suffrage for the indefinite future had been settled by disfranchising amendments to state

[14] Gunnar Myrdal, *An American Dilemma* (New York, 1944), I, 461–64.

[15] Louis M. Hacker and Benjamin B. Kendrick, *The United States since 1865* (New York, 1932), 64.

[16] Paul H. Buck, *The Road to Reunion, 1865–1900* (Boston, 1938).

[17] Frederick Douglass, cited in *Journal of Negro History*, Vol. IV (January, 1919), 56–57.

constitutions.[18] The legend reached its ultimate extreme in a book written in 1926 entitled *The Advancing South* and containing a chapter called "The Ebbing Tide of Color."[19] It survives today in the assertion of an Arkansas editor that the increased voting of Negroes in the Democratic primaries makes the race "a potent, positive factor in the region" and makes "the passing of the one-party system inevitable."[20]

These sanguine hopes have not been fulfilled. The South has not given the Negro the liberty and equality accorded him elsewhere; the one-party system and the Negro question have not been eliminated from politics; the color line has not ebbed. Southern culture, as Donald Davidson said in 1938, "has an enormous vitality, even in those attitudes which sociologists call survivals: its ways of humor, its 'stubborn bantering threats to outsiders,' and various 'defense mechanisms.'"[21] Numerous cultural factors, together with "a certain revivification of sectional antagonisms," declared the South's leading sociologist in 1936, have "contributed to an apparent solidifying of the regional culture."[22] There have been changes, but, as Stark Young wisely observed in 1930, the changing South is still the South.

It is well to warn against taking optimistically the pronouncements of Southern progressives. Frequently they are rare specimens protected by aristocratic family connections or by the isolation of academic or editorial sanctums from the mass sentiments around them. Gunnar Myrdal scornfully notes that the Southern liberal is afraid of "the deadly blow of being called a 'nigger lover'" and therefore likes to keep the Negro out of sight in agitations designed for the benefit of the race.[23] Liberal pronouncements on the national or sectional level of group organizations are not likely to be implemented on local levels. Myrdal contrasts the bold words and actions of the central office of the National Association for the Advancement of Colored People with the timidity of this association's chapters in

[18] James W. Garner, in *Studies in Southern History and Politics* (New York, 1914), 367–87.

[19] Edwin Mims, *The Advancing South* (New York, 1926).

[20] Harry S. Ashmore, in *The Southern Packet*, Vol. IV (November, 1948), 1.

[21] Davidson, *The Attack on Leviathan*, 302.

[22] Howard W. Odum, *Southern Regions of the United States* (Chapel Hill, 1936), 531.

[23] Myrdal, *An American Dilemma*, I, 470.

Southern towns.[24] He also notes that white ministers are not likely to burden their congregations with the liberal exhortations on the race question which they are supposed to bring back from the general assemblies of their churches.[25] When such exhortations are brought home, they are not likely to be taken seriously. Observant persons realize the indifference of the thousands who each Sunday attend the Bible classes of the South to the liberal and even radical study materials which national church organizations put into their hands. "In the sphere of religion," Richard M. Weaver observes, "the Southerner has always been hostile to the spirit of inquiry. He felt that religion which is intellectual is no religion."[26]

The facts do not justify the claim that the history of North-South relations since 1865 has been a record of steady decline in the intersectional asperities. An examination of the evidence reveals a series of ups and downs in an everlasting battle between the forces making for sectional reconciliation and those making for sectional estrangement.

The let-us-have-peace sentiments at Appomattox were followed by the hates of Reconstruction. Indeed, the bitterness created by this attempt to give Negroes some share of the American dream of equality was more lasting than that created by the antecedent bloodshed. The good will created by the surrender of the North in 1877 on the Reconstruction issue was matched by the ill will created by the Lodge Force Bill of 1890 and by the disfranchising amendments to the Southern state constitutions. The intersectional and interracial friendship created by Booker T. Washington was dimmed by the affronts of Theodore Roosevelt and the muckrakers to the Southern standards of caste.

The sense of national pride engendered in Southern hearts by the election of Woodrow Wilson and the victories of World War I was followed by an attack on the South which has been characterized as "more abusive and unrelenting than anything the Southern States have experienced since the last Federal soldier was withdrawn from their soil."[27] There were the Ku-Klux exposures, ridicule of South-

24 *Ibid.*, II, 823-24.

25 *Ibid.*, 869.

26 Richard M. Weaver, "The Older Religiousness of the South," *Sewanee Review*, Vol. LI (Spring, 1943), 248.

27 Davidson, *The Attack on Leviathan*, 315.

ern political and religious attitudes, and the uncovering of alleged abuses of justice. The good will engendered between Franklin D. Roosevelt and the South was followed by legislation which affronted the traditions of the region. The willingness of the South to bear its share of the armed crusade to impose American ideals of equality upon Japan and Germany was followed by the demand that the South apply this ideal to the Negro. There was created an atmosphere of suspicion and alarm over Northern intentions.

In 1930 a group of twelve writers known as the Southern Agrarians supplemented a justification of the right of the South to maintain its historic identity with the belief that the South they esteemed was nearer the reality than the progressive South praised by the liberals. The twelve understand that national standardization has not annihilated the fundamental differences of their section. They know that even though the modern Southerner joins the Westerner and Northerner in adopting a common type of automobile, house, and clothes, he has not necessarily surrendered his distinctions of thought and emotions; that reading the same book and attending the same school do not necessarily eliminate provincial thinking. They understand that the conversion of many educated Southerners to the logic of liberalism does not imply a willingness to put aside inherited habits and to live according to the new logic. They know, for example, that few of the many who talk against race prejudice are willing to suffer the penalties of violating customary racial barriers; that few who believe that the cause of liberalism can be promoted by having two political parties are willing to incur the displeasure of their conservative neighbors by joining a political party other than the Democratic.

Examination of many of the phases of the institutional life of the New South reveals a constantly recurring condition: despite the changes which the catastrophe of 1865 made inevitable, the distinctive culture of the section was never destroyed. In politics, to cite the most obvious example, the South responded to the suggestion that the Negro be given the equalities mentioned in the Declaration of Independence by reducing the race to political impotence. The opening, since 1937, of the Democratic primaries to the Negroes by the federal courts effected a change more technical than actual. While there was a considerable increase in colored voters, the new majority of Southern States these leaders decreed that Southern voters merely won the privilege of ratifying procedures already determined by white majorities. An unchanging caste system generally prevented the Negro from becoming a candidate for office or from advocating policies contrary to the will of the whites. The sum total of his political gains to date are favors from municipal authorities, one member of the Kentucky legislature, one member of the Richmond City Council, and one member of the North Carolina Board of Education.

A lasting break in the political unity of the white race is the fond hope of the friends of Negro uplift. Thereby would it be possible for the minority race to hold the balance of power between white factions. Such a break has not come. It was threatened in 1928, when five states of the so-called Solid South voted against the Democratic candidate for President. When in the election of 1932 the name of the objectionable candidate was removed from the ballot, the Southern States voted unanimously for Democratic candidates and repudiated the leaders of the 1928 bolt. Again in 1948 was there a threat to political unity when the Southern people disapproved the desire of the Democratic presidential candidate to extend certain civil rights to Negroes. The people left to the leaders of the state machines the determination of the method to meet this emergency. In the interests could better be served by supporting the nominee of the traditional party; the voters fell in line. In four states the machine leaders felt that local interests could better be served by supporting an independent candidate; the voters fell in line. Thus in no Southern state was white solidarity sufficiently broken to make the Negro vote important.

Although concessions were made to the liberal spirit in regard to the Negro, the South remained adamant in the matter of greatest importance. The bonds of caste, by which the Negro was kept subordinate and underprivileged, were weakened in few respects. In the middle of the twentieth century it was still possible for the demagogue to win office by campaigning against Negro rights; for whites to take jobs away from blacks when members of the superior caste desired them; for business opportunities and employment in the newer industries to be white monopolies; and for Negroes for all practical purposes to be excluded from the professions of politics,

law, and engineering. The average white still had three tones to
his voice: a normal tone for whites; a "mammy voice" for Negroes
with whom he was familiar, and a haughty tone for strange Negroes.
The progress of the blacks in health and education was brought
about by the intervention of benevolent whites, not through the
efforts of the blacks themselves. The major equality which the blacks
possess is the right to migrate, to move from job to job, from country
to town, from South to North.

Since the Civil War, there has been a steady decline in what the
ante-bellum traveler Frederick Law Olmsted called "the close co-
habitation and association of black and white." Immediately after
the war the two races separated in churches, and for the cultural give
and take of the plantation was substituted a dual school system which
sealed off the children of one race from the other. Gradually it became impossible for a white person to teach in a Negro school without losing caste. No longer did the two races have what William
Faulkner calls "the same parties: the identical music from identical
instruments, crude fiddles and guitars, now in the big house with
candles and silk dresses and champagne, now in the dirt-floored cabins
with smoking pine knots and calico and water sweetened with mo-
lasses."[28] The whites have been able to implement a growing aversion
to intimate contact with the blacks through the use of labor-saving
devices and through the spread of progressive notions concerning
the dignity of labor. Despite Supreme Court decisions, immutable
social custom makes for increased residential segregation, especially
in the newer sections of the cities. In many places the blacks live so
far away from white settlements that the whites find it impractical
to hire them as servants. In fewer numbers are blacks sitting in the
balconies of white theaters or patronizing white physicians and den-
tists. It is now almost possible for a middle-class person to live many
years in a Southern city without contacts with blacks.

One of the most persistent beliefs about the South is that the
Negro is in a constant state of revolt against the social pattern of
the section. Despite a vast literature to the contrary, the facts of
history refute this assumption. As a slave the black man never attempted general insurrection and did not run away often. "The
slaves," says a historian of the Confederacy, "supported the war

---

[28] William Faulkner, *Absalom, Absalom!* (New York, 1936), 98.

unanimously (albeit somewhat involuntarily)."[29] It is now proved that outside compulsions rather than inner ambitions prompted the political insubordinations of Reconstruction. Their artificial character is proved by the fact that they were not accompanied by social insubordinations and by the fact that they disappeared as soon as the outside compulsions were removed. Indicative of the willingness of the rank and file of the blacks to accept the *status quo* are the words of a conservative demagogue who knew the Negro well. If the election of governor of South Carolina were left "entirely to the Negro vote," declared Cole L. Blease in 1913, "I would receive without trouble 75 to 90 per cent."[30] In communities in Virginia, North Carolina, and Tennessee where the blacks have made wide use of the suffrage, there have been social and economic gains for the race but no assault on white supremacy. This fact is one of the main arguments advanced by Southern Liberals in favor of giving the blacks the suffrage. Of late, the prospective Negro voters have abandoned the comparatively independent Republican party in order to join a party completely dominated by their white neighbors. They vote, not for Henry Wallace and others who practice race equality, but for those who at best render only lip service to this principle.

That the Negroes are not in revolt against the white pattern of civilization is illustrated by their conduct in a field of action in which they possess perfect freedom. This is religion. They voluntarily imitate the whites in this. They join the whites in maintaining the orthodoxies and in creating a black counterpart to almost every one of the white denominations. If the masses of the whites are Baptists or premillennialists, so are the masses of the blacks; if the upper-class whites are Episcopalians or Presbyterians, so are the upper-class blacks. If the Catholics, Unitarians, and Congregationalists make little headway among the whites, the same is true among the blacks. If skepticism and atheism make little appeal to Southern whites, the same is true of the Southern blacks. Among them there is no relapse into paganism, either African or of other types. The lessons taught from the Bible by the slave masters are still the Negro faith.

Southerners cherish to the highest degree a great American

29 Robert S. Cotterill, *The Old South* (Glendale, 1936), 317.

30 *Message of Governor Cole L. Blease . . . January, 1913* (Columbia, South Carolina, 1913), 13.

superstition: that the school is a social panacea. If the unsuspecting stranger studies the plans of the section's schools, he may conclude that the purpose of these institutions is not only to make Southern youths into Northerners but also to make them into communists of the variety Plato describes in *The Republic*. Textbooks written in the North give an anti-Southern bias to instruction in history, literature, and speech, and the school seemingly is attempting to usurp many of the functions of child nurture traditionally belonging to the home.

But among Southerners there is the education which does not educate. This result is caused partly by the temperament of a people inclined to be leisurely and even Philistine. It is caused also by the survival of overwhelming traditions. Northern bias in textbooks is offset by less formal and perhaps more effective indoctrination in local ideals which survive the regimentation of the schools. Many Northern teachers in Southern schools feel obligated, not always reluctantly, to acquire the regional bias. The home, not the school, determines the cultural outlook of Southerners. It is remarkable how seldom the problems raised in the classroom are discussed in the market place or around the dinner table; how perfect is the freedom of speech enjoyed by the teacher because few bother to repeat the teacher's opinions; and how unused is the public to listen to the collective opinions of teachers or students; and how even lessons in a subject so "scientific" as cooking have difficulty in changing the home diet. How little the college affects its surroundings is revealed by the fact that the voluntary reading habits of the college community are nearly the same as those of the nonacademic community. Proof of this comes from the comparison of the books and magazines sold in corner drugstores.

The South accepts Northern dictation in literary matters more completely than in other fields. A book, even one about the South and by a Southerner, wins little attention from Southerners unless published in New York. In order to win the approval of New York, the Southern author sometimes feels obligated to use a critical realism or romantic irony which involves a repudiation of the Southern past. Many among educated Southerners commit a major crime against intelligence; instead of letting their opinions of state or section grow out of their own observations, they accept the opinions of New

York journalists as paraphrased for them by their local newspapers.

There is danger, however, of overemphasizing literary materials in measuring the outlook of a people as nonliterary as those of the South. Most Southern readers ignore the realistic writings, nourishing themselves on the self-flattery of historical romance. Many among the minority who read the new realism do not connect it with life, regarding it as a vicarious escape into a sentimental world which they do not actually wish to enter. Moreover, the new school of Southern writers belongs to the South to a greater degree than earlier critics realized. This was expressed in the sensational success of *Gone With the Wind,* an obvious glorification of the Old South. It is now realized that behind the stinking vulgarity of Erskine Caldwell lies a lusty and even humorous appreciation of the Southern poor white; that behind the seemingly unreasoning violence of William Faulkner lies a legend of the South as patriotic as it is pessimistic; that James Branch Cabell, despite his irreverence, is able to move among medieval legends with a sense of continuity with aristocratic Virginia; and that Ellen Glasgow, despite her bleak landscape and progressive hopes, has compassion for her unprogressive Virginians.

Forces work against the apparent progress from rural stagnation to urbanization. Southerners who move from country to city and factory do not surrender their rural ideals. In the South the country conquers the city as effectively as elsewhere the city conquers the country. The larger Southern cities grow, the less do they become cities in the cultural sense; unlike the cities of Europe and the North, they do not emphasize such urban arts as the theater, the drama, and music; nor do they have good cooking in public places. This is because a larger and larger proportion of their inhabitants possess rural backgrounds and are naturally most interested in country pleasures. The wealthy of the new Southern cities spend their surpluses on farms, country estates, horses, hogs, hunting, and city houses in country style.

The march toward America's ideal of democracy is stayed that the splendid legend of the Old South might be preserved. "Perpetually suspended in the great haze of memory, it hung, as it were, poised, somewhere between earth and sky, colossal, shining, and incomparably lovely."[31] The attitude of the old agrarian aristocracy

[31] Wilbur J. Cash, *The Mind of the South* (New York, 1942), 124.

continued to be a part of the Southern tradition, not only in the thirty-five years after 1865 but also into the twentieth century. Everyone who claimed to be a planter was metamorphosed into a Marse Chan or a Squire Effingham. "The Southerner feels," wrote William Van Conner in 1948, "that the ante-bellum world possessed values and a way-of-life in which the needs of the whole human being could be more readily satisfied than they could be in our industrialized society."[32]

Ancestor-hunting became an important activity. "Even today from Virginia to Texas," wrote William A. Percy in 1941, "ten thousand crepuscular old maids and widows in ghostly coveys and clusters are solving such insoluble problems."[33] Many persons tie themselves to baronial planters and some—if we accept the word of James Branch Cabell and Stark Young—trace descent from the Ten Lost Tribes of Israel. Such an attitude tends to create an atrophying pessimism; an incomplete and frustrated region, as William Faulkner puts it, a region vainly trying to recover its identity, vainly trying to relive its legendary past. This attitude also possesses constructive social functions. A consciousness of illustrious forebears gives satisfactions not unlike those of religion to old people without material assets. It gives justification to the ambitions or attainments of self-made men, freeing them of inferiority complexes and getting them into the best society. It gives rise to the cult of antique furniture, the reproduction of which is the most appreciated thing of beauty the twentieth-century South produces.

The changing South of the legend works both ways. Changes in the direction of national uniformity are accompanied by changes in the opposite direction. Important among the latter is the disappearance of the fear of the hot climate inherited from European ancestors. This is because of the invention of artificial ice and refrigeration and because of the elimination of such climatic evils as malaria, yellow fever, and hookworm. The habiliments of the ancestors have been replaced by looser and lighter garments. The Victorian modesty of the maiden has been replaced by a nakedness almost as complete as that of a pagan goddess. The South has learned to regard the sun as a beneficent god instead of a cruel tyrant. Its

---

32 In Tate, *A Southern Vanguard*, 94.
33 William A. Percy, *Lanterns on the Levee* (New York, 1941), 38.

curative properties are now regarded as a protection for rural Southerners against lack of sanitary devices.[34] Sun baths are indulged in for two reasons: because of health and because of an aesthetic revolution which holds that a brown skin is more beautiful than a fair one. The acme of Southern comeliness is blue eyes, blond hair, and bronze skin.

Many of the regional characteristics herewith listed are survivals out of a dark past and are persistently condemned by outsiders. If they are defended by Southerners, it is with fundamental qualifications. The South of the twentieth century has no intention of declaring "a positive good" those aspects of its behavior which affront the national majority. It, however, finds it not only possible but practically wise to defend as "positively good" certain of its peculiar ambitions and tendencies. There are certain developments which, unlike those behind the proslavery argument of the Old South, do not run counter to the liberal sentiments of the outside world. The South, long accused of tyranny against others, can, with a show of reason, accuse others of tyranny against it.

"Positively good" is the demand that the section be allowed to adjust its artistic expressions to the climate and temperament of its people. Because of the tyranny of books and magazines imported from strange climates, Southerners are prompted to construct artificial lakes, treeless lawns, and low-roofed houses without porches or blinds. These lakes are often mosquito-infested and slimy or muddy; the lawns are often bare and unkempt; and the houses are often uncomfortably hot for six months of the year. Southern suburbs often possess the chaotic appearance of a parade of circus cages. The newer public monuments sometimes stress the sensational and the realistic. Comfort and inherited taste demand a return to the tangled garden, to shade-giving trees, to the porches and high-roofed halls of antebellum homes, and to public monuments in which the classical ideals of the section are respected. Southerners have as much right to their peculiar tastes as do other peoples.

One of the prices the South pays for its progressive industrialization is increasing servitude to Northern capital. New York has grown into the most autocratic city-state of modern times, with the Southern province of the United States as one of its important colonies. The

[34] Vance, *Human Geography of the South*, 361.

great financial houses of that and kindred cities control most of the region's strategic industries, having sent out a second and third generation of carpetbaggers to found factories or to purchase those already existing. The Southern industries owned and controlled by outsiders include the region's railroads, its coal fields, its iron reserves, its electric power, and its gas and oil resources. The existence of Northern patent monopolies and the absence of local machine manufacturing permit outside direction even of industries locally owned. Manufacturing is confined mainly to the elementary processes. The South fabricates its own cast-iron pipes, steel rails, bridges, and oils; but not its hardware, locomotives, automobiles, clocks, radios, dynamos, drugs, and many other finished products requiring the highest skill to produce and bringing in the highest profits.

Retail profits are siphoned out of the section by Northern-owned chain stores. Only a few of the "specialty" articles made excessively profitable through national advertising are controlled by Southerners. The Southern businessman is a mere factor or agent of Northern principals, who control both production and distribution. His function is to sell the gasoline, automobiles, mechanical refrigerators, alcoholic beverages, clothing, insurance policies, and a hundred other articles endeared to the Southern public through advertising. Some of these articles are as worthless as the wooden nutmegs the Yankee peddler is said to have imposed upon the public in ante-bellum days. The burden of these purchases on a relatively poor people is injurious. In 1937 an economist estimated that the South was paying out a billion dollars annually in excess of its income.[35] It balanced its credit by selling property to investors from other sections of the country, by borrowing, by going bankrupt, and by destroying forests and lands to secure immediate incomes.

Apparently there is no effective remedy for this situation. The federal government, through its policies of protective tariffs, constitutional immunities to corporations, railroad rate discriminations, and patent monopolies, customarily favors the older manufacturing centers of the country. The possibility of the South's revolting against its debtor status, in the manner of the Revolutionary planters against their British creditors, is ruled out by the outcome of the Civil War. That Southern leaders are able to reconcile the sons and grandsons

[35] Daniel C. Coyle, in *The Virginia Quarterly Review*, Vol. XIII (Spring, 1937), 192.

of those who followed Robert E. Lee and William Jennings Bryan to the economic domination of the North caused an eminent historian to cry out bitterly in 1942: "We are confronted with a paradox more amazing and ironical than any ever conjured by the imagination of Gilbert and Sullivan. The people of the South, who all their lives have suffered deprivations, want and humiliation from outside finance imperialism, followed with hardly a murmur of protest leaders who, if indirectly, were nonetheless agents and attorneys of the imperialists."[36]

However, there are protests which excite the moral sympathies of those liberals the world over who condemn colonial exploitation. William Faulkner may be creating in his hideous character Popeye a compendium of the rape and corruption which alien finance capitalism visits upon this novelist's section. Academicians like Walter P. Webb of Texas and Howard W. Odum of North Carolina furnished the facts concerning the South's plight; President Franklin D. Roosevelt's National Emergency Council and Governor Ellis G. Arnall of Georgia have broadcast these facts.

Some economists regard the Roosevelt-Truman policy of heavy expenditures by the federal government a means of lessening the annual excess of expenditures over receipts which an uncontrolled system of capitalistic enterprise imposes upon the South. It is believed that the levying of huge federal income taxes according to ability to pay, and the expenditure of these revenues according to the degree of human need, mean a shift of resources from the wealthier North to the poorer South. The federal expenditures of the period of World War II and its aftermath created an unparalleled prosperity which has resulted in a greater proportional increase in Southern incomes and has allowed Southerners to retire a considerable portion of their debts. Southern ports like Hampton Roads and New Orleans impinge upon the commercial monopoly of New York City. The partial victory of Arnall against freight-rate discriminations may presage a reversal of long-established federal policies of favoritism to patrons of Northern carriers. The Tennessee Valley development is a magnificent gesture by the federal government toward redressing the grievances of the South against the rapacity of the financiers who

[36] Benjamin B. Kendrick, in *Journal of Southern History*, Vol. VII (February, 1942), 49.

captured the section's electric power. The success of this experiment may lead to its duplication in other areas as an additional means of redressing the balance against the Southern and other regional economies.

Under the direction of Southern entrepreneurs one great Southern industry has annexed the whole United States as its province. This is tobacco under the direction of the Dukes and the Reynoldses. Other comparable successes are Coca-Cola and patent medicines. The South's most mature industry, cotton textiles, has learned to make fabrics of the finest quality, and under the trade names of Cannon, Dan River's, and Avondale is capturing profitable national markets. These may be followed by triumphs in other fields; for Southern labor is growing more skilled and Southern business more cunning. The workingman is astir with the obvious intention of exacting the highest possible wages from employers, be they local or Northern. The Southern farmer is giving up his traditional conservatism to form trade agreements and crop-reduction compacts to exact the highest prices from Northern consumers.

Perhaps the greatest threat to the integrity of the regional life is that the South will succumb to bribes offered by the wealthier section of the country. There is precedent for such behavior. Robert E. Lee's refusal to accept a sinecure from a Northern business concern did not prevent other former Confederate generals from doing so. The Reconstruction period was scarcely over before these men and other leaders of Southern opinion took action which had the earmarks of scalawagism. Northern business leaders invaded every Southern state, offering the gospel of prosperity. They invited the local leaders to what one historian has picturesquely called the Great Barbecue. These leaders, with a few exceptions, took their places at the table in order to participate in the profits of the new business. They became the agents or hired attorneys of the invading capitalists. The Great Barbecue continues to the present, with the table growing longer and longer to make room for a greater variety of Southern leaders. The hospitality grows so generous that a recent Georgia writer believes that both sides in the struggle for the control of state affairs receive financial support from the capitalists.[37]

[37] Calvin Kytle, "A Long, Dark Night for Georgia?" *Harper's Magazine,* Vol. CXCVII (November, 1948), 57–58.

Southern educators receive subsidies from the capitalistic philanthropies of the North for the purpose of carrying on research which, at least by implication, discredits the traditional race and social distinctions of the South. Inherited concepts of states' rights are set aside in order that Southern politicians, businessmen, farmers, and commoners may share in the ever increasing federal bounties. Donald Davidson thinks that under the reforming zeal of federal social planners the Tennessee Valley may become a region of forests, pastures, and lakes in which the once busy grower of tobacco or cotton will be "a tipped purveyor and a professional friend to tippling fishermen."[38]

That the South is willing to sacrifice moral and even religious scruples for the proverbial mess of pottage is illustrated by the repeal of prohibition. A five-decade battle against Demon Rum culminated in every Southern state's giving its consent to the Eighteenth Amendment. Some who felt that they knew the region well believed that prohibition had become the Eleventh Commandment, a fruition of the Southern combination of puritanism and reticence. The unexpected happened. All the Southern States except Mississippi and Oklahoma repealed prohibition. A New York dominated national administration wanted the revival of the liquor industry as a means of escaping the Great Depression of 1929. Revenue-hungry Southern politicians saw in the revived liquor traffic a rich source of income. The South Carolina legislature, half-repentant over its violation of a righteous heritage, re-enacted prohibition on condition that substitute revenues be found for the inevitable losses. No substitutes were found, and South Carolina continued wet.

"I wish," said a Georgia professor recently, "that Miss Millie would come back to life and drive the rascals out with her broomstick." He was referring to Mildred D. Rutherford, a publicist who defended the South by sharp attacks on Northerners, and to the imported critics of Southern ways in Southern universities who have created a feeling of inferiority among Southern youths. These critics make comparisons between the region's creature comforts and those of the rest of the nation: the comparative scarcity in the South of house paint, plumbing, hospital beds, individual wealth, balanced diets, neat lawns and barns, magazine and newspaper readers, new

[38] Donald Davidson, *The Tennessee* (New York, 1948), II, 305.

automobiles, and the thousand and one conveniences and tricks which are more plentiful in the North. The critics have established the legend of a gully-washed land inhabited by a lazy and contented people.

The South has listened to these criticisms and derived much benefit from them. It does not wish to experience again the privations of the eighteen-sixties, when an attempted revolution cut its communications with the more progressive section of the United States. At the same time, thoughtful Southerners feel that there is room for intelligent criticisms of the complaints of outsiders. Perhaps many current adverse comments on the South are mere repetitions of British travelers' condemnation, a hundred years ago, of Kentucky for being shabbier and poorer than neat and very rich Ohio. Such criticism is as unintelligent as condemning a citizen of a town as a wastrel because he is not so rich as his richest neighbor. That the South today is not so richly endowed with wealth and creature comforts as the rest of the richest country on earth does not prove that the region below the Potomac is poor and unprogressive. This region, indeed, is fabulously rich compared with the neighboring countries of Central and South America, richer than any large area of the world outside the United States.

It is time to be philosophical about the comparative backwardness of the South. History and geography explain it in part. An additional explanation is that the people of the section, in the interest of worldly ease or Christian ideals, prefer contentment to chasing after material values which do not lead to paradise. "In taking on work," says a discerning student of the sectional differences, "the new South has not forgotten everything else."[39] The Southerner's conception of wisdom is not gratified by spending his idle moments keeping his house and garden perfectly neat, as many Northerners do; his sense of values calls for recreations, even dissipations, at the expense of physical perfections. The self-respecting Southerner, unlike the self-respecting Northerner, is not absorbed by the need of saving for old age. If the worst comes, the Southerner can achieve social security at the expense of usually willing relatives.

Recent American history is characterized by renewed challenges

[39] Norman Foerster, in *North Carolina Historical Review*, Vol. XXIII (April, 1946), 224.

to the principle of regional self-determination. Northern political parties, vying for leadership in what Americans call democracy, are again demanding the blotting out of many of the South's racial distinctions. The South is able to strike back with a good chance of being able to maintain its traditional position. It feels that the Constitution of the United States is on its side in matters of intimate concern. It believes that America is not ready to become a consolidated democracy at the expense of the federal republic. It believes that it possesses the right to deal with the blacks within the limits of the national conscience; that its liberal apologists and critics are correct in asserting that it is making progress in ironing out race discriminations; and that its violations of democratic concepts in respect to the blacks are in reality no worse than what takes place in the North. The good Southerner is constantly discovering cases of ill treatment of Negroes in such places as Detroit, St. Louis, and Chicago.

The pressures in favor of national standardization have been great and the surrenders numerous. One social critic finds in the South "a sheer love of the up-to-date," a conscious going "after a streamlined industrialization that is elsewhere not so expressly planned," and "a triumphant 'progressive' education which progresses even faster than in the North and which has been rushing school systems off into a life of sin as fast as they are born."[40] Nevertheless, the South is proud of the fact that for sixty years it has been able to couple an unsuspected loyalty to the nation with customs and folkways which vary most from the national monotony pictured by Sinclair Lewis. The region below the Potomac retains its own manners, its own speech, its own temperament, and the multitude of subtle peculiarities by reason of which the uniformity of the section with the nation turns out to be more a myth than a reality. The Southern people, says a distinguished historian and critic after a ten years' absence from North Carolina, "impress one at once with their different voices, different accent, their sense of manners, the courtesy which appears in all classes, their organic folksiness (as if of one family), their awareness of the past as a force both hampering and helping."[41]

[40] Robert B. Heilman, in Tate, *A Southern Vanguard*, 127.
[41] Foerster, in *North Carolina Historical Review*, Vol. XXIII (April, 1946), 222.

BIBLIOGRAPHIC NOTE

Definitions of the South on historical principles are: Ulrich B. Phillips, *The Course of the South to Secession* (New York, 1939); Avery O. Craven, *The Repressible Conflict* (Baton Rouge, 1939); William E. Dodd, "The Emergence of the First Social Order in America," *American Historical Review*, Vol. XL (January, 1933), 217–31; William G. Brown, *The Lower South in American History* (New York, 1902); and John Crowe Ransom, "The South Defends Its Heritage," *Harper's Magazine,* Vol. CLIX (June, 1929), 108–18.

The whole gamut of regional differences is run in Francis B. Simkins, *The South Old and New: A History, 1820–1947* (New York, 1948). Other attempts at histories of the South from a regional or a national viewpoint are William B. Hesseltine, *The South in American History* (New York, 1942); Benjamin B. Kendrick and Alex M. Arnett, *The South Looks at Its Past* (Chapel Hill, 1935); and Julian A. C. Chandler and others (eds.), *The South in the Building of the Nation* (13 vols., Richmond, 1909–13). Four volumes of Wendell H. Stephenson and E. Merton Coulter (eds.), *A History of the South* have been issued by Louisiana State University Press out of a projected ten. The interaction between the culture and the society of the region is brilliantly set forth in Wilbur J. Cash, *The Mind of the South* (New York, 1942); Vernon L. Parrington, *The Romantic Revolution in America, 1800–1860* (New York, 1927); Shields McIlwaine, *The Southern Poor-White* (Norman, 1939); and Edgar T. Thompson, "The Natural History of Agriculture in the South," in David K. Jackson (ed.), *American Studies* (Durham, 1940).

The distinctive history of the Old South is described with resounding emphasis in Robert S. Cotterill, *The Old South* (Glendale, 1936); Ulrich B. Phillips, *American Negro Slavery* (New York, 1918), and *Life and Labor in the Old South* (Boston, 1929); William E. Dodd, *The Cotton Kingdom* (New Haven, 1919); and James G. Randall, *The Civil War and Reconstruction* (Boston, 1937). Phases of ante-bellum life are treated in Clement Eaton, *Freedom of Thought in the Old South* (Durham, 1940); William S. Jenkins, *Pro-Slavery Thought of the Old South* (Chapel Hill, 1933); Francis P. Gaines, *The Southern Plantation* (New York, 1923); E. Merton Coulter, *College Life in the Old South* (New York, 1925); Richard M. Weaver, "The Older Religiousness of the South," *Sewanee Review,* Vol. LI (Spring, 1944), 244–50; John D. Wade, *Augustus Baldwin Longstreet* (New York, 1924); and William P. Trent, *William Gilmore Simms* (Boston, 1892). The exaggeration of the cultural differences of the Old South is corrected by Charles S. Sydnor, *The Development of Southern Sectionalism, 1819–1849* (Baton Rouge, 1948); and Fletcher M. Green, "Democracy in the Old South," *Journal of Southern History,* Vol. XII (February, 1946), 2–23.

For a comprehensive history of the New South, one must await the appearance of C. Vann Woodward's and Rupert B. Vance's volumes in Stephenson and Coulter (eds.), *A History of the South*. Brief but intelligent treatments are Walter L. Fleming, *The Sequel of Appomattox* (New

Haven, 1919); and Holland Thompson, *The New South* (New Haven, 1919). Paul S. Buck, *The Road to Reunion, 1865–1900* (Boston, 1937) sustains the thesis of the progressive nationalist. Biographies which grapple with the problems of the section are C. Vann Woodward, *Tom Watson, Agrarian Rebel* (New York, 1938); Francis B. Simkins, *Pitchfork Ben Tillman: South Carolinian* (Baton Rouge, 1944); Raymond B. Nixon, *Henry W. Grady* (New York, 1943); and Daniel M. Robison, *Bob Taylor* (Chapel Hill, 1935).

Recent definitions of the Southern province are: Count Hermann Keyserling, "The South—America's Hope," *Atlantic Monthly,* Vol. CXIV (November, 1929), 605–608; Norman Foerster, "Iowa, North Carolina and the Humanities," *North Carolina Historical Review,* Vol. XIII (April, 1946), 222–27; Jonathan Daniels, *A Southerner Discovers the South* (New York, 1938); and the essays by Malcolm Cowley, Robert B. Heilman, and Herbert M. McLuhan in Allen Tate (ed.), *A Southern Vanguard* (New York, 1947).

Books of personal experiences testify profusely to the regional differences. They are: Sir George Campbell, *White and Black* (New York, 1879); Albert B. Hart, *The Southern South* (New York, 1910); Ludwig Lewisohn, *Up Stream* (New York, 1923); Marietta M. Andrews, *Memoirs of a Poor Relation* (New York, 1927); Julian R. Meade, *I Live in Virginia* (New York, 1935); John A. Rice, *I Came Out of the Eighteenth Century* (New York, 1942); William A. Percy, *Lanterns on the Levee* (New York, 1941); and Katherine D. Lumpkin, *The Making of a Southerner* (New York, 1947).

The best way to know the South intimately aside from living there is to read the social novels. Its whole history comes to us in the imaginative reconstructions of Ellen Glasgow and William Faulkner, especially in the former's *Romance of a Plain Man* (New York, 1909), *Barren Ground* (New York, 1925), and *Vein of Iron* (New York, 1935); and in the latter's *Absalom, Absalom!* (New York, 1936), *Sartoris* (New York, 1929), and *The Unvanquished* (New York, 1938). Intimate segments of the regional life are also derived from Thomas S. Stribling, *Birthright* (New York, 1922), *Bright Metal* (New York, 1928), and *The Store* (New York, 1932); Marjorie K. Rawlings, *The Yearling* (New York, 1938); Margaret Mitchell, *Gone With the Wind* (New York, 1936); Corra Harris, *The Circuit Rider's Wife* (New York, 1910); Ben S. Robertson, *The Red Hills of Carolina* (New York, 1942); and others too numerous to mention.

The classic description of the regional differences is Rupert B. Vance, *Human Geography of the South* (Chapel Hill, 1932). This work is supplemented by Howard W. Odum, *Southern Regions of the United States* (Chapel Hill, 1936), and *The Way of the South* (New York, 1947); and Rupert B. Vance, *All These People: The Nation's Human Resources in the South* (Chapel Hill, 1945). The region is analyzed with unparalleled comprehensiveness from the viewpoint of its major problem in Gunnar Myrdal, *An American Dilemma* (2 vols., New York, 1944). Bold refutations of the many publicists who have condemned or minimized the regional differences are Twelve Southerners, *I'll Take My Stand* (New York, 1930); and Donald Davidson, *Attack on Leviathan* (Chapel Hill, 1938).

Chapter 5

The Spanish Southwest
An Example of Subconscious Regionalism

John W. Caughey

THERE are regions in the United States–New England, the South, and the Great Plains, for example–which have fixed and obvious boundaries and therefore exactness of meaning. But the term Southwest, with or without the adjective Spanish, is by contrast a variable which has meant almost all things to all men. Prudence therefore suggests that anyone proposing to talk about this region should begin by searching for a definition.

The political approach is not of much help, since there is no Southwestern unit intermediate between the states and the nation, nor has there been such a unit since the brief appearance of the Comandancia General de las Provincias Internas of the seventeen-seventies and eighties. And, although there is a Southwest to and for which Nature does certain things differently than for other parts of the United States, its geographical boundaries are blurred rather than sharp and ordinary maps do not make it clear.

Another possible approach is through appeal to authority. In recent years the term Southwest has been bandied about by a multitude of persons who should know. Charles F. Lummis, Lansing Bloom, Erna Fergusson, and company have given vigorous endorsement to the principle that the Southwest is New Mexico–centered. The Texas State Historical Association issues a journal called the *Southwestern Historical Quarterly,* but is content to have it pure Texas. J. Frank Dobie, in his course and syllabus on the life and letters of the Southwest, starts with Texas, but is willing to expand as far as the trail herds went. In the "Southwestern Historical Series," Ralph P. Bieber, LeRoy Hafen, and Arthur H. Clark took a stance in Missouri and looked south and west, chiefly down the Santa Fe Trail into New Mexico, but incidentally at Colorado, Arkansas, Texas, northern Mexico, and California. The editors of *Look,* in their series of picture books on American regions, marked off a Southwest beginning in Texas and stopping in Arizona. The Rockefeller Foundation, the host "once removed" of this conference, has compromised on a dual answer to the question. It has chartered a research program at the Huntington Library on a transmontane, trans-Rocky Southwest, and another at the University of Oklahoma on a Southwest bounded by the thirty-seventh parallel and the Gulf, the Mississippi and the Continental Divide.

By implication, at least, W. P. Webb in *Divided We Stand* and E. G. Mezerik in *The Revolt of the South and the West* point to a much larger Southwest. They discuss a common plight and a unity of interest for the historic South and the western half of the nation. They come, therefore, virtually to the conclusion that the Southwest is that part of the United States—about three-fourths—which is not the favored Northeast.

Still another approach, to which I as a historian turn by instinct, is to look for definition by history.

The first fact encountered is that the southern half of the United States, along with much more land south of the border, came into history through the visits of early sixteenth-century explorers, men such as Ponce de León, Ayllón, De Vaca, De Soto, Coronado, and Cabrillo. Likewise, it was the Spaniards, a century or two later, who first occupied much of this territory.

In the late eighteenth century, when the United States emerged as a nation, these lightly garrisoned Spanish provinces were its neighbors both on the south and on the west. Furthermore, thanks to the reforms of the enlightened Charles III, these were provinces of a revitalized Spanish Empire, an empire less fabulous than it had been a quarter-millennium earlier in the golden age of the conquistadores, but now reaching its greatest territorial extent. In 1789, in fact, when Washington was inaugurated President, the United States was confronted by the reality of a Spanish Southwest that began at the Georgia-Florida frontier, swept through the Creek Indian country to the Tennessee, thence to the Ohio and the Mississippi, and wound up north of Nootka on the Pacific. Spanish title and control thus spread over most of what we now call the South and over the entire trans-Mississippi West, an area that closely approximates the Webb-Mezerik South and West.

As soon as there was a United States and even before, the Americans and their governments betrayed an irresistible impulse to encroach upon these sparsely settled borderlands. Emboldened by the distresses of Europe and heartened by the vigor of American growth, diplomats challenged Spanish rights in the Old Southwest and, in the Treaty of San Lorenzo in 1795, picked up clear title as far as the thirty-first parallel and the Mississippi. In its pattern of Spanish retreat and American advance, this treaty set a motif that was to be repeated with variations all across the continent—in West and East Florida; in Louisiana, where Napoleon arranged a brief interregnum; in Oregon, contested also by Russia and Britain; in Texas, the Mexican Cession, and the Gadsden Purchase.

The expansion into the territory of Spain (and her legatee, Mexico) was relentless and rapid. Mid-nineteenth century saw it accomplished, the final steps taken in the brash certitude of Manifest Destiny. The territorial enlargement of the United States, mostly by taking over lands that once were Spanish, is a fact of great significance. The corollary may be even more important: that for the United States there has always been a Spanish Southwest.

Throughout the vast area once held or claimed by Spain, more or less of a Spanish heritage is discernible today. It may be in place names, in vocabulary, in the choice of sites for settlements, in law or customs, in agricultural methods, or in actual population. Over much of the area the reminders of Spain have worn thin. They are most in evidence in the states adjacent to the Mexican boundary from Texas to California.

Out of this apparent jumble of geographic, political, didactic, and historical fact, a Southwest emerges, which, as I see it, stretches from central Oklahoma and Texas to southern California. Much of Colorado, Utah, Nevada, and northern California belong, so that it embraces the lower left-hand quarter of the parallelogram that is the United States. Geometrically, at least, this is an incontrovertible Southwest. In other respects as well it constitutes a genuine region. A number of the traits most characteristic of it penetrate farther afield; many, for example, are shared with the states and territories of northern Mexico. But there remain other traits, some of them Spanish in derivation, which are the core of Southwestern regionalism.

As a setting for analysis of these regional characteristics, a rapid review of Southwestern history seems in order.

In the beginning, of course, throughout the hemisphere were the Indians, their civilization wonderfully diverse, remarkably provincial. Ethnology, however, discerns a regionalization in culture areas, each characterized by pervading similarities and by contrasts to the traits and patterns of other areas. Of the dozen or fifteen such areas in pre-Columbian America, two account for most of the territory here labeled Southwest: the California–Great Basin area reaching from central and northern California to the Great Salt Lake, and the Pueblo-Southwestern, its center with the Pueblo Indians, but raying out to Utah, Colorado, Texas, Chihuahua and Sonora, Baja and southern California. The pre-Columbian civilization of this south-western quarter of the present United States thus was distinguishable from that to the north and the east. In the Pueblo center, incidentally, it had the highest population density of the entire United States. Presumably if Indian culture was to exert any influence on post-Columbian America, some carry-over of its regionalism would be entailed.

The first intrusion of Europeans into this region came three-quarters of a century before Jamestown and a century and a quarter before the earliest entry in the history of Wisconsin. Álvar Núñez Cabeza de Vaca showed the way. Cast ashore on the Texas coast after a thwarted attempt at settlement in Florida, he was servant, almost slave, to the Indians, rose to be a trader and a medicine man, and finally traipsed across the continent and got back to civilization (in the form of a band of Indian-hunting Spaniards) on the west coast of Mexico. His tales of the north led to a probing by Friar Marcos and Estevanico and to more extensive *entradas* by Cabrillo, Alarcón, and Coronado, while De Soto and Moscoso, working out of Florida, advanced to the eastern margin of the area. With these first recording agents, the history of the Southwest begins. The reports taken back to Mexico, however, could not compete with the actual riches of the Aztec and Inca lands, and consequently occupation was deferred until considerably later.

When Spanish occupation did occur—after 1598 in New Mexico,

1687 in Pimería Alta, 1697 in Baja California, 1718 in Texas, and 1769 in Alta California—the age of the conquistadores had given place to empire-building of quite a different sort. Imperial authority had made itself paramount. Advance into a new province was determined, not by a rugged-individualist, gold-hungry *adelantado,* but by a calculating government. This later advance, in every instance, was more for the sake of erecting defenses for Mexico and the Caribbean than because of the intrinsic attractions of the new lands. The settlements began as frontier garrisons; they were staffed by government employees, particularly soldiers and missionaries. The most fundamental procedure was the effort to Christianize and civilize the Indians into useful citizens of the Spanish Empire, but beyond that, imperial policy did not call for building up much more than a token occupation of these northern borderlands.

At their maturity they had approximately these contours: in religion, orthodox Roman Catholic, though with some admixture of Indian belief and practice; in government, loyal to and dependent upon the orders and appointees of the king; in economy, practicing simple Spanish agriculture supplemented by whatever could be carried over from Indian methods; and in society, achieving a blend of Spanish and Indian customs. Nowhere in the course of the American westward movement did there develop settlements so unified in religion, so subordinate to imperial or national authority, or so committed to the principle of the preservation and incorporation of the Indians.

Except for the brief experiment of the Comandancia, these colonies were individually run by military, civil, and religious officers directed by the viceroy at Mexico City. Up to the end of the Spanish epoch (in 1821) they were only incidentally brushed by foreign contacts—a St. Denis (French, 1715) in Texas, the Mallet brothers (French, 1739) in New Mexico, a horse-trading Philip Nolan (1785) in Texas, an otter-hunting William Shaler (1804) in California, a courtly Rezanov (Russian, 1805) in California, and an inquisitive Zebulon Montgomery Pike (1806) in New Mexico. By the end of the Spanish epoch there were third-generation Spaniards in California, fourth- and fifth-generation Spaniards in Texas, and ninth- or tenth-generation Spaniards in New Mexico.

The onset of the Mexican period cut off effective control from the old viceregal capital, but of course a strong momentum of Spanish custom carried on. The abandonment of the old restrictive system and the breakdown of the supply lines from Mexico opened doors to foreign trade. Russians and English had some success in California, but it was chiefly American enterprisers who seized the opportunity: Boston droghers in California, and Missouri merchants on the trail to Santa Fe. Commercial annexation of California and New Mexico to the United States was achieved by these men. They were soon joined by the leather-shirted mountain men who poured across the unmarked boundary in quest of beaver pelts, and by thousands of pioneer settlers moving into Texas and a much smaller number venturing all the way to California.

In 1836 the Texas Americans raised a lone-star flag and defied Mexican rule. A decade later a handful of California Americans made similar use of a one-star flag, though in theirs the star was eclipsed by a bear. Meanwhile in 1844 the voters of the United States had given James K. Polk what he interpreted to be a mandate for expansion. The lame-duck Congress and President acted on the annexation of Texas, diplomatic pressure yielded clear title in the Pacific Northwest, and the Mexican War permitted Polk to square out the nation with the seizure and retention of New Mexico and California and their intermediate environs. The advance to the Pacific encompassed the new Zion of the Mormons and brought them back into the jurisdiction of the United States, which in these few years had increased its territorial holdings by more than 60 per cent.

The American century began with many problems of adjustment to the new regime. Texas and California had a few thousand and New Mexico a larger number of residents of Spanish persuasion who, at least in the two latter provinces, were covered by treaty guaranties. The Anglo-Americans already on hand and those who came in '49 and the fifties, notwithstanding the democratic and tolerant qualities that F. J. Turner imputes to the frontier, too often took a hostile and discriminatory attitude toward these older residents.

Out of what probably would have been a process of gradual change and development, the Southwest was shaken by the discovery of gold in California in 1848. A rush ensued that quickened interest in the entire Southwest. Soon the Westerners were clamoring for a mint, for immediate settlement of Mexican land titles, for prompt

Indian control, for a transcontinental wagon road, and for a railroad to the Pacific. Within the next few years these things and much more were accomplished. Mining of gold and also silver spread to Nevada and Colorado, in lesser degree to Arizona and New Mexico, and up the Rockies to Alaska. Mining boomed California cattle raising, prompted a great development of wheat farming, created a market for Pacific Coast lumber, gave excuse for the forced runs of the clipper ships, justified improvement of the steamer service by Panama, led to transcontinental stage lines and the Pony Express, and was an argument for federal support of Pacific railroads.

In Texas and Indian Territory, meanwhile, southern plainsmen began to farm the prairies, while in Utah the Mormons resorted to irrigation to make a garden in the desert. Without benefit of theocratic leadership, California made important additions to its irrigated lands, and New Mexico continued to utilize the dams and ditches inherited from its Indian and Spanish epochs. From Texas the range cattle industry spread west as well as north. Throughout the Southwest, too, the buffalo hunter was busy, and the United States Army was fighting Indians and trying, at first without much success, to point the moral of reservation life.

By 1890, when the frontier is supposed to have made its disappearance, the Southwest was "filled" with perhaps two million inhabitants. The last Indian war had been fought, the open-range phase of the cattle industry was over, the railroad builders had practically completed their mission, San Francisco felt itself an old metropolis, and Los Angeles was clearing its head after the orgy of its first great real estate boom. By this date admission to statehood was a completed process in the Northwest as well as throughout the East; yet, in the Southwest, of the eventual eight states only four were functioning. In the studied judgment of their peers, Oklahoma had too many Indians, New Mexico too many Spaniards, Utah too many Saints, and Arizona not enough of any sort of people to be entrusted with statehood.

Came the twentieth century and, in time, statehood, the automobile, the truck and tractor, the refrigerator car, the airplane, and the radio. Factors such as these facilitated development of an agriculture in several parts of the Southwest specializing in perishables for rapid delivery to eastern markets. Several of them cut down the time lag, if not always the cost, of maintaining contact with the rest of the world. Joined with the warmth and sunshine of the region, they encouraged the habit of looking to the Southwest as a sanatorium. With dude ranches, Indian tours, parades, fairs, expositions, excursions, rodeos, frontier days, national parks and monuments, desert spas, and Hollywood, they have greatly enlarged the tourist crop.

The twentieth century has seen the Southwest far outstrip the rest of the nation as an oil producer. This has been the period of gargantuan dam building, huge and intricate projects for carrying water to parched lands and thirsty cities, and equally stupendous projects for hydroelectric generation and transmission. In such matters, as well as in harbor improvement, highway construction, and bridge building, twentieth-century engineers have put their mark on the Southwest.

Stimulated by the experiences of two world wars, the Southwest has redoubled its efforts to develop industry. In motion-picture making, airplane manufacture, and Indian curios it has gained great success. In shipbuilding it earned temporary acclaim. In the making of such things as furniture, garments, and tires, it has done at least moderately well. During the forties two great steel plants rose at Geneva and Fontana, California. The uncertainties that attend their future illustrate the complications that absentee ownership, branch plants, patents and licenses, freight rates, interest rates, and federal interference cast athwart the aspirations of the Southwest for an industrial development of its own. But, whatever the control, industrial expansion has gone forward.

The new agriculture, the new industry, the expanded service trades, catering to tourists as well as residents—these are the elements largely responsible for the rapid population growth of the Southwest in the decades since 1890. The current estimates run to approximately twenty-five million.

In this Southwest it is possible to identify a number of distinguishing characteristics. The people, for example, at least if taken en masse, are distinguishable from those of any other quarter of the United States. First, by reason of history and propinquity, it is the part of the United States preferred by those of Spanish extraction or background. In number of Mexicans, Los Angeles is second only to

Mexico City. Arizona and Texas have large contingents, and New Mexico has so many whose language is Spanish that its legislature is still bilingual.

Second, the Southwest has at least four-fifths of the Indians surviving in the United States. In part this is due to the system of Indian removal which shunted Southeastern Indians into what is now Oklahoma. In part it is traceable to the large and flourishing Indian groups of pre-Columbian times. Spain's well-intentioned program of preserving the Indians may have helped in New Mexico and California. More important, doubtless, was the fact that American settlement of parts of the Southwest, particularly in New Mexico and Arizona, was delayed until the United States Indian Office was functioning with effectiveness for the protection of the Indians.

Of Orientals, likewise, the Southwest has the most. In still other respects, the region has a cosmopolitan population.

Probably more significance attaches to the fact that for more than a century a regional characteristic has been large volume of in-migration. Some have come in response to superficial attractions, such as the dry warmth and the stars of Hollywood. Others have surrendered to the blandishments of our chambers of commerce and our realtors. A substantial number came because of the vaunted pleasures and comforts of Southwestern life. Still others saw job opportunity or business opportunity and came aswarming. Literally, therefore, the people of the Southwest have not yet had very much time to get acquainted with each other or to figure out, in all instances, how best to make use of the region.

The Southwest is something of a paradox of oldness and newness. It has a large number of first Americans and some towns that date back far beyond Columbus. Two of its states, California and New Mexico, got their names sooner than any others of the forty-eight except Florida. The colonization of the Southwest began a long time ago; yet the major impact of American development of the region has been felt only recently, chiefly indeed in the twentieth century. In these circumstances it is not surprising that the Southwest showed high receptivity to technological improvements: in the seventies and eighties to the railroad, the six-shooter, the Winchester, and the windmill, and more recently to the automobile, the airplane, the aqueduct, the high-tension line, and the junior college.

For a long time it has been customary to speak of the colonialism of the Southwest. With payrolls of its frontier agents the Spanish Empire was willing to subsidize its colonies in this area. When the United States took over, it did some subsidizing through its Indian program and its grants for transportation improvement. The Southwest made relatively modest response in the form of direct taxes paid to the federal treasury, but it poured out a wealth of raw products—gold, silver, buffalo hides, beef, wheat, wool, etc.—which added greatly to the national wealth. The part of the public domain located in the Southwest was also an asset to the nation, and particularly to the national government.

In our day, new sorts of federal contribution have been devised: aid in education, road building, and harbor improvement; expenditures for the national parks; federal planning and leadership in water and power development; and federal outlay for research. Statistically, however, these additions are far more than counterbalanced by the exploits in the Southwest of the Collector of Internal Revenue. Meanwhile the Southwest has greatly stepped up its raw-products output, especially in oil, oranges, cotton, fruits and vegetables, fish, and copper. With the continuing export of wheat, beef, and wool, this smacks of economic colonialism, notwithstanding the concurrent flowering of a certain amount of manufacturing.

Economic colonialism, in the sense of exploitation of the region's resources for the benefit of interests nearer the seat of government, certainly is still a fact. The Webb-Mezerik analysis, though spread on a broader canvas, applies to the Southwest. It points to discrimination through the tariff system, patents and patent-leasing, interest rates, freight rates, pricing, absentee ownership, and absentee management. The facts appear to be as stated. That there is a measure of well-being in the Southwest in spite of this exploitation is variously attributed to the obtuseness of its people; to the vast resources of the region, especially in fertile soil, minerals, and oil; and to the ingenuity with which production has been widened and built up.

When I first came to the Southwest, I was most impressed by its vastness and openness, not to say emptiness. "This is the country," the saying ran, "where you can see farther and see less. . . ." There are spots in the Mojave Desert and Nevada and the Navajo country where the adage still holds, but for much of the Southwest its truth has deteriorated on both counts. There are more people, buildings, and enterprises to see, and through industrial fumes the visibility is impaired. But the Southwest is still big, and it is still remote. Not so isolated as once perhaps, no longer the "Too Far West," but still handicapped by the cost in time and money of its regional logistics. Much has been done to shrink distances. The Southwest would like to see still more accomplished.

The major fact about the Southwest undoubtedly is that it is subhumid. Limited water supply, more than any other one factor, sets the ceiling on agricultural development, on industrial capacity, and on the population that can be supported. As concerns the water problem, one may generalize that the easy things came first and have been done (the Pueblo ditches from the Rio Grande, the artesian wells in the Pecos Valley, the initial diversion of Colorado River water into the Imperial Valley); the hard things took a little longer but also have been done (the Owens Valley Aqueduct, the Salt River project, the Moffat Tunnel waterway, and San Francisco's Hetch Hetchy); the impossible tasks were postponed, but several have been tackled and some have been finished (Boulder Dam, the Los Angeles Metropolitan Aqueduct, and the Central Valley project). Ahead lie mostly still more impossible projects, such as piping the Mississippi to Los Angeles, squeezing the salt out of the ocean, or making rain.

Water is the Southwest's biggest problem. Except on a partial and localized basis, no other region can make that claim.

In the United States of our time, so many forces are nationwide in their impact that regionalism cannot be a matter of absolute differences. All parts of the country listen to the same commentators and advertisers, read the same columns and news dispatches, see the same films and comics. All have participated in the last several wars and elections. All have a share in federal policy-making and in the national debt. Our society, furthermore, is fluid and we are highly foot-loose individuals. Rolling about by automobile, bus, train, and plane, we see to it that no section has a chance to gather much moss of provincialism.

In the light of these circumstances, the measurable distinctiveness of the Southwest in its population, its high incidence of technological advance, its economic colonialism, its specialized pursuits, its handi-

caps of size and remoteness, and its critical shortage of water constitutes it beyond cavil as a region.

Peculiarly, the inhabitants of this area seem to be relatively in-
nocent of regionalism. Whereas millions proclaim "I am a Texan," or
"I am a Californian," almost no one boasts "I am a Southwesterner."
Why, I do not know. Perhaps because the phrase is too much of a
mouthful. Perhaps because the Southwest is not and never has been
a political unit, an officer-electing unit, a taxing unit. Perhaps because it has had several local literatures instead of one that was as
integrated as New England's. Perhaps because no single newspaper
has ever spread its tentacles through the region as has "The World's
Greatest Newspaper" in the Midwest. Perhaps because the Southwest
has never been embattled as was the South.

I submit that greater consciousness of regionalism would help the
Southwest. It might help in combating the ogres of exploitation from
the Northeast, as has been suggested. More certainly it would help
in meeting the region's internal problems. A united front in preserving the natural beauty of the Southwest, in readying it as a
vacation land, and in welcoming tourists would be good business
and better hospitality. The habit of outdoor living, to which the
climate of much of the region invites, suggests the utility of a regional
approach to domestic and public architecture and to apparel design.
Conservation of timber, of which the region is short, of arable soil,
and of minerals, which are not inexhaustible, is frequently of moment
to much more than the immediate locality or even the state. The
water problem in particular will almost have to be faced as one for
the region instead of as an assortment of little problems susceptible
of local solution or neglect.

Whether the utility of the regional approach will eventually
create an effective Southwestern regionalism is another matter. The
loyalties to the several states are already deeply ingrained. Some have
as much as four hundred years of history back of them. Yet the state
lines throughout the Southwest are, every one of them, artificial. And
the hyperloyalty of a synthetic Californian, recently arrived from
the Midwest, may indicate that, with proper conditioning, an equivalent devotion to the Southwest could be engendered in the course
of much less than four centuries. The regional publishing now
occurring at Norman, Dallas, Albuquerque, Stanford, and Berkeley,

and the regional studies in progress at Oklahoma and the Huntington Library connote a scholarly recognition of the reality of the Southwest as a region. It may be that a grass-roots recognition will follow.

BIBLIOGRAPHIC NOTE

The nearest approach to a bibliography on the Southwest as a region is J. Frank Dobie, *Guide to Life and Literature of the Southwest* (Dallas, 1943). An imposing array of works is cited, and the comments are warm and pungent, but there is comparative neglect of the westerly part of the region and of the twentieth century. A generation ago Charles F. Lummis acted as self-appointed spokesman for the Spanish Southwest. His vehicles were the editorial columns of *The Land of Sunshine* and *Out West,* and his books, such as *The Land of Poco Tiempo* (New York, 1893) and *Flowers of Our Lost Romance* (Boston, 1929). Erna Fergusson, *Our Southwest* (New York, 1940) analyzes New Mexico and its environs. Green Peyton, *America's Heartland: The Southwest* (Norman, 1948), though not always convincing in its interpretations, scans the area from the Gulf to the Rockies.

General description is available piecemeal in the state Guides assembled by the Writers' Project of the Works Progress Administration and in the more impressionistic volumes in the "American Folkways" series: Stanley Vestal, *Short Grass Country* (New York, 1941); Donald Day, *Big Country* (New York, 1947); Haniel Long, *Piñon Country* (New York, 1941); Edwin Corle, *Desert Country* (New York, 1941); and Carey McWilliams, *Southern California Country* (New York, 1946).

Southwestern history is likewise embodied chiefly in works that have time limitation—for example, Herbert E. Bolton, *The Spanish Borderlands* (New Haven, 1921) and A. B. Thomas (ed. and tr.), *Teodoro de Croix and the Northern Frontier of New Spain, 1776–1783* (Norman, 1941); and in books on the individual states—for example, Rupert N. Richardson, *Texas, the Lone Star State* (New York, 1943); E. E. Dale and M. L. Wardell, *History of Oklahoma* (New York, 1948); Harvey Fergusson, *Rio Grande* (New York, 1933); John Walton Caughey, *California* (New York, 1940); and Robert Glass Cleland, *From Wilderness to Empire* (New York, 1944), and *California in Our Time* (New York, 1947). A dozen or more volumes of Hubert Howe Bancroft, *Works* (39 vols., San Francisco, 1882–91) are Southwestern history. A useful work with stress on the frontier stages is Rupert N. Richardson and Carl Coke Rister, *The Greater Southwest* (Glendale, 1934).

Most of the states in this region support journals of local history. There are also literary journals, such as the *Southwest Review* (Dallas) and the *New Mexico Quarterly* (Albuquerque), which shed periodic light on the culture of the region. Sources and monographs by the thousands are also pertinent, and some expressly deal with regional problems—for example, Walter P. Webb, *The Great Plains* (Boston, 1931) and *Divided We Stand* (New York, 1937; 2nd ed., Austin, 1944); and A. G. Mezerik, *The Revolt of the South and the West* (New York, 1946).

Chapter 6

The Pacific Northwest

Lancaster Pollard

Iɴ sᴏᴍᴇ respects the history of the Pacific Northwest dis-
closes most distinctly those qualities typical of all United States
regions.[1] Here the pattern of structure and change is relatively clear.

The Pacific Northwest is pulled together by a river, or watershed,
system. Although divided into east and west by mountain masses,
it is geographically similar throughout its north and south reaches;
and the eastern and western sections have the river system in common.
This geography has continuously exerted an effective regionalizing
influence. Furthermore, that influence has been strong during those
periods when the impulse of unifying cultural forces was limited.

During the period of the first major, and in many ways decisive,
growth—from 1843 to 1885—the Pacific Northwest was relatively
isolated. Consequently, the culture that developed there was largely
local and more "characteristic" than would seem likely in a community composed of people from many regions and several nations. The
settlers came from the Middle West; from the Old South and New
England, either directly or by way of Illinois, Iowa, and Missouri;
from Canada, the British Isles, Germany, and the Scandinavian
countries. Yet they were blended into a surprisingly homogeneous
group. This is especially noticeable in Oregon, as compared to Washington, where population increased slowly until 1885.

Those conditions of geography and settlement in isolation helped
to establish a regional culture during the years when technology was
weakening or altering regional characteristics elsewhere.

Since this paper approaches the region as a historical development, it may be well to emphasize that "history happened fast" in

[1] Superior numbers refer to notes and bibliographical references at the end of this
chapter.

the Pacific Northwest. Changes that stretched over centuries in New England or the Old South occurred in decades here. Nevertheless, the pattern of growth, except for the time element, followed an outline in many respects typical of other regions of the United States. The rapidity, the "concentration," of development accentuated not only the novel but also the common, and thereby facilitates their examination.

The intent of this paper is to trace Pacific Northwest history, to try to discover its dominant phases, and to analyze them as regional factors. Sometimes what appears as positive statement is only tentative. Much research and writing must yet to be done to prove or condition it. With that proviso this essay is offered.[2]

If history is change, the agent of that change is communication in all its conditions and methods. A region is an area of relevant, accordant change, an area of synthesis. A region's borders are the effective limits of communication. Geographically, politically, economically, and aesthetically, those limits are varied. They are usually blurred and overlapping. But the borders of a region are the boundaries of agreement. That "agreement" involves many factors, such as similarity of economic opportunities through geographic resources or local tastes and demands, and the feeling of "area-kinship" that comes from familiar association and sharing common problems.

Before the industrial revolution and the accompanying revolution in land use, in transportation, and in communication, the original surface conditions of the earth were strongly determining and regionalizing factors in the life of man. Of that long period it may be said that rivers created regions. Rivers were routes of communication; river valleys were fairly self-contained economic areas, and were centers of cultural ferment.

The earliest settlements in the Pacific Northwest were fur-trading posts, and they were always on rivers, near or at their mouths on the coast and, wherever possible, at the confluence of two streams in the interior. In this region, however, the trading posts in only a few instances became our modern cities. They were located where the fur trade demanded, for the efficiency of that almost purely frontier industry. Most of them were abandoned as, decades after their establishment, cities grew up, sometimes near them, but usually on sites nearer convenient landings for farm produce, or at falls for industrial power.

The valleys of the Willamette River and its small tributary streams in Oregon were the first of those areas of continuous expanding settlement. In the valley of the Willamette the retired servants of the Hudson's Bay Company took up farming. For Americans it was the end of the Oregon Trail. The settlers who came by ship, after landing at Fort Vancouver—on the north bank of the Columbia above the mouth of the Cowlitz and across from the mouth of the Willamette—made their way up the valley to build a new society among people of their own kind.

Certainly it is significant that almost all the present cities of major importance in the region are river cities and were founded before 1880. They were situated on the Columbia or its lower tributaries and on Puget Sound, and, with the exception of Vancouver, were started in the late eighteen-forties or early fifties.

Rivers were basic in the next decade, after the Yakima Indian War had ended and the interior was again opened to settlement. Walla Walla, Washington, not on but near the river, and where land and river routes met, became a supply center for the Idaho-Montana mines. The mining town of Boise, Idaho, was on the same river as Fort Boise of the fur-trade and Oregon Trail periods, and about thirty miles from the post.

In the eighteen-seventies another handful of cities were established: Spokane, Washington, at the falls on the river of that name, but in anticipation of the coming of the transcontinental railroads; Pendleton, Oregon, growing from a trading station on the Umatilla River close to the confluence of joining streams; and Missoula, Montana, located a few years earlier but developing into a town after 1870, situated on Clark Fork a few miles above the junction of that stream and the Bitterroot River.

This pattern might seem to overemphasize the importance of rivers in centering settlement and in creating regions until the early growth of the Old South and New England is recalled. In the settlement that made them and made them regions, rivers held a comparable place and influence. There is a lag in time, but the Pacific Northwest was a region in relative geographic isolation a hundred years after such isolation had ended on the Atlantic seaboard.

There are, of course, limitations to this concept that rivers made regions, and that mountains made sections.

The Mississippi River valley should on this basis be a region. It isn't. During the early period of settlement there the area was too big to be effectively unified by the existing communication facilities. Southerners and Northerners took their intellectual habits with them and could not, even had they wished to do so, have carried on a frequent and full communication of ideas. Again, the economies of the upper and lower river rested upon differing technologies, at tracted differing groups, and encouraged differing societies. Small base was provided for a river-valley region. Later and more rapid settlement was accompanied by two other conditions: the people themselves were in a flux of movement, and they expressed growing political antagonisms that yielded to neither space nor time.

The Great Plains, also, in part contradict this "river concept"; however, they were not effectually occupied until after the railroads and the telegraph—streams of steel and copper—had penetrated their formerly harsh wastes and provided adequate communication facil ities. Also, the comparable economy and way of life made easier the spread of the feeling of likeness.

So far, attention has been given principally to geographic forces in Pacific Northwest history. Two elements no less important than geography have been disregarded. One is this: ways of making a living are kinds of isolation and in themselves are limitations of communication. The other is this: ways of thinking are also kinds of isolation and also constitute limitations of communication. They are in themselves areas of kinship.

Both enter as much or more—today much more—than geographic factors into the creation of a region. Geographic determinism is not the explanation of regions. It overlooks people and the fact that different groups have adapted themselves in different ways to the same or a similar environment. It disregards cultural climates and technologies that have changed, and are today decisively changing, geographic environments and some of the characteristics of geographic regions. In brief, geographic regionalism is not historical; it assumes a static society or one molded by physiographic conditions entirely.

In American history ways of thinking are, chronologically, cer-

tainly of primary importance. It is obvious that the differences between the Dutch, French, Swedish, and English settlers, and the
natives of the Old South or New England, are almost wholly differences of mores and knowledge. The variation in tools, in imple-
ments for exploiting the resources of the land, was minor when
compared to the contrast in attitudes toward nature and man. The
differences between the Old South and New England, and between
those regions and others later settled, stem perhaps as much from the
beliefs and social attitudes of the people as from the land and its
yield.

Those viewpoints were in their essentials relatively constant during the early decades of the westward movement, and were certainly
so during the settlement of the Atlantic seaboard. New Englanders
did not change their ways of thinking when they crossed the Appalachians or the Mississippi, nor did the people from the Old South
or the Middle States. The opening of new economic and social opportunities did not alter fundamental attitudes toward man's place
in the universe or his relationships with his fellows.

Cultural change was slow. Technologies and the accepted systems
of belief were fairly constant. Difficulties of transportation that
stopped far movements resulted in people carrying with them the
ideas and habits of "home," no matter where they settled. Adjustments were made to geography, it is true; but few settlements were
made in a radically dissimilar geographic area until after advances
were made in technology, or until after old and long-accepted beliefs were challenged.

Settlement of the Pacific Northwest started late. If the fur trade
be taken as the beginning, it was 1811, the year before Louisiana
became a state; if the coming of the first Americans of permanent
residence, it was 1834, two and three years respectively before
Arkansas and Michigan entered the Union, two and four years before
Wisconsin and Iowa territories were created. Settlement was rapid
after the "great migration" of 1843. And it was a settlement in such
isolation that ways of thinking and behaving were strongly influenced
by the local cultural environment.

Two groups of people settled and principally gave the Pacific
Northwest its cultural pattern.[3] Both groups carried with them the
inherited viewpoints of the regions from which they came. But,

brought together here, where they must perforce live together, they came to have a new point of view. Sometimes the change was subtle, sometimes obvious, but it resulted in a composite way of thinking and, through that, a region.

Southerners usually came over the Oregon Trail. Some were Southerners one generation removed, who arrived by way of Missouri, Illinois, and Iowa, and some came directly from the Old South. They scattered throughout the region, although often tending to locate, as more relatives and neighbors came, in transplanted communities. Studies illustrate this community move as, for example, from one county in Kentucky to one county in Washington. The settlers were usually farmers, but more than a proportionate share were politicians. During the period before the War Between the States, farmers were moving westward, seeking cheap land through pre-emption claims; after the depression of 1837, many jumped the two thousand miles to the free and fertile land of Oregon. During the same period, the Democrats were in control of the federal government; Democratic appointments and patronage in Oregon encouraged the Southern politicians to look to that fruitful field.

Of the many who might be chosen to represent the politicians, perhaps Joseph Lane is typical though outstanding. Born in Buncombe County, North Carolina, he moved to Indiana and became active in politics there. A hero of the Mexican War, he was appointed first territorial governor of Oregon, where he served later as commander in Indian wars and as senator. He was the vice-presidential candidate on the proslavery Democratic ticket of 1860. Retiring from politics, he lived the rest of his life on his Oregon farm.

New Englanders—and people from Atlantic slopes of the Middle States—more frequently came by ship, took land along the river banks, and laid out towns to which they gave New England or border-state names. Moving up the Willamette from its junction with the Columbia, the major cities are Portland (by the flip of a penny not "Boston"), the metropolis of Oregon and one of the two large cities of the region; Salem, the state capital; Albany; and Harrisburg. A majority of the leading businessmen and industrialists were in this group. The missionaries and more influential ministers also were, either directly or by one or two stops, from New England. Being the educational and cultural leaders, and often adept politicians themselves, the ministers shared with the politicians the direction of public affairs.

The Catholics were another group that was an early force, and their numerous presence helped to give the Pacific Northwest its present character. Most of the retired Hudson's Bay Company employees were Catholics. Catholic missionaries came almost with the Protestant. There were some early conflicts, but the Catholics, also, were an accepted and conditioning group. In fact, until 1840 there were as many Catholics as Protestants in the Pacific Northwest, and as much French as English was spoken here.

The first books published by Americans beyond the tier of states on the west bank of the Mississippi River were from a Protestant mission press located near present Lewiston, Idaho. The first newspaper on the Pacific Coast was a Democratic party organ published in Oregon City. The oldest college in the region is still a Methodist institution. The first hospitals were Catholic institutions. A Congregational clergyman, Rev. George H. Atkinson, was, almost literally, the "father of public education" in Oregon. Until the end of the period of isolation, these groups—New Englanders, Southerners, and Catholics—made up the great bulk of Pacific Northwest population. Eventually they blended.

One factor contributing to this homogenizing was geographic: the settled region was small and geographic elements were almost uniform. Another factor was geographic and technological: the isolation and the lack of extended communication facilities made for community life and activity in a dominating degree. Another was also geographical and technological: ways of making a living were similar throughout the region, and not specialized. Another was social: settlers had to associate with neighbors, if they were to associate with anyone, no matter what the differences in background.

There was Dr. Dorsey S. Baker, to take a "successful" example. Trained in medicine, he did not practice it in the Pacific Northwest. Instead, during the eighteen-sixties and seventies he was a merchant, a cattleman, a banker, a railroad builder, and a lumberman, most of his career centering about Walla Walla, Washington. Or a man might be a governor and engage also in "large milling and mercantile enterprises," according to a contemporary puff; but, in fact, George Abernethy, governor in the provisional government, was a country storekeeper and small-town miller in Oregon City, Oregon. Rich man, poor man, all associated as equals, at least in the chance that their positions might be equalized or reversed.

Another strong human factor in making the settlers into a region-group was intermarriage between Southerners and New Englanders and between shifting economic classes. In those mixed families conflicting traditions and beliefs were compromised, and on a local basis.

How decidedly, and quickly, the settlers came to regard themselves as a region-group is illustrated by their attitudes during the War Between the States. Although the Democrats were the majority party, both before and in several elections immediately after the conflict, the region voted Republican and was Union during the war decade. There was some belligerent talk but no fighting in the region.

Sometimes, however, the too-fervent advocate found it advisable to change his residence. Cincinnatus Hiner Miller, later well know as Joaquin Miller, edited so virulent a pro-Confederacy newspaper that he was forced to move to another town. There he set himself up as a lawyer, was elected a judge, and began the writing of poetry— some on the clean pages of the court's bound record books, perhaps while giving judicial attention to the litigation before him.[4]

There was talk of creating an independent Pacific Coast republic, which, although it did not go beyond talk and not much of that, did indicate that the older American regionalisms were being conditioned by a new one.[5]

In addition to all this, there was the subtle, hard-to-measure, but possibly fundamental, factor that may be called area-kinship.[6] This is the feeling of acquaintanceship, of at-home-ness, with your fellow regionalists, which most persons feel but which is difficult to demonstrate. It is, probably, a combination of earlier-mentioned factors, with ease and completeness of communication being strongest. The first generation of settlers in Oregon talked the same language geographically, economically, and socially, if not linguistically. They might not know each other, but they had many things in common: ideas, work, and acquaintances, possibly including each other's relatives.

This area-kinship is not restricted to geographic areas. It tends to create intellectual and economic regions, also. The average Method-

ist is more at home with Methodists wherever he may be than he is
with Catholic fathers of his own city. A historian, who might feel
a bit ill at ease hearing his razor-wielding barber in another region
damn the Yankee or the Klan, is comfortable, even smugly so, on the
foreign campus. Bankers are bankers everywhere, as are corporation
directors and motion-picture stars. Labor unions, the National Association of Manufacturers, and—less successfully—political parties
are kinds of kinship regions.

During the period of Pacific Northwest history now under review,
those "regions" were of minor importance, and are noted here to
anticipate later discussion.

Until the close of the eighteen-eighties Portland, Oregon, was
the metropolis of the region, the center of economic and social life
both "east of the mountains" (the Cascade Range) and west of them.
Portland was the home office of the river transportation monopolies;
the big bank was there; there was the Newmarket Theater. In that
opera house, opened in 1873, many of the world's great artists played;
to see those performances, people came from as far as two hundred
miles. Such new towns as Walla Walla, Yakima, and Wenatchee in
eastern Washington, Umatilla and Pendleton in eastern Oregon, and
the Snake River settlements were largely tied to Portland by the
Columbia River and its tributaries. The people spreading into mining and farming districts often ventured from the Willamette Valley,
and their new communities were in a wide sense suburbs of the
valley. The coming of the railroads changed that congruity.

The first railroads built in the region were local and in effect
continuations of the river transportation systems. The one constructed by Dr. Baker between 1872 and 1875, from Wallula on the
Columbia to Walla Walla, opened a rich wheat area; but its trains
were feeders to the steamboats, and the railroad itself was soon
purchased by the river transportation company. Twelve years later
a railroad was completed between Portland and San Francisco,
bridging the mountains between the heads of navigation on the
Willamette and Sacramento rivers. Between those two dates, in
1883 and 1886, transcontinental lines reached Portland, and Tacoma
and Seattle on Puget Sound.[7]

Those railroads ended the region's isolation. They brought a flood of people whose national or regional backgrounds were often different from those of the people already there. They opened new districts for agriculture and made possible the expansion of existing industry. The provision of that transportation—and communication —facility had immediate and tremendous effects upon the Pacific Northwest, in areas changing some of the earlier regional characteristics. Some of those changes are represented statistically in the table below.[8]

GROWTH OF THE PACIFIC NORTHWEST

	1880	*1890*	*Percentage of increase*
Population			
Oregon	174,768	313,767	*80*
Washington	75,116	349,390	*380*
Idaho	33,600	84,385	*160*
Value of industrial products			
Oregon	$10,900,000	$41,400,000	*280*
Washington	3,300,000	41,800,000	*1100*
Idaho	1,000,000	1,400,000	*40*
Value of agricultural products			
Oregon	$13,200,000	$22,600,000	*65*
Washington	4,200,000	14,000,000	*230*
Idaho	1,500,000	3,800,000	*150*

It is not only the great increase in population—160 per cent for the region, exclusive of western Montana—that strikes attention. More significant is where the people went, better than 60 per cent of the immigrants going to Washington Territory. The great majority of those went to the Puget Sound communities: Seattle's population grew during the decade from 3,533 to 42,837; Tacoma's from 1,000 to 36,006. In contrast, Portland, although gaining in population, dropped in numbers gained and in percentage of increase, growing from 17,557 to 46,385.

In Oregon the new population was absorbed into the community and did not materially alter the cultural pattern. Several eastern Oregon counties gained considerably in number of residents, but the bulk of the newcomers settled in "the valley." All, excepting in some degree the residents of southward-turned Klamath County, looked to Portland and Salem, the economic and political capitals. Many of the new settlers in and around such Inland Empire towns as Yakima and Wenatchee were at the time more closely bound in every way to Portland than to Puget Sound.

The change was in Washington, and especially in the Puget Sound area, which is still somewhat of a regional island in the Pacific Northwest. Since it was to that area that most of the newcomers came, they submerged the local, regional culture. The result was that Washington Territory—created in 1853 and admitted as a state in 1889, only a few years after the provision of adequate transportation and communication facilities—and in particular its western portion, underwent a second frontier period that was hardly ended a generation later.

The people themselves were different. American settlers in Washington were a generation older than those who built up Oregon, and, while still mainly from the Middle West, were a people culturally in transition to a much greater degree than were the early settlers. They were in a very large proportion people on the move, with relatively short geographic, and confused regional, backgrounds. Their ideas also were in the process of change that led to the Populism of the eighteen-eighties and nineties. They were less frequently neighbors from "back home." In short, they were, before coming to the Pacific Northwest, regionally unsettled and of no, or of confused, area-kinship.

Also, there was a larger proportion of foreign immigrants than formerly, especially from the Scandinavian countries. To promote that immigration, Oregon and Washington, as well as the railroad and steamship companies, distributed advertising literature.[9] No area received more Swedes and Norwegians in proportion to the already resident population than Washington, which to this day ranks third in Scandinavian population. Language difficulties, differences in cultural background, and the tendency to locate in "closed" communities and to intermarry within the clan—all hampered communication, which depends upon comparable ways of thinking, and slowed the absorption of thousands of those persons into the area-kinship group.[10]

Another condition that slowed the regionalizing of western Washington was the amount of time required to clear the land, to build houses, and to provide physical services for this wave of newcomers. Few hours were available for cultural activities. In addition, economic activities were too disparate to permit such general integration as had taken place in the older, slower moving, agricultural communities. In many instances, those then resident and holding land on the Sound became proprietors and the newcomers became laborers.

Also important was the influx of out-of-region capital into Washington and into Idaho and western Montana. Such capital creates a responsibility, not to the region which it enters, but to the home bank. Profits do not stay to build up the region, and employees are caught in conflicting loyalties and needs. The capital and those who worked for it were colonists: they were the means of exploitation, necessarily and despite regional feelings that might develop. Perhaps unconsciously, some firms made it a practice to move managers about, thus impressing upon them that they were "company men" whose interests and loyalty were to a corporation more than to a region or a community.

Oregon was principally "home-owned" and continues so. The largest department store in Oregon is still in the possession of the founding families, who have used their wealth for their community. The largest department store in Washington has become a branch; the second largest, one of a chain. Of the two largest Washington dailies, both in Seattle, one is a Hearst paper and the other is partly "foreign" owned. Of the two largest Oregon dailies, both in Portland, one is still owned by the family of the founder; the recent sale of the other was widely regarded as somewhat scandalous. Although the Weyerhaeuser Timber Company has large land holdings in Oregon, much of the timber in the state is locally owned and sawed. The reversion of the Oregon and California Railroad timberlands, which are being opened on a co-operative basis to private operators for sustained-yield cutting, will, apparently, make secure the economic position of these smaller local companies. Much of Washington's land went to the railroads, and through them to the eastern lumber companies or operators. Even in agriculture, although not a great deal of data has been gathered, the same difference—home ownership versus "foreign" ownership—seems to hold.[11]

In brief, the coming of the railroads ended the isolation of the Pacific Northwest but did not integrate the region. The railroads were interregional, not intraregional, transportation and communication facilities. They disrupted the developing regionalism. By so doing, they emphasized the fact that a region is a growth from within—the development of area-kinship—not a change promoted from without.

During that same period when outside capital and its influence were important, another force was gathering strength. That was specialization, with its emphasis on restricted group, rather than regional, coherence.

Ways of earning a living are a kind of area-kinship and set up limits to effective communication. Specialization tends to create confined areas of familiarity in the economic field and also in the social; it interrupts the broader communication that characterizes a region in the usual meaning. In effect, specialized ways of making a living create new "regions," which take on local color but whose borders are not local.

The period of Pacific Northwest history opened by the railroads was marked by the beginning of full economic development. It was also marked by both the centrifugal tug of foreign finance and the disintegrating influence of specialization among groups. That situation was not unique to the Pacific Northwest. Transregional realms were being established everywhere by capital and labor combinations.

Some indication of this segregation into groups, and the consequent weakening of regional consciousness, is to be found in much legislation between 1885 and 1930. Those acts, while revealing the influence of the affected groups, were also an effort to bring them, at least politically, into the region. The formation of labor unions and the passage of laws about labor are, perhaps, as good a key as any to that period and change.

During the eighteen-eighties the Knights of Labor were represented in the Pacific Northwest. However, the number of specialized laborers was not then large enough, nor was their specialization sharp enough, to bring the Knights success.

After 1890, when organizers of the American Federation of Labor entered the region, labor organization progressed rapidly and labor's influence increased. By 1900, there were between thirty and thirty-five American Federation of Labor locals in Oregon; during the next decade, between fifty and fifty-five more were incorporated. In Washington the number was larger, being fifty-odd by 1900, with at least forty-five being incorporated in the two years 1901 and 1902. In this latter year "130 unions reported." With the backing of many unorganized workers and a fair portion of "the public," labor was strong enough to secure the creation of a Labor Board in Oregon in 1903, and in Washington in 1905, although Washington had had a labor commissioner since 1899. In those same years, laws were passed to improve labor's position. As early as 1901, Seattle had a labor newspaper, the *Union Record*.[12]

Most of those early locals were decidedly craft organizations, from cigar makers and saddlers to barbers and boilermakers. Usually their members were long-time residents of the communities in which they worked and still in a measure thought of themselves as regional citizens.

That was not true of union members during World War I, when tens of thousands of workers were imported into Seattle and Portland from all over the United States. The union was to them the region. Most intended to, and did, return "home" when shipbuilding and other war industrial activity stopped. The general strike in Seattle during 1919 was an expression of group consciousness as opposed to regional kinship.

Interesting and odd in this phase of the region's history was employer-worker relationship in lumbering, pre-eminently the regional industry. The American Federation of Labor had attempted with little success to organize mill and woods workers; what little success did accrue was in the mills among settled laborers. The lumberjack was a wanderer, going from camp to camp. Frequently he had no "home," being a sort of forest gypsy, and often a rough individualist. During World War I the Industrial Workers of the World found him a convert or fellow traveler, and a period of strikes and slowdowns followed under the leadership of that organization. A truce was effected under the semipatriotic Loyal Legion of Loggers and Lumbermen; but the normal employer-worker "peace" was not established until years later, when automotive transportation and changed logging techniques turned the old-time lumberjack into a semipermanent resident of some town and very often into a family man.[13] Although this change in labor was not fully felt until during and after the depression of the nineteen-thirties, by the mid-twenties it was well under way. Group loyalties were being conditioned by a sense of area-kinship.

Although the initiative, referendum, and recall were adopted in two states before Oregon, that system of direct legislation became known as "the Oregon system"—perhaps because of the dramatic fight over the subject there. Adopted in Oregon between 1903 and 1910, and in Washington in 1912, that "system" was an effort on the part of the people to recapture in politics, then the most apparent field, a kind of regional action. It was intended to meet the situation caused by the use of financial and special-group influence in the legislature, and was a campaign for home rule. Certainly it is significant that initiative measures in Washington and Oregon are often similar, deal with the same problems, and often meet with comparable degrees of acceptance from the voters.[14]

Related to this circumstance, is the extraordinary independence of voters in the Pacific Northwest. The block of votes called "independent," "other," or "floating" has since 1896 averaged twice as high in Washington as throughout the nation, and 50 per cent higher in Oregon. The important thing is that it is mostly cast for regional, as opposed to national, candidates—seemingly the triumph of regional feeling over national sentiments.[15]

It is difficult to say to what extent better communication facilities, such as the automobile and the telephone, helped in this general reuniting of the people; obviously they helped greatly. The Pacific Northwest is uniquely dependent upon highway transportation. When the railroads were building, the population was small and scattered. The terrain is rugged, even when water grades are followed. Despite the construction of many intraregional lines during the nineteen-twenties, there are still many good-sized towns and many areas without railroad connections. On the other hand, the highway systems, constructed in the main after 1915, are excellent and afford good coverage of the entire region.

The new communication system serves both commerce and social life. Forest-, mine-, and farm-to-market roads have made possible the further expansion of all kinds of economic activity. They have facilitated the combining of far-scattered one-room schools into modern consolidated schools where children of many families associate together. They have served to pull communities together, and to tie those communities to one another.

That the Pacific Northwest was again coalescing into a region is perhaps best demonstrated in its literature, especially in its literature after World War I. In Oregon the phases of history so far discussed are not so sharply marked in the literature of the state as they are in Washington, the latter state having undergone another "frontier" period between 1885–90 and 1915–20. The settlers of Oregon were strongly inclined to take their pens in hand and often turned out near first-rate material. There were, however, characteristics of the literature that did reflect the regional period of its composition, noticeable in Oregon and striking in Washington.

During the eighteen-nineties and the early years of the twentieth century, in both of these states and in Idaho, there was a veritable flood of usually indifferently written volumes in praise of the pioneer days and the pioneers. Those who had got the feel of the region before the confusing tidal wave of newcomers, were preaching their sermons. During the nineteen-twenties the newcomers came to feel at home also, and began to express their sentiments. James Stevens, Nard Jones, Archie Binns, Vardis Fisher, Anita Pettibone, Allis McKay, Joseph Kinsey Howard—and the list could be long continued—are creating a true regional literature. Often it is distinguished in style; usually it is marked by a "characteristic" feeling. A handy package of both the writing and the feeling is the collection of essays published under the title *Northwest Harvest*.[16] Even if this literature expresses nothing else, it reveals a self-conscious sense of area-kinship.

Possibly the recent literature has some psychological relationship with the pioneer-praising books of a generation earlier. For the current period of Pacific Northwest history, like the thirty or so years following 1885, is again one of distraction and change.

There have been two immigrations into the region in the last two decades, one of them very large.

During the depression of the nineteen-thirties there was a considerable movement out of and within the region as well as into it.

The combined population of Oregon, Washington, and Idaho increased from 2,963,000 in 1930 to 3,351,000 in 1940. Also, in Montana there was a marked movement of residents from the eastern to the western part of the state. The population figure does not, however, indicate the number of newcomers, of whom it is estimated some 240,000 came into the region between 1930 and 1938. Probably half of that number were included in the 36,000 families who came from dust-bowl areas, and most of whom continued here as farmers. Between 1940 and 1948 the population of Washington increased from 1,736,000 to 2,148,000, and that of Oregon, from 1,089,000 to 1,476,000. Allowing for natural increase, there remain an estimated 700,000 newcomers, an increase of 25 per cent in less than a decade. Of these, approximately 350,000 moved into the Seattle and Portland areas.

Those who came during the depression were, for the most part, families—in the main, farm families. They came hoping to stay; made efforts to fit into their new communities, with which they had much in common; and were quickly absorbed.

Although there were many families among the war workers, there were as many single men. These were in a position somewhat like that of the old-time lumberjack, except for required union association. Housed in barracks, 6,000 in one project alone, or left to find rooms in already overcrowded cities and towns; two-thirds of them working shifts outside the regular work day; all strangers—they lived lives segregated in part, and almost wholly outside the normal routine of the community. The families were located in war housing projects. Vanport, a suburb of Portland, had a population of as many as 35,000–40,000 men, women, and children, and was for years Oregon's second largest city. The Hanford-Richland area, the "atomic bomb home" in southeastern Washington, grew from a few hundred farmers and villagers to 51,000 organized workers during the war, and has today perhaps 35,000 residents. Most of the war workers intended to "go home" after the war; they were exploiters from other regions, bringing strange ways of thinking with them. They lived in their own towns in what was often socially a state of isolation. Furthermore, they were not welcomed and were frequently subjected to social discrimination. They were islanded in almost every way. Being so situated and treated, they could not readily become a part of the older communities about which they were clustered.[17]

After the war, many of those workers took a well-earned vacation on their unemployment compensation, and stayed . . . and stayed. Of those who returned home—usually families—many soon came back to the Pacific Northwest. Some have found work in the new postwar industries. Their position is somewhat improved from the viewpoint of becoming regionalized, but is not good. Housing shortages and other limited public utilities still keep them much in their own congested areas where they are of no region.

In a very true sense the Pacific Northwest is in a new frontier period. It is an industrial frontier. Its centers are towns and a limited number of factories. It is a frontier of new and often different people; and even of new towns and cities. The overwhelming majority of older residents dislike this disturbance of their formerly comfortable, easily ordered, and well-understood way of life.

Yet one kind of region is already taking shape, a region whose limits are those of efficient economic service. Here that service is based upon the river system. Even the Puget Sound communities, two or three hundred miles from the Columbia and separated from it by a mountain range, are knit into the river-region system by a power grid and interwoven economic interests. The region taking shape is a management, an administrative, region. It is based on hydroelectric power, and its area is defined with surprising sharpness. Except for its extension into part of British Columbia and for the small California-looking Klamath River district, it is the historical "Oregon country," the political Pacific Northwest.

This economic service region is not, however, purely—though it is principally—a power service region. Land and water uses are involved: farming and forestry, fishing and river transportation, no less than manufacturing. To a much greater degree than in the Great Plains, the variety of the total economy here complicates the problem of efficient management.

The kinship region is today more difficult to define. The inflowing people, now almost wholly American and from the Middle West, have not yet been absorbed into the older population, and so have not taken on the local characteristics existing when they came. Nor have they effected much noticeable alteration in the social patterns that they found. Their semi-isolated communities are to long-time residents a sort of objectionable or questionable tourist attraction; they themselves are somewhat in the position of being visitors to Boise or Olympia or Salem.

Other conditions slow the mergence of the kinship-area. The bulk of the newcomers are specialized labor; their association tends to be—partly because of residence—within their own group. This is not, of course, unique to labor, but is common to the professions as well. In the Northwest, however, as in many older industrial communities in the East, it is strengthened by the fact that the new labor is "foreign." Again, the majority of the late comers are Democrats and—less so in Seattle—suspect as radicals; whereas the natives were and are decidedly independent in politics, they distrust New Dealers and "Federalist" Democrats.

Nevertheless, similarity of economic problems; the absorption, though slow, of "alien" groups into the cultural region; increasingly wider regional communication by travel and the local press, by local education and literature—all these are, by present indications, again bringing the Pacific Northwest together into a region. It will not be the region of 1880 or of 1920.

In the preparation of this paper, a pattern of regionalism seemed to emerge. In the Pacific Northwest it has always been founded on what is here called, for want of a better word, area-kinship. It was first determined by physical communication routes, by river systems, as much as by what mores men had grown up with; the restrictions of isolation brought the people together, changed them, and gave them much in common. Then followed a period of confusion, when came different people of different work and thought, and isolation was broken down. From those decades evolved a regionalism in some respects unlike the preceding, made possible by new technologies of every kind. As often self-conscious differences were lessened or erased, the people again were at home among themselves and felt that they "belonged" to this region. The following expansion of the new communication facilities—radio, national distribution of consumer goods, and, most recently, inescapable international connections—might have been expected to negate what had in the past made regions. In the current history of the Pacific Northwest, this is not so. There is a limit to what a people can comprehend in feeling as well as accept in logic. That limit is the reaches of area-kinship, of understanding, of effective communication.

A region is not a static thing of geography or, today, an unchanging society. In history it is an area of coherent, relevant change. Its boundaries are those of common problems and interests. There is a variable mixture of elements in this: land and labor, people and heritage; it ends as essential agreement in community life.

NOTES AND BIBLIOGRAPHICAL REFERENCES

1. It is my belief that definitions should conclude discussions and not precede arguments. However, a note on my usage of the word "region" may remove some preliminary questions.

To me a "region" and a "section" are essentially the same thing; the difference is only a way of looking at them as fields of action. An easy—and therefore wrong—definition might go: Regions are made by rivers, sections by mountain ranges. But that is only saying that a region is an area "pulleyed together." All regions are separated more or less, if not by geographic mountains, then by ranges of thought and economic activity. Sections are, in this view, regions in opposition, in active competition or conflict. And that in itself tends to strengthen regionalism, or area-kinship. To call a region a section is to emphasize its apartness from other regions; to call a section a region is to emphasize its self-consistency.

The true difficulty is to determine what are regions in total and what are often called subregions. A subregion may be a part, in different ways, of several regions. A region may even include what I call "islands," small areas often very unlike the surrounding community. In the Pacific Northwest, Seattle is something of an island, as are Richland and the Jordan Valley.

But the meanings of my usage should be apparent in the paper itself.

2. Three histories of the Pacific Northwest have been published since 1905: Joseph Schafer's *History of the Pacific Northwest* in that year; G. W. Fuller's *A History of the Pacific Northwest* in 1931; and O. O. Winther's *The Great Northwest* in 1947. The latest revision of Schafer's book is now thirty years old, but it is still useful as an outline up to, say, 1890. Fuller's book is badly proportioned, but contains considerable material on the history of the area east of the Cascade Range; his book is, in fact, a rewriting of his history of the Inland Empire. Winther's book is good in proportion and in its use of recent monographs and articles; the first edition was, however, full of nagging errors, was often unbalanced in emphasis, and was cluttered with displays of inconsequential and superficial erudition. Winther has now (1950) revised this book and added

much pertinent material, corrected a reasonable number of errors, and made it a better book than it was in the first edition.

Histories of the Pacific Northwest States have their limitations also. Except for Lancaster Pollard's two-volume history of Washington (1937), they are textbooks or WPA Guides if recent, and if older are far out of date—most of them, in fact, deal skimpily if at all with the period since 1880. The Guides are useful but were not intended to be histories. For Idaho the best book—in fact, the only one—that covers the entire period to date is the textbook by C. J. Brosnan, *History of the State of Idaho*, written in 1918 and well revised in 1936. For Oregon and Washington the two books that attempt a full-length history are Pollard's texts, *A History of the State of Washington* (1941), revised in 1943, and *Oregon and the Pacific Northwest* (1946). The latter book carries a lengthy bibliography which lists most of the sources—not specifically referred to here—used in the preparation of this paper.

Much of the basic data of the region's history has not yet been worked into articles or monographs, although the *Oregon Historical Quarterly* and the *Pacific Northwest Quarterly* together publish close to six hundred pages yearly—and the *OHQ* is now (1950) in its fifty-first year.

3. Although the largest group was from the Middle West, the families of that group were seldom more than one generation from New England or the Old South or, in smaller numbers, the Middle States. Among them, however, the synthesizing of cultures that was to be so strong in Oregon was well begun.

George H. Himes, for nearly fifty years assistant secretary and curator of the Oregon Historical Society after its founding in 1898, interviewed more than seven thousand settlers who arrived before 1857. From the data compiled on biographical cards for these people, he estimated early immigration to have been 50 per cent from the Middle West, 33 per cent from south of the Mason-Dixon Line, 6 per cent from New England, and 11 per cent from twenty-two foreign countries, the great majority of the latter from the British Isles, Canada, and Germany. Later census figures substantiate his findings.

4. Biographical studies of locally prominent men are rare. For studies of the lives and work of the men mentioned see: Sister W. Margaret Jean Kelly, *The Career of Joseph Lane, Frontier Politician*, a Ph.D. dissertation published by the Catholic University of America Press, 1942; *Forty Years a Pioneer, Business Life of Dorsey Syng Baker*, written by W. W. Baker, the son of the subject, and privately published by Lowman and Hanford, Seattle, 1934; Harr Wagner's *Joaquin Miller and His Other Self*, published by the Harr Wagner Publishing Co., San Francisco, 1929. For Abernethy there is no sketch, even, of his life, but many scattered references through volumes of the *OHQ*. The Library of the Oregon Historical Society contains much manuscript material by each of the persons mentioned, including the court record—poetry—political speeches—true confessions volumes of Miller; an interesting article on the poet is H. C. Thompson's "Reminiscences of Joaquin Miller and Canyon City," *OHQ*, Vol. XLV (December, 1944), 326–36.

5. There are some contemporary letters in the Oregon Historical So-

ciety library that refer to the "Pacific Republic," which has been discussed in passing in articles in the *OHQ,* Vol. IV (June, 1903), 105–106; and Vol. XII (December, 1911), 329–30. There are other articles in the same quarterly devoted entirely to the subject: Dorothy Hull, "The Movement in Oregon for the Establishment of a Pacific Coast Republic," Vol. XVII (September, 1916), 177–200; and Joseph Ellison, "Designs for a Pacific Republic, 1843–63," Vol. XXXI (December, 1930), 319–42.

6. "Hard to measure" is a mild way, indeed, of stating the difficulties of describing the existence and force of "area-kinship." I recently tried to conduct a seminar on the subject, using first books by regional authors and then editorials in selected regional newspapers. The results were meager enough but did plainly indicate that the feeling does exist.

7. A comprehensive survey article, rich in references to sources, is Randall V. Mills, "A History of Transportation in the Pacific Northwest," *OHQ,* Vol. XLVII (September, 1946), 281–312.

8. Other tables compiled from census reports plainly show this change.

OREGON	1880	1890	1910
Total population	174,768	313,767	672,765
Oregon born	67,942	111,850	225,102
United States born	144,265	256,450	559,629
Foreign born	30,503	57,317	113,136

Ten leading states from which settlers came

Missouri	10,754	15,329	25,456
Illinois	7,804	14,043	27,942
Iowa	6,969	12,478	28,242
Ohio	6,201	11,551	20,030
California	6,011		18,184
New York	5,443	9,450	16,115
Indiana	5,055	8,332	
Pennsylvania	3,342	6,599	
Tennessee	2,469		
Wisconsin	2,118	5,519	18,755
Michigan		4,067	
Minnesota		3,482	16,499
Washington			17,508
Kansas			15,937

Five leading countries from which settlers came

Germany	5,034	12,475	17,777
Ireland	3,659	4,891	
Canada and Newfoundland	3,019	6,460	12,394
England	2,960	5,679	7,995
Scotland	1,129		
Sweden		3,775	10,099
Norway			6,843

WASHINGTON	*1880*	*1890*	*1910*
Total population	75,116	349,390	1,141,990
Washington born	19,348	54,227	262,694
United States born	59,313	267,227	623,055
Foreign born	15,803	90,005	256,241

Ten leading states from which settlers came

Oregon	6,583	12,803	29,569
Illinois	3,228	17,653	51,163
Missouri	3,160	12,359	38,665
New York	2,981	16,065	31,706
Iowa	2,866	14,512	47,862
Ohio		13,882	32,849
Wisconsin		11,443	47,267
Pennsylvania		11,123	26,296
Minnesota		11,040	52,198
Kansas		9,043	
Michigan			38,089

Five leading countries from which settlers came

Canada	2,856	17,412	39,263
Ireland	2,243		
Germany	2,198	15,399	29,382
England and Wales	1,846	11,530	19,413
Sweden and Norway	1,228		
Sweden		10,272	32,195
Norway		8,334	28,363

Differences in the character of the populations of the two states are apparent.

The foreign born in Oregon were about 16 per cent of the population throughout the period 1880–1910; in Washington they were approximately 20 per cent in 1880, 26 per cent in 1890, and 22 per cent in 1910. According to the 1940 census, foreign-born residents were approximately 12 per cent of the population of Washington and 8 per cent of the population of Oregon.

American settlers in Oregon in 1850 had come, in order of diminishing numbers, from Missouri, Illinois, Indiana, Kentucky, Ohio, New York, Virginia, Iowa, Tennessee, and Pennsylvania. For Washington the census of 1870 lists states of birth of settlers in order of numbers—Oregon, New York, Illinois, Missouri, and Ohio—naming those states only. Again for 1880 only five are listed.

9. The Oregon Immigration Commission, with the aid of Henry Villard, issued five promotional pamphlets in German and one each in Swedish, Norwegian, and Danish. Arthur J. Brown discusses "The Promotion of Emigration to Washington, 1854–1909," in the *PNQ*, Vol.

XXXVI (January, 1945), 3–17. See also Carlton C. Qualey, *Norwegian Settlement in the United States* (pp. 188–196), published in 1938 by the Norwegian-American Historical Association.

10. There is more material bearing on this point than anyone has had time to catalogue, let alone survey.

There are the authors such as Ernest Toefil Skarstedt, who wrote in Swedish, volumes on the Swedes in Oregon and Washington (Lancaster Pollard, "A Check List of Washington Authors," *PNQ*, Vol. XXXI [January, 1940], 80–81), and Hans Bergman, who wrote in Swedish and in English *History of the Scandinavians in Tacoma and Pierce County (ibid.,* 13).

There was the foreign-language press. An incomplete list includes, with date of founding:

Norwegian: *Nordlyset,* 1847; later absorbed by the *Washington Posten,* 1886, which is still being printed in Seattle.

Swedish: *Vestra Posten,* 1887, still being printed as a weekly in Seattle; *Svenska Posten,* which is a combination of several *Postens* founded after the *Vestra,* and which is still being published in Seattle.

Finnish: *Unsi Katamas,* published in Astoria from 1881 to 1890; *Laimetar,* started in 1890 at Astoria, but inconsistently published to 1906; *Tyomies,* a radical paper begun in Astoria in 1907 and published there until moved to Wisconsin in 1930, in which year the editor and several staff members were deported to Russia as Communists.

German: *Deutschezeitung,* 1867, published in Portland until 1884; *Nachtricten,* 1890, the successor to *Freie Presse,* 1885. There were many German papers during the early years of the century, but most suspended during World War I and the rest, with one or two exceptions, died during the depression of the thirties. Two religious papers, published by the Benedictine Fathers at Mt. Angel, Oregon, *St. Joseph's Blatt* and *Armen Seelen Freund,* have a circulation of about fifteen thousand today.

Oriental: Both Japanese and Chinese language newspapers came into existence during the eighteen-nineties, but apparently none continues publication today except as a bulletin.

Italian: Inadequate records indicate that the first established, but no longer published, were *La Stella,* 1922, Seattle, and *Da Tribune Italiana,* 1926.

11. So far as I know, the effort has not been made, even in one field, to determine the proportion of out-of-region and local capital investments. The examples given in the text can be, of course, only indicative; however, they can be easily increased by adding the livestock industries, fruit and vegetable processing, fisheries, etc.

The following statistics for 1939 are from the 1940 *Census of Manufactures,* III, 847, 1047. They are, again, only indicative, especially since the classifications do not make a distinction between out-of-region and in-region capital. Presumably most of the "central-administrative-office (plural unit)" type of ownership or control represents out-of-region capital; "independent (single unit)" is very largely local.

		No. of estab-lishments	No. of wage earners	Value of products	Value added by manufacture
Corporate ownership or control					
Central-administrative	Oregon	313	22,868	$168,182,705	$69,536,623
	Washington	543	47,795	397,267,685	166,423,723
Independent (single unit)	Oregon	640	27,878	137,645,942	73,538,979
	Washington	1,055	31,572	180,400,363	91,904,976
Noncorporate ownership or control					
Central-administrative	Oregon	58	506	4,507,308	1,459,777
	Washington	79	1,225	8,631,308	3,078,574
Independent (single unit)	Oregon	1,237	12,370	55,038,481	27,639,365
	Washington	1,536	9,732	50,350,453	25,230,990

If my interpretation is indicative, these figures would signify that the value of goods produced by local manufactures in Oregon was approximately 52 per cent of the total; in Washington, approximately 36 per cent. The percentage of "local" employees is even more striking, for Oregon being approximately 63 per cent; for Washington, approximately 35 per cent.

These are insecure estimates, I know, but they accord with my impression of the over-all production, an impression based upon studies of the lumber and fishery industries. See Pollard, *A History of the State of Washington* (1937), II, 7–33, and "The Salmon Cannery of Oregon, Washington and Alaska," *Americana*, Vol. XXXVI (Fourth Quarter, 1942), 638–68.

12. The second biennial report (1907) of the Bureau of Labor Statistics and Inspector of Factories and Workshops for the State of Oregon (the bureau's full title!) contains the statistics cited for Oregon and much valuable—and amusing—data.

13. Norman S. Hayner's "Taming the Lumber Jack," *American Sociological Review*, Vol. X (April, 1945), 217–55, discusses the changed status of the lumber workers.

14. Claudius O. Johnson, "The Initiative and Referendum in Washington," *PNQ*, Vol. XXXVI (January, 1945), 29–63, and "The Adoption of the Initiative and Referendum in Washington," *PNQ*, Vol. XXXV (October, 1944), 291–303. The *Oregon Blue Book* carries a list of initiative and referendum measures with votes for and against.

There are, it is amusing to note, some sharp differences, not so much in vote percentages as in majorities: in the election of 1948, for example, "conservative" Oregon voted down a "liquor by the drink" initiative while "radical" Washington passed it. However, in such matters as social security, school support, etc., there is a close parallel in voting.

15. Unpublished studies by the writer. The vote for President and for governor in Washington and Oregon illustrates this especially. Both states have at times gone overwhelmingly Democratic for national candidates and yet elected Republican governors by almost as large, or even as large, a majority. Off-year elections, notably in Oregon but also in Washington, most plainly express local as different from national interests and attitudes.

16. See Pollard, "Washington Literature: A Historical Sketch," *PNQ,* Vol. XXIX (July, 1938), 227–54; Helen Hitt, "History in Pacific Northwest Novels Written Since 1920," *OHQ,* Vol. LI (September, 1950), 180–206; and Alfred Powers, *History of Oregon Literature* (1935).

17. Of the several studies of depression and war-job migration perhaps the best are the census volume *Population, Internal Migration 1935 to 1940, Social Characteristics of Migrants;* Pacific Northwest Regional Planning Commission, *Recent Migration into the Pacific Northwest* (1938); Elon H. Moore, "Oregon Population Changes from 1945 to 1948," *Oregon Business Review,* Vol. VII (April, 1948), 1 ff.; Washington State Department of Health, "Estimated Population of Washington by Counties and Cities, as of July 1, 1948," *Current Washington History,* Vol. VI (November, 1948), 7–9.

The census study reports a total native in-migration of 159,816 for Oregon and 187,212 for Washington between 1935 and 1940, totals that would be considerably increased if in-migrants for 1930 to 1935 were added. Total out-migration from Oregon was 82,371; from Washington, 103,861. The number of persons moving to farms is reported as 62,111 in Oregon and 63,148 in Washington. The rural-farm out-migration was 9,406 from Washington and 8,974 from Oregon. This indicates that of the net native in-migration gain of 159,756, farm families accounted for 106,-879. That figure does not include the census "rural-nonfarm" figures.

Part III

Regional Aspects
of American Culture

Introduction

John Fabian Kienitz

In his survey of Carolingian art, Roger Hinks expresses the opinion "that some regional influence, whether of landscape or climate, exercises a pressure constant in itself, though meeting with a varying degree of resistance." For the period of time that this art covers, the years from A.D. 800 to 900, Hinks finds a regional distribution for the painting and sculpture of Western Europe. Concerning the fine arts it is safe to say there has always been a regional influence, and it seems to me that this sign of place is all the more acute and winning when it occurs, so far as we can tell, without conscious effort to make that influence manifest.

The architecture of the United States, perhaps more convincingly than either painting or sculpture, has had from its beginnings to the present day an attractive and one might say inevitable regional foundation of style. We have always had, and may we always continue to have, a tradition of wood in New England, of brick in Virginia, and of stone in Pennsylvania. A concern for a naturally local material seems to go with a conscious desire to build adequately for the most part, and sometimes superbly, in keeping with the physical environment.

Throughout a life devoted to architecture and its history, Rexford Newcomb has maintained a keen interest in the architecture of the Southwest, from which interest stems his plea for the learned continuation of what he calls, rightly, a Mediterranean style. This style comes to this region from regional characteristics which are apparent as one moves over California, Texas, and Arizona. During the second half of the nineteenth century, the regional expression in building disappeared and suffered a long neglect because of a somewhat thoughtless *ad hoc* construction that had only the shabbiest kind of utilitarianism in mind. For the Southwest as well as for other geographical entities, the passing of the initial exploitations brings builders and clients alike to a reflective pause; and out of the new contemplation that appears as a resource of mind, after 1900 we arrive at a realization, in the Southwest and elsewhere, that there was something good here to begin with and that this something is worth our care. Accuracy in regional distinctions is the merit of Rexford Newcomb's studies in the Spanish architecture of the Southwest. Here, it seems to me, lies the justification of our research in the fine arts of a region: with their help we are enabled to maintain a tradition with reason and tact. So true is this that now in Arizona, to name a single state, we are able to get, without fanfare or trace of parochial chauvinism, a domestic and public building style which is an adroit synthesis of the old arts and crafts of building with the new science of comfort of the modern age. Far from being a servile or utterly abject dependence on the primitive past, regional study of architecture gives rise to the richest possible accommodation to climate and place. It adds to the native force of the original building style something of the more leisured grace that ought rightly to be added to it. And so it avoids frontier restrictions or the excesses of a temporarily fashionable fiat.

When the regional paintings and philosophies of Grant Wood, Thomas Hart Benton, and John Steuart Curry came to the attention of the larger public, there was a real danger that this art and thought might come to be overvalued. This actually happened, much to the dismay, as I know from conversations with Curry and Wood, of the artists themselves. It was the opinion of Grant Wood that his painting ought to be considered the personal choice of a man who spoke not for a region but for himself. He would have been pleased had he lived to know what we know, namely, that his paintings of Iowa folk and scenes have an instantaneous and universal appeal, not for Iowa and Americans alone but for the world. He would have agreed with those who say that there are no geographical stops for the emotions and that a small idea may carry far if it is well presented.

The first response, of antagonism or approval, placed regional painting in a bad light and evil company. But here again the consequences of an original excess were not all of them disastrous. The attention paid to regionalism among its twentieth-century pioneers brought us, characteristically, to a new interpretation of our earlier painting and particularly of that art as we have it in the nineteenth century. Here the publications of E. P. Richardson have been invaluable. For he has, in his books and as a director of an important museum, rehabilitated our artistic achievement, using in part a regional measure as a control. The result is a new enjoyment of the painting of the past, and, again, a more reasonably critical approach to an understanding and evaluation of the more recent painting.

As for artists themselves, the overblown fantasies once showered over Wood, Benton, and Curry have died a natural death to be replaced by a more appealing attention that is now given to young painters the country over who paint most effectively out of their own experiences. In doing so they often hit upon an idea, a sequence of thought and feeling, which serves to rekindle for all of us the delight we have had in passing through the varieties of American place. Of these younger painters, in the second and third generations of regionalists, it may be said that a sense of the environment is a factor in their making rather than what it was once in danger of becoming: an excuse for the cruelest and most dictatorial kind of provincial expression.

For regionalism in literature, Benjamin T. Spencer has assembled a marvelous and attractively detailed structure of fact. In our literature and painting alike, there waits the material for regional documentation. Richardson and Spencer have carried a proper emphasis to the past, and we learn from them that what is taken by the uninformed to be of recent concern, actually has roots in our Yankee beginnings and will, somehow, remain with us in the future. Spencer has been a patient and observant voyager in time. He has accumulated the fact out of which elaborate theory may be made. His thoroughness is his, and our, best control; it makes or should make it impossible for those who come after in this field, either to take regionalism lightly as a constant phenomenon in our literature or to deny its importance as one of the prime sources of creative inspiration.

Chapter 7

Regionalism in American Literature

Benjamin T. Spencer

Regional literature in contemporary America is the off-
spring of literary nationalism, which in turn is the child of the
Romantic movement. As the American Revolution whetted the desire for a national literature and the American scene called for indigenous expression, such European critics as Herder and Madame
de Staël gave philosophical sanction to native impulse by viewing
literature as the organic product of a national culture. Consequently,
for a century and a half American authors have sought a distinctive
American utterance which, as Longfellow declared in 1832, would
bear the stamp of "those distinguishing features which literature
receives from the spirit of a nation—from its scenery and climate, its
historic recollections, its government, its various institutions . . . and,
in a word, from the thousand external circumstances, which . . . give
it a marked and individual character, distinct from that of the literature of other nations."[1] In the nineteen-forties, Archibald MacLeish
echoed Longfellow's nationalistic doctrine by urging an "adaptation
of an art of letters developed in Europe to the experience of life in
a country geographically, meteorologically, socially, psychologically,
and otherwise unlike the country and the life of Europe."[2]

In the early decades of the nineteenth century, American writers
perceived that those differences in climate, history, occupation, and
institutions which had wrought in America a nationality distinct from
that of England were also in the vast new continent effecting further
distinctions. United politically though the nation might be, the
homogeneity in manners, traditions, folkways, and sentiments from

[1] Henry W. Longfellow, in A. T. Rice (ed.), *Essays from the North American Review* (New York, 1879), 321–22.

[2] Archibald MacLeish, *Yale Review*, Vol. XXXI (Autumn, 1941), 64.

which belletristic literature was likely to derive its nurture and flavor, was to be found most surely in the states or several regions. Accordingly, literary sentiment in the first half of the century proceeded to Hawthorne's cry in the eighteen-fifties that America had "no limits and no oneness; and when you try to make it a matter of the heart, everything falls away except one's native State."[3] Inevitably the American imagination, eager to embrace the nation, found itself thrown back upon its diverse cultural communities. In the eighteen-twenties and thirties, historical novels in the manner of Scott celebrated the origins of restricted areas like New England; the overtones of romance were sought along the Hudson; and numerous magazines appeared consciously proclaiming their regional commitments through such titles as the *New England Magazine*, the *Knickerbocker*, the *Western Monthly Review*, or the *Southern Rose*. Thus for over a century the regional impulse has been an active force in American letters. Inasmuch as the major products of this impulse have been subjects of frequent treatment, the present essay will seek rather to understand the concept of regionalism primarily through an exploration of its historical development. Through such a process, it is hoped, both the validity and the limitations of the mode may be suggested; and thereby the promise of regionalism in current literary practice may be more soundly assessed.

In its first phase, in the generation preceding the Civil War, the regional impulse in literature felt especially obliged to come to terms with the nationalistic spirit. Accordingly, under varying terminology the authors and critics of the eighteen-thirties and forties expounded the concept of a national literature as the aggregate of sectional utterances. For Timothy Flint in Ohio the instinctive affection for one's natal spot or for that portion of the country invested with the associations of home constituted "nationality"; but between such *amor patriae* and affection for the Union, he was careful to say, there is no conflict. The Yankees and Southerners he regarded as having this "nationality" to an especial and admirable degree lacking among Westerners. Wherefore, his *Western Monthly* he designed as an "humble offering to the life of our country in general, and of the West in particular." The "nationality" which Flint assigned to the

[3] Cf. Nathaniel Hawthorne, *Works*, Riverside ed. (Cambridge, Massachusetts, 1914), X, 456; XI, 470.

Southern character, John Pendleton Kennedy attributed more narrowly to the Virginian, and this "old nationalism," as he termed Virginia's "once peculiar . . . cast of manners," seemed to him to merit faithful portrayal from one who had studied his subject on the spot. The distinctive habits and "exclusive American character" of states other than the Old Dominion, he feared, were fading into a uniform insipidity through an assimilation of "foreign usages"; disappearing were those "homebred customs" which "strengthen local attachments and expand them into a love of country."[4]

Though Benjamin Drake preferred the term "region" to "nationalism" or "section," an expectation of somewhat greater sectional autonomy appears in his plea to the alumni of Miami University in 1831 for "co-operation in weaving the coronal of Backwood's literature." The region is as yet unexplored by the native writer, said Drake, as he enumerated the aboriginal, the natural, and the social themes which might well form the literary character of the Mississippi Valley and render it distinct from "the lighter and more superficial productions of other regions. . . . Instead of transmontane sentiments and opinions, without discrimination, to be moulded to the circumstances of this valley, our literature should be the result of the political, moral, and physical condition of things by which we are surrounded."[5] The title of his brother Daniel's address two years later at Transylvania, "Remarks on the Importance of Promoting Literary and Social Concert, in the Valley of the Mississippi, as a Means of Elevating its Character, and Perpetuating the Union," was apparently intended to forestall possible charges from some of the members of the Literary Convention of Kentucky that he might encourage a sectional literature which would subserve a Western confederacy inimical to the Union. Regarding the Western States (including western Pennsylvania and western Virginia) as geographically and economically and hence culturally bound together in an organic region and at the same time as the "cement of future adhesion among all the states," Drake insisted that this West could best serve the Union by becoming "united with itself." These states were a "natural confederacy" which should achieve unity in "social feeling, literary

[4] Timothy Flint, *Western Monthly*, Vol. II (June, 1828), 10, 12, 13; John P. Kennedy, *Swallow Barn* (New York, 1851), 8–9.

[5] Benjamin Drake, "An Address . . . September 27, 1831" (Cincinnati, 1831), 7, 11, 14.

institutions, and manners and customs"; they were to become a "brotherhood," a "literary and social communion, like that which New England presents"; they were to amalgamate all, including European immigrants, "into one social compound." Toward this end, concluded Drake, "we should foster western genius, encourage western writers, patronize western publishers, augment the number of western readers, and create a western heart." When this is done, he argued, "the union will be secure, for its centre will be sound." Despite the references to the political weight of the West, Drake's conception of a homogeneous society "connected by nature in the great valley" is more fundamentally akin to the organic principles of modern regionalism than to a divisive sectionalism. Certainly most spokesmen for literary regionalism today would renounce little of the literary program which his "confederacy" involved.[6]

In the South, Daniel Whitaker was of similar mind. As one of the most consistent editorial spokesmen for a literature which should "breathe a Southern spirit, and sustain a strictly Southern character," he thought of Southerners as a people. Yet Whitaker was aware that even the most distinctive literature of this people must inevitably involve characteristics common to the larger circle of all works in English. The Southern author, he contended, however, could not write genuine American literature except by writing Southern literature; by selecting, "as far as practicable, . . . topics of a local character, bearing directly upon the customs, peculiarities, and general tone of thinking, which prevail in this section of the country." Like Kennedy and the Drakes, he was eager in the decade of the eighteen-thirties to demonstrate the compatibility of sectional expression with the more inclusive interests of the country, with the American idea, and with an American literature. Hence his conclusion:

> But in a country so extensive as ours . . . diverse laws and customs—different pursuits and variety of opinions resulting from these pursuits—inequalities of climate, producing corresponding developments of genius and character—will and do . . . affect the intellectual character of a people, and give a peculiar tone to its literature. To this extent, and to this extent only, will the literature of the South partake of striking and original features.[7]

6 Daniel Drake, "Remarks on . . . Literary and Social Concert" (Louisville, 1833), 16–19, 25, 26.

7 Daniel K. Whitaker, *Southern Literary Journal*, Vol. I (September, 1835), 58.

It is not surprising that Whitaker as editor of the *Southern Rose* reprinted the sardonic remarks of the Charleston *Mercury* on "this twaddle about literary prospects founded on the quantity of 'dirty acres' that we [Americans] possess." For the *Mercury*, like Whitaker, was convinced that "when we do create an original literature, it will not be general but sectional in its character; . . . [and] far from embodying the universal characteristics either of our country or its inhabitants, it will spring up in nooks and corners, deriving its power and worth from its being characteristic, not of the nation, but of its own circumscribed home."[8] The national literature, reiterated the *Magnolia* in 1841, is like the bow of the covenant, and the South, like other sections, must contribute its distinctive shade toward the perfection of the whole. Since the arrangement of society, the productions of the soil, the climate, and hereditary feelings all produce their effects on the mind, Southern literature will bear "the impress of this contrariety from the North." Yet such *"characteristics . . . do not . . .* constitute *sectional* literature, that, [*sic*] is based on prejudice," the *Magnolia* emphatically declared, proclaiming that it knew only "one common country, one common literature, built up by American labourers, upon American mind." Thus, though in critical discussion the terms "nationality" and "section" and "region" were a somewhat unfixed currency, the desideratum of sectional critics through the early eighteen-forties generally was a national literature which should be, to use the phraseology of the "new regionalists" a century later, not that of a "federation of conflicting sections but a homogeneity of varying regions."[9]

Although apologies for such a sectional literature, like sectional titles for periodicals, appeared more frequently in the South and West than in the established literary centers of the New England and Middle States, the concept of a national literature as an aggregate of complementary local, state, or sectional works was not confined to the former sections. New England, it is true, most persistently identified her own as the representative utterance of America rather than as one of several co-ordinate voices in the national harmony. Yet Margaret Fuller granted the local features of Hoosier, Sucker, and

[8] *Southern Rose,* Vol. VII (August 3, 1839), 398–99.

[9] *Magnolia,* Vol. III (November, 1841), 524; Howard **W.** Odum and Harry Estill Moore, *American Regionalism: A Cultural-Historical Approach to National Integration* (New York, 1938), 41.

Wolverine life to be "worth fixing"; and on "the lately peopled prairies" she deplored the absence of compositions founded on regional history and relevant to pioneer experience. Emerson, having besought attention for the "meal in the firkin; the milk in the pan," applauded Downing and Crockett. Yet pre–Civil War New England authors, despite their sectional consciousness, referred seldom to a New England literature. They were interested rather in glimpsing the oversoul in any object or in creating an American literature through any native media. Hence Whittier's disparagement of his early *Legends of New England;* hence Hawthorne's declaration that *The House of the Seven Gables* did not pretend to "describe local manners," that it had much more to do "with the clouds over head than with any portion of the actual soil of the County of Essex."[10]

Although the *Knickerbocker* deplored certain aspects of sectional literature, especially the Western and Southern tendency to puff works of local origin, the New York writers were generally disposed to accept a regional substructure in the erection of a national literature.[11] The early Knickerbockers had zealously explored and assessed the literary veins in the Hudson River region, though they did not wage a campaign, as later regionalists might have done, for a New York or Middle States literature. It was in the spirit of the early Knickerbockers, therefore, that at mid-century the influential New York *Literary World* declared editorially that to be "sectional . . . in an American writer of fiction is undoubtedly a merit. For in our extended country, it would be next to impossible for a writer to identify himself with the individualities of the different quarters." The time would come, the *World* prophesied, when not only the "sections" such as the Hudson, the Mississippi Valley, and the "storied rocks of New England" would have been portrayed; "every State, as well . . . , will have found its peculiar painter and historian."[12]

As the prophecy of the *World* implied, the ante-bellum conception of varied indigenous literatures was by no means an adjunct of a divisive sectionalism. Hence as new organic cultural regions emerged from the traditional sectional entities, each became ambitious for

[10] Margaret Fuller, *Papers on Literature and Art* (New York, 1846), I, 105; II, 130; Ralph Waldo Emerson, *Works*, Riverside ed., I, 111; Hawthorne, *Works*, III, 15–16.
[11] *Knickerbocker*, Vol. XVIII (November, 1841), 461–62.
[12] *Literary World*, Vol. II (October 23, 1847), 282.

characteristic literary utterance. From the older South, Alexander Meek, a frequent spokesman for both an American and a Southern literature, detached the early Southwest (Alabama, Mississippi, and Louisiana) and proffered a "humble guide-book" to this "almost un-cultured territory in which the Historian, the Novelist, and the Poet may find the richest incentive for the highest exercise of their respective vocations." Resentful of the anthologists' neglect of this "far South-West," the *Magnolia,* in the early eighteen-forties, also proclaimed the region to be "prolific in incentives to high intellectual effort" and its scenes and temper to be worthy of literary treatment. Like the Southwest, in the eighteen-fifties the Far West was becoming conscious of its distinctive themes and character, and after mid-century a Pacific literature evolved as the proud complement of a Western literature.[13]

Thus throughout the eighteen-thirties and forties, a considerable body of critical thought was devoted not only to the nurture of sectional literature but also to the reconciliation of sectionalism and nationalism in American letters. Perhaps no single figure bespoke more consistently the inclusive ideal than Simms. Declaring his criticism as "national" as his poetry and fiction, the *Literary World* in 1847 pronounced him "truly American." A characterless work cannot be national, Simms argued, and the channel to nationality is through the sections: "If we do not make *our* work national, it will be because we shall fail in making it *sectional.*" There had never been, nor could there be, he said, a national literature "not made up of the literature of distinct sections." Though Whitaker had analogized sectional distinction in the national literature by the colors of the bow of the covenant, Simms, like Hayne, preferred to think of a "republic of letters" in which each section would have its representative. An American author could scarcely be expected to escape one of the strongest impelling forces of the human mind, the *genius loci,* he concluded; and the "let alone" principle of the national democracy seemed to him properly to encourage both the individual and the sectional elements which would lend the requisite imprint of originality to American works.[14]

13 A. B. Meek, *Romantic Passages in Southwestern History* (New York, 1857), *iv;* *Magnolia,* Vol. II, N.S. (June, 1843), 357, 359.

14 *Literary World,* Vol. II (October 23, 1847), 282; [William Gilmore Simms], *Magnolia,* Vol. IV (April, 1842), 251–52 (Though the article is unsigned, previous editorial

From W. T. Coggeshall, Western anthologist and Ohio state librarian, however, came equally comprehensive pronouncements regarding the varied hues and richer flavor which sectional consciousness would nurture in the national letters. In his decision to discourse at Ohio University in 1858 on "The Social and Moral Advantages of the Cultivation of Local Literature," Coggeshall disclaimed any fear of "an imputation of 'sectionalism,' " for it seemed axiomatic to him that any literature which lived, represented "the spirit of a people" and in "that sense it must be 'sectional,' or local; in a word, native." Like Simms and Hayne, he contended that within a nation which has widely varying characteristics "a Republic of Letters may be a confederacy of individualities." A genuine local literature, he concluded, however, was threatened both by colonial-mindedness and by exploitation of sensational elements in the area; hence he protested against the identification of Western literature with tomahawks, bear-hunting, bandits, and the like; and he denounced the "servile dependence on the Atlantic States" which undervalued home productions. The poetry and romance peculiarly inherent in the traditions, settlement, and natural advantages of the West seemed to him not yet sufficiently to have animated the literature of the section; the epic, the lyric, and the pastoral which reposed in Western legend and scene had remained unsung.[15]

As mid-century approached, despite the pervasive tendency to resolve the sectional principle in literature into a national asset, despite the large fund of politically innocuous themes which the sectionalists espoused, sectional literature inevitably became divisive. For a genuine sectional (like a national or regional) literature, as Simms remarked, "asserts the character of its people, speaks to their wants and represents their honorable interests"; it reflects social sympathies, moral hues, and political temper.[16] So long as the moral principles are generalized in historical fiction or didactic poem, so long as the sectional character is embodied in symbol or in romance or in realistic depiction of manners, sectional literature becomes only

---

announcements, style, and points of view all indicate Simms's authorship.); *Views and Reviews* (New York, 1845), I, 17–19; Paul Hamilton Hayne, *Russell's Magazine*, Vol. III (April, 1858), 78–79.

[15] W. T. Coggeshall, "The Protective Policy in Literature" (Columbus, 1859), [3], 4, 9–10, 17, 28.

[16] [Simms], *Magnolia*, Vol. IV (April, 1842), 251; *Views and Reviews*, I, 19.

potentially—but not actively—an antinational force. When the culture of an area involves the doctrine of either economic or moral domination, however, then the organic literature of that people must enhance the principle and accelerate its political embodiment. And at such times, as Simms recognized, sectional literature ceases to be merely a complementary color in the spectrum of a national literature; it becomes a counterweight in the scale of sectional interests.

"We are quite sure that, ere long, there will be two schools of literature divided by this river [the Potomac]," wrote N. P. Willis in 1835, "as different from each other . . . as that of England from that of France." Within a few years Southern editors were beginning to demand a literature of their own to counteract the "smuggled literature" which was slipping into Southern firesides from the "incendiary madmen" across the Potomac; Lowell's *Biglow Papers* and Whittier's "Massachusetts to Virginia" were proclaiming the moral superiority of the New England character and society; Coggeshall was reminding Western authors that since their central valley was the "heart of the Republic," they had "a new opportunity" to "give tone to the entire system." As sectional principles intensified into sectional issues and ultimately found political implementation, editorial policies of magazines were inevitably colored by the bias of the section in which they were formulated. Thus the *Atlantic Monthly,* announcing itself as an "exponent of what its conductors believe to be the American idea," was by editorial intention "the new literary and anti-slavery magazine"—an intention which was readily discerned and countered in the South. In such an atmosphere the aesthetic merit of works with nonpolitical regional themes and settings could scarcely be judged objectively. Hence New York authors complained of New England discrimination, Southern authors felt themselves arbitrarily discounted by Northern publishers, and Western authors resented the snubbing of the East.[17] More dangerous to "the fine sweet spirit of nationality" than the double allegiance of state-nation is that of section-nation, warned Rufus Choate in 1858: "There is an element of regions antagonistic to nationality."[18]

[17] N. P. Willis, *Athenaeum,* No. 375 (January 3, 1835), 12; *Magnolia,* Vol. III (January, 1841), 43–45; Coggeshall, "The Protective Policy in Literature," 27. For the contentious sectionalism of the magazines, cf. F. L. Mott, *A History of American Magazines* (New York, 1930), II, 106 ff., 495 ff.

[18] Rufus Choate, *Addresses and Orations* (Boston, 1884), 489, 490, 492.

Although the hopes for a comprehensive national literature through a co-ordinate representation of the scenes and sentiments, and of the manners and legends, of the several sections were not to be fully realized before the Civil War, the pervasive concept was not unaccompanied by performance. The fact that the literary mode of the day was romantic rather than realistic (as recent regionalism has tended to be) does not invalidate the regional impulse and temper everywhere present in ante-bellum American letters. In New England, Whittier, Catharine Sedgwick, Hawthorne, and Sylvester Judd had all represented in poetry or fiction something of the natural background and the texture of life and character in Massachusetts. In New York, not only had Irving resurrected much of the latent Dutch lore of the Hudson, but also Cooper in *Satanstoe* and Paulding in *The Dutchman's Fireside* had explored pre-Revolutionary regional manners and folkways. From humorists like Seba Smith in Maine and Augustus Longstreet in Georgia had come in the eighteen-thirties a more realistic focus on contemporary habits, character, and speech—a mode which throughout the century was to pull American literature toward the earthiness of some restricted scene. In Virginia, George Tucker's *The Valley of the Shenandoah* (1824) and Kennedy's *Swallow Barn* (1832) had comprehended much of the detail and spirit of agrarian Virginia, and W. A. Caruthers' *The Cavaliers of Virginia* (1834) had inaugurated a century of romances in which Virginian authors unabashedly paid tribute to a proud code. Farther south, Simms invoked the muse of local history to portray much of the Carolinian past; but he also took more realistic account of frontier material in the tales of *The Wigwam and the Cabin* (1845) and in a version of the famous Kentucky tragedy, *Beauchampe* (1842). And in the "Southwest," J. B. Cobb, contending that his little town of Columbus was "a miniature of the world," followed Longstreet somewhat sedately in composing his *Mississippi Scenes* to demonstrate the wisdom of bringing "the imagination from its *wandering* flight to our own homely firesides."[19]

What is now generally characterized as regionalism in American literature was thus omnipresent in concept and practice in the generation which preceded the Civil War; and many of the literary axioms of twentieth-century regionalists, such as the view that "the

[19] J. B. Cobb, *Mississippi Scenes*, 2nd ed. (Philadelphia, 1851), 26–27, 32.

Great American Novel must be a composite of regional novels," were critical commonplaces among sectionally conscious authors a century ago.[20] The normal maturation and refinement of ante-bellum regionalism, however, not only was deflected by civil conflict but also was colored by the influx of new literary modes in the last generation of the century. Accordingly, literary regionalism entered its second phase. With the Union victory, with the reaffirmation of the American idea, with the treasonable taint which attached to sectionalism per se, the impulse toward limited and homogeneous cultural communities which had been a formative element in ante-bellum sectionalisms generally went underground and emerged as "localism." Affianced to a young and avowedly objective but confident realism, localism bred "local color."

The nostalgic re-creations of ante-bellum life in New England, South, and West would seem to discount Waldo Frank's contention that the Civil War was the "death-spasms of all the sections, of all our pasts."[21] Yet clearly American authors of the new literary generation were inclined to distrust the literary pattern designed to serve the old sectional entities; and hence they delimited their scope of reference to small and politically impotent communities. The ante-bellum utterances which had sprung from long immersion in, and loyalty to, a sectional culture (like those of Simms or Hawthorne) yielded to more detached exploitations of regional novelties for a nation which, having solidified its political unity, could apparently abandon itself to delight in its cultural diversity. A new group of Southern writers took especial care to disassociate themselves from the sectional taint. Throughout the South lie untouched and original materials, wrote Joel Chandler Harris in 1879, but the author who mines them will not care "one copper whether he is building up Southern or Northern Literature, and he will feel that his work is considerably belittled if it be claimed by either on the score of sectionalism." For to Harris the sectionalism "that is the most marked feature of our modern politics can never intrude into literature. Its intrusion is fatal, and it is this fatality that has pursued and overtaken and destroyed literary effort in the South. The truth might as well be

---

[20] Cf. the quotations of William Allen White and Oliver La Farge, in Odum and Moore, *American Regionalism*, 168, 169.

[21] Waldo Frank, *The Re-Discovery of America* (New York, 1929), 65.

told. We have no Southern literature worthy of the name, because an attempt has been made to give it the peculiarities of sectionalism rather than to impart to it the flavor of localism."[22] This attack on native materials from what he called the "artistic standpoint" Harris advocated as a literary practice for all areas of the country; but his conviction regarding its especial pertinence to the South was evidently shared by Mary Noailles Murfree (Charles Egbert Craddock), who explicitly informed Aldrich that her stories were local, that they had no political bias and no "sectional purpose to serve," that their aim was the delineation of a unique society. The expatriate movement which flourished contemporaneously was merely the obverse side of the same distrust of organic native cultures of which the old sectional literatures had been a part. The literary result of such distrust was, as Gertrude Atherton long ago observed, a "Geographical Fiction," of which the center was primarily neither plot nor passions but the exploration and exposition of a new area.[23]

The figures who dominated American literature in the closing decades of the century—Howells, Eggleston, Twain, Garland, Taylor —all propagated and in varying degrees practiced the new localism. They tended to be of James Whitcomb Riley's mind on the "proper spirit" of the American voice: it was to be a mass of disparate provincial and local utterances, with the "old classic splints . . . loosened and taken off," with "the long-cramped mental members . . . limbering at the joints . . . and striking straight out from the shoulder." For Howells this decentralization of American letters through local realism was a counterpart of the decentralization of American life; and this "growth of our literature in Americanism" he "watched . . . with intense sympathy," supposing that it would lead to a more authentic national product than would attempts to fulfill the pretentious specifications for the "great American novel" or to embody inclusive American traits. "Our very vastness forces us into provincialism of the narrowest kind," he said, and hence "only the general taste" of our literature could be uniformly American.[24] Such a

[22] Julia C. Harris (ed.), *Joel Chandler Harris, Editor and Essayist* (Chapel Hill, 1931), 45–47.

[23] E. W. Parks, *Charles Egbert Craddock* (Chapel Hill, 1941), 79; Gertrude Atherton, *Lippincott's Magazine*, Vol. L (July, 1892), 114.

[24] James Whitcomb Riley, *Letters*, ed. by William Lyon Phelps (Indianapolis, 1930), 49–51; William Dean Howells, *Literature and Life* (New York, 1902), 174–77; *Harper's*

literature, Howells supposed, needed none of that sustenance and unity supplied by the cultural homogeneity which had been impressed on the old sections by climate and topography and racial heritage.

When Hamlin Garland first visited Howells, in the eighteen-eighties, he received encouragement for the principle of veritism which was taking shape in his own mind. To be great, Garland told Howells, American literature "must be national and . . . to be national, [it] must deal with conditions peculiar to our own land and climate." Eggleston, Cable, Harris, Jewett, Wilkins, and Harte seemed to Garland to be "working (without knowing it) in accordance with . . . [this] great principle," dealing with local life which they knew best and cared for most. Garland was "strong for native art" based on the same critical principle.[25] Both the older and newer "sectional" authors like Kennedy and Stowe re-created regional life from a devotion to the "old nationalisms." The local colorists of the post–Civil War generation, like Riley and Eggleston, however, professing respect primarily for the verifiable and observable fact, even in the representation of dialect, were less concerned about reliance on, or reflection of, a pervasive regional culture. The contrast between *Swallow Barn* and *The Old Swimmin'-Hole and 'Leven More Poems* suggests the constriction which the local colorists accepted.

In assuming that the local realists were working without conscious adherence to the "great principle," however, Garland was surely in error. Harris's adherence to provincialism was explicit; and Eggleston admittedly derived his literary creed from Lowell's *Biglow Papers,* the Flemish realists, and the environmental doctrines of Taine. "I have wished to make my stories of value as a contribution to the history of civilization in America," Eggleston wrote in 1873, referring to his attempt to portray "correctly certain forms of American life and manners." Thus, conceiving the novel to be a combination of history and art, he treated what he termed "Western back-country districts" fundamentally as would a social historian of the region. Yet to free America from the "habitual imitation of that

Magazine, Vol. LXXXIII (July, 1891), 317–18; Vol. LXXXVI (December, 1892), 150–55; *Current Literature,* Vol. VIII (September, 1891), 1–3.

25 Hamlin Garland, *A Son of the Middle Border* (New York, 1928), 387; *Roadside Meetings* (New York, 1930), 32, 59.

which is foreign," Eggleston added, American writers must represent the "spirit" as well as the "forms" of American life. Through this provision for the "spirit" of native life, for "art" as well as for "history" in his fiction, he frequently succeeded, as in *The Circuit Rider,* in suggesting a regional context more comprehensive and unified than did the local colorists of the dominantly picturesque. Yet so close were his literary principles to those of Howells that his 1892 Preface to *The Hoosier Schoolmaster* might have been an addendum to *Criticism and Fiction*: "The taking up of life in this regional way has made our literature really national by the only process possible. The Federal nation has at length manifested a consciousness of the continental diversity of its forms of life. The 'great American novel' . . . is appearing in sections." [26]

Yet Eggleston's *The Hoosier Schoolmaster* was surely not "perhaps the first deliberately regional novel produced in this country," as Ferris Greenslet has supposed it to be. For if such works as Simms's many border narratives and James Hall's *The Harpe's Head* (1833) be disqualified on the score of their romantic coloring—though both writers were motivated by regional literary pride—cogent claims may be made for Harriet Beecher Stowe's *The Pearl of Orr's Island* (1862) or for Henry Ward Beecher's *Norwood; or, Village Life in New England* (1867), which not only are replete with New England local color, folkways, manners, codes, and occupations, but also are explicitly conceived to reflect those New England influences, traditions, and convictions which produced a genus, as Beecher observed, not only distinct from that of other sections but highly individualized within the area. Yet a surer claim could be made, perhaps, for a conscious regional matrix in Bayard Taylor's *The Story of Kennett* (1866). Presaging the major tenets which Howells was to submit for the development of American fiction, Taylor built his novels on the premises that "the proper province of fiction" is not "what ought to be, or might be . . . but what is"; that a "representation of 'American life'" need not be "an unmitigated glorification of the same"; and that no single work can "contain every feature of that complex national being, which a thousand volumes could not exhaust." Specifically, in *The Story of Kennett* Taylor proposed not only to repre-

[26] Edward Eggleston, *The Mystery of Metropolisville* (New York, 1873), Preface; *The Hoosier Schoolmaster* (New York, 1892), Prefaces to 1st and Library eds.

sent the "elements of life in a simple, healthy, pastoral community" in Pennsylvania—elements which he, like the local colorists, acknowledged to be "incorrect of American life, in its broader sense" but nevertheless "locally true"—but also to copy the pastoral landscape "field for field, and tree for tree" and the "common dialect" of the country as he had heard it.[27] Though the plot is laid in the past and is at times melodramatic or idyllic, so is that of *The Hoosier Schoolmaster*. Indeed, if one *raison d'être* for the genuinely regional work is that it comprehends and submits the order of a community as a point of stability amid the complicated issues of the larger world, then *The Story of Kennett,* with its substratum of Quaker faith, may have more convincing claims to legitimacy among early regional novels than *The Hoosier Schoolmaster*.

For the increasing suspicion during the last decades of the century that the local-color version of regionalism lacked conceptual unity and imaginative range, the proponents of the mode had a stock answer: human nature is everywhere the same, and the faithful portrayal of an obscure provincial contains the universal story. Conceiving literature as operative on a plane of intelligence more refined than that of the political life of the nation, the local colorists in the main preferred the detachment of generalized principle and sentiment allowed by the remote and the picturesque, and thus they avoided confronting those controversial themes which adherence to an inclusive national or a sectional literature would have involved. Though professed realists, the local colorists, ironically, supplied for most of their readers a romantic respite in the Great Smokies, or in a pioneer village, or in a Maine fishing port. In a nation where political issues had recently bred costly strife, the natural inclination was to find the universal in the innocuously provincial. Even Lowell, who had so conspicuously employed his poetry in behalf of the American idea as he conceived it, soon after the Civil War argued that, since democracy is too abstract an influence for literary treatment and inspiration, the "novel aspects of our life under our novel conditions may give some freshness of color to our literature." Yet though literature uses the life immediately at hand, said Lowell, its

27 Ferris Greenslet, *Under the Bridge* (Boston, 1943), 36; Henry Ward Beecher, *Norwood* (New York, 1868), 1–2; Bayard Taylor, *John Godfrey's Fortunes* (New York, 1864), *iii–iv; The Story of Kennett* (New York, 1894), *iv–v.*

unity is "infinitely distant"; its theme, as was Dante's, is Man; and the difference of angle at which life is seen in Minnesota and in India is "almost inappreciable."[28]

This union of novelty and universality, this doctrine of an "artistic literature, the only literature possible under our modern conditions," became a reiterated note in the critical apologies of the local realists. No other place affords better opportunities than Atchison, Kansas, for knowing life, wrote Edgar W. Howe, for this or any town in America contains in its local history those strange incidents which have their peculiar counterparts in Tolstoy or Daudet: "The human story is much alike in every clime and every age." Among his rural neighbors Harris detected "the human nature that underlies all types of life" and that makes Mrs. Poyser as common to Georgia as to New England. In New Orleans, Lafcadio Hearn agreed with Harris that American authors would find "the natural blossoms of human life" amid the "wild plants" of the common people rather than in the "hothouse growth of fashionable intellectuality." In the Far West, Millicent Shinn, editing the *Overland Monthly,* perceived the development of an "American school" of fiction in the serious artistry with which a new group of native authors studied human nature by its differences but thereby enticed the reader to find the common humanity beneath; and Bret Harte, in his later years reflecting on the design of his early stories, supposed that he had attempted to exhibit not only the novel incidents and settings of California but also the universality of his characters' problems. From the Midwest, Garland, admitting the local colorists' concern with social differentiations, believed nevertheless that Americans were coming to see "that something heroic is not incompatible with flippancy and vulgarity, and that a local scene or character if painted faithfully becomes universal"; and Eggleston, defending the usefulness of correct delineations of temporary and specific manifestations of American life and manners, remarked also the need to be true to human nature in its permanent and essential qualities. Among the Eastern critics, Howells, more cognizant of the climate of national opinion out of which the trend toward narrow constriction in literature had grown, acutely observed that the American

[28] James Russell Lowell, *Works,* Standard ed. (Boston, 1899), II, 148–52.

novelist sought "the universal in the individual rather than the social interest."[29]

The vogue of local color, with its tendency to insulate literature from the dominant social currents of the national life, could not of course entirely dispel the sectional interests, traditions, and attitudes which had gradually coalesced before the Civil War. In the South, older writers like Hayne and Cooke persisted in aligning Southern literature with the ante-bellum character of the South; and Thomas Nelson Page allowed this same character to shine blatantly through his local-color surfaces. In the eighteen-eighties, Midwestern authors, romantic as well as realistic, by forming "The Western Association of Writers" recognized the common interests and points of view which continued to give cultural cohesion to the Ohio Valley. Annually for twenty years the association met to further its aim of stimulating an indigenous regional literature free from domination of Eastern critics and from the stamp of the Eastern mind.[30] The term "sectional" indeed lingered in the vocabulary of critics like Stedman and Scudder; and frequent references of lesser critics to such qualities as the *must* which is the keynote of Southern novels and the *ought* which pervades New England fiction betray the impact which the old sectional cultures had made on the national mind. American literature, according to such sectional-minded critics, would be stronger if it were a composite, not of the infinite diversities of localism, but of the virility of the North, the audacity of the West, the breeziness of the Pacific, and the languid sensitiveness of the South.[31]

The local-color version of American regional literature was thus largely a corollary of what Howells called the centrifugal forces at work in American life during the generation after the Civil War. The power and stability which the Union victory had conferred

29 E. W. Howe, *Plain People* (New York, 1929), 184–85; Joel Chandler Harris, *Life and Letters* (Boston and New York, 1918), 204–205; Lafcadio Hearn, *Editorials*, ed. by C. W. Hutson (Boston, 1926), 149; [M. Shinn], *Overland Monthly*, Vol. I, N.S. (April, 1883), 431; Bret Harte, *Cornhill Magazine*, Vol. VII, N.S. (July, 1899), 8 ff.; Hamlin Garland, *Literary News*, Vol. IX (August, 1888), 237; Edward Eggleston, *The Mystery of Metropolisville*, 7; William Dean Howells, *Criticism and Fiction* (New York, 1891), 128.

30 Cf. *Indiana Magazine of History*, Vol. XXIX (1933), 187 ff.; and *Critic*, Vol. VI, N.S. (October 2, 1886), 162.

31 Cf. E. C. Stedman, *Century*, Vol. XXX (May, 1885), 38 ff., and H. Scudder, *Atlantic Monthly*, Vol. LII (November, 1883), 704; Anna Dawes, *Critic*, Vol. XI, N.S. (June 5, 1889), 1; *Current Literature*, Vol. I (July, 1888), 1.

upon the political arm of the nation, as Scudder observed, created an atmosphere of national confidence which at once encouraged a fluidity in social life and permitted an infinite series of literary explorations of a society which could be diversified because its center was strong. American novelists never get beyond "bits of local and provincial painting," wrote General John W. Ames in the early eighteen-seventies, because they do not have the homogeneous, compact, and hierarchical society of the English to serve as a subject. "In a word, there is no *American* social novel because there is no *American* society," the General concluded. "And let us trust neither the one nor the other is imminent."[32]

To the climate of such opinion one may legitimately trace, perhaps, not only the emergence of local, detached themes but also the addiction to dialect and to the short story in the last decades of the century. The proponents of a national literature, from the days of Noah Webster, had often regarded an American language, distinct and standardized, as an indispensable instrument of an American culture. Sectional or racial dialect had of course been a frequent and accepted element of authentic color in the ante-bellum novel. But with Eggleston, Harris, Page, and Riley provincial diction and pronunciation were regarded as such salient ingredients of literary merit that the most painstaking effort was expended upon giving them authenticity. Such precision in dialect, said Howells, is a refreshing contribution to American literature and an evidence of a healthy decentralization. As this indulgence in diverse dialects afforded a linguistic index to the absence of a commanding national culture, so even by contemporary analysts the preference for the short story as a vehicle was attributed to the absence of a homogeneous national character. As a medium to express the diverse local units which were accepted in the aggregate as American society, the "great American novel" seemed to the local colorists irrelevant and pretentious, as the consistent tenor of their references to it shows. For the range of experience which they wished to embrace, the short tale with an abundance of dialect ordinarily seemed to suffice.[33]

[32] H. Scudder, *Atlantic Monthly*, Vol. LVII (February, 1886), 271; J. W. Ames, *Overland Monthly*, Vol. XI (December, 1873), 505.

[33] Howells, *Criticism and Fiction*, 135–38; Mariana G. Van Rensselaer, *Lippincott's Magazine*, Vol. XXIII (June, 1879), 754ff.

The decentralization of American literature over which Howells had presided, bearing its fruit in the hundreds of dialect sketches in the magazines of the eighteen-eighties and nineties, found its most comprehensive apology near the end of the century in Garland's *Crumbling Idols* (1894). Homer and Shakespeare seemed to Garland merely early milestones in a past which was "a highway of dust"; the American writer would ignore these crumbling idols, would commit himself to the doctrine of Progress, would accept the new gospel of individual expression, veritism, which held that "each locality must produce its own literary record, each special phase of life utter its own voice." Like Eggleston, Garland valued literature as the record of social change and supposed the vitality of even Homer and Horace to lie in their ability to catch "the differentiating element," to paint those unique surfaces which in turn belong to each epoch and locality. "Local color is the royal robe," he concluded; and since each age is its own best interpreter, it need never "express fundamentals, but [rather] . . . its own minute and characteristic interpretation of life." Yet for all his effort to evoke in America local literatures which would catch the "little different angle" at which the "sun of truth strikes each part of the earth," for all his conviction that the word "difference" held the promise of future art, Garland was forced to admit that within large cities and within limited areas there were common experiences and habits which would issue in regional literatures. Writers of New England, the South, the Middle West, and the Pacific Coast, he said, would fasten on the "subtle differences" presented by the life of their own decade and area. Through such literary pluralism, Garland was confident, each section would be delivered from the dogmas of the past and from the domination of the East; each region would have in the spontaneous reflection of its life a literature which would touch its inhabitants more deeply than would the "sinking" Shakespeare; and thus and thus only would a democratic American literature be born.[34]

Across the country Garland saw a partial fulfillment of his prescription for a fresh national literature, though not always with the implications of progress which he equated with a changing society.

[34] Hamlin Garland, *Crumbling Idols* (Chicago, 1894), 22, 54, 57, 62, 77, 147–51, 167–68, 188; *Forum*, Vol. XVI (October, 1893), 166.

In New England, from the pens of Rose Terry Cooke, Sarah Orne Jewett, and Mary E. Wilkins Freeman, was accruing an account of a region where poverty and disease afflicted the tenements of industrial cities and where a gentle melancholy or repressive pride marked a declining rural culture. In the Southern highlands, the picturesqueness of dialect could not entirely allay the bleakness which formed the substratum of the stories of Craddock and Harris. And in the Midwest, Howe's *The Story of a Country Town* (1883) and H. B. Fuller's *The Cliff-Dwellers* (1893) gave respectively to the plains and to Chicago the same veracious treatment which Garland in *Main-Traveled Roads* had applied to the farm life of the Middle Border. Nor was Garland's the only major voice, at the turn of the century, which continued to espouse the focus on a delimited region. H. B. Fuller, impressed by the "noble background" of Wisconsin, urged Garland to "do for this country what Thomas Hardy has done for Wessex." Riley admonished aspiring Indiana authors to be "positively veracious" in their use of dialect and to write down "Jes' as they air—in Country and in Town"—the Hoosier poems which lie about as thick as hoptoads when it rains. Adherence to such local realism seemed to Howells to have made Riley "a very great artist," one who afforded "a more entire liberation to our native genius than we have yet realized," one "who could have come in no other time or place than ours." In turn, however, Howells acclaimed as first among the Midwestern poets the Kentuckian, Madison Cawein, because his local pieces dealing with feuds and with the Klan and his faithful portraiture of Midwestern landscape showed him to be "deeply rooted in the life of the region."[35]

Many of the writers whom Garland applauded as local colorists, however, acknowledged a literary impulse deeper than the desire to record the social problems of a region. Like Sarah Orne Jewett, they were disturbed rather than heartened by the passing of "certain phases of provincial life"—disturbed as Stowe and Kennedy and Richard Malcolm Johnston had been in previous decades. As tributes to the distinction and integrity of a tradition of regional character,

---

[35] Hamlin Garland, *A Daughter of the Middle Border* (New York, 1921), 208–209; Riley, *Letters*, 178–80; William Dean Howells, *North American Review*, Vol. CLXVIII (May, 1899), 588; William Dean Howells' Foreword to Madison Cawein, *Poems* (New York, 1911).

stories like Jewett's "The Gray Mills of Farley" were focused on the continuity of "fundamentals" which Garland disparaged rather than on the sociological change which he considered the veritist's proper theme. In a country which is too large to be expressed, said Norman Hapgood in the late eighteen-nineties, the American author may most readily attain greatness by being a part of a culture which has its roots in the soil: "He talks about the simple, universal subjects, and his environment is given inevitably, without conscious effort, in every line he writes." With this experienced regionalism as opposed to an applied and self-conscious local color, Mark Twain concurrently aligned himself. No native novelist is competent to "generalize the Nation," he said; and since an author's whole capital is the "slow accumulation of *unc*onscious observation—absorption"—he becomes merely another superficial foreign observer "when he steps from the State whose life is familiar to him." At the turn of the century, upon richer historical bases than veritism allowed, Ellen Glasgow, too, was inaugurating her comprehensive portrayal of Virginia life, as she later declared, not as a disciple of local color but in revolt against it. For "literature, like life, must spring from roots," she believed, and her interest was in "the enduring fibre of human nature" as she observed it in the life about her rather than in "the superficial picturesqueness of local color." And in the Far West, though agreeing with the local colorists that America is a union but not a unit and hence that it "is only possible to make a picture of a single locality," Frank Norris nevertheless renounced as culturally incidental the "'red shirt' literature of western life," and in *The Octopus* and *McTeague* sought rather to comprehend something of the deeper "idiosyncrasy" of his region, something of the "play of unleashed, unfettered passionate humanity" in the peculiar economic and social atmosphere of the Far West.[36]

Thus, a generation before the advent of the new regionalism of the nineteen-twenties, the regional current in American letters en-

[36] Cf. Sarah Orne Jewett's 1893 Preface to *Deephaven* (Boston and New York, 1894); Norman Hapgood, "Home Culture for Americans," *New England Magazine,* Vol. XIII, N.S. (February, 1896), 725–26; Samuel Langhorne Clemens, "What Paul Bourget Thinks of Us," in *How to Tell a Story* (New York, 1897), 187–88; Ellen Glasgow, *A Certain Measure* (New York, 1943), 48, 67; Frank Norris, "Two Uncollected Essays," *American Literature,* Vol. VIII (May, 1936), 190–98, and *The Responsibilities of the Novelist* (New York, 1903), 87.

tered a third phase: there developed the awareness that America was "tremendously sectional even yet," to use Norris's phrase, and that an American literature must evolve from a more substantial immersion in the experience and culture of the several areas than local color or veritism had encouraged. Yet local color would seem to be not so much a prelude to literary regionalism as a mode of embodying regional diversity, which, in the generation following the Civil War, was weighed and found wanting. The marked reversion to the romantic at the turn of the century did not signalize an impulse to escape the contemporary, but to understand and order it in terms of a central and durable tradition, in terms of a "usable past." Discontent with surfaces, as Norris confessed, regionally conscious American writers felt impelled to seek a fictional "truth" other than reportorial accuracy. Mary Johnston, Hopkinson Smith, and Ellen Glasgow in Virginia, James Lane Allen in Kentucky, Maurice Thompson and Booth Tarkington in Indiana, and Frank Norris and Gertrude Atherton in California were all attempting, with varying degrees of skill and insight, to present the substrata of regional character or the substructure of regional history which lay below the eccentricities of dialect and manners. Nor was aboriginal influence ignored. The *genius loci* of the Great Lakes region was enriched by the Indian tales and legends recounted by Mary Hartwell Catherwood. And in Maine, Charles Godfrey Leland, who in the early eighteen-sixties in *Sunshine in Thought* had been an evangel of rootless objective realism, now attempted to supply the one deficiency in the "sweet charm . . . which haunts the hills and valleys of rural New England"— those "ties of tradition or folk-lore" which permit the writer to feel "'heart-intimate' with the scenery." Thus considerably earlier than Mary Austin's efforts to infuse the rhythms of the Navajo into an Amerindian art in the Southwest, Leland was seeking to derive "Amerindian metres" from the "Algonkin" dialects and was urging instruction in Indian languages and traditions at the universities so that Americans might achieve that accord with their land which centuries of aboriginal life had wrought and which aboriginal poetry and mythology had expressed.[37]

The counterromanticism at the end of the century did not, therefore, signify an abandonment of the regional attack on Ameri-

[37] Norris, *The Responsibilities of the Novelist*, 215, 220–22; C. G. Leland, *Kulóskap the Master* (New York and London, 1902), 14–18.

can materials; it rather sought a more comprehensive strategy. In the early eighteen-nineties the dominating figure in the Western Association of Writers, Maurice Thompson, counted it no treason to the literary independence and utterance of the West when he charged Garland's veritism with fostering "blood-raw vulgarity done up in 'dialect'"; and perhaps he only pointed to Garland's inevitable and imminent disillusion with the barrenness of veritism when he asked, "What light is verity seen by? . . . What shirt sleeve bumpkin, proud of his illiteracy, will ever sing the true song of the plow?" Only "hothouse metropolitan critics" could suppose that Riley's representation of "Hoosier civilization" is realistic, Thompson pertinently observed; for it was Riley, he contended, who was in effect a romancer—a romancer in picturesque language.[38]

By the mid-nineties, Garland's zealous efforts to nurture indigenous compositions were largely supererogatory. As Edward Everett Hale, Jr., observed, the writing of local stories had become "as natural as the whooping cough," and thousands were being spawned for every servile attempt at a blank-verse tragedy. The real issue for American authors was no longer the validity of provincial materials or the benefit that derived from the use of one's own experience, as both Hale and the *Atlantic* observed. The demurrer of the romanticists was that verbal photography does not constitute the sum of literature. Hence confirmed devotees of regional materials, like Cable and Kate Chopin, insisted not so much on renouncing veritism as on pushing beyond it. The "field" cannot save the American author, concluded Cable at fifty; he must find amid the human passions "the universal self." The reflection of social problems and local color are not sufficient motives to insure literary survival, wrote Kate Chopin in criticism of *Crumbling Idols;* human impulses do not change. To John Burroughs, too, Garland seemed to have erred "a little in thinking this honey will be better than any ever made before." The bee's product is honey and not mere nectar, he reminded the veritists; and just as honey from Florida and California and Michigan will possess distinctive flavors derived from the locale, so every literature will bear the unique impress of the "facts of race, of country, of time, of conditions." Yet into this fund of historical fact the writer must secrete the formic acid of his imagination, Burroughs

[38] Maurice Thompson, *Independent,* Vol. XLV (October 12, 1893), 1361; Vol. XLVI (March 29, 1894), 391; Vol. XLVII (May 9, 1895), 616.

contended, if the product is to be more than the nectar of barren realism. In Burroughs' metaphor the romantic addendum to local color was comprehended.[39]

Although this counterromanticism at the end of the century affected regional writing by expanding its sensitivity beyond sociological veritism, it did not therefore necessarily debilitate the regional impulse. It extended regionalism vertically, as it were; it did not so diffuse it horizontally as to dissolve it. It supplanted the mode of Edward Eggleston with that of his brother, George Cary, who in such novels as *Two Gentlemen of Virginia* and *The Warrens of Virginia* avowedly attempted a faithful picture of life in the region but eschewed phonetic representation of old Virginia speech as both futile and foolish. The opposition to the regional literary emphasis came rather from traditionalists, who insisted that American letters must be disciplined by European literary experience, and from nationalists, who insisted that America's young literature needed to be impregnated by the confident vigor of the whole national development. "The effect of physical-geographical environment on literary production is mostly nil," wrote Ambrose Bierce in contempt of Garland's "corn-fed enthusiasm" for a new Western literature; "racial and educational considerations only are of controlling importance." A distinctively Western literature could only be "distinctively illiterate," Bierce argued; and a "writer who knows no better than to make or try to make his work 'racy of the soil' knows nothing of his art worth knowing." Whereas Cable concluded that a writer's "field" could not "save" him, Bierce went further to affirm that the field was unimportant and the manner was everything. The "New Movement" in American letters under Riley seemed to him to have become the Dominion of Dirt, in which the Muse was threatened with the humiliating embrace of yokels who filed their teeth with their tongues. The "somnolent nigger" and "clay-eating cracker," uninteresting to Bierce in life, became no more interesting to him in the "Reporter School" of fiction.[40]

[39] Edward Everett Hale, Jr., *Dial*, Vol. XVII (June 1, 1894), 12; *Atlantic*, Vol. LXXVI (December, 1895), 840–44; George Washington Cable, *North American Review*, Vol. CLVIII (January, 1894), 22; Kate Chopin, quoted in D. S. Rankin's *Kate Chopin* (Philadelphia, 1932), 141–44; John Burroughs, *Dial*, Vol. XIX (November 1, 1895), 239–40.

[40] George Cary Eggleston, *Two Gentlemen of Virginia* (Boston, 1908), Preface; *The*

As the end of the century approached, however, the local and regional literary focus was subjected to intense distrust, more from a renascent national spirit than from a traditionally disciplined taste in authors like Bierce. By the mid-nineties Theodore Roosevelt was already remarking both the dangers to national unity inherent in an "unwholesome parochial spirit" in the arts and also "the futility of talking of a Northern literature or a Southern literature, or an Eastern or a Western school of art." Nor in a "full and ripe literary development in the United States," Roosevelt observed, is the location of literary centers of any consequence. That Howells' and Garland's doctrine of decentralization of the arts had, in the course of a generation, acted as a retarding influence in America's growth toward a homogeneous and distinctive New World character, became the conviction of many men of letters as well as men of affairs. In the *Atlantic,* Paul Leicester Ford, whose carefully wrought *Janice Meredith* exemplified the renascent interest in national history, protested American writers' preoccupation with the particles of the river bed to the neglect of the great veins of national gold. And in the *Century,* the popular Emerson Hough, convinced of America's great mission, lamented that the great wave of nationalism had not extended into literature and overwhelmed that literary "sectionalism which shows upon the one side superficiality and superciliousness, upon the other resentment and suspicion." Even regionalists like James Lane Allen admitted the need of a more inclusive literature to supplement what he regarded as the indispensable genre pictures of Negroes and Creoles and other variant types in the common life of America. This larger desideratum in American letters at the turn of the century, Allen contended, was the delineation of the "utmost embodied excellence of our social institutions," the Anglo-Saxon gentleman of the New World. The sum of regional literatures did not seem to him to have reflected the national genius: "The largest creations of our national art are less than the realities of our national experience."[41]

Warrens of Virginia (New York, 1908), Preface; Ambrose Bierce, *Collected Works* (New York and Washington, 1911), X, 41, 42, 44, 63, 242; XI, 174, 176, 178, 182–83.

[41] Theodore Roosevelt, *Forum,* Vol. XVII (April, 1894), 198–99; Paul Leicester Ford, *Atlantic Monthly,* Vol. LXXX (December, 1897), 728; Emerson Hough, *Century,* Vol. LIX (February, 1900), 506–507; James Lane Allen, *Bookman,* Vol. IV (October, 1896), 119–21.

When, after the confused and impotent first decade of the century, the veins of both local color and nationalistic romance had proved their thinness, American literature around 1912 manifested the strength of a second renascence; but this one was not sustained by the regional consciousness so indubitably as had been that of the preceding generation. Sometimes under the stimulus of European literary modes and masters, sometimes in despair over the barrenness of an increasingly mechanized society, American authors fled to Europe or to the soil; but they did not at first tend to identify themselves with, or to suppose their strength derived from, regional culture. Until the middle nineteen-twenties, the writer or critic who had become disillusioned with metropolis or cosmopolis generally staked his new faith in the locale or the village; in his vocabulary appeared the term "local" rather than "sectional" or "regional," though mere local color had clearly had its day. His interest in the local became transcendental rather than realistic: like Emerson, through the meal in the firkin and the milk in the pan, he did not care to paint rural manners so much as to glimpse universal truth. Harold Stearns, envisioning a national drama, wrote of the blending of mind and soil which comes from "years of loving localism" and bespoke for American writers the "courage to grasp the nettle of our own life." William Carlos Williams, encouraged by the Maine poems of Wallace Gould and confident that "a man can be a poet anywhere under any circumstances," advised other writers to use the land at their feet. "From the shapes of men's lives imparted by the places where they have experience, good writing comes," wrote Williams in the nineteen-twenties. "One has to learn what the meaning of the local is, for universal purposes. The local is the only thing that is universal." No doubt Dreiser, too, was expressing agreement with such a principle when, in the latter part of *The Genius*, he had a French critic find one of the signs of immaturity in American art to be the omission of that "sense of the universe in miniature." Thus, in its fourth phase, American regionalism narrowed into the channel of a "loving localism." [42]

In the decade of World War I, therefore, the regional shone for

[42] H. Stearns, *Seven Arts*, Vol. I (March, 1917), 519, 521; W. C. Williams, *A Novelette and Other Prose (1921–31)* (Toulon, 1932), 117; Theodore Dreiser, *The Genius* (Garden City, New York, 1923), 226.

the most part through the local. That at times the local adumbrated the cultural pattern of a state or a cluster of states, such works as Anderson's *Winesburg, Ohio* or Frost's *North of Boston* or Zona Gale's *Miss Lulu Bett* are all reminders. Yet the first thought seems to have been to establish roots rather than to flower into comprehensive regional expression. John Dos Passos in 1916 remarked America's loss, due to an all-enveloping industrialism, of the "earth-feeling, the jewelled accretions of the imagination of succeeding ages," which in older literatures had served as a woof on which "individual artists may work the warp of their own thoughts." Contemporaneously, Waldo Frank railed at those importers of foreign dramatic modes who never seemed to "learn the need of roots" in American life. And even the cosmopolitan critic James Huneker concluded that the American novelist would be cosmopolitan at his own risk, that if he "cuts loose his balloon he is in danger of not getting home again." By 1925 the anthologist W. S. Braithwaite, after more than a decade of assessing the luxuriant growth of American poetry, in retrospect could properly observe that localism had been the dominant motivating spirit of the twentieth-century renascence. To Braithwaite this process of "absorbing local backgrounds" suggested also that the poets at least were growing more "sectionally imaginative," were finding a different "primary emotion" in each section; and yet he likewise concluded that "America is as various as her forty-eight states" in "materials, experiences, character, and temper," and that "each detail of this variety" should be "made a whole in itself, and not the fragment of a whole which can never be represented as a unit."[43]

In Braithwaite's casual identification of local and state and sectional is posed the question of whether the local is synonymous with or leads to the subregional literature of states or portions of states, to the regional literature of larger geographical and economic units, to the national character as a whole, or to the universal. The answer is probably that it allows a focus on any of these levels, but that a "loving localism" by no means insures the regional. Thus Sinclair Lewis affirmed that his *Main Street* (1920), despite its

[43] John Dos Passos, *New Republic*, Vol. VIII (October 14, 1916), 269–71; Waldo Frank, *Salvos* (New York, 1924), 98–99; James Huneker, *Unicorns* (New York, 1917), 82–84; W. S. Braithwaite, *Anthology of Magazine Verse for 1925* (Boston, 1925), x–xi.

abundant Minnesota verisimilitude, was not a regional study but rather a projection of "Main Streets everywhere"—in the Carolina hills or upstate New York—the end of a tradition of civilization chiefly to be found in small towns throughout America. In Heyward's *Porgy* (1925), on the other hand, the local dialect and relationships of Catfish Row would scarcely seem to be representatively Carolinian or Southern or national, but rather, Charlestonian. Miss Glasgow's local detail in *Barren Ground* (1925) would seem to catch characters and issues which embrace the larger area of her own state, and which perhaps reach out regionally into the whole agrarian South.

In the Midwest, Vachel Lindsay's localism, however, was not directed primarily toward either regional or national interpretation, but rather toward the universal insight. Out of the little communities, he felt, might radiate a purity of sensibility in a democratic art which would regenerate the character of the nation and, at last, that of the world. And though he judged the dispersed agrarian society of South and West to be the natural seedbed of such a redemptive literature, his "West-of-the-Mississippi, West-of-the-Alleghenies gospel," as he termed it, was pointed toward an "Art Revolution" which would place in power Artists who love Beauty and God. When Lindsay wrote of the Sante Fe Trail, he did not follow Garland's prescription of sociological veritism, but rather his own doctrine in *Adventures While Preaching the Gospel of Beauty*: "They [American artists] should, if led by the spirit, wander over the whole nation in search of the secret of democratic beauty with their hearts . . . overflowing with the righteousness of God." Proclaiming that "every State is to have its Emerson, its Whittier, its Longfellow, its Hawthorne," Lindsay bespoke for the West and South the transcendental localism of the New England Renaissance rather than a disinherited and delimited regionalism. As his ally Lindsay recognized Percy MacKaye, whom he thought also "born to evangelize the whole of America" for such community artists. And, indeed, concurrently MacKaye was attempting civic masques and folk plays to nourish a local drama, whether metropolitan or rural. These masques and plays were considered but a "foretaste of the eventful realization of the democratic ideal, when art will be made not only for the people, but also by the people." Such community drama, MacKaye believed, is "the ritual of democratic religion," and its "life-meaning . . . is universal."[44]

In this atmosphere of transcendental localism, subregional materials, such as those of *Winesburg, Ohio,* were likely to emerge as exhibitions not primarily of regional mores but of larger tendencies or deficiencies in modern Occidental men everywhere. Such works, like Hawthorne's, may legitimately be termed "regional" if the milieu rather than the basic plane of reference is the determinant of definition. "In the trade of writing the so-called new note is as old as the world," wrote Sherwood Anderson in 1914, proclaiming the right of the "new man . . . to speak out of the body and soul of youth." Indeed, Anderson's revolt was made explicitly against the Howells-Eggleston-Garland view of fiction as a kind of social history whose vitality inhered in a reflection of the idiosyncrasies of its time and place. "In all the world there is no such thing as an old sunrise, an old wind upon the cheeks," he asserted by way of protest against the writer who looks outside himself for materials. With "a feeling that the great basin of the Mississippi River . . . is one day to be the seat of the culture of the universe," Anderson, like Lindsay, tried to give a "sense of infinite things" in the commonplace Midwestern world. The same distrust of a narrowly focused and self-conscious localism was shared by another "regionalist," Stark Young, who, as editor of the *Texas Review,* charged that "reeking [of the soil] is a modern affair, conscious, heavy with journalistic sweat" and "apt to be an exploitation." The worthiest literature, he supposed, like Anderson, "reek[s] of the whole world," and the imagination most profitably dwells on that common plane which runs horizontally through Texas and Ohio and middle France. "While life strives to get out of the corner, all our critics try to push our lives back into a corner," added James Lane Allen at the end of a literary career that had been notable for fusing man and his environment in the bluegrass region of Kentucky. "Well, how many New Jersey passions have they?"[45]

Though the word "regional" infrequently occurs in the vocabu-

[44] Sinclair Lewis, *Main Street* (New York, 1920), Preface; Vachel Lindsay, *Letters . . . to A. Joseph Armstrong,* ed. by A. J. Armstrong (Waco, 1940), 30, 42, 47, 71, and *Adventures While Preaching the Gospel of Beauty* (New York, 1914), 16–17, 174–76; Percy MacKaye, *Community Drama* (Boston and New York, 1917), 7, 11, 54 ff.

[45] Sherwood Anderson, *Little Review,* Vol. I (March, 1914), 23; Vol. I (April, 1914), 16–17; Vol. VI (October, 1918), 4, 6; Stark Young, *Texas Review,* Vol. I (June, 1915), 80–81; James Lane Allen, *The Landmark* (New York, 1925), 12.

lary of the American writer in the early nineteen-twenties, Huneker's
view that America is a "chord of many nations" was in effect occasionally accepted as a valid metaphor for a condition which justified
a mild sectionalism in letters. But few authors had firm enough hold
on, or confidence in, either sections or subregions as homogeneous
cultural entities to venture to make them the controlling factor in
plot and character and atmosphere. Contrasting American cities and
sections with the long-compacted culture upon which a French or
English author might premise his work, Conrad Aiken remarked
in the early nineteen-twenties that American authors could not even
"regard a section like New England . . . as a definite environmental
factor, say 'y,' and . . . conclude . . . that any poet who matures there
will inevitably be representable as 'y p.' "[46] But young and, at the
time, obscure writers and critics already had begun in the South and
West a revaluation of American literature which was to reaffirm the
need for the man of letters to relate himself to a cultural area larger
than the village and smaller than the nation. The organic cultural
relation which the ante-bellum author had found pre-eminently in
New England, but also in the Middle States, the South, and the Ohio
Valley, was being sought in the beginnings of the "new regionalism."
Though Lindsay had preached the gospel of local art in *The Village
Magazine* (1910) and in *Vision* (1912), the little magazines in the West
in subsequent years began to extend their horizons. Harriet Monroe's
Poetry (1912———), though by no means confined to Midwestern
themes or authors, protested the literary bondage in which New
York held Chicago and condemned the long-established Chicago *Dial*
for its indifference to the intellectual life of a vast and rich region.
With more explicit intentions of giving the Midwest a voice, however, John T. Frederick launched the *Midland* in Iowa in 1915; and
in 1920, H. G. Merriam in Montana, through the *Frontier,* made a
"pioneer endeavor to gather indigenous northwest materials." In
1924 the *Southwest Review* emerged from the older *Texas Review*
to bespeak more consistently the cultural interests of a region. Moreover, national journals like the *American Mercury,* through essay
and story and poem, encouraged assessment of American literature
within the distinctive categories of the states. By the mid-twenties a

[46] Huneker, *Unicorns,* 83; Conrad Aiken, in H. Stearns (ed.), *Civilization in the
United States* (New York, 1922), 216.

new mosaic of regional bases for American literature was being designed across the land, and American writers, building though they
were on long-established foundations, felt a zestful reassurance in the
"new regionalism."[47]

The new regional consciousness to which such magazines as the
Midland were both index and stimulus was a development of localism
on which Lindsay and Sherwood Anderson seized as the surest
deliverance from an industrialized and standardized society. What
the regionalists of the late nineteen-twenties and thirties added was,
in effect, a skepticism of William Carlos Williams' doctrine of the
imaginative efficacy of the "objective immediacy of our hand to
mouth existence." Through such spokesmen as Donald Davidson
in the South and Ruth Suckow in the Midwest and Mary Austin in
the Southwest, the regionalists contended that sustenance for American letters can best be found in the values of a deep-rooted and
homogeneous culture. This cultural unity they, like Hawthorne,
could scarcely define in national terms. As the regionalists sought to
renew organic ties not only with an area of the land but with the
human values which had accrued upon it, concurrently the proletarian authors insisted that American literature must accept and
help codify an inevitable machine economy, and the expatriates, re-
volted alike by the crassness of bourgeois capitalism and by the
barrenness of the provinces, fled for a few experimental years abroad.
Indeed it is not surprising that in Paris the editor of the expatriate
magazine *transition* should remark the dangerous tendency in "cen-
tralisation . . . unless curbed by a regional consciousness," should
deplore the destruction of regional peculiarities in America, and
should declare "the indigenous . . . a catapulting force" toward the
universal.[48]

Of these three divergent but related responses to the machine in
America, only the regionalist has any commanding vitality today.
Yet the other two in a measure have augmented and colored the
current of modern regional literature. Finding foreign soil un-
congenial, many of the temporary exiles, like Allen Tate and Louis

[47] Harriet Monroe, *A Poet's Life* (New York, 1938), 314. For the influence of other
little magazines, see Frederick J. Hoffman, Charles Allen, and Carolyn Ulrich, *The
Little Magazine* (Princeton, 1946), 128–47, 260, 376.

[48] William Carlos Williams, *Contact*, Vol. I (May, 1932), 109; E. Jolas, *transition*,
No. 14 (Fall, 1928), 182.

Bromfield and John Gould Fletcher, returned to become apologists for their respective regions. On the other hand, the proletarian movement, withering on the rocky soil of ideological clichés, scattered seeds of class and racial consciousness which took root in the regional fiction of such authors as Caldwell and Steinbeck. The literary reversion to the regions, undertaken in revolt against an industrial society during the nineteen-twenties, was accentuated in the financial depression of the thirties when American writers were frequently forced back to both a cultural and a physical reliance on the land. Moreover, the depression contributed to a regional or subregional attack on American materials, through the WPA Guides, which focused attention upon the history and traditions of the separate states and gave hundreds of amateur and practiced authors who compiled the Guides an introduction to themes near at hand.

What, then, is the new literary regionalism which, gaining momentum in the late nineteen-twenties, became one of the dominant literary principles of the thirties and which, despite the national consciousness engendered by the war, remains a potent influence in the early fifties? In the first place, as Carey McWilliams has aptly observed, it is not nearly so new in theory or practice as many of its adherents suppose it to be.[49] Indeed, such judicious regionalists as Robert Penn Warren and Mary Austin have observed that a century ago in Nathaniel Hawthorne regional writers in America had a pre-eminent exemplar. Expansion of material and refinement of attack have of course increased the range and subtlety of the new regionalists. In state folklore and historical societies and in sociological studies of habits and biases of numerous areas, has accrued an assessment of American life from which modern regionalists may be expected to draw dividends of authenticity. And for the delineation of responses to regional environment, Henry James and D. H. Lawrence and Gertrude Stein, among others, have provided disciplines which have generated more sensitive perceptions than the prevailing modes of a century ago may have usually allowed. The new regionalism is indeed to be credited with gains over its antecedents; but it is a growth, not a discovery. As it has been for over a century, literary regionalism is the omnipresent and evolving

[49] Carey McWilliams, *The New Regionalism in American Literature* (Seattle, 1920), 25–26.

regional consciousness reflected through the current literary mode. When the mode is inadequate, as is local color, the total impact of regional forces is slighted; but the impulse toward regional expression is not thereby permanently impaired.

In the second place, the new regionalism is diverse in theory and practice and aim. In the older areas—the New England and the Middle Atlantic States—there is the least reliance upon organized and explicit regionalism, though the Maine stories of Mary Ellen Chase and of R. P. Tristram Coffin, the Vermont novels of Dorothy Canfield Fisher, and the upstate New York narratives of Walter Edmonds have certainly been directed toward the exposition of regional character and background. In the South, members of the erstwhile Agrarian group, such as Robert Penn Warren and Allen Tate and John Crowe Ransom and Donald Davidson, have declined to accept as definitively regional what they regard as an elementary use of local color in works like Heyward's *Porgy,* and have insisted instead on a Southern tone and style and point of view as the touchstones of Southern literature. In the Midwest, regional tendencies are apparently not co-ordinated by any such organization as the old Western Association of Writers, but the works of Walter Havighurst, August Derleth, Paul Engle, Ruth Suckow, and others reflect a temperate faith in the literary substance to be found in a realistic representation of both manners and codes in the past and the present. Next to the South, the Southwest has been the most vocal during the past two decades; and, with the *Southwest Review* and the *New Mexico Quarterly* as organs of discussion, Mary Austin, Oliver La Farge, J. Frank Dobie, Stanley Vestal, B. A. Botkin, and numerous associates have encouraged not only an exploitation of the traditionally virile aspects of the life in the region but also an absorption of rhythms and values as indigenously fashioned by centuries of Mexican and Indian experience with the land itself. To the north, the recently established *Rocky Mountain Review* has revived many of the issues of the early nationalists who tried to design a unique literature for a land with magnificent scenery but few "moral associations." And in the Northwest, periodic writers' conferences now wrestle with the same problem in that territory. Indeed, in view of the diverse stages of indigenous culture in the several areas, more accurately the new regionalism might be termed the new regionalisms.

Thus, united though they are in a common revolt against remote metropolitan dominance, the variance among the regions in racial stocks and topography and cultural maturity has issued in diverse emphases and concepts and programs of literary strategy. From the Southwest, for instance, has come the steadiest insistence on the use of folk and aboriginal materials. In editing the several volumes of a regional miscellany, *Folk-Say* (1929–32), in Oklahoma, B. A. Botkin represented folk sources as a means of recovering and sustaining not only the native character of the region but also a living speech as embodied in the oral word. He described regionalism, as contrasted with local color, as a retrospective and detached effort to derive a new American myth from the commonality of the folk. Concurrently in Texas, Samuel Asbury, who in the spirit of Vachel Lindsay had preached a community art through his *Texas Nativist* leaflets in 1914–15, insisted that a mass of deeply felt and perhaps inferior folk expression must precede the arrival of a genuine American art which will supersede the current passive culture.[50] Writers like Stedman and Howells who have tried to escape going native have in reality been expatriates working on American soil, the repatriated John Gould Fletcher has added; and the tragedy of American literature is that it has had no folk tradition, no voice of the uneducated and unsophisticated and unspoilt people to oppose the Babbitlike industrialist. To Fletcher, as to Asbury, the great American poetry will be an "end-product"—a recapitulation and assimilation and enlargement of a humbler folk expression.

Yet the hazards to literary maturity in a retrospective folk emphasis have been assessed by other regionalists and critics, such as Donald Davidson in the South, Ruth Suckow in the Midwest, and Carey McWilliams in the Far West. Such a preoccupation, Davidson fears, could lead the regionalists not only to a futile attempt to recover creatively such folk arts as the ballad but also to an ivory tower where they would decline to "confront the total and moving world." Sensitive to the same stigma of social irresponsibility with which regional literature has been branded by the proletarian critics, Miss Suckow, both through a major novel and through explicit comments, likewise has sought to turn regional writing from the folk to the

[50] Cf. B. A. Botkin, *Folk-Say* (Norman, 1929); McWilliams, *The New Regionalism*, 15–20; Samuel Asbury, *Southwest Review*, Vol. XV (Winter, 1930), 216–17.

folks—to the same sturdy norms of regional values and conduct which Whitman besought in the nation as a whole. How difficult and inconsequential are efforts of the modern author to will himself into the naïve, Carey McWilliams has observed, the Irish Renaissance should remind regionalists disposed to rely on the folk cult. Indeed, not only have many regionalists deplored excessive preoccupation with folk themes; they have also maintained that a living regional literature, unlike local color, must be inclusive enough to reflect and clarify pertinent social issues. Even John Gould Fletcher, who would allow a large reference to folk sources, has concluded that regionalism is only an enlightened kind of sectionalism in which the writer indulges in an "impure and human" activity involving the political and social interests of his region.[51]

Although one of the dominant assumptions accounting for the regional literary movement has been the unembraceable diversity of the national life, the writers who have confined themselves to the major regions have not always found the uniformly established character and manners toward which they have looked. In rural New England, time and a relatively stable racial and moral heritage have given regional authors a firm cultural context from which to work during the past century. In the South, however, the cultural leaven of a minority race has posed a more intricate problem. The Negro, though his social plight has been accorded especial attention by Caldwell and Stribling, by Lillian Smith and Richard Wright and others, has achieved something of a cultural autonomy through his folk songs; and his folklore has received sympathetic adaptation through Joel Chandler Harris and Roark Bradford. But in more sensitive and inclusive adumbrations of Southern culture, William Faulkner, without condescension and without sentimentality and without the caricature of dialect, has pictured the Negro as an integral part of an organic regional development—as a being in the process of time wrought upon inexorably by his environment but also in a measure determining it, as both the victim and partial creator of the South. But in the Southwest, the Indian and the Mexican thus far

---

51 John Gould Fletcher, *Southwest Review*, Vol. XIX (July, 1934), 429–34; Donald Davidson, *The Attack on Leviathan* (Chapel Hill, 1938), 238; *Hound and Horn*, Vol. VI (July–September, 1933), 564–65; Ruth Suckow, *The Folks* (New York, 1934), *passim*, and *Scribner's Magazine*, Vol. LXXXVIII (September, 1930), 245 ff.; McWilliams, *The New Regionalism*, 22–24.

have fared somewhat differently. Through centuries of regional experience antedating that of the people whose civilization now dominates them, they have seemed to Mary Austin to supply the cultural design of the Southwest in that they represent "the mutual adaptations of a land and a *people*." Yet, as many Southwestern regionalists admit, the dichotomy of cultures has scarcely been resolved; vigorous twentieth-century conquistadores continue to impose "derived notions of the good life upon the land." The Anglo-Spanish-Indian elements have not been culturally fused even to the degree that the Anglo-Negro elements have been synthesized in the Southeast; and though the Amerindian traits have been enumerated, classified, and extolled, they must remain largely the stuff of local color until they have ceased to become an embellishment and have become integrated into the unconscious outlook of the region. Even such sympathetic narratives as *Laughing Boy* and other Indian stories of Oliver La Farge do not convincingly ease what Dudley Winn has called the "Southwestern regional straddle."[52]

Regionalism as it is conceived and practiced by its more thoughtful exponents, one may confidently suppose, is not an evanescent enthusiasm soon to fade as a forced and premature growth in American letters. In accordance with its own principle, as it were, its roots are in native soil, and through a century of maturation it has been shaped by the mental climate and physical structure of the country. Although it has been fertilized by foreign techniques, it is not, as was the orthodox proletarian formula, a transplanted exotic. Contemporary regionalism in literature, however, has its seedbeds in the old sections, though few regional plants attained maturity in the ante-bellum era. But were Simms and Timrod and James Hall and Ellery Channing now alive, they could find the chief articles of their literary faith fulfilled in the major regionalists of their respective sections. Across the century, both groups have intended a regional expression that would transcend Garland's report of a unique locality, an expression that, as Mary Austin says, would be *of* a region, not merely *about* it.[53]

[52] Mary Austin, "Amerindian Verse," in W. S. Braithwaite's *Anthology of Magazine Verse for 1926* (Boston, 1926), 104–105; *Southwest Review,* Vol. XIV (Summer, 1929), 474–75; Dudley Winn, "The Southwestern Regional Straddle," in *Southwesterners Write* (Albuquerque, 1946), 285, 288.

[53] Mary Austin, *English Journal,* Vol. XXI (February, 1932), 106–107.

In fact, the new regionalists have generally accepted as the principle of growth in regional literature Emerson's century-old dictum: "A literature is no man's private concern, but a secular and generic result." Eager as are the writers in newer regions like the Rocky Mountain States to achieve a sensitive reflection of the unique social and physical character of their area, they do not minimize the role which they must concede to time. Nature must bite deeper into Rocky Mountain authors before they can create much more than nature myths and "westerns," Wilson O. Clough has concluded in the *Rocky Mountain Review*. The regional writer, he adds, is "one to the country born, of the second or third generation. . . . Authentic regional expression is a matter of living and of absorbing landscape and character into the unconscious."[54] Similarly, in California, Genevieve Taggard has observed that an inadequate absorption of the Pacific Coast immensities into the imagination has led Western (like other American) poets to commit the literary sin of "deliberateness." And in the South, echoing Timrod's contention nearly a century ago that a Southern literature is to be recognized by "the tone and bearings of the thought, in the drapery, the colouring," both John Crowe Ransom and Cleanth Brooks have accounted the piney woods and swamps and plantations and feuds as incidental to that Southern mentality which, born of generations and reflected in the very texture and cadence of style, will mark the authentic regionalist. Of the literary benefits conferred by such a deeply grounded regional experience in the South, the work of William Faulkner would seem an increasingly sure affirmation; for Faulkner's imagination, a sensitively organic product of the land which it reports, in its thorough embrace of the region past and present has also comprehended much of the universal, "pregnant with values," which, as Harold G. Merriam in editing the *Frontier* declared, springs from the specific fact. Such a principle, however, is as old in American literature as the New England regionalism of a century ago; for from E. T. Channing at Harvard both Emerson and Thoreau undoubtedly learned that to attain the universal mind, they must "pass through the discipline . . . of common things near at hand . . . ; of influences the most accidental."[55]

---

[54] Emerson, *Works*, XII, 260; Wilson O. Clough, *The Rocky Mountain Reader* (New York, 1946), 415–16.

[55] Genevieve Taggard, *Continent's End* (San Francisco, 1925), *xxviii–xxix;* Henry

Thus the regionalists have been their own best critics. In the new regions of the West, especially, they have soberly recognized that self-conscious literary movements involve the danger of turning young authors toward the reportorial, the strained, the artificial; but such a danger, they assume, is an inevitable accompaniment of a proper attempt to discourage literary colonialism and to assess the literary fund of material peculiar to any region. In the older Southeast, one of the most confirmed regional authors, Marjorie Kinnan Rawlings, has taken an even more severe view of narrowly designed regional efforts. Such a literature she condemns as "perhaps as spurious a form of literary expression as ever reaches print"; for to hold up a people naked as literary specimens, she asserts, is not to express but to betray the region. Like Miss Rawlings, Robert Penn Warren has expressed a prevalent Southern concern that regionalism, as an "ism," may encourage the reportorial curiosity at the expense of the creative imagination; that it may cultivate simple-mindedness and limit sensibility; that it may relinquish inherited resources of speculation and relax critical standards. No literature can be mature without the regional consciousness, Allen Tate has recently said; but the regional principle, if it is not to breed provincialism, must be corrected and sublimated by some "supra-political culture" such as the classical-Christian tradition.[56]

Literary regionalism is therefore today a diversified movement, bred by the cultural pluralism of a vast nation and by the cultural deficiencies of an industrial-urban society. No easy, arbitrary formula can be fashioned to satisfy the discriminating reader as to the legitimacy of a book which pretends to be regional. Is *Death Comes for the Archbishop* a regional novel? Not for Mary Austin. Is *Porgy* a regional play? Not for the Agrarians. Hence, the present essay has sought not to illustrate some narrow conclusion regarding regional literature but rather to show it as an evolving mode operating on

---

Timrod, *Essays* (Athens, Georgia, 1942), 88; John Crowe Ransom, *Virginia Quarterly Review*, Vol. XI (April, 1935), 187–89; Cleanth Brooks, *ibid.*, 308–10; Harold G. Merriam, quoted in *College English*, Vol. VI (October, 1945), 12; E. T. Channing, *Lectures Read to the Seniors in Harvard College* (Boston, 1856), 267–68.

[56] Marjorie Kinnan Rawlings, "Regional Literature in the South," *College English*, Vol. I (February, 1940), 384–85; Robert Penn Warren, "Some Don'ts for Literary Regionalists," *American Review*, Vol. VIII (December, 1936), 147–50; Allen Tate, *Virginia Quarterly Review*, Vol. XXI (Spring, 1945), 263, 269.

divers planes appropriate to the cultural maturity of the area. Its definition must be elastic enough to include the meticulous local chronicling of Sac Prairie by August Derleth, the recovery of regional origins in Vardis Fisher's *Children of God,* the quiet evocation of the Southern temper to Katherine Anne Porter's *Old Mortality,* and the eclectic exploration in depth of Indiana culture in what would seem to be an attempt to write the great regional novel—*Raintree County.* As the literary nationalists long ago agreed that a national literature is contingent on the achievement of a national culture and character, so a regional literature will be firm and predictable to the degree that a region and its people have come to terms. A regional literature is the articulation of those terms. If they are patiently and wisely achieved, they will not go unnoticed in other regions and in other lands.

BIBLIOGRAPHIC NOTE

A complete bibliography of literary regionalism in America would fill a large volume. The preceding footnotes include many of the important illustrations and analyses of the movement. The following list is limited to a few of the works which best define the movement or reflect its historical development.

BIBLIOGRAPHIES

Coan, O. W., and R. G. Lillard. *America in Fiction.* Stanford University, 1945. Under "Farm and Village Life," pp. 22–55, this annotated bibliography gives a sectional classification to those works which reflect the distinctive flavor of the Northeast, the Middle West, the Plains and the Northwest, the South, and the Southwest and California.

Leary, Lewis (ed.) *Articles on American Literature Appearing in Current Periodicals, 1920–1945.* Durham, North Carolina, 1947. Most of the important recent articles on regionalism are listed in a special section, pp. 308–13.

Spiller, Robert E., and others. *Literary History of the United States.* New York, 1948. Vol. III, 304–25, contains an excellent bibliographical summary of the major regional works and critical treatments thereof.

ANTHOLOGIES

Flanagan, John T. (ed.) *America Is West.* Minneapolis, 1945. The gradual maturing of a distinctive literary utterance in the American heartland during the past century is here convincingly illustrated in typical treatments of such aspects as the Indian, frontier, farm, river, and small town.

Pearce, T. M., and A. P. Thomason (eds.) *Southwesterners Write*. Albuquerque, 1946. Thirty-two modern Southwestern authors are selected to show "the intermingled patterns of living and the contrasting currents of thought in the modern civilization of Oklahoma, Texas, New Mexico, and Arizona."

Sterling, G., Genevieve Taggard, and James Rorty (eds.) *Continent's End*. San Francisco, 1925. This collection of Far Western poetry, with introductory essays by the three editors, throws light upon the problems as well as the assets which the Pacific Coast offers the poet.

Warfel, H. R., and G. H. Orians (eds.) *American Local Color Stories*. New York, 1941. Although this volume does not draw a sharp line between local-color and regional compositions, it affords an excellent representation of the diversity of the American scene as it has been captured by some thirty-five authors from James Hall to Zona Gale.

Warren, Robert Penn (ed.) *A Southern Harvest*. Boston, 1937. This representative selection of twenty-odd short stories from Southern writers includes authors as varied in theme and manner as Jesse Stuart, Caroline Gordon, Thomas Wolfe, William Faulkner, Erskine Caldwell, and Roark Bradford.

West, R. B., Jr. (ed.) *Rocky Mountain Reader*, New York, 1946. In narratives, poems, and essays, such writers as Wallace Stegner, Vardis Fisher, W. O. Clough, Bernard DeVoto, and Norman Macleod explore and demonstrate the literary resources in Mormon, Indian, mining, and physical backgrounds peculiar to the region.

HISTORY AND CRITICISM: BOOKS AND PAMPHLETS

Chittick, V. L. O. (ed.) *Northwest Harvest; a Regional Stocktaking*. New York, 1948. Based on a writers' conference held in Portland in 1946, this volume of analyses by fifteen authors from the Northwest and elsewhere assesses both the limitations of the regional approach in general and the literary potentialities of the Northwest in particular.

Dobie, J. Frank. *Guide to Life and Literature of the Southwest*. Dallas, 1943. One of the nation's leading regionalists has here appraised the hundreds of books which deal with such distinctive cultural influences in the Southwest as backwoods humor, Texas rangers, cowboys, bad men, mining and oil, and buffalo.

Garland, Hamlin. *Crumbling Idols*. Chicago, 1894. The most comprehensive apology for local realism or "veritism," to use Garland's term, whereby American writers were to aim for a spontaneous report of their own social and physical environment rather than to concern themselves with any human constants.

Glasgow, Ellen. *A Certain Measure*. New York, 1943. Miss Glasgow's thoughtful exposition of the principles governing her literary career and of the origins of her Virginia novels is perhaps unequaled as a commentary on the process by which regional materials may be used to show the "enduring fibre of human nature."

McWilliams, Carey. *The New Regionalism in American Literature.* Seattle, 1930. This chapbook offers an acute examination of some of the manifestations and claims of the movement in the nineteen-twenties, especially in the West, and describes the need in American culture which it fulfills.

Nicholson, Meredith. *The Hoosiers.* New York, 1900. This study of the most active and cohesive of the subregional groups at the turn of the century, by one of their number, affords an index to the varied uses of and attitudes toward local materials at the time; and it suggests something of the part which state lines have always played in America in determining literary communities.

Rusk, R. L. *The Literature of the Middle Western Frontier.* New York, 1925. The two volumes of this work are detailed and indispensable aids for the understanding of the first currents of regional expression through various forms and channels in the early Middle West.

CRITICAL ESSAYS

Austin, Mary. "Regionalism in American Fiction," *English Journal,* Vol. XXI (February, 1932), 97 ff. One of the most discriminating essays in its analysis of the literary benefits conferred by an authentic regionalism which is of rather than about the area.

Brooks, Van Wyck. *On Literature Today, Opinions of Oliver Allston.* New York, 1941. In the chapter "Nationalism and Regionalism," pp. 256 ff., Brooks rejoices in the "rise of regional feeling" as one evidence of that "self-identification with the local group" which will redeem American literature by ridding it of colonialism and by attaching it to the "primary life" of the country.

Davidson, Donald. "Sectionalism in America," *Hound and Horn,* Vol. VI (July–September, 1933), 561 ff. This essay, later expanded in *The Attack on Leviathan* (Chapel Hill, 1938) and elsewhere, gives the essence of Davidson's cogent interpretation of regionalism as the "condition of literary realization" in America and as a redemptive counter-agent to a "characterless and synthetic Americanism."

Fletcher, John Gould. "Regionalism and Folk Art," *Southwest Review,* Vol. XIX (July, 1934), 429 ff. An attempt to reconcile the views that regionalism provides the necessary local and folk bases for the mature artist and yet is also an enlightened sectionalism.

Hoffman, Frederick J., Charles Allen, and Carolyn Ulrich. *The Little Magazine.* Princeton, 1946. Chapter 8, "Regionalism and the Little Magazine," though it probably overestimates the role of the little magazines in the regional movement of the past generation, contains valuable material on the *Midland* and other important regional periodicals; and the Bibliography, comprising the latter half of the volume, contains useful data on all regional journals between 1891 and 1945.

Levy, Babette. "Mutations in New England Local Color," *New England*

Quarterly, Vol. XIX (September, 1946), 338 ff. This analysis of the constants and also of the changing emphases in the works of Stowe, Cooke, Freeman, and Jewett suggests that these local colorists succeeded in encompassing a wide range of New England life.

McDowell, Tremaine. "Regionalism in American Literature," *Minnesota History*, Vol. XX (June, 1939), 105 ff. After making a brief historical survey of the movement, the author offers a suggestive assessment of its relation to the national and to the universal and draws a distinction between regionalism and local color and pseudo regionalism.

Odum, Howard, and Harry Estill Moore. *American Regionalism*. New York, 1938. In Chapter 7, "Literary and Aesthetic Regionalism," the authors review some of the varieties and principles in modern literary regionalism and correlate them with the six major regions with whose cultural differentials the volume is concerned.

Ransom, John Crowe. "The Aesthetic of Regionalism," *American Review*, Vol. II (January, 1934), 290 ff. An exposition of the way in which a regional culture develops slowly from foreign cultural importations modified by the topography and the economic character of the area.

Southwest Review, Vol. XIV (Summer, 1929). This issue is devoted to a symposium on the potentialities of a regional literature in the Southwest, with moderately sanguine views taken by Stanley Vestal, H. M. Jones, B. A. Botkin, and J. Frank Dobie; with a negative view from Albert Guerard; and with a most positive and comprehensive view from Mary Austin.

Virginia Quarterly Review, Vol. XI (April, 1935). The entire issue is devoted to Southern literature, with essays, stories, and poems from Ransom, Warren, Tate, Elizabeth Madox Roberts, Stark Young, Cleanth Brooks, and others, who give impressive evidence of the literary art and criticism which have sprung from the Southern regionalists during the past two decades.

Chapter 8

Regionalism in American Painting

E. P. Richardson

T HE other contributors to this symposium have traced the rise of the regional concept and described some of the areas which, by administrative practice or popular usage, are accepted as more or less established regional units in American life. They have had to deal with the objective phenomena of geography, climate, economic and political life, and the way in which these gave rise to regional forms of social organization and finally to regional concepts.

But I have to deal with a field of the imaginative life of this country. The objective phenomena of geography and economics do not translate themselves so clearly into the subjective field of the imagination—indeed, sometimes they do not translate themselves at all. The place where a man lives may determine what crops he can grow, or what he does for a living. But there is no automatic connection between the rivers, mountains, or plains of man's habitat and the imaginative life of man's mind.

Painting is a language. Mankind has erected languages of communication and expression upon each of the main senses—sight, hearing, and touch—through which we are in touch with our environment and our fellows. Painting and sculpture are imaginative languages based on sight and touch, as words are a language of the sense of hearing. But painting, as a language, has not been used in American life for practical purposes, as speech has been. Its task in American life has been to express the personal and imaginative conceptions of the individual artist, not the social beliefs and experiences of the race.

Painting is also an art without the practical elements of architecture. Its materials are the same in all climates. A picture needs no adaptation to a Wisconsin winter or a Texas summer, as does the form of a house. The regional influences of climate and geography do not affect its practice as they affect architecture. Nor has it been used, like literary skill, to give expression to the strong practical currents of thought in which the life and conflicts of political sections have been expressed. There is nothing in painting comparable to the antislavery writing of the New England romanticists, or to political oratory.

There is not even a theory of regionalism in painting. There is nothing to correspond to the debate which has been going on in American literary criticism for the past 125 years, so well described in Benjamin T. Spencer's paper, on the merits of regionalism versus nationalism, expatriatism, proletarianism, and various other anti-regional theories of literary creation. The theoretical debate in the field of painting has been a simple one, between American nationalism, on the one hand, and loyalty to various cosmopolitan styles and points of view on the other.

Yet there is a geography of culture. My task is to show to what extent it exists in the field farthest removed from those objective phenomena described by Fulmer Mood, and where even the subjective force toward regionalism which Lancaster Pollard called "the feeling of area-kinship" can hardly be said to exist.

As an index of culture, painting exists throughout the entire length of American history. This point needs emphasis. Painting is a contemplative activity and a somewhat uncommon skill. At the time of the first settlements it was still largely organized as a craft, in the workshop-apprentice pattern. It is rather remarkable, therefore, to find that painting and drawing accompanied the first explorers in the sixteenth century. Rodrigo de Cifuentes, an artist, accompanied Cortez on his expedition into Honduras in 1525; a French artist, Jacques Le Moyne, came to Florida about 1564 with the Huguenot expedition under Laudonnière; John White, an artist of exceptional interest, came to Virginia with Raleigh's first colony in 1585; Samuel de Champlain illustrated the journals and reports of his travels with his own drawings. When the first permanent settlements were made in the seventeenth century, painters appeared in them very early, well within the lifetime of the first settlers. Thus painting has a continuous history in American life from the first explorers until the present.

The men who made the first permanent settlements in the seventeenth century brought with them the arts and skills to which they had been accustomed in their homelands. Among the arts and the handicrafts established here in the earliest colonies was the art of portrait painting, which was a normal feature of seventeenth-century middle-class life in Holland and England. There are more than four hundred likenesses extant of Americans born before 1700. The greater part of these were painted in America. In view of a probable loss, which I should estimate to be very great, through neglect, fire, and other causes, this shows a very considerable activity in the early colonies.

The interesting point, for this discussion, is that painting appeared in several different forms.

First, the English settlers in Puritan New England brought with them the English tradition of family feeling and a liking for family portraits. The style of these portraits was English provincial, modified at the close of the century by an echo of the English baroque introduced into England by Van Dyck and Lely. The basis of the popularity of the portrait in New England was family feeling. But there was also in the Calvinist temper a strong interest in human character, which revealed itself in an unusually large number of portraits of old age, or of striking though unhandsome faces. Character rather than beauty governed the artist's approach.

On the Hudson there was a settlement of the most pictorially gifted of all the Northern, Protestant peoples. The Dutch in the seventeenth century produced a great school of painting, on the highest technical and spiritual level of achievement, and astonishingly profuse in range and in quantity. The names of more than eight thousand Dutch seventeeth-century painters are known. The Dutch settlers brought to the Hudson a sober, provincial, but solidly competent version of their realistic portrait tradition. The bust portrait of Governor Stuyvesant in armor, in the New-York Historical Society, shows the virtues of this tradition. The significant thing about the Dutch settlements is that the craft of painting at once struck root and, by the early years of the eighteenth century, an indigenous school of rudely trained but observant and sensitive painters was active on the Hudson River. One painter family, the Duyckincks, can be traced from 1638 until the Revolution.

In the Middle Colonies a different tradition appeared among a mixed population of English Anglicans and Quakers and Swedish Lutherans. The key figure here was Gustavus Hesselius, born of a distinguished family of Swedish clerics and intellectuals (Swedenborg was his cousin). He came to the Delaware River in 1711 with his brother, who was to be pastor of the Swedish church at Christina, now Wilmington, Delaware. Gustavus Hesselius settled in Philadelphia but worked as far south as Virginia. He brought to the Middle Colonies the tradition of the Italianate Dutch painters of the school of Utrecht, who were in the eighteenth century widely admired through the whole Baltic Protestant world. How different this tradition was from the rather grim portrait tradition in Calvinist New England may be seen by the roll of Hesselius' activities: the first religious painting, a "Last Supper" for an Anglican church in Maryland; the first classical literary subjects, a "Bacchanal" and a "Bacchus and Ariadne"; and the first notable portraits of American Indians, in which one may see, perhaps, the dawn of an ethnological interest and a hint of the rise of scientific thought in Philadelphia. And in addition to being a painter, Hesselius was a builder of pipe organs. The Peale family of artist-scientists, who dominated the Philadelphia scene in the early years of the Republic, represented this same combination of artistic, scientific, and mechanical interests on a higher level, as Benjamin West represents the same interest in ideal, narrative subjects.

Finally, in the Southern tidewater colonies, there took root in eighteenth-century plantation society the English landed gentry's interest in the aristocratic portrait, used as a decoration in the fine rooms of the family mansion. This tradition was so congenial to the Southern life that it reigned supreme from the beginning of the eighteenth century to the Civil War. Like New England portraiture, Southern tidewater portrait painting had a basis in strong family feeling. But it was a relatively impersonal style, in which the decorative effect of fine clothes and graceful posture outweighed the interest in human character.

Thus, the art of painting began in the United States with four regional flavors: (1) the New England interest in portraiture, which flowered in Copley and Stuart; (2) the indigenous Dutch love of painting; (3) a many-sided aesthetic tradition blended of ideal, decorative, scientific, and mechanical interests in the Middle Colonies, where Benjamin West, Charles Willson Peale, Rembrandt Peale, and Robert Fulton were to appear; (4) a decorative portrait tradition in the plantation colonies which remained alive until the end of that phase of Southern life.

The first period of our national life, from the close of the Revolution to the outbreak of the Civil War (1780–1860), coincides with the neoclassic and romantic periods of painting. The neoclassic period was brief and disrupted by the Revolution and the long period of post-Revolutionary adjustment. Some of the best talents of the pre-Revolutionary period, Benjamin West and J. S. Copley, were drawn to London, not out of political sympathy, but because they found there a greater opportunity for patronage and personal development. Thus there appeared for the first time a force which is the opposite of regionalism and which has fought a long battle against regionalism throughout American history—the attraction of the highly developed professional centers of Europe.

It was inevitable that as American life grew from provincial to national level, and as artists of first-rate talents appeared, American artists should become ambitious to acquaint themselves with the highest developments of their art, as seen in the picture galleries and the active artistic life of the great cities of Europe. The development of American institutions of art was slow. The first annual exhibitions of painting appeared in Philadelphia in 1805, Boston in 1827, and New York in 1826, but the first art schools in the modern sense were not established until the eighteen-seventies in Philadelphia and New York. The development of the art museum was even slower. The great American museums of today were not founded until after the Civil War, when the concentration of population and wealth brought a new period of American urban life. The Metropolitan Museum was organized in New York in 1870; the Boston Museum in the same year. The Corcoran Gallery, Washington, was built in 1860 but was used by the quartermaster's department during the war and restored to museum use in 1869. There followed the establishment of other museums: Philadelphia in 1875, Cincinnati in 1880, Detroit in 1884, and Chicago in 1899. These institutions did not reach maturity until the early decades of the twentieth century.

As a result of the slow development of the professional schools and institutions of art, American painting has been marked by a dichotomy between the urge to develop an imaginative interpretation of American life and the urge to learn about the latest developments in Europe and to adjust our professional life to that of Europe. American artists have tended to fall into two classes. There have been the brilliant cosmopolitans—like Benjamin West, Allston, Whistler, Sargent, and Mary Cassatt—who studied abroad and who sometimes remained abroad, sometimes returned home to represent the American form of the international art of their day. This type at its best has made a brilliant personal contribution. At its worst it constitutes the mass of pasticheurs who have characterized modern cosmopolitan civilization, especially since the growth of rapid communication in the past hundred years. Then there have been the solitary individualists, like Winslow Homer, Thomas Eakins, and Albert Ryder. But this has led me ahead of my story.

The four regional traditions which we saw established in the Colonial period were the basis of the first period of our national culture. New England contributed to neoclassic painting the portrait art of Stuart and the patriotic narrative compositions of Trumbull. In New York, a descendant of Hudson Valley Dutch folk artists, John Vanderlyn, became the first American disciple of the school of Paris, and the first of a native school of good portrait painters appeared there. In Philadelphia the Peales dominated the scene, with their combination of artistic and scientific interests. In the South the taste for portraits was gratified chiefly by artists who emigrated there from other regions, although Charleston produced in Fraser a portrait miniaturist of the first rank.

But after 1800, there appeared a sudden flowering of creative energy as remarkable as it was unforeshadowed. The first professional European art critic to visit this country was Anna Jameson, in 1837. She was astonished at the way the country seemed to have poured its energy into painting: "The country seemed to swarm with painters," she said. In the Romantic period, from 1800 to 1860, the art of painting became diffused over the whole continent. As the native population spread westward along the great inland rivers and across the plains to the Pacific coast, painters went everywhere with them, painting the portraits of pioneers, farmers, and frontier dignitaries; studying the landscapes, the Indians, and the birds and animals of the great new continent. The most vigorous artistic life was in the older regional centers of the northeast. But by the end of the period, there was hardly a city of any size, from Portland, Maine, to San Francisco; from Albany and Buffalo, Detroit and Chicago, to New Orleans, which did not have a number of painters at work in it. The chief subjects were portraits, landscapes, genre scenes of American life, illustrations of American romantic literature, with a considerable infusion also of European travel and of illustrations of the romantic past. To some extent these artists addressed themselves to a national audience through the medium of the American Art Union, a lottery scheme which in the eighteen-forties distributed engravings and original pictures country wide. But by and large, in the absence of a national journalism of art, these artists addressed themselves to a restricted regional audience. They had their studios in Chicago or St. Louis, Cincinnati or Albany, and those who desired to have a portrait painted or to buy a landscape went to see the favorite local painter.

One other aspect of this period remains to be mentioned. As the population spread rapidly across the continent, and was widely diffused on lonely frontier farms, remote from all the institutions of organized society, men and women with a natural gift for the arts continued to appear from it. Sometimes these boys or girls, born in cabins on lonely frontier clearings or tiny river settlements, might grow to manhood, as Chester Harding did, before discovering that the art of painting existed. Others, like Bingham or Whittredge, seemed to be guided to their own vocation from their wilderness birthplace by an instinct as sure as the homing instinct of a wild animal. This continuous springing up of artists wherever the spreading stream of settlement flowed, seems to show that a certain percentage of the population is born with a natural tendency toward the arts, just as others are born with a tendency toward law, medicine, or mechanical skill.

The tendency of the succeeding period—of objective realism and impressionism, lasting roughly from 1870 to 1914—was altogether in the opposite direction, toward centralization of the artistic life of the country. The rise of New York to a dominant position, as the only place where an artist could achieve national reputation or commercial success, as the focus of the art trade and of the journalism of art, went steadily through this period.

In part, this was merely a reflection of the gigantic forces of consolidation—the railroad, the telegraph, steam power, machine manufacturing, finance capitalism, the mass life of cities—which had their focus in New York. In part this was the reflection of a new intellectual climate. The Philadelphia Centennial of 1876 was a kind of turning point. It symbolized the end of the first century of national life. It illustrated the wonders of the machine. And it turned the eyes of the country outward toward Europe and Asia, and away from the old sources of national culture. The Romantic movement faded away rapidly. The railroad and the ocean steamship opened the world to easy travel. The era of the photograph had come. Photographs of Paris and Rome, of the Nile and India and Japan, brought home the lure of exotic arts and unfamiliar scenes. Travel became a passion with the American wealthy and the American intellectual.

Before such a profusion of new possibilities, the earlier, simpler outlook was lost. Faced with a thousand novel impressions, it is no wonder that artists became self-conscious and eclectic. The same process took place in all countries of the Western world. In England, France, Germany, and Italy, also, the old national culture was replaced by a new cosmopolitan culture. New York became the port of entry for this culture into America, and the center which drew to itself the greater number, indeed almost all, of the American painters of outstanding talent.

The artists most honored during their own lifetime, in this new period, were the brilliant cosmopolitan artists who lived abroad, like Sargent and Whistler, or artists like Duveneck and Chase who taught here the new techniques of painting which they had studied abroad. New York became the center of the American Impressionists, who brought home the brilliant new style of the *avant garde* in Paris.

At its best, this period offered a very attractive and stimulating fresh outlook. At its worst it was a period of triumph for the pastiche —the skillful display of good taste and souvenirs of travel, without any roots in deep imaginative experience. But it impoverished the life of all other centers by draining away the natural artistic leaders to New York. And within the period itself there were powerful protests against its rootless eclecticism. The artists who are most honored today are the strong, sober individualists—Homer, Eakins, and Ryder. These men all took refuge in solitude, either self-imposed or forced on them, in order to find in solitary meditation their own interpretation of life.

New York, in spite of its dominance, was never absolute. Philadelphia, Boston, and Chicago formed influential local centers. There were artist colonies elsewhere—in California, in Indiana, in New Mexico, at New Hope in Pennsylvania, and in Provincetown. Yet it is difficult to escape the conclusion that the vitality of the lesser centers reached its lowest point during this period, and that the life of the majority of American cities was impoverished by the excessive centralization of the best artistic talent in one place.

In the twentieth century, this cosmopolitan culture has continued and indeed been intensified. The dominant trend in painting today is the American branch of the École de Paris. The school of criticism associated with it believes today that art is wholly a universal and international human language and that it is intellectual treason to the progress of humanity to believe in, or emphasize, nationality or regionalism in art.

There have been two other phenomena, contrary to this tendency, in twentieth-century painting. The first is nationalism. A sharp protest against the expatriate tendency of American painting was made in New York City in 1908 by a group of painters, led by Robert Henri, whose credo was the aesthetic richness of everyday American life— "the esthetic significance of the elevated and the skyscraper, city crowds and rows of flat houses," as one of them put it. Some of these men, like Glackens, Luks, and Sloan, were Philadelphia-trained men, who had felt the tradition of Eakins; George Bellows was a recruit from Ohio. This protest aroused opposition at first. These painters were labeled the "Ash Can school." Gradually they achieved a welcome and a national recognition. Yet the protest of the New York Realists has had little influence, partly because they were not painters of the first rank, partly because the brilliantly pyrotechnic explosion of new styles in twentieth-century Paris was more attractive to artists than their local program. Only five years after their first exhibit, in 1913, the Armory Show was held, which introduced European post-

Impressionist painting to America; and New York has been ever since more associated with the American developments based on the school of Paris than with the native scene. There is much good painting in New York. But the New York school, if such exists, presents no unified character except its experimentalism and cosmopolitan culture.

A second protest group appeared in the nineteen-thirties in the Middle West. Thomas Benton, Grant Wood, and John Steuart Curry were the leaders of this movement, which again asserted the value of the American scene against European nonrepresentative painting and against the influence of the cosmopolitan taste of New York City. I think it is not unfair to say that this movement has disintegrated as rapidly as the preceding one. And so, probably, will any other movement of protest. Art is a positive and creative aspect of the imagination. Protests based upon fear, or hostility, have no creative base.

Nonetheless, there has come about today quietly, almost unnoticed, an enormous degree of decentralization in the activity of American painters. New York has not wholly lost its primacy. It is still the home of the largest concentration of painters. It is still the center of the art market and of the journalism of art. Yet the creative activity of the country is now (1950) as widely diffused as it was before 1860. This has come about not as a result of sectional jealousies and in a spirit of hostility to national or international artistic life, but as a result of natural, organic development. In Boston, Philadelphia, and Washington; in the Deep South, the Middle West, the Pacific Northwest, and the Desert Southwest; and in San Francisco and Los Angeles, are active regional centers.

This activity is regional as a matter of practical convenience, not as a result of theory. It has become physically impossible to focus the artistic life of a nation of 150,000,000 people in one spot—New York or any other city. During the period of consolidation, while New York was the chief center for exhibitions, there arose also three or four other large annual exhibitions—in Philadelphia, Pittsburgh, Washington, and Chicago—which were looked on as covering the national scene and including all the artists of national importance. A striking feature of the past twenty years has been the increase in number and importance of other local, state, and regional exhibitions. Hardly any state is today without an annual state exhibition, held in the principal art museum of the state. In the more densely populated states, there are several regional annual exhibits. In Ohio, for example, Cleveland, Cincinnati, and Youngstown hold local or regional exhibits of a high level of quality, while regional annuals of lesser importance are held in half a dozen other cities. The same story is repeated in most of the larger states. The increase in the number of exhibitions has resulted from an increase in the amount and quality of painting done in local centers, demanding an outlet.

An index of the regional diffusion of painting is offered by the rise of art museums, which has been one of the striking features of American community life since World War I. To the museums founded in the later decades of the nineteenth century have been added hundreds of others, large and small. Very active institutions are found today all through southern New England, the Middle States, Maryland, and Virginia. The South has a number of small institutions, with the most active growth taking place in Florida. In the Old Northwest—Ohio, Michigan, Indiana, and Illinois—are many active art centers. The Great Plains States—Minnesota, Iowa, Nebraska, Missouri, Kansas, Oklahoma, and Texas—all have active regional centers. In the Rocky Mountain States, Colorado stands out as the only active state. In the Southwest, both Arizona and New Mexico have colonies of artists and show vigorous activity. On the Pacific Coast there are many good painters, many institutions, and many exhibitions, from Seattle and Portland to San Francisco, Los Angeles, San Diego, and Santa Barbara in the south.

Several factors have produced this immense diffusion of the art of painting. The first of these is the slow growth of the professional organization of the painter's art, until now there are excellent art schools, museums, and exhibitions all over the country. It is no longer necessary for the student to go abroad, or even to go to the eastern seaboard, to enjoy excellent educational facilities and to study the great art of the world. A second factor was the federal government's patronage of art in the nineteen-thirties, which, though largely a failure in its immediate results, yet made it possible, by patronizing art on a national scale, for a whole generation of painters to gain a start professionally in their own region, without first going to New York to gain a reputation there. The talent of the country was allowed to take root in its own region, instead of being drained off to one spot. The third factor has been the growth of the arts on the college campus and the consequent diffusion throughout the country of not only well-trained art critics and art historians, but painters, sculptors, and craftsmen of all sorts. All of these factors seem to have operated without special forethought, as a result of the spontaneous and organic growth of American life, rather than as a planned decentralization. The situation in which we find ourselves is that of an immense outpouring of energy, so widespread that it is prominent everywhere except in parts of the South and the thinly populated Rocky Mountain region.

Yet I do not believe it would be possible to offer a survey of American painting at present which would show any clear regional trends, or schools of thought, or styles. There are no deep-rooted local schools. There are only individual artists who may for a time seem to give an individual flavor to the work of their community; or loosely connected groups of artists, which dissolve as easily as they are formed. National unity, and the unity of the climate of the mind that prevails throughout Western life, are stronger than any of these vague local associations.

Regionalism may be said, therefore, to be a relatively superficial phenomenon in the field of American painting, compared with its strong, objective existence in other fields. It does not exist as a theory. It seems to have no existence in the shape of firmly rooted regional trends of styles. There is the fact, however, of a great decentralization in the professional and institutional life of this art. There is significant work being done in every region. This activity takes form in any one of the current modes of painting, which exist without regional boundaries throughout the Western world, as well as in valiant personal styles. If regional and local loyalties are weak, there is a healthy diffusion of hope, self-confidence, and vigorous activity in many centers. The regional character of this activity is a kind of Emersonian self-confidence, a belief that it is possible for the artist to do good work, and to achieve spiritual greatness, wherever he may find himself at home.

Chapter 9

Regionalism in American Architecture

Rexford Newcomb

Human experience is predicated upon geography. In fact, human history makes little sense unless it is read in the light of geography. Scholars have been all too prone to compart knowledge and to separate essentially related phenomena. Thus frequently has architecture been divorced from its environment and considered apart from that environment. This is most unfortunate, for architecture, if it is anything, is a function of environment and, like other expressions of human life, cannot be fully understood outside that context.

Inseparably linked as it is with its backgrounds, architecture reflects, as do few other arts, the life and thought of a race, a place, or an age. A careful examination of the relationship between any architecture and its environment, geographic or human, will bear out the truth of this statement. Therefore one who would adequately appraise any style or period of architecture must understand not only the history, the genius, and the social and religious customs of its builders, but also the geographic, geologic, and climatic conditions of the land of its inception.

In no country is so wide a diversity of architectural expression to be encountered as in the United States, and in no country can the causes of that diversity be more readily discovered. The reasons are clear. Our nation is a far-flung sisterhood of states with varying climates, topographies, and physical resources and with mixed ethnic relationships. The resulting regional patterns of thought and folkways are marked, in spite of increasingly rapid means of communication and transportation.

Opened to settlement at a time when the leading nations of the Old World were seeking lands for exploitation, America became a theater for colonial development by the French, the English, the Dutch, and the Spanish, with later infiltrations of Quakers, Swedes, Scotch-Irish, and Germans. Once the country was able to offer wider social and economic opportunities than those afforded by their homelands, America became a mecca also for the Welsh, the Irish, Italians, Poles, Portuguese, and various other nationalities who came in increasing numbers.

Except the Spanish, most of these peoples settled upon the Atlantic seaboard. But once that seaboard was comfortably settled, the more daring and restless elements sought new opportunities and the chance of fortune in the regions beyond the Appalachians. Spreading first to Kentucky and Tennessee, these pioneers soon entered the present states of Ohio, Indiana, Illinois, Michigan, and Wisconsin, then called the Northwest Territory. When the public lands in these areas were taken up, it was the trans-Mississippi territories of Missouri, Iowa, Minnesota, Kansas, and Nebraska that beckoned. Then came the drive to the Pacific Northwest over the Oregon Trail, the settlement of the Mormons in the valley of the Great Salt Lake, and the expansion by way of the Santa Fe Trail to our Hispanic Southwest.

Following the trail breaker, trapper, and trader, came the farmer and the mechanic; and soon lands that were once called "the great American desert" were converted into profitable farmsteads and cattle ranges. Thus America has witnessed a colorful pioneer pageant the like of which no other country in the world has experienced.

It is well known that pioneer communities have never been noteworthy for developed artistic expressions, and only in those sections of America settled long enough to have produced a reasonably integrated culture has architecture reached anything like an adequate expression. These regions are not great in area when compared with the vast American domain. In large sections of the nation, architecture is still in what may be termed a pioneer stage. But staunch and tough fibers, the making of a real national architectural fabric, are assuredly being spun; and out of the background of a history that must potently influence whatever we do for today and for tomorrow, is emerging an efficient and adequate expression of modern American life and thought. But there are still many exotic threads in this fabric.

It is important to remember that architecture is always strongly

influenced by past building experience, and that forms eloquent of
one environment are frequently carried from that environment to less
receptive situations with the passage of peoples. How amusing thus
becomes an English Gothic cathedral in Singapore or a New Mexican
Colonial hacienda in the Mohawk Valley of New York. Moreover,
acquired building tastes and habits are frequently projected beyond
their natural habitats by architectural literature. The whole cult
of the classical revival was propagated by means of the literature that
grew out of the rediscovery of

> ... the glory that was Greece,
> And the grandeur that was Rome.

But the copying of styles of past architecture—a practice inspired
by a romantic nostalgia—even though it may have a regional distribution, is not to be confused with regionalism itself. One has to
look through the superficial charms of the Greek Revival in New
York or in Alabama to discover whether or not there are real regional
differences.

Turpin Bannister points out: "Regionalism is often confused with
provincialism. They should be clearly distinguished. Provincialism
is the parochial and half-understood reflection of styles radiated
from the great metropolitan style centers. The products of provincialism may be quaint, naïve, and amusing, but they lack the
vitality, spontaneity and promise of future growth characteristic of
truly regional products."

If we accept Bannister's definition, we must conclude that much
of what has transpired in American architecture is mere provincialism.
On the other hand, even though our architecture was originally
imported from Europe, it soon reacted to the changed environment
to exhibit indigenous qualities of its own. "The European tradition
was still clear, but the product could only have materialized in the
new locale." Some of these distinctions upon regional bases we shall
attempt to point out.

When the English colonists first reached our shores, rural England had not as yet embarked upon that revival of classic architecture
which had already set in at London and the larger centers. The rural
districts still employed medieval types of structure.[1] Many of the

---

[1] Henry C. Foreman, *The Architecture of the Old South, Medieval Style*, chap. i.

colonists came from rural districts where wood was still plentiful and buildings were of the time-honored "half-timber" construction. The frames of such buildings were assembled upon the ground, then raised into place and pinned together with heavy dowels. The interstices were filled with "wattle and daub" or with rough mud bricks of clay and straw called "cats." Sometimes sun-dried and, upon occasion, even burned bricks were used for filling, the resulting "half-and-half" wall being plastered inside with whitewashed clay, and covered upon the exterior by a coating of lime plaster.

The colonists were thoroughly familiar with this type of structure and, finding wood plentiful in the New World, they employed it widely. But this wattle and daub, satisfactory enough in genial Old England, would not do in the rigorous climate of New England. Thus environment stepped in to alter an historic architectural procedure. Thereafter, the colonists rived, split, or sawed out a covering of "clapboards," with which they sheathed the exteriors of these half-timber houses to shed the water and keep out the wind. So efficacious were these clapboards that they were universally adopted and became an important feature of subsequent American wooden architecture. Clapboarding, now universally produced in long lengths on machines, comes down to our day in what we call weather-boarding or siding.[2]

The rigorous climate is likewise to be noted in the compact plans evolved in New England. The chimney was placed in the center of the building, the fireplaces for the various rooms opening into it. This arrangement conserved heat and stiffened the frame.

In time, the central chimney was crowded out of its place by an axial corridor or hall which was projected through the middle of the house, the rooms flanking it on either side. From this hall a stairway, more or less elaborate, led to the upper stories, while the fireplaces with their respective chimneys were relegated to positions at the ends of the house. With this symmetry of plan came also a gradual infiltration of classic details and proportions. Thus the somewhat bleak, bare, and puritanical Early American house gave way to the classically inclined Georgian residence.[3]

But whatever the change, in obedience to climate the New Eng-

[2] Rexford Newcomb, *The Colonial and Federal House*, 36.
[3] *Ibid.*, 30–35.

land plan remained compact, and when more room was needed, the house went up instead of out. This was accomplished by the adoption of the two-plane or gambrel roof. This change permitted greater space in the attic, which, in effect, now became a third living floor.

When, following American independence, prosperity came to the seaport cities and wealthy shipowners built pretentious homes, even then the house did not expand laterally. The gambrel was replaced by a full third story, crowned by a balustrade-enclosed roof with a so-called "captain's lookout" from which a mariner with glass might discover whether or not his ship had arrived in port. Curiously enough, when New England architectural patterns traveled westward, the "captain's lookout" went along. Thus today one discovers these features atop houses in the Middle West which afford vistas no more exciting than broad fields of wheat, soybeans, and corn.

In the Middle Atlantic region, colonial architecture contrasted markedly with that of New England. Here, in the absence of splendid white pine, brick made of local clays was widely employed, except in certain sections of Pennsylvania, where structures of native stone, roofed with local slates, became the rule.[4] So potent has been the influence of the staunch old houses of the Philadelphia-Germantown area that to this day houses are erected in this time-honored vernacular.

Farther south, in Maryland and Virginia, where the climate induced a different social and economic system, the effects are plainly seen in houses admirably adapted to life on the great maritime plantations where cotton and tobacco were raised and where large numbers of black men carried on most of the hard labor of production. In this genial climate and under a favorable social organization, architecture became formal, balanced, and aristocratic. Plans became extended and detached. It made little difference how far the kitchen might be from the breakfast room or dining room, for there were plenty of servants to take the steps, and covered dishes to keep the food warm. Thus the kitchens were usually far removed from the apartments of the master's family.

The housing of these slaves called for special arrangements. On some plantations, slave families lived in small individual cabins; on others, in long ranges of "quarters." The personal servants of the

4 *Ibid.,* chap. iii.

master's family ate in the kitchen of the "big house," which was, of necessity, large. Often there were two kitchens, one in the main house and a detached kitchen where baking, preserving, and the like were carried on.

In Virginia the plans are more open and detached than in Maryland, in some cases the service departments being completely separated from the main house. Larger openings, lower roofs, and open two-storied porticoes reflect the climate of this sunny littoral. In the Carolinas, Georgia, and Alabama, the same open forms were prevalent but with local variations. In this section the two-story portico, like that on the Miles Brewton house in Charleston, was very popular. After the Revolution, and especially during the Greek Revival period, porticoes with columns two stories high became the fashion. Thus, in the South, geography and a different social order produced concomitant changes in architectural expression.[5]

Another interesting European influence upon American architecture is encountered in those portions of the Atlantic seaboard settled by the Dutch. Dutch influence centered on Manhattan Island, but it extended up the Hudson, into Connecticut, and into Long Island and New Jersey. Here the Dutch built stone town houses with stepped gables, and compact and thrifty farm structures. The more prosperous Dutch houses were two rooms deep, crowned by a roof of low slope with deep projections front and rear. This overhang was soon extended in such a way as to form a true porch or, as it was later called in the New York area, a piazza. Many consider this the origin of the American veranda or porch.

The Dutch also appropriated the gambrel roof, to which they imparted a peculiar slope resulting in a form which to this day is called a "Dutch" roof. These old Dutch buildings have a substantial, homelike air that reflects in every line the national qualities of their builders. In certain sections of New York and New Jersey, these forms still potently influence the line and massing of modern residential structures.[6]

Another region of transplanted culture was that of the colonial

[5] *Ibid.,* 29–30.

[6] Rexford Newcomb, *Modern Architecture with Particular Reference to the United States,* 57–67.

German settlers who concentrated in eastern Pennsylvania, where they were for the most part farmers. Here the quaint, picturesque, and substantial buildings which they erected still impart a genuine touch of the Old World to the American scene. While they utilized local materials, the German builders handled these with that thorough regard for craftsmanship that has always characterized the architecture of their homeland. The Pennsylvania Dutch interior was simple but colorful. A deep, clear blue, combined with an intense yellow, crude reds, and deep greens, was a favorite color scheme. Furniture, fabrics, and accessories all exhibited vivid hues. Thus Pennsylvania and America have been enriched by this German contribution which, like the Dutch Colonial, has decidedly influenced the residential architecture of the mid-Atlantic region and indeed that of regions beyond the mountains.[7]

French occupation of territory in what is now the United States was slight, but in the settlements at Michilimackinac and Detroit, Michigan; Vincennes, Indiana; Cahokia, Kaskaskia, Fort Chartres, and Prairie du Rocher, Illinois; St. Louis, Ste Genevieve, and St. Charles, Missouri; and along the Mississippi to New Orleans, definite French traits are to be found in the architecture. Of these areas, Louisiana was most profoundly influenced, and a visit to the *Vieux Carré* of New Orleans is almost like a trip to some provincial town of old France. To Louisiana was added a second French increment when the Acadians from the country around Grand Pré, Canada, were removed thither. Thus "Cajun" traits are to be traced in the present-day language, folkways, government, and institutions generally.

But for the more indigenous architectural developments we are indebted to the French families who received large land grants and who under the institution of slavery built up great plantations. These interesting old plantation mansions along the Bayou Teche and the lower Mississippi between New Orleans and St. Francisville are eloquent reminders of that unique landed aristocracy developed under French and Spanish protection.[8]

French Colonial houses in the upper Mississippi Valley were of

[7] *Ibid.,* 67–75.

[8] Natalie Scott and William P. Spratling, *Old Plantation Houses in Louisiana.*

simple arrangement—two or three rooms placed side by side, each with a door opening upon a *galerie* that extended across the front of the house. Sometimes these *galeries* flanked two sides of the structure and often completely surrounded the house. Three types of construction were prevalent in this region: *poteaux en terre,* a sort of loose stockade of vertical posts set in the ground with stone and mortar infilling; *poteaux sur sole,* a more carefully built wall of squared posts set upon a sill with stone foundation; and solid stone masonry. The roof of the *galerie* was pitched lower than that of the main house, the result being a two-plane roof with a decided flare at the bottom. Excellent examples of French construction are still to be seen at Cahokia, Illinois, and Ste Genevieve, Missouri.[9]

The principal regional traits of the Louisiana house are two: it is always raised above the ground, and a *galerie* encloses one or more sides of the structure. In the smaller houses the main floor is raised only two or three feet to permit a free circulation of air; in the larger structures the living floor is up one story. This, of course, is to avoid dampness in the living areas.[10] The *galerie,* though perfectly reflective of the Louisiana scene, was widely used in the French Illinois country, also, where it appears to have been imported by way of Canada. Indeed, two-story *galeries* were not infrequent in old St. Louis.

The facts that this country became American territory through the Louisiana Purchase of 1803 and that many of the great Louisiana plantation houses were built after American occupation should not disturb us, for while this excludes them from the Colonial category chronologically, it certainly does not culturally. Here, perhaps more completely than elsewhere in America, metamorphosed geography and history live down to the present.[11]

The habitat of our Spanish Colonial architecture contrasts markedly with that of other European types so far discussed. It includes vast sun-drenched, semidesert areas in the present states of Texas, New Mexico, Arizona, and southern California, with settlements

[9] Charles E. Peterson, "Early Sainte Genevieve, Missouri, and Its Architecture," *Missouri Historical Review,* Vol. XXXV (January, 1941), 207–32.

[10] Buford L. Pickens, "Regional Aspects of Early Louisiana Architecture," *Journal of the Society of Architectural Historians,* Vol. VII (January–June, 1948), 33–36.

[11] J. Frazer Smith, *White Pillars,* chap. vi, vii.

also at St. Augustine and Pensacola, Florida, in Georgia, and along the Gulf Coast. Here, principally through the leadership of the Franciscan friars, who organized great ecclesiastical establishments and built up vast landed estates, Spanish institutions and customs were introduced.

Spanish Colonial architecture, while it was expressive of the pioneer life and setting which gave it birth, was nevertheless the result of a long heredity which markedly influenced its expression. That heredity is traceable back through Mexico to the mother country, Spain.

But in Spain itself architecture had already experienced a vari-colored career. The country was originally inhabited by the Iberians, who were doubtless a division of the great early Mediterranean race. Into Spain eventually came the Greeks, the Phoenicians, and the Romans, who, when their power waned, were succeeded by the Visigoths. In the early eighth century the Visigoths were conquered by the Moors; and the Moors, in turn, were driven out, after seven hundred years of occupation, by the successors of these very Visigoths whom they had driven northward into the Pyrenees. Thus Spanish blood, Spanish institutions, and Spanish architecture were definitely cosmopolitan.[12]

When the Spaniards arrived in Mexico, naturally they began to build in the fashion of the Spanish homeland. They appropriated few, if any, of the ancient Aztec forms, although, through the employment of native Indian artisans, a certain barbaric splendor was in time imparted to Mexican Colonial architecture. And indeed a reflection of this filtered through to the provincial churches and other structures that were eventually built in the American Southwest.

Meeting peculiar environmental conditions in each of the future American states to which it spread, this age-old Spanish-Mexican style was in each situation modified to produce a new regional variant. For instance, California, with her wide range of climate, her maritime geography, and her variegated flora, permitted architectural forms that would appear exotic in New Mexico or Texas. Here the simplest of shapes, enhanced by a wonderfully clear and vibrant atmosphere and the deep shadows which a vivid sunshine induces, make un-

[12] Rexford Newcomb, *The Old Mission Churches and Historic Houses of California*, chap. viii.

necessary the elaborate forms and minute detail called for by less brilliantly lighted landscapes.[13]

The architecture of Arizona, on the other hand, was allied more closely with the Sonoran types of northern Mexico and partook of a certain regional desert quality which recalls, perhaps more forcefully than anything else encountered in America, the desert architecture of Moorish North Africa. Here the roof—in California always a crowning glory of red tiles—became so flat as not to figure in the perspective, except on churches where low masonry domes were used.[14]

Again in New Mexico we encounter an entirely different architectural expression. Here the Spaniards found a sedentary Indian population which had already developed an appropriate native architecture. Thus, when the conquistadores employed these Indians to build structures with European plans and utilities out of native materials, there resulted a new regional type, half Spanish, half Indian, the like of which has been nowhere else evolved.[15]

In Texas, along the Gulf Coast, and in Florida new exposures and different conditions were encountered. The result was other regional variants of this adaptable and cosmopolitan style, so appropriate geographically and racially to the large Hispanic areas of the American Southwest.[16]

Recent years have witnessed a revival of the Spanish Colonial, not in any strict archaeological fashion, but as a living style and with correct deference to its regional variations. Excellent modern examples of the style can be seen in most of our states which were once parts of the Spanish domain. In two states, California and Florida, this sun-begotten architecture has been so well adapted to modern American living that it has become a vital, new style. Combining as it does echoes from more than one Mediterranean land, the author, in 1928, proposed the term Mediterranean to designate this cosmopolitan vernacular.[17] Since that time, much has developed in New Mexico, where a highly regional Santa Fe school flourishes, and in Texas and Arizona, where local regional types are perpetuated.

13 Rexford Newcomb, *Spanish-Colonial Architecture in the United States,* 34–35, plates 51–94.

14 *Ibid.,* 32–33, plates 47–50.

15 *Ibid.,* 29–31, plates 29–46.

16 *Ibid.,* 25–28, plates 1–28.

17 Rexford Newcomb, *Mediterranean Domestic Architecture in the United States.*

What these states have done and are doing, an informed citizenry and an artistically alert architectural profession may do for other areas of our country.[18]

America's great intermountain area was settled from two sources. Ohio, southern Michigan, northern Illinois and Indiana, southern Wisconsin, and parts of Iowa and Kansas were peopled mainly by Northerners, while Kentucky, Tennessee, and the New South were recruited from Virginia and the South Atlantic seaboard.

With this westward movement of peoples—one of the great treks of human history—building forms known in the East reached the Middle West for the first time. However, the settlers in the western country could not immediately duplicate the structures which they had left behind in their home states. For the first few years they resorted almost exclusively to the log cabin. This type of structure, which played so large a part in the development of the West, was of north European origin and was first introduced into America by the Swedes who settled on the Delaware River in 1638. Eventually adopted by the Pennsylvania Germans, the Scotch-Irish, and other restless folk who settled the West, it became the universal structural form in all pioneer wood-bearing sections of the country. In fact, "the log cabin was exactly what the pioneer needed." It was "a type of habitation that could be built of materials taken from the land in clearing it" for cultivation. It could be "put together with the same tool used in felling the trees; and it presented a combination of economy and convenience admirably adapted to the westward movement." Houses, jails, schools, churches, and courthouses alike were built in this manner.

The early cabins were of one or two rooms, but by the addition of appendages they were considerably amplified. Often the Southern settler orientated his home so that the prevailing summer breezes were directed through a "dogtrot" porch connecting the kitchen and the main cabin. Such a breezeway was a pleasantly cool spot in summer. It served as the family washroom, complete with bench for water bucket and wash basin, and as a storage place for the kitchen firewood. Chimneys were at first of logs.

The next development came with the construction of squared-

[18] Newcomb, *Spanish-Colonial Architecture in the United States*, 36–39, plates 95–130.

log structures of one or two stories with stone foundations and stone or brick chimneys. In plan these houses were not unlike types found beyond the mountains. In fact, after clapboards became available, many a house of such construction was converted into what, from all outward signs, appears to be a framed house.[19]

Eventually the settlers turned to the more permanent materials; and in Kentucky, particularly in the bluegrass region, small houses of stone or brick appeared. In time these smaller habitations became tenant houses or slave quarters, and the master built for his family a great brick mansion. Brick came into vogue about 1786, just as the Georgian manner went out of use and the Federal style came in. As a result, Kentucky has many excellent examples of such architecture,[20] as have Tennessee and other parts of the New South.[21]

Some of the pioneers who came over the mountains into Kentucky and Tennessee eventually pushed onward to become settlers in Ohio, Indiana, and Illinois. This settlement antedated the movement of New Englanders westward and was largely participated in by those Southern hunter-pioneers who, having seen service in the Indian wars, were accustomed to rough life in the open. The Ohio and the Mississippi formed the highways by which many of these backwoodsmen came westward. Gradually they chopped their way northward and westward along the wooded banks of the tributary streams, not as yet venturing out upon the open prairie.

These settlers covered roughly the southern half of the states mentioned, there meeting emigrants from New England and the Middle Atlantic who, after 1830, swarmed into the northern areas. These settlers from the South, recalling the open, airy structures of their home states, erected houses as nearly as possible like those which they had left behind. The settlers from New England built structures similar to those in which they had dwelt beyond the mountains.

South of a line roughly marked by the Old National Road, one still finds this architecture of Southern lineage. It exhibits a predilection for brick as a structural material, a symmetrical arrangement of structures and their wings and appendages, detached service

---

[19] Rexford Newcomb, *Architecture of the Old Northwest Territory*, chap. vi.
[20] Rexford Newcomb, *Old Kentucky Architecture*, plates 5–89.
[21] Clifford H. Cochran, *Grandeur in Tennessee*, 1–19.

buildings, classical frontal porticoes, open two-story galleries, wide central halls, and high ceilings.[22]

North of this line are buildings of Yankee lineage. Many who had lived in Early American homes, i. e. homes erected before 1720, in Massachusetts and Connecticut built edifices of a similar plan in northern Ohio, despite the fact that such houses had passed out of fashion in the East seventy-five years before. Moreover, since carpenters were no longer versed in Early American carpentry, they dressed these old-fashioned plans out in the latest Federal-style forms. To be sure, as time went on, these compact New England plans were modified to accord with life as it was lived in the West and with the changed climatic scene. Thus Yankee architecture spread across the Middle West.[23] It is to be remembered, however, that Yankees sometimes settled in southern situations, like Marietta on the Ohio, and that Southerners, upon occasion, penetrated to northern points like Galena, Illinois.

The accent upon religious freedom in Article I of the Ordinance of 1787 encouraged sects of all kinds to settle in the Northwest Territory. Thus came Moravians, Mormons, Rappites, Zoarites, Mennonites, Dunkers, Shakers, Quakers, and Catholics, besides adherents of all sorts of Protestant faiths, each faith bringing its own type of meetinghouse, a little white church or a temple. The result was a variety of ecclesiastical architecture.

On August 1, 1792, the governor and judges of the Northwest Territory adopted an act "directing the building and establishing of a court-house and county jail . . . in every county." By this legislation the officials of the territory provided an architectural setting for the legal business of the region. In the rural districts of the Old Northwest these structures became, as often they remain today, the most important edifice within a county.

Article III declared: "Religion, morality and knowledge, being necessary to good government and the happiness of mankind, schools and the means of education shall forever be encouraged." Out of this provision and the subsequent enabling legislation, grew the public school system and the many colleges and universities, denominational and otherwise, that early arose in this region.

[22] Newcomb, *Architecture of the Old Northwest Territory*, chap. vii.
[23] *Ibid.*, chap. viii.

In addition to the movement of Americans into the Old North-west, we must mention also marked infiltrations from Europe, with concentrated settlements here and there. As early as 1826, Timothy Flint remarked the curious mixture of races and classes in the West, all commingled in "a spirit of adventurous enterprise." What a melting pot the Northwest was to become during the next forty years can be fathomed only by an examination of European immigration into the area during these years. Hither came Cornishmen to the lead mines of southwestern Wisconsin, Welshmen to Ohio and Wisconsin. The Irish settled in great numbers in most of the states; and there were heavy concentrations of Germans at Cincinnati, Chicago, Milwaukee, and St. Louis; and German-Swiss at Highland, Illinois, with other settlements at Vevay, Indiana, and New Glarus, Wisconsin. The Dutch came to Holland, Zeeland, and Grand Rapids in Michigan, also to Wisconsin and Illinois; the Norwegians to northern Illinois and southeastern Wisconsin; and the Swedes and Danes to Illinois, Wisconsin, and Minnesota.[24]

Where concentrated, each of these groups has to a degree in-fluenced architectural expression, sometimes as to style, again as to plan and arrangement, but more frequently as to construction and craftsmanship.

When the Northwest Territory was opened, architecture upon the Atlantic seaboard had passed through the Colonial period, al-ready described, and the Federal style—a sort of American Empire—was in vogue. This was to prevail until about 1820, when the Greek Revival set in.

This latter somewhat archaeological manner, introduced into America by Benjamin Henry Latrobe (1764–1820), became the principal American architectural vernacular between 1820 and the Civil War. American builders knew little about Greek construction, but they employed current methods of building to achieve the clas-sical forms which they copied from builders' handbooks which circulated widely. Marble, the popular antique material, was, of course, out of the question, but templelike structures of stone, brick, and even of wood were erected to serve as residences, churches, and public buildings. In general, it was the Greek Revival—in its hey-day during the developing period of the Old Northwest—which

24 *Ibid.,* chap. ii.

followed the log cabin when better homes could be built.[25] The Greek Revival exhibited wide regional adaptations.

Another style coming to us from England was the Gothic Revival. Beginning as a style for churches, this romantic vogue was used mainly for residences, schools, and college buildings. Little was understood of medieval construction, however, and whatever Gothic quality was achieved was the result of copying medieval ornamental details from imported architectural handbooks. Of course all of this has little to do with regional expression, except as local usages and traits emerged within the confines of a revived historical medium.

Meanwhile the tide of settlement moved westward. In 1836, four hundred and fifty steamboats helped bring to Chicago throngs of Easterners, most of whom outfitted here for the journey onward. "The Yankees," says Nida, "quickly took possession of all the woodlands and knowing little of how to farm the open prairie, refused to abandon the timbered regions until all were taken. Then some moved out on the higher prairies and fortune smiled on them."[26]

Building a home upon a treeless prairie was not an easy task. If the prairie was near a wood, logs for a house might be purchased. But often there was no timber and the settler had no funds with which to buy. So he had to content himself with indigenous materials. Thus the sod house came into being. Such houses were made of sods two feet long, eighteen inches wide, and four inches thick. Cut out with a spade, they were laid in a wall much like bricks and held together with wooden stakes driven through two or more courses. If a roof of shingles could not be secured, the pioneer had to content himself with a covering of turf or straw. However, the introduction of sawmills in the timbered portions in time solved the problem and frame houses replaced the sod cabins.

By this time the balloon frame, invented by a Chicago Yankee, George Washington Snow (1797–1870), to save precious lumber, had come into use. First employed in the fast-growing town on Lake Michigan in 1833, the balloon frame soon spread over the prairies and in time became, as it is today, the typical constructive scheme for light timber buildings.[27] Presently roads, canals, and eventually

25 *Ibid.*, chap. xi–xiii.

26 William Lewis Nida, *The Story of Illinois and Its People*, 168.

27 Alfred Theodore Andreas, *History of Chicago*, I, 504–505.

railroads made possible a wider distribution of structural materials.

The story that has been related of architecture in Ohio, Illinois, and Indiana was repeated upon every new frontier of the American plowman. In Minnesota, Kansas, and Nebraska the log cabin and sod house were followed by frame houses of questionable utility and little artistic merit, these, in time, to be supplanted by better-planned and happier structures. And so the story has run in each new community—an evolution from the flimsy, crude, and ugly to better and more appropriate types.

As civilization moved westward across the continent, the transplanted New Englandism of the Old Northwest, together with purer strains carried thither from New England itself, reached the Pacific slope. At Astoria, Oregon City, Portland, Salem, and other early settlements in the new Northwest, Anglo-Saxon architectural notions, modified to meet local conditions, brought forth simple and well-proportioned structural types. Plentiful wood in the Pacific Northwest again made possible the cabin of horizontal logs which is to this day manifest in the Mountain States. This same wood made possible also the jigsaw monstrosities of the Victorian era.

Many a Yankee family settled in Hispanic California, where the old houses which they reared exhibit a happy commingling of the forms appropriate to the use of adobe as a building material with utilities characteristic of New England. Thus resulted the so-called Monterey style—a type which combines the heavy adobe walls, the overhanging balcony, and the patio of Spanish precedent with the deep-revealed double-hung windows, the picket fences, and the roofs of split shingles reminiscent of New England.[28]

Another type, currently enjoying a revival, is the Western ranch house, which incorporates traits growing out of American building experience upon the great sheep and cattle ranches of the West and Southwest. Nor must one omit the ubiquitous wooden bungalow, allegedly of Oriental (Indian) origin, which blanketed the Pacific Coast, then swept the nation to the detriment of more appropriate and indigenous cottage types in many regions.

In addition to the well-defined regions discussed above, there are many fringe areas where cultures meet with resultant mixed architectural expressions. Texas is a good example with its clear references

[28] Newcomb, *The Colonial and Federal House,* 35.

to the Old South, Negro life, Mexican infiltrations, and ranch life. Here the wood building of the eastern pineries gives over to adobe construction as one moves southwestward. In Utah, also, the Yankee building habits of the Mormons were refashioned to include the adobe and granite construction which a new habitat afforded. The results were striking.

The rapid industrialization which followed the Civil War radically affected our social and artistic continuity. We witnessed the rise of industrial cities in what had been largely an agrarian scene and the accumulation of great fortunes from lumber, meat packing, grain, steel, oil, and manufacturing. The bulk of the nation's business came into the control of great corporations. Labor became highly organized, and struggles between labor and management developed. These were indeed important changes. The old order was passing; a new order was replacing it.

From this time on, more careful social and economic planning became necessary. This resulted in antitrust laws, civil service reforms, the regulation of public utilities and common carriers, workmen's liability, child labor laws, collective bargaining of labor, arbitration of labor disputes, the imposition of income taxes, and the enfranchisement of women.

Meanwhile, over the nation swept every architectural fad, native or imported, that reached our Atlantic seaboard. First it was the French Renaissance of Richard Morris Hunt (1828–95), first native-born American to obtain a diploma from the École des Beaux Arts in Paris. His work, based upon a study of French chateau architecture and the pavilions of the Louvre, bristled with towers, turrets, and mansard roofs. His W. K. Vanderbilt house (1879–81) in New York, while beautiful architecturally, was neither American nor regional.[29]

Shortly, H. H. Richardson (1836–86) returned from Paris to practice in Boston. Using the time-honored Romanesque monuments of southern France and northern Spain as models, he designed robust stone structures of picturesque mass and romantic interest. His masterpiece, Trinity Church in Boston, was widely acclaimed and, as a result, he received commissions for buildings throughout the na-

[29] Newcomb, *Modern Architecture with Particular Reference to the United States,* 127–31.

tion. In fact, the vogue for the Richardsonian Romanesque became so pronounced that in the eighteen-eighties and nineties it was proclaimed the national style.[30]

Soon Charles Follen McKim (1847–1909) returned from study abroad to enter a three-year tenure in the office of Richardson. Following this experience he joined Mead and Bigelow in New York City in the practice of architecture. In 1879 the firm of McKim, Mead, and White was formed when Stanford White replaced Bigelow. Rejecting the popular Romanesque, McKim, Mead, and White practiced a variety of refined classic design based upon the French *néo-Grec*. This change was most acceptable to a nation schooled to the quiet simplicity of the Greek Revival and already tired of the restless, if picturesque, silhouettes of Richardson and Hunt. The Neo-Classic of McKim achieved a genuine rebirth in the snow-white buildings of the Chicago World's Fair of 1893, and from then on the nation welcomed designs of classic purity for its schools, libraries, courthouses, and other public structures.[31]

To be sure, these were not the only styles in which architects attempted to express the nation's changing social needs. Indeed, added to this battle of the styles were experiments in Neo-Gothic, Neo-Byzantine, Neo-Colonial, and even Neo-Egyptian. The results of these changeful modes are plainly visible in cities throughout the country, and the picture is not a happy one. The whole approach appears to have been at fault. For one thing, the architectural profession, having become unified nationally about this time, began to exert an important role in American culture. Too much emphasis was placed upon style as such, rather than upon functional solutions of our building problems. Indeed, it was generally believed that there should be a unified national style. How wrong these tenets were it remained for men like Louis Sullivan and Frank Lloyd Wright to demonstrate later.

If Boston and New York may be said to have been the foci of post–Civil War architectural activity, under the leadership of Sullivan that focus was to shift to Chicago and the Midwest. Born in New England, Sullivan was trained at Massachusetts Institute of Technology and in Paris. In 1881 he came to Chicago, where he joined in

30 *Ibid.*, 131–37.
31 *Ibid.*, 141–54.

a partnership with Denkmar Adler to practice architecture. Having announced his philosophy that architectural form should follow function, Sullivan proceeded to apply this logic to the solution of professional commissions entrusted to his firm. Meanwhile he converted to his doctrine of architectural independence a group of brilliant young architects who had been attracted to Chicago by the building activity that followed the Great Fire. Among these were Frank Lloyd Wright, Dwight Perkins, George G. Elmslie, Irving K. Pond, Hugh Garden, George Maher, Max Dunning, Walter Burley Griffin, and others who constituted the little group of modernists who came to be known in architectural circles as the Chicago school.

Out of the work of these men and a group of followers, there grew a regional type which emphasized horizontal lines and wide overhangs and was widely hailed as the prairie style. Except for the work of Wright, who has never surrendered, a revived traditionalism spelled doom for this movement. However, Wright's sons, his pupils Barry Byrne and George Fred Keck, and younger disciples carry on in an independent vein.

While this Chicago school concerned itself largely with aesthetic considerations, others were pioneering in the means to an expression of functional form in newer structural materials, like steel and concrete, which luckily at this time became economically available to American builders. This movement was participated in by three prominent firms of architects who sought to house the growing business of the Illinois metropolis in multiple-storied structures. The heads of these firms and the men most importantly associated with this development were William Holabird (1854–1923), William Le-Baron Jenney (1832–1907), and Daniel H. Burnham (1846–1912).

Before 1883, masonry structures were of the Richardsonian wall-bearing type. Late in that year, Jenney was commissioned to design the Home Insurance Building. In this edifice, for the first time in history, Jenney carried the weight of his structure not upon the walls but upon a skeleton framework of iron concealed within the walls—cast-iron columns and wrought-iron I beams. While this building was under construction, the Carnegie-Phipps Steel Company turned out the first of its Bessemer steel beams and asked permission to substitute these for iron beams in the upper floors. This agreed to, the Home Insurance Building in Chicago became the first of all skyscrapers and the progenitor of a movement that was to culminate in New York's Empire State Building. Other Chicago buildings in this line of development were the Tacoma Building (1888), the Rand-McNally building (1889), which was the first to have an all-steel frame, and the Monadnock Block (1891).

For some time, however, engineering and aesthetics went separate ways, and these early skyscrapers were sheathed in traditional raiment. It remained for Adler and Sullivan, in the Wainwright Building in St. Louis (1891), first to express adequately the structural frame of the building in its external lines. This was achieved by giving the vertical members, which carry the main loads, dominance over the horizontal members, which carry the loads of one floor only.

Carrying this idea further, Sullivan succeeded in expressing in even more beautiful external form the internal steel structure of the Guaranty Trust Building in Buffalo, New York (1895). This noble and practical demonstration of his doctrine of function versus form set a precedent that was to shape all subsequent skyscraper design.[32]

Meanwhile new materials, new systems of construction, and new inventions—further results of industrialization—came to influence American life and architecture. Consider the consequences of the internal-combustion engine and its derivatives, the automobile and the airplane. In the wake of these inventions came garages, private and public, filling stations, great automotive factories, parking areas and buildings, hangars, airports, superhighways, and a streamlining of life in general. Ponder also the possible architectural implications of aluminum, enameled steel, glass, plastics, air conditioning, radio, and television! Thus, in spite of fitful fads of eclecticism and flash backs to traditionalism, an architecture expressive of current American life and thought is definitely, if slowly, emerging. Today the emphasis is less and less upon the superficialities of style and more upon living, functional forms. The important trends in architecture are not the result of personal caprice, but the product of deep-moving social forces; whatever its pattern, there is an abiding continuum that indelibly stamps American architecture as truly American.

From what has been said, it will be discerned that there are two forces at work in American architecture—one centrifugal, the other centripetal. The first comes about through our strong democratic

[32] *Ibid.*, 187–205.

nationalism, a fairly common pattern of folkways, easy means of communication and transportation, a wide distribution of architectural information in periodical literature and books, new nationally distributed inventions, and a general gregariousness of thought which prompts the Smiths of Kansas City to want a house like that of the Joneses in Santa Barbara. These factors tend to break down regional differences.

The second force results from our extended geography, with corresponding climatic variations, topographies ranging from desert to alpine, and vegetation ranging from semitropical to north temperate. If nature were allowed to take her course, regional differences, both social and artistic, would be far more pronounced than they are.

In view of all these variables, a unified national architectural expression is not to be expected or desired. In our American states, society will never be identical, and, even if it were, climate and other environmental factors would prevent a uniformity of architectural expression. Architecture is a living, dynamic social expression. Creation is not yet complete. New and significant regional forms are yet to be expected.

BIBLIOGRAPHY

Andreas, Alfred Theodore. *History of Chicago.* 3 vols. Chicago, 1884–86.

Cochran, Clifford H. *Grandeur in Tennessee.* New York, 1946. Illustrated with 110 plates and drawings.

Foreman, Henry C. *The Architecture of the Old South, Medieval Style, 1585–1850.* Cambridge, Massachusetts, 1948. A study of the beginnings of architecture in the Old South, paying particular attention to early types of construction practiced in the colonies. Indispensable to one who would understand the earliest building procedure of our English colonists. Illustrated.

Frary, I. T. *Early Homes of Ohio.* Richmond, Virginia, 1936. Excellent for an understanding of the movement of seaboard architectural forms into the Old Northwest. The many illustrations include churches, courthouses, and banks, in addition to residences.

Hamlin, Talbot. *Greek Revival Architecture in America.* New York, 1944. A complete and competent study of the architecture of the classical revival in the United States. The material is arranged geographically, permitting the reader to make regional comparisons. Illustrated.

Kimball, Fiske. *American Architecture*. Indianapolis, Indiana, 1928. A brief survey, distinguishing variations upon stylistic and regional bases. Illustrated.

──────. *Domestic Architecture of the American Colonies and of the Early Republic*. New York, 1922. A complete and competent treatise upon the career of domestic architecture throughout the Atlantic seaboard colonies. Contains a chronological chart, listing the important houses with dates and authorship where established by documents, also copious notes upon the individual houses. Amply illustrated.

Newcomb, Rexford. "A Brief History of Rural Architecture in the United States." *President's Conference on Home Building and Home Ownership*. Washington, 1932. A brief outline of the history of rural architecture upon a regional basis. The influence of environment and social pattern upon the architecture of the principal regions is pointed out. Illustrated.

──────. *Architecture of the Old Northwest Territory*. Chicago, 1950. A detailed study of early architecture in Ohio, Indiana, Illinois, Michigan, Wisconsin, and a part of Minnesota. Amply illustrated.

──────. *The Colonial and Federal House*. Philadelphia, 1933. An analysis of the elements of Colonial and Federal houses with illustrations of their salient features and a discussion of their regional adaptations.

──────. *The Old Mission Churches and Historic Houses of California*. Philadelphia, 1925. A study of the California variant of the Spanish Colonial style against its environmental background, physical and social. The outstanding traits of the style are analyzed and discussed. Illustrated.

──────. *Spanish-Colonial Architecture in the United States*. New York, 1937. An analytical study of Spanish Colonial architecture and its regional variants in Florida, Texas, New Mexico, Arizona, and California. The features of the regional types are catalogued and illustrated and lists of the important monuments are furnished. Some 36 of the 130 plates of illustrations are devoted to modern exemplars of these regional types.

──────. *Old Kentucky Architecture*. New York, 1940. A survey of Kentucky architecture from the log cabin days down through the Colonial, Federal, Greek Revival, and Gothic types to the Civil War. A short letterpress sketches the evolution of Kentucky types and cites important examples. Some 130 plates illustrate the typical monuments.

──────. *Mediterranean Domestic Architecture in the United States*. Cleveland, Ohio, 1928. A volume of 224 plates and brief letterpress setting forth the regional adaptations of domestic architecture in the United States based upon the Spanish and related Mediterranean precedent.

──────. *Modern Architecture with Particular Reference to the United States*. New York, 1939. An outline digest of the salient features of the different periods and regional variations of American architecture, with lists of important examples and complete bibliographies.

Nida, William Lewis. *The Story of Illinois and Its People*. Revised ed. Chicago, 1930.

Peterson, Charles E. "Early Sainte Genevieve, Missouri, and Its Architecture," *Missouri Historical Review,* Vol. XXXV (January, 1941), 207–32. A discussion of French architecture and building in the Illinois country, with an analysis of the salient features of this regional type.

Pickens, Buford L. "Regional Aspects of Louisiana Architecture," *Journal of the Society of Architectural Historians,* Vol. VII (January–June, 1948), 33–36.

Raymond, Eleanor. *Early Domestic Architecture of Pennsylvania.* New York, 1931. Illustrated.

Scott, Natalie, and William P. Spratling. *Old Plantation Houses in Louisiana.* New York, 1927. Journeys to the important plantations along the Mississippi from New Orleans to St. Francisville, on Bayou Lafourche, and in the Teche country. Text with sketches of the houses.

Shurtleff, Harold R. *The Log Cabin Myth.* Cambridge, Massachusetts, 1938. Investigates the origin and career of the log cabin, which was highly important in the American westward movement.

Smith, J. Frazer. *White Pillars.* New York, 1941. Early life and architecture of the lower Mississippi Valley, particularly Tennessee, Mississippi, Alabama, and Louisiana, with plans and drawings and copious notes on the important houses. While there are no photographs, the delightful sketches give an excellent idea of the architecture of the area.

Tallmadge, Thomas E. *The Story of Architecture in America.* New York, 1927. Treats of American architecture in its entirety with frequent references to its regional differences. Excellent for a general survey.

Chapter 10

Linguistic Regionalism

Hans Kurath

Language is a complicated system of signaling meanings by means of words, phrases, sentences, and larger utterances.

Language serves the purpose of communication within a society so as to produce co-operation and mutual understanding among its members in all activities, ranging from the performance of manual tasks to the development of rules of conduct, scientific procedures, the propagation of ideas and ideals, and the dissemination of all types of information among the members of the group.

Speech forms and their meanings are conventional, as are the sounds of which they consist. Each member of a speech community pronounces the forms in much the same way as other members of his group and applies them to similar situations, i.e., he uses words, phrases, and sentences in generally accepted senses. Growing up in a certain society, he acquires the speech habits of his elders and his associates. Intimate contact among the members of a group produces uniform usage; social or geographic separation results in divergent usage. If language is to serve its purpose as a means of communication within a society, the language habits or speech ways of the members of that society must be relatively uniform.

Speech habits are specific and they are shared in a large measure by all the inhabitants of a region or by all members of a social group. Hence, the linguist, by selecting representative speakers and recording their usage, can determine accurately the geographic and the social dissemination of hundreds, if not thousands, of individual features of speech—words, word forms, constructions, and pronunciations. When he compares the dissemination of these individual features, he soon discovers recurring patterns of distribution. For instance, he finds that certain words are current only in eastern New

England, in the Hudson Valley, on Chesapeake Bay, in the Virginia piedmont, or in the southern upland (the Appalachians); or that their regional spread is focused on these areas. Or he discovers that certain expressions are found in all of the New England settlement area, extending from the Atlantic or the Connecticut River westward to the Great Lakes and beyond, but not in Pennsylvania or farther south, while others are current throughout the Pennsylvania settlement area but not in the New England area or the old plantation country of the South. This discovery of the recurrent patterns of distribution results in "spotting" the major speech areas and their subdivisions.[1]

Thereafter he undertakes to assemble all the features that are characteristic of the several areas identified, drawing a boundary—isogloss—for each one of them and then combining the isoglosses of these features. He soon finds that these isoglosses rarely coincide exactly over their entire extent; rather they form more or less close-knit bundles, coalescing here and there and flaring elsewhere. These bundles of lines constitute the boundaries of speech areas, which may be rather sharply defined, as in northern Pennsylvania (between the New England and the Pennsylvania settlement areas) or along the Blue Ridge in Virginia (between the Southern and the Pennsylvania settlement areas); or they may have the character of a transition belt, as between eastern and western New England, along the waist of New Jersey, in central West Virginia, or in the upper piedmont of the Carolinas.

In setting up speech areas, the linguist follows a well-established scientific procedure: he samples usage systematically throughout the area under investigation; he delimits the dissemination of each feature of speech separately on the basis of his survey; and then he assembles speech boundaries showing similar trends. Thus he arrives at a well-founded conception of the extent of the several speech areas,

---

[1] All statements regarding the distribution of speech forms in the Eastern States are based on evidence provided by the collections of the *Linguistic Atlas of the United States,* a research project of the American Council of Learned Societies. The collections for the eastern United States, formerly at Brown University, are now at the University of Michigan. The *Linguistic Atlas of New England* (Providence, Rhode Island, 1939–43) has been published in six parts; also a *Handbook of the Linguistic Geography of New England* (Providence, Rhode Island, 1939). For this paper I have drawn extensively on my *Word Geography of the Eastern United States* (Ann Arbor, 1949).

THE SPEECH AREAS
OF THE EASTERN STATES

THE NORTH

1 Northeastern New England
2 Southeastern New England
3 Southwestern New England
4 Upstate New York and w. Vermont
5 The Hudson Valley
6 Metropolitan New York

THE MIDLAND

7 The Delaware Valley (Philadelphia Area)
8 The Susquehanna Valley
9 The Upper Potomac and Shenandoah Valleys
10 The Upper Ohio Valley (Pittsburgh Area)
11 Northern West Virginia
12 Southern West Virginia
13 Western North and South Carolina

THE SOUTH

14 Delamarvia (Eastern Shore of Maryland and
   Virginia, and southern Delaware)
15 The Virginia Piedmont
16 Northeastern North Carolina (Albemarle
   Sound and Neuse Valley)
17 The Cape Fear and Peedee Valleys
18 South Carolina

0   25   50
SCALE IN MILES

the character of the boundaries separating them, and of the relations between the areas so delimited.[2]

Since speech is employed in all the activities of a people, ranging from the performance of the chores of daily life to scientific procedures and literary composition, all aspects of the material and the spiritual culture of a people and their history must be reflected in it somehow.

Man takes his speech ways with him wherever he goes. Thus the Yankee farmer from western New England introduced his way of talking English into upstate New York and the entire Great Lakes basin. The cotton planter of the South Atlantic States carried varieties of Southern speech westward into the Gulf States and up the Mississippi Valley; and Pennsylvanians continued to speak their varieties of English—and German—when they settled the southern upland, the Ohio Valley, and the central plateau extending westward from the Appalachians to the Ozarks. These three major streams of westward migration created the three major speech areas of the eastern half of the United States.[3]

Whenever these three major streams mingled on the frontier, as in the middle part of Ohio, where New Englanders and Pennsylvanians settled side by side, or in West Virginia, where Southerners took up land alongside the Pennsylvanians, new blends of older types of American English developed in the course of several generations. This resulted in rather wide transition belts between the major areas, in which features derived from several different dialects are current. From what we find in the Eastern States, which have been systematically investigated for the *Linguistic Atlas,* it is clear that speech boundaries are most sharply defined on the Atlantic slope, in the original colonies; and that more and more extensive overlaps—transition belts—occur the farther west one goes, as the result of the progressive mingling of settlers having different speech ways.

Internal migrations in the areas that experienced extensive in-

[2] The scheme of the speech areas of the eastern United States, set up in this manner, is presented on the accompanying map.

[3] Representative examples of words restricted to the Northern area, the Midland area, or the Southern area are given in the table at the end of this paper. Regional words may, of course, be spread over any combination of these major areas or over one of the major areas and adjoining subareas.

dustrialization during the nineteenth century, such as southern New England, and the accumulation of population in cities and urbanized areas, have broken down many older speech differences by eliminating or reducing the currency of back-country expressions. As a result, the rural northeastern part of New England now stands out against the industrialized sections of eastern Massachusetts in word usage and in pronunciation.

On the basis of the isoglosses for more than four hundred regional, or local, words we find that there are two speech boundaries of the first degree of importance in the eastern United States. One runs in a westerly direction through northern Pennsylvania, separating the Northern from the Midland area; the other runs in a southwesterly direction along the Blue Ridge in Virginia, separating the South from the Midland.[4]

Boundaries of the second degree run (1) in a northerly direction from the mouth of the Connecticut River to the Green Mountains in Vermont, (2) from the fork of the Susquehanna in Pennsylvania (Sunbury) to Sandy Hook in New Jersey, (3) from Dover in Delaware in an arc through Baltimore to the Blue Ridge near Harpers Ferry, (4) from the lower James in Virginia through the piedmont of North Carolina to Roanoke in the Blue Ridge, (5) between the Peedee and the Santee in South Carolina, (6) along the northern watershed of the Kanawha in West Virginia, and (7) from Roanoke in the Blue Ridge through the piedmont of North Carolina to the Blue Ridge in South Carolina.

The secondary boundary running from the East Branch of the Susquehanna in northeast Pennsylvania to Sandy Hook in New Jersey may be regarded as the eastward continuation of the boundary between the North and the Midland. To the north of it lie the New England settlements in northeastern Pennsylvania and in East Jersey.

The secondary boundary running from Harpers Ferry on the Potomac by way of Baltimore to Delaware Bay, passing south of Dover, Delaware, is the northern sector of the boundary between the Midland and the South; while the secondary boundary running from the gorge of the James River in the Blue Ridge through the upper piedmont of the Carolinas is its southern extension. To the southeast

4 See the map.

of this major speech boundary lies the plantation country of the South with its distinctive speech ways.

The other secondary boundaries and the lesser boundaries divide the three major speech areas into more or less clearly characterized subareas: eastern New England versus western New England; the Hudson Valley versus western New England and upstate New York; eastern Pennsylvania (Philadelphia area) versus western Pennsylvania (Pittsburgh area); Delamarvia versus tidewater Maryland and Virginia; the North Midland (Pennsylvania) versus the Shenandoah Valley and West Virginia; the Virginia piedmont versus eastern North Carolina; the Cape Fear–Peedee area versus the Neuse-Albemarle area to the north and the greater part of South Carolina to the south. Some of these subareas are more distinctive than others, e.g., eastern New England, metropolitan New York (a subdivision of the Hudson Valley area), Delamarvia, the Virginia piedmont, and South Carolina south of the Peedee.

In general one can say that the coastal area, the oldest in point of settlement, is the most highly diversified in speech. In eastern New England we find that Narragansett Bay (Rhode Island), Cape Cod, the Merrimack Valley, and the coast of Maine all have distinctive local expressions. On Chesapeake Bay, the Eastern Shore often differs from the Western Shore; and on the Western Shore of Virginia the Northern Neck, the Middle Neck (between the Rappahannock and the James), and the Norfolk area not infrequently differ in usage. In the Carolinas we find equally clear subdivisions: Albemarle Sound, the Neuse Valley, and the Cape Fear and Peedee valleys all have characteristic local expressions.[5]

The reasons for this great diversity in usage on the seaboard would seem to be the prolonged isolation of these early settlements in Colonial days, continued difficulties in intercommunication be-

---

[5] Examples of local expressions:

Narragansett Bay: johnnycake, 'griddlecake'; dandle, 'seesaw'; eace worm, 'earthworm.'

Narragansett Bay and Cape Cod: tempest; scup (a fish); cade, 'pet lamb.'

Cape Cod: apple grunt (an apple dessert); cleave-stone peach, 'freestone peach.'

Merrimack Valley and Essex County: mud worm, 'earthworm'; orts pail, 'garbage pail.'

Eastern Shore: hand horse, 'near horse'; corn stack, 'corncrib'; cocky horse, 'seesaw.'

Albemarle Sound: trumpery room, 'storeroom'; cookie, 'doughnut'; Sunday baby, 'illegitimate child.'

cause of the deep indentation of the coast, loss of progressive (younger) elements in the population during the westward movement, and conservatism resulting from pride in the long past and fondness of "olden days."

The southern upland (the South Midland), the upper Ohio Valley (western Pennsylvania and northern West Virginia), and up-state New York are linguistically much more uniform than the coastal section, and the boundaries between them have rather the character of transition belts—i.e., the isoglosses are widely spaced. They were settled in fast-moving and overlapping waves shortly before and after the Revolutionary War; hence the larger speech areas and the flowing boundaries.

We may anticipate a progressive enlargement of the speech areas, greater uniformity within the areas, and widening transition belts between them, the farther west we go. The rapidity of expansion during the nineteenth century and the mingling of the streams of settlers from the East would tend to produce that effect. Nevertheless, the wide-meshed survey of the Great Lakes basin, which is now in progress, shows that the boundary between the Northern and the Midland speech areas (the New England and the Pennsylvania settlement areas), which is so clearly defined in its course in northern Pennsylvania, is well marked all the way to the Mississippi River. It runs as a rather loose and tangled strand of isoglosses through north central Ohio, as a neat bundle of lines in northern Indiana, and then swerves southwestward through Illinois in the direction of St. Louis, the lines flaring out progressively.[6]

The westward extension of the boundary between the Southern and the Midland areas is yet to be determined. One expects it to follow the northern boundary of the Cotton Belt, which was largely settled from the plantation country of the South Atlantic States.

Speech areas are not stable. Their boundaries advance or shrink.

[6] Hans Kurath, "Dialect Areas, Settlement Areas, and Culture Areas in the United States," in C. R. Ware (ed.), *The Cultural Approach to History* (New York, 1940). Alva L. Davis, "A Word Geography of the Great Lakes Area," University of Michigan dissertation (1948). Both Kurath and Davis base their findings on the survey of the Great Lakes basin and the Ohio Valley which is now in progress under the direction of Albert Marckwardt of the University of Michigan and with the collaboration of Frederic G. Cassidy of the University of Wisconsin and Harold Allen of the University of Minnesota.

Often they advance in one sector while they recede in another. The shifting of old boundaries can be clearly demonstrated for most of the areas in the Eastern States that have a prominent population center: eastern New England (Boston), the area surrounding metropolitan New York, eastern Pennsylvania (Philadelphia), the Virginia piedmont (the old fall-line ports—Alexandria, Falmouth, Richmond) and the low country of South Carolina (Charleston).

Massachusetts Bay words have been carried southward into the area of the Plymouth Colony to such an extent that Old Colony words often survive only on Buzzards Bay and on Cape Cod. The southern half of Essex County, too, has been largely merged into the Boston area. New words, such as "tonic" for carbonated soft drinks, have spread throughout the Boston wholesale area. By this process of radiation from the dominant center of Boston, old local usage has been and is being replaced by regional usage.

The spreading influence of the speech of metropolitian New York on Long Island, in southwestern Connecticut, in the lower Hudson Valley (to the Highlands), and in East Jersey (to the upland) is clearly traceable in the progressive elimination of New Englandisms from Long Island and East Jersey and in the replacement of old Hudson Valley words in the lower part of the valley. Even more striking is the introduction in these areas of New York City pronunciations, of which the well-known diphthong in words like "bird" and the loss of r in words like "hard" are most readily noticed, but by no means the only ones. The extension of metropolitan New York pronunciations to the surrounding areas is easily traced because of the many unique features of metropolitan speech. Commuting, trade relations, and the cultural prominence of this great population center all have a share in disseminating its speech habits.[7]

Philadelphia influence in a westerly direction was rather effectively blocked until fairly recent times by the barrier of Pennsylvania German settlements in the Great Valley and the Lancaster Plain. But evidence of a more recent spreading of words to the Susquehanna Valley is not wanting.[8] On the other hand, Philadelphia expressions have spread southward to the very door of Baltimore,

---

[7] Yakira H. Frank, "The Speech of Metropolitan New York," University of Michigan dissertation (1948).

[8] Disseminated from Philadelphia to the Susquehanna Valley: pavement, 'sidewalk'; baby coach, 'baby carriage.'

which did not rise into prominence until after the Revolution, and they have been carried far beyond the old settlement boundary on the Eastern Shore of Maryland and in Delaware, creating here a transition belt of spaced isoglosses between the Midland and the Southern speech areas.[9] As a result, the speech of Delamarvia shows a unique blending of old local features, old Southernisms, and imported Midland features.

The fall-line ports of Virginia form the center of a well-defined and rather uniform speech area, the Virginia piedmont. The influence of this area extends northward to Annapolis—even to Baltimore—and it is strongly felt in the Virginia tidewater. On these points of land on Chesapeake Bay we still find expressions that occur also on the Eastern Shore and on the Carolina coast, but they have been, and still are, yielding ground to piedmont expressions.[10]

On the other hand, the Norfolk area has escaped piedmont influence, partly because of its old trade connections with Albemarle Sound, partly because of the historic antagonism between the fall-line ports and Norfolk, the only deep-sea port of Virginia. To this day, the Norfolk area—the so-called South Side of Virginia—is linguistically most closely akin to the northeastern section of North Carolina.

As the influence of such important centers of trade and culture expands and extends the areas in which they are located, the adjoining areas shrink and may ultimately be completely submerged. The "Down East," Cape Cod, eastern Long Island, the Catskills, the Virginia tidewater, and various sections of the South Atlantic coast are in this situation. They lack important centers of their own, they are mostly sparsely settled, and many of the younger generation seek larger opportunities elsewhere. Such recessive or relic areas have great importance for the student of the history of our language because they preserve usages that formerly were current over much larger areas.

The linguistic acculturation of the Dutch (Holland Dutch) in the Hudson Valley and of the Germans (Pennsylvania Dutch) in eastern Pennsylvania and derivative areas is a part of the general trend from local to regional—and to national—usage, which gained momentum

[9] Examples: blinds, 'roller shades'; smearcase, 'cottage cheese'; worm fence, 'rail fence'; cornhusks.

[10] Some Virginia piedmont expressions that have encroached upon the tidewater area: nicker, 'whinny'; croker sack, 'burlap bag'; snake doctor, 'dragonfly.'

after the creation of the Union and was progressively accelerated by improvements in transportation and communication, by the growth of urban centers, and by compulsory attendance in the public schools.

The transition from Dutch and from German to English—i.e., to regional types of English—involved a rather prolonged period of bilingualism during which English words and phrases were more or less freely introduced into the Dutch or German spoken in the home and among neighbors, especially expressions concerned with social and political institutions and activities peculiar to America, the administration of justice, etc.; and during which Dutch and German words and phrases for things of the intimate life of the family and the farm—such as cookery, social customs, parts of the house and the barn, and calls to cattle and horses—were carried over into their English. After the foreign language was given up, the English current in the Dutch and the German settlement areas retained some of these foreign expressions and turns of speech. But even these relics were largely eliminated in the course of several English-speaking generations.

In the Dutch settlement area, where only a handful of old-timers in Bergen County, New Jersey, still know Dutch, very few Dutch relics have survived to this day;[11] but several Dutch expressions that had spread beyond the Dutch area in Colonial times or during the first half of the nineteenth century (during the bilingual period) are firmly established.[12]

In the Pennsylvania German area the situation is very different. In the Great Valley and the Lancaster Plain, and on the lower Susquehanna, where these Germans from the Palatinate and other parts of southwestern Germany settled in compact communities in the half-century preceding the Revolution, Pennsylvania Dutch is still widely spoken in the home and in transacting the affairs of the farming communities, although English is the usual medium of communication in the urban centers and in dealing with strangers. The hold of this folk dialect of German on this area has been substantially strengthened by the creation of a folk literature, written in Pennsyl-

[11] Some Dutch relics and words modeled on the Dutch: kip! (chicken call); pot cheese, 'cottage cheese'; hay barrack, 'roofed haystack'; sawbuck, 'sawhorse'; sapbush, 'sugar-maple grove.'

[12] Dutch expressions now current in the Hudson Valley and adjoining areas: stoop, 'porch'; cruller, 'unraised doughnut'; sugarbush, 'maple grove.'

vania Dutch, since the middle of the nineteenth century. It seems, therefore, highly probable that the Great Valley of Pennsylvania will remain bilingual for generations to come.

The English spoken in this bilingual area shows many Germanisms, outright borrowings as well as expressions modeled on German.[13] These Germanisms are less numerous in the Susquehanna Valley than in the Great Valley, and they are rapidly fading out in the Shenandoah Valley and on the Yadkin, where bilingual speakers are few.[14] West of the Alleghenies only scattered relics are found.[15]

The acquisition of English by the Germans in the Pennsylvania settlement area, the co-existence of German and English over longer periods leading to two-way borrowing, the gradual abandonment of German in favor of English, and the consequent fading out of Germanisms in the English spoken in this area form a chain of events paralleled in many other sections of our country: in the French settlements of Louisiana, in the Spanish settlements of the Southwest, and in the numerous German and Scandinavian settlements in the Middle West. The mode and the tempo of this linguistic acculturation vary, but the sequence of stages is much the same everywhere.

In conclusion, I should like to emphasize the fact that linguistic geography is a branch of cultural geography. Speech is an important element in the cultural heritage of any society; hence, the determination of the regional dissemination of speech ways is of great importance in delimiting culture areas. It may well be that the linguistic geographer has an advantage over the scholars who deal with other aspects of regional culture—such as political institutions and social customs, the architecture of farmhouses and barns, farming methods, food habits, and songs and tales and other forms of folk art—because speech ways are specific ingrained habits of every individual in a community, which any trained observer can readily record. In any event, linguists have made extensive surveys in Europe and more recently

[13] Expressions current in the English spoken in the bilingual Pennsylvania German area: smearcase, 'cottage cheese'; ponhaws, 'scrapple'; thick-milk, 'curdled milk'; (school) leaves out, 'lets out'; saddle horse, 'near-horse'; vootsie! (hog call); rainworm, 'earthworm'; toot, 'paper bag.'

[14] German relics in the Shenandoah Valley: vootsie!, saddle horse; in western North Carolina: vootsie!, saddle horse, rainworm.

[15] German relics found west of the Alleghenies: ponhaws, school leaves out.

REGIONAL WORDS

x *in general use*
/ *frequent*

	NORTH				MIDLAND					SOUTH			
	Eastern New England	Western New England	Upstate New York	Hudson Valley	Delaware Bay	Eastern Pennsylvania	Western Pennsylvania	West Virginia	Western North Carolina	Delamarvia	Virginia Piedmont	Eastern North Carolina	South Carolina
pail	x	x	x	x									
boss! (cow call)	x	x	x	x									
johnnycake, 'corn bread'	x	x	x	x									
angleworm, 'earthworm'	x	x	x	/									
stoop, 'porch'		x	x	x									
buttonball, 'sycamore'		x	x	x									
hasty-pudding, 'mush'	x	x	x										
teeter board, 'seesaw'	x	x	x										
haycock	x	x	x	x	x	x	/			x			
whetstone	x	x	x	x	x	x	x			x			
whinny	x	x	x	x	x	x	x						
string beans	x	x	x	x	x	x	/						
cornhusks	x	x	x	x	x	x	x						
blinds, 'roller shades'					/	x	x	x	/	x			
skillet, 'frying pan'					x	x	x	x	/		/		
snake feeder, 'dragonfly'					/	x	x	/	/				
sook! (cow call)						x	x	x	x				
smearcase, 'cottage cheese'					x	x	x	x	/	x			
run, 'creek'					x	x	x	/			/		
stone fence					x	x	x	/		x			
bucket, 'pail'					x	x	x	x	x	x	x	x	x
s(w)ingletree, 'whiffletree'						x	x	x	x	x	x	x	x
corn pone, 'corn bread'						/	x	x	x	x	x	x	x
polecat, 'skunk'						x	x	x	x	x	x	x	x
light-bread, 'wheat bread'								x	x	x	x	x	x
clabber								x	x	x	x	x	x
you all								/	/	x	x	x	x
light-wood, 'kindling'										x	x	x	x
turn of wood, 'armful'										x	x	x	x
low, 'moo'										x	x	x	x
co-wench! (cow call)										x	x	x	x

in America, and they have developed a scientific method of sampling speech ways, of delimiting speech areas, of determining trends in usage, and of interpreting linguistic conditions and events with reference to settlement history, trade areas, population centers, and such cultural agencies as the schools and the press. Since the close correlation between speech areas on the one hand and settlement areas and trade areas on the other has been pretty well established, it would seem that the scheme of speech areas that has been worked out for the eastern United States on the basis of the survey made for the *Linguistic Atlas of the United States* can be a valuable guide in any attempt to delimit the culture areas of that section of our country.

BIBLIOGRAPHY

Bach, Adolf. *Deutsche Mundartforschung.* Heidelberg, 1934.

Bloomfield, Leonard. *Language,* chap. v, xix. New York, 1933.

Dauzat, Albert. *Essais de géographie linguistique.* Paris, 1921.

Frings, T. "Sprachgeographic und Kulturgeographie," *Zs. f. Deutschkunde* (1930), 564.

——— and E. Tille. "Kulturmorphologie," *Teuth.,* Vol. II, 1–18.

Gamillscheg, Ernst. *Die Sprachgeographie und ihre Ergebnisse für die allgemeine Sprachwissenschaft.* Bielefeld and Leipzig, 1928.

Jaberg, K., and J. Jud. *Der Sprachatlas als Forschungsinstrument.* Kritische Grundlegung und Einführung in den Sprach- und Sachatlas Italiens und der Südschweiz. Halle, 1928.

Kretschmer, P. *Wortgeographie der hochdeutschen Umgangssprache.* Göttingen, 1918.

Kurath, Hans. A Bibliography of Linguistic Geography, in Hans Kurath and others, *Handbook of the Linguistic Geography of New England.* Providence, Rhode Island, 1939.

———. *A Word Geography of the Eastern United States.* Ann Arbor, 1949.

———, B. Bloch, and G. S. Lowman. *Linguistic Atlas of New England.* 3 vols. Providence, Rhode Island, 1939–43.

——— and M. L. Hanley. "Progress of the Linguistic Atlas of the United States and Canada." Annual reports of progress, beginning 1931, in the *Bulletin of the American Council of Learned Societies.* Washington.

Pessler, W. "Grundzüge zu einer Sachgeographie der deutschen Volkskunst," *Jb. f. hist. Volkskunst,* Vol. II, 44.

Pop, S. *La dialectologie.* 2 vols. Louvain, 1950.

Roedder, E. C. "Linguistic Geography," *Germanic Review,* Vol. I, 251–308.

Schrijnen, J. *Essai de bibliographie de géographie linguistique générale.*
  Nimêgue, 1933.
Wagner, K. *Deutsche Sprachlandschaften (Deutsche Dialektgeographie,*
  Heft XXIII). Marburg, 1927.

Part IV

The Concept of Regionalism
as a Practical Force

Introduction

John M. Gaus

People live in organizations that call upon them for mutual contributions toward the supplying of some common services. These services, and the organization, are related to a given area. A family lives somewhere, although in recent years that may seem to be too large a claim! A city, county, national state, is somewhere, with boundaries fixing its legal jurisdiction. But however boundaries may be drawn, there will be some factors of geography, history, and technology that do not coincide with them. A river, or a region of common factors of soil and climate, will embrace more than one political entity. Changing technologies in transportation will spill a city into the country, and, aided by techniques of refrigeration, will widen the potential milkshed; or will make wilderness areas available for recreation for city dwellers.

The Roman Empire in the West and its successor in the East, and the Roman and the Greek Orthodox Catholic Church, left cultural heritages that have profoundly influenced world affairs for centuries. As Turner reminded us, we may observe in the contemporary development of our own sections in the United States the processes of nation-building which we dimly discern in the Europe of a thousand years ago.

The legislator, the administrator, and the judge of today, like their counterparts in every kind of human association, are constantly confronted with the problem of reconciling function of service with area.[1] Their problem is one both of theory and of condition. The

---

[1] Note the recent statement of this phase of government by James W. Fesler, Professor of Political Science and Research Professor in the Institute for Research in Social Science, University of North Carolina, in his *Area and Administration* (University, Alabama, 1949).

discrepancy between newer functional need and older areal boundary is often so great that some grow out of patience with the traditional boundaries, speak of them as "unreal" and "unnatural," and urge the creation of new ones. Two comments should be made about this. First, the often derided political jurisdiction is as much a region as one determined by climate. Once a political boundary is drawn, human interests—political ambitions, areas of common services, and tax rates—adhere to it. It becomes as "natural" a fact as a rainfall line, which may also be affected by human intervention in the form of new types of land management. Second, the creation of a new region apparently more "natural" for the function or service desired, may adversely affect the existing community life by overcomplicating machinery and creating rival claimants to loyalty, taxes, and resources.

Nevertheless, the task of political invention is thrust upon the world by the growth of population and its interdependence, its pressure on resources, and its concentration in metropolitan regions. Thus Great Britain established a Boundary Commission to review its local government areas; Western Europe is exploring some form of federation to achieve economic betterment and collective security; and the U.S.S.R. and Eastern Europe and Northern Asia are laboratories in the problems of regions.

The practical force of regional factors is illustrated throughout the history of our federal system, which now includes national, state, and local units as basic units that are interwoven by law, administration, and party organization. Within these main lines are constantly evolving new combinations such as the Port of New York Authority, the Boston metropolitan agencies, the Tennessee Valley Authority, and the regional units of national and state government departments and regional committees within departments, as illustrated in those of the Department of the Interior. Nor is this all; the fact that some problems are peculiarly affected by conditions outside our national jurisdiction explains our acceptance of international agreements that also reflect the federal principle.

Turner's address at Chicago was in 1893. In the same year appeared a collection of papers edited, and in part written, by Robert A. Woods, entitled "The City Wilderness." These studies of Boston pointed to the emergence of metropolitan regions, a wilderness yet to be adequately explored and given order.

Perhaps we shall invent a new regional political unit for such regions. Perhaps we shall invent a process of program planning and budgeting within the national administrative and legislative systems that better reflects the need for adapting national policies to specific application locally. We may find some solutions in the co-operation of groups of states and of counties, through compacts, joint services, and co-operation in policy-making and execution with regional offices of national departments. Such procedures and devices are alike in the search for a better relation of function to area. In John Dewey's meaning of the word "public," we shall be facilitating newly emerging regional publics to recognize and organize themselves. The artists and the social scientists need each other for wisdom in that enterprise.

This symposium is evidence, in the variety of interests and regions represented, that the practical problems of regions are widely recognized and studied. We have all had Turner much in our minds here. Let me conclude with some of his wise observations on our theme:

The significance of the section in American history is that it is the faint image of a European nation and that we need to re-examine our history in the light of this fact. . . . What is now needed is co-operation between geographers who have come from geologic training to an interest in the regional aspect of human geography; the statisticians who have aimed to divide the nation into convenient sections for census data; the politicians, economists and bankers who have tried to map the Federal Reserve Districts; the railroad experts; business men in general; the historians; the students of literature and society—to make a more adequate survey of what are actually the natural regions in human geography as shown by human action. . . . I make the suggestion that, as the nation reaches a more stable equilibrium, a more settled state of society, with denser populations pressing upon the means of existence, with this population no longer migratory, the influence of the diverse physiographic provinces which make up the nation will become more marked.[2]

[2] Frederick Jackson Turner, *The Significance of Sections in American History* (New York, 1932), 50, 205, 313.

Chapter 11

The Tennessee Valley Authority

Gordon R. Clapp

T HE affairs of the world, troubled as they are, have placed this country in a new role. America's breadbasket has new mouths to feed, at home and abroad. Our basic industries of steel, aluminum, chemicals, and heavy goods have new markets thrust upon them; our capacity to produce is under stress at many points to supply materials fast enough and in quantities large enough to meet all demands. Electric power supply is skating on the thin ice of a too small margin of reserve practically everywhere; power shortages are the rule, not the exception.

These few examples describe what the experts call a "tight economy." And over it all hangs the constant specter of a world and national emergency that would require—if it should come in spite of our efforts to prevent it—a sudden expansion of production from this country's already heavily pressed soils, industries, and sources of basic energy.

We have built a great pyramid of productive organization in this country; it has reached higher and higher levels in the past ten years. We are called upon now to go back and redesign the base—to make it broader so it may support an even higher structure. The development of the natural resources of our great river valleys is a part of that job.

But greater production from a better mobilization of our physical resources is not enough. The methods, the ways and means, we devise to use modern technology in the redesign and reorganization of our physical assets will affect our freedom. The big question at this point is this: Can we be more expert, more nearly scientific, in the treatment of our physical resources and at the same time multiply the opportunities for man to exercise his free will?

It is against this background that the story of the Tennessee Valley has gained a new significance in the minds of many people. For the story of the Tennessee Valley demonstrates clearly that a sound expansion of our ability to produce must include a new approach to the development and use of our basic natural assets—rivers, soil, forests, and minerals. The experience of the Tennessee Valley also demonstrates that the genius of experts, engineers, and managers can be blended with the democratic aspirations of the people of a whole region to increase the sense and reality of human freedom.

When the TVA was established by the Congress and the President in 1933, the Tennessee Valley had a long history of difficulties and problems. Consider these states, within and across whose boundaries the Tennessee River forms and flows: Virginia (the southwest portion), North Carolina (the western side of the Appalachians), Tennessee (east, lower central, and west), Georgia (the northwest corner), Alabama (the northern part), Mississippi (the northeast corner), and Kentucky (the western and a bit of the southeastern part of the state). Agricultural and raw materials for export were the main source of wealth. The Tennessee River, the fourth largest in volume of stream flow in the country, was a great river; but it was a destructive force, not a friend. In the wintertime, it poured devastating floods upon the valley and swelled the flood crests on the lower Ohio and Mississippi rivers. In drier seasons, the flow was too small to support navigation or to turn the few turbines in its path. The agricultural lands of the watershed had suffered from long cropping, poor land-management, and erosion. The forest lands, which even today cover more than half the valley, had been depleted, as in many other regions, through poor cutting practices, lack of protection against fire, grazing, and general neglect.

Yet a realistic appraisal of the Tennessee Valley's resources revealed a land of promise. The Tennessee River was a potential asset, and the people of the region knew it. They had sought to bring about its development for more than a hundred years before TVA. In 1918, the federal government built nitrate munitions plants and, to supply them with power, built a large steam plant and began the construction of Wilson Dam. The dam was to produce power, and, with its lock, was to make navigation possible over the famous

Muscle Shoals. But the nitrate plants were never used during World War I, and Wilson Dam was not completed until several years later. This idle national investment at Muscle Shoals formed the nucleus of the present TVA development.

The TVA was established because it seemed apparent that the problems and opportunities of the Tennessee Valley required some one agency to do what no other existing federal or state agency was equipped or authorized to do. TVA was set up to plan and carry out a program for control and use of the erratic waters of the Tennessee River system; to see the river as a unit and the region as a whole; to live in the valley and to work with and strengthen state and local agencies in their service to the people; and to aid the enterprise of private citizens in removing the barriers and obstacles that were creating scarcity and destruction in a region of abundant but idle resources.

As to the Tennessee River, TVA was directed to plan, build, and operate a system of dams for the maximum amount of flood control, the maximum development of navigation, and, so far as was consistent with these two purposes, the maximum generation of electric power.

In eighteen years, TVA has constructed eighteen major dams and has integrated them in operation with ten previously existing dams, some purchased from a utility company and some owned by a private corporation but operated under TVA direction by agreement. The Tennessee River is now controlled from the headwaters of its tributaries in the Great Smoky Mountains to its mouth at the Ohio.

The present system of twenty-eight dams and reservoirs provides nearly 11,700,000 acre-feet of storage for flood control at the beginning of the flood season each year—that is about January 1. In the twelve years since Norris Dam was first placed in operation, the TVA reservoir system has averted more than $45,000,000 in flood damage at Chattanooga alone. This sum, not counting damage averted at other points on the Tennessee or in the lower Ohio and Mississippi basins, is equal to more than one-quarter of the total TVA investment in flood-control facilities. In the lower Ohio and Mississippi basins, the TVA system can reduce crests by two and one-half to three feet. This provides protection in those basins to 6,000,-000 acres of rich bottom land outside the Tennessee Valley, and will reduce the frequency of flooding on an additional 4,000,000 acres.

A 630-mile navigation channel has been created, on which traffic is breaking records regularly—508,000,000 ton-miles in 1949. This is an increase of fifteenfold when compared with river traffic before TVA began its work.

In 1933, the major traffic consisted of sand and gravel, dredged from the river bottom and transported relatively short distances, and of forest products—railroad ties, rough lumber, etc.—moved by barge, chiefly in the lower part of the river. Now the modernized river, a series of lakes connected by locks of high lift, carries goods of higher value for longer distances—petroleum from Louisiana and Illinois; automobiles from Michigan; grain from Missouri and Kansas; and aluminum, fertilizer, coal, and iron and steel articles from the Tennessee Valley to the upper Mississippi Valley. This new commerce is discovering again the affinity between the Southeast and the great Middle West.

The dams which control the floods and keep the channel open also produce hydroelectricity. The TVA electric power system today generates over ten times as much electricity as the area produced in 1933—more than 17,500,000,000 kilowatt-hours of energy annually for 1,145,000 consumers over an area of 80,000 square miles. New customers are receiving service at the rate of 10,000 per month.

The integrated development of the Tennessee River system has provided more economical flood control and more economical navagation facilities than could have been achieved by single-purpose developments. The power sold from the same system of dams brings the federal government a return averaging more than 4 per cent annually on its investment in power facilities.

In doing these things, the TVA has demonstrated a new approach to the development of a river. Let me explain by two examples.

The operation of a water-control system is a complicated assignment. A great many considerations enter into the daily, weekly, and monthly decisions on the storage and release of water. The requirements of navigation may sometimes call for special water releases on short notice. Shoreline farmers, recreation interests, fish and wildlife experts, and malaria-control agencies all have a special concern in how water is regulated in the reservoirs. Sometimes the various uses of water and the management of reservoir levels for one objective or another seem at cross purposes; more often the conflicts may be found, upon exploration, to be more apparent than real. The TVA, charged as it is with the operation of the system as a unit, has to resolve these conflicts in the most efficient and prudent manner. It cannot escape responsibility by passing the buck to some other agency, for no other agency shares control of the river's flow.

A similar problem of drawing unity from conflict arises in planning the dams. The genius of specialization lies in the precision with which a particular part of a problem may be analyzed. But specialized analyses, if they are to be understood and reflected in beneficial action, must be related to the logic and workability of schemes of broad context. The world of resources exists for people to live and grow in—not as a pile of pieces for experts and special groups to distribute among themselves. A river system and the climate and terrain which give it being are a case in point. It is not difficult to imagine the confusion that would follow if three separate groups of engineers, each responsible to a different agency, attempted to develop a river for navigation, for power, and for flood control; there would be endless competition for favorable dam sites, perpetual bickering over the storage and release of water, and so on. But when one group of engineers, united under a single management, is charged with developing the river for all three purposes, plus a concern for every possible auxiliary benefit, the job is half done; the flood-control engineer, the navigation expert, and the power engineer pool their special talents and devise a system that will do justice to each purpose within the limits set by the engineering facts and the policies set forth in law.

These examples may seem trivial. But the truth they illustrate is important as this country looks ahead to the development of its great river valleys. Experts frequently disagree so sharply that the layman is led to believe that either the one or the other must be right. He is told variously that when a river is dammed the fish are damned; that flood-control dams cannot produce electricity; that measures to control malarial mosquitoes are detrimental to fish and wildlife. As a rule these disagreements spring from an inadequate understanding of the facts common to the specialized experience and knowledge of the other expert's field. A unified management with transcending responsibilities can lead the contending experts into a fruitful search for facts and experience that will frequently break down the rigid theories marking the jurisdictional boundaries of professional isms. In the absence of unified management in the planning stage of river development, these disagreements among experts are pitched prematurely into the arena of political decision. The farmers who want electricity from the river are told they must win out over the cities which want protection from floods. The conflict among experts is the signal and the fuel for conflict and division among the people. Public decision frequently is stalemated and badly needed developments are delayed. Sometimes these disagreements are compromised by pressures that do violence to good engineering, to say the least, and at worst, betray the expectations of the people.

Thousands of millions of dollars and man-hours and countless tons of materials will be required to harness our rivers, rebuild our soils, and protect our forests. How these programs are planned and how these plans are carried out can affect the cost and the benefits in thousands of ways. If these developments freeze forever into costly concrete and steel, the unresolved or hastily compromised disagreements of various schools of experts, if the planning of the rivers is unrelated to the problems of the land, the nation will pay too much for too little, and opportunities for more freedom, more human growth, will be restricted or frustrated.

The TVA has responsibility for a regional result; it must bring these conflicting expert points of view together in the region. The experts do not have to refer their disagreements to separate sources of final professional authority in Washington. When TVA's recommendations go to Congress, the debate there is not about engineering. The debates in Congress are, as they should be, arguments about public policy, which is a high political function and responsibility beyond the scope of TVA's assignment. When TVA's recommendations are built into dams and river channels, TVA is and can be held accountable for the results because it must help make the estimated multiple benefits for the future come true.

The role of the TVA in the development of the region is twofold. It has undertaken and carried out activities that were too great, or too broad in scope, to be accomplished by state or local agencies or by private enterprise. Our great rivers do not respect state lines; engineering plans must encompass the whole river if plans are to be sound, operations unified, and great investments beneficial.

"Divide and conquer" may work in the strategy of human conflict, but we cannot tame and harness rivers by such a cynical and primitive device. Nor should we try to separate a river from its influence and effect upon the regional community that lives in and around its watershed. A river put to work can energize a whole hinterland if there is regional leadership searching for the unity of people and their environment. Thus the real measure of success of the TVA is in the extent to which the people of the region take hold of the new opportunities created by a useful river.

What has been going on in the Tennessee Valley for the past eighteen years is by no means solely a federal accomplishment. By the processes of joint study and discussion, consultation, negotiation, agreement, and action, the TVA and more than one hundred local, state, and federal agencies; scores of quasi-public bodies, business groups, farm organizations, and labor unions; and literally thousands of Valley citizens have arrayed themselves in a loose and flexible but tough federation of effort to put the resources of the Tennessee Valley to work.

For example, the construction and operation of an integrated system of dams and supporting steam plants, of which TVA has several, make for economical and efficient production of power. But the distribution of that power is not in the hands of TVA. One hundred forty-five municipal and co-operative organizations, locally owned and managed, buy power at wholesale from TVA under explicit long-term contracts; these local agencies distribute the power to 1,145,000 ultimate consumers at resale rates agreed upon by both parties. The people of the region, individually and through their own organizations, put the power to work in accordance with their own needs and desires.

Here is another example: The dams on the Tennessee River, in addition to the main objectives of flood control, navigation, and power, opened the way for the establishment of a recreation industry, and the people of the region are beginning to do something about it. Nearly thirty state, municipal, and county parks, along with quasi-public developments by church groups, boy and girl scouts, and other organizations, dot the lake shores. Up to January 1, 1950, the people of the region had invested approximately $21,000,000 in parks, pleasure craft ranging from fishing boats to cabin cruisers, boat docks, resorts, and other recreation facilities. The fish and game laws governing this TVA domain are the laws of the respective states, enforced by state officers. The TVA reservoirs have not obliterated any state powers or boundaries.

Agricultural development provides another good example of how the TVA works. The TVA, by the terms of the act which established it, has improved and operates the Muscle Shoals chemical plants to produce munitions in time of national emergency and phosphate and nitrogen fertilizers for farmers during peacetime. At its laboratories and in its chemical plants, TVA has worked out new processes and produced new materials which help meet the need for phosphates.

These new products must be tested under actual farming conditions before they are ready for general use. TVA turned to the established agencies of the region—the land-grant colleges and the state extension services, aided by the United States Department of Agriculture. With these agencies and hundreds of farm communities, TVA worked out the plan for test-demonstration farms in which individual farmers, chosen by their neighbors, have mobilized in soil-conservation groups and are testing TVA's products. In return for the materials, the test-demonstration farmers work out new systems of farm management, emphasizing soil- and water-conserving practices which phosphate makes possible. The test-demonstrations are open to study by neighboring farmers.[1] As one farmer put it, he was running a "miniature experiment station" for his community.

There are scores of instances where whole communities join in area test-demonstrations, planning together for community betterment based on increasingly wise use of their soil resources. Row crops, conducive to erosion, are coming down off the slopes to the flatter lands, and are being replaced by pastures or close-growing cover crops which hold water on the land and protect the soil.

Very few of the test-demonstration farmers ever see a TVA man

---

[1] On June 30, 1948, there were 11,676 test-demonstration farms in the Tennessee Valley receiving TVA fertilizers, and 3,629 outside the valley. The total number of test-demonstration farms established since the program was started was then 64,479.

from one end of the year to the other; yet, through their state extension services and county agents, these farmer-citizens are a dynamic part of the general program of development envisioned by the Congress when it set up the TVA eighteen years ago.

Now for a few observations by way of conclusion. In the Tennessee Valley the TVA has provided the unifying influence, the sense of cohesion and direction, which is necessary to a comprehensive program for conservation and development of natural resources. It has stimulated the interest of state and local agencies and opened new opportunities for them to serve.

The TVA has strengthened, rather than weakened, state and local initiative. Figures compiled from state reports in 1950 show that operating expenditures of state agencies concerned with resources had increased fivefold between 1933 and 1948—from $11,000,000 to $59,000,000. The states of the Tennessee Valley region are bearing an increasing responsibility for seeing that resources are fully and wisely used.

The states and the TVA, working together, stimulate the growth and expansion of private enterprise; in the Tennessee Valley private economic development is proceeding at a faster rate than in the country as a whole. A score of indices can be cited to identify this as a fact.[2] But in the context of the present discussion the cumulative convictions of the people of the region tell more than the statistics of economic progress. The people of the Tennessee Valley will tell you they are on the way: they are rebuilding their region; the frustrations of the past have been replaced by the changes of the present and the promise of the future.

[2] In 1933 the per capita income in the Tennessee Valley was 40 per cent of the national average; in 1947 it was 60 per cent of the national average. The income of individuals in the Tennessee Valley increased more rapidly than in the country as a whole. In total income payments, the increase in the nation between 1933 and 1947 was 138 per cent; in the Tennessee Valley, it was 245 per cent. The Tennessee Valley increased its manufacturing activities (these are all privately owned enterprises, of course) more rapidly than did the country as a whole, or the Southeast, or the seven Southeastern States lying partly in the Tennessee Valley. The Valley had 163 per cent more manufacturing plants in 1946 than in 1933; the seven Valley states had 132 per cent more, and the nation 95 per cent more. The number of wage earners in manufacturing had increased 140 per cent in the Valley, 94 per cent in the Valley states, and 100 per cent in the nation.

The very essence of the TVA idea is a strong faith in this thesis: The whole country benefits as each region builds a stronger economy upon the native characteristics and resources that mark it as a region.

There is an additional benefit in this approach to the problems of harnessing a river and mobilizing the resources of its watershed. The TVA, accountable as it is to the whole nation, also provides a means by which the region can be studied, described, and understood as an integrated whole. And because this is so, the relationships among regions, and between one region and another, can be analyzed and understood in better perspective.

The mainspring of the working machinery of the TVA as an agency of the federal government is this: TVA's responsibilities run to a single region; its officials and employees live and work and make decisions in the very climate of the regional community, not as agents of a distant central office, but as employees of a localized, regional agency; the TVA acts as a nucleus of regional effort in which state and local governments and private initiative gain new strength and new functions in building a stronger region.

In expanding the base of our productive enterprise, we should remember that our resources have a site—they are localized. Our human energies, if they are to be used effectively, must be mobilized around the places where these resources exist.

The area where we work with the resources we have must be defined to the scale of our comprehension. Otherwise our understanding of the problems becomes too abstract to produce action. It is here that the concept of the region has significance. Regions can, of course, be variously defined—by a watershed, by a tier of states, or by the application of a score of indices. The significance of the idea of the region, however, lies not in the definition, for no definition can be wholly satisfactory, but in the search for unity—unity in a common cause for work and action. What makes a region is that its components are more closely related to each other than they are to the components of other geographic areas. There is similarity, therefore, in the problems and in the factors which create them. There is similarity in the needs and the opportunities present throughout the region.

From these fundamental similarities a sense of cultural neighborhood emerges. And in the context of cultural affinities people find it easier to reach general agreement on what courses they must follow to improve their lot. They cast their government in forms that are intended to meet their needs; they develop customary ways of thought and expression reflecting their environment and rooted in it; and they may undertake joint action to reach their common ends. The pattern of action can be valid and impelling, in the large, throughout a region, since it is woven out of common resources, common problems, and common aims. What one part of a region learns will have meaning for other parts of the same region. The lessons of success and failure here and there within the area begin to impart momentum and direction to the region as a whole.

Our search, then, is for regional patterns, patterns in which man achieves a productive partnership with the factors of his environment, so that his use of resources is creative and redounds to the benefit of all men. Such patterns emerge from a knowledge of what resources are and what the laws of their use demand. Out of this knowledge we must build a working scheme, a multiplicity of plans of how to get from here to there, a guide to action that will move toward the ends on which regional understanding and agreement have been set.

In harnessing a regional agency to the physical facts and the human aspirations of a region, we need to temper impatience with a careful sense of self-restraint: a full and faithful understanding that resource development is not a job for a self-appointed elite of experts, scientists, and administrators, no matter how competent they are or how beneficent their intent. The life, liberty, and pursuit of happiness of the people depends on their resources and how they use them; the people, in accord with the most elementary principle of freedom, are the ones to determine what they will do and how they will do it. The regional program, however sanctified by the judgment of experts, will have meaning only if the farmer, the banker, the workman, the manager, the editor, and the teacher share in the analyses of problems and opportunities which suggest the region's purpose. They are the ones whose daily action, delay, or apathy, whose knowledge or ignorance, whose vision or selfishness, will decide what happens to our resources and how we shall use or destroy them.

The TVA as an instrument of regional development serves in full accord with this democratic idea. As Howard Odum has said,

"I don't know of any other strategy anywhere which provides facilities so well for both exploring and solving the increasing complexity of the relation between government and business as a regional program such as TVA. We are already in structural process of working together before we know it." [3] The fact is that the establishment of the TVA represented no extension of federal powers, no encroachment upon the rights of the states or the local communities. Search as one will through the act creating the TVA, he will find there no authority and no activity which the federal government is not already exercising or carrying on in other regions throughout the United States.

TVA has no coercive powers. It issues no orders or directives; it has no authority to do so. And it needs none; it wants none. TVA cannot compel the people of a region to hew to the line of some super plan, devised on high and handed down by fiat; nor would it want such powers. As the TVA reported to the Congress in 1936: "The planning of the river's future is entrusted to the TVA. The planning of the Valley's future must be the democratic labor of many agencies and individuals, and final success is as much a matter of general initiative as of general consent." [4]

The TVA method recognizes and practices the belief that there is no end to the process of public definition of how the job is to be done. Agreement on general direction in a region can and should be reached. But within the understanding about man's relationships with nature, and with agreement on direction, the people of the Tennessee Valley will constantly be defining and redefining how and with what devices they are going to propel themselves toward the foreseeable goals they have selected. The TVA, as an instrument of research and action in the hands of the people, provides a rare opportunity for the principle of self-help for local and community autonomy and development, and affords means of balancing people with institutions, freedom with resources. Thus our ultimate end is never fixed. This is as it should be. Means and methods can escape the blighting curse of uniformity if we recognize and place high value upon the latent and unlimited ingenuity of man's mind.

Our responsibility in our time is to establish and strengthen the

[3] Howard W. Odum, in a letter to Gordon R. Clapp, February 16, 1949.
[4] *Annual Report of the Tennessee Valley Authority*, 1936, p. 2.

processes by which we and our children can keep open a wide choice of development. Our chances of success and forward movement are great if our devices of public administration accommodate and nourish the diversities within and among regions. The TVA as a device of public administration can work and adapt itself to almost any definition of regionalism, since its flexibility provides easily for an integration of many factors. Howard Odum has summarized the idea in these words: "It is an American heritage that the nation will be strong because of the strength and integration of its diverse regions. Genuine regionalism concerns itself with the relation of regions to the total more than with the mere priority of regional advantages."

Unity of purpose and uniformity in action or behavior are not the same thing. Unity for a common purpose can discover and apply a regional will; diversity can add strength and versatility to the abilities of our regions and the larger community of the nation.

Chapter 12

The Great Lakes Cutover Region

Walter A. Rowlands

F IRST let me describe quickly and in broad outline the essential geography of this great region of ours. Half again as large as the New England States, it is a region of 57,000,000 acres of land covering 86 counties, 1,500 townships, and some 3,000 school districts and has a population of more than one and one-half million people, mostly rural. It contains the greatest iron-ore deposits in the United States and some of the best limestone in the country. Even before World War II, lake traffic at the Sault Ste Marie locks amounted to 88,000,000 tons annually, valued at $900,000,000. To move this amount of freight required the use of 700 registered lake vessels. This was more than the total of all the freight which passed through the Panama, Suez, Welland, and New York Barge canals in a single year.

Most of the region ranges from 800 to 2,100 feet above sea level. Its topography is typical of a glaciated country—gravelly moraines and pine plains, swamps and ridges, and fertile soils. The annual rainfall varies from 25 to 35 inches. The temperature ranges from extremes of 50° below zero to a summer high of 105° F. It is rugged country. It has been governed successively by the French from 1650 to 1763, by Great Britain from 1763 to 1783, and by the United States since 1783, when the region was officially transferred by treaty.

Speaking of the Great Lakes in his recent book of that name, Harlan Hatcher said:

The name is apt. No other adjective describes the expanse of the region or the activity of this greatest body of fresh water in the world. The lakes are great in size, great in commerce, great in engineering, great in history and romance, great in cities and industries along their shores, and great in interest and in beauty. They are not so much a region as an area.

They are not local—they are international. The lakes serve as a boundary between the United States and Canada, yet they do not separate two nations—rather, they join together two great peoples.

Walter Havighurst, in his book *Land of Promise,* said, "Time has brought many changes to the land that once was the Northwest, but is still a new country, restless, vigorous, not yet settled into permanence."

On the other hand, J. B. Martin, in his book *Call It North Country,* said: "It's an old country—men were claim jumping in the iron fields before gold was found at Sutters Mill in California. By the time President Lincoln was calling for 75,000 volunteers, the copper kings were sending labor lookers to Europe to bring in a fresh supply of workers."

This great region has witnessed both abject poverty and fabulous wealth. From rags to riches, it was a region of ambitious men and rugged and ruthless individualism. In the heyday of lumbering, in the vicinity of Bay City and Saginaw, Michigan, upwards of one hundred millionaires were created. In Muskegon, Michigan, forty millionaires were made in two seasons of logging alone. Yet, in 1934, 34 per cent of the population of the Upper Peninsula of Michigan was receiving relief. In one section of the Upper Peninsula at the depth of the depression, almost 75 per cent of the population was on relief. In all three states, the relief problem was most severe in the cutovers.

In 1890, lumber production in the Lake States was 35 per cent of the nation's total; today it is but 4 per cent. The logging industry provided the needed material for shipbuilding, for manufacturing, and for building a nation of homes; yet the lumberjacks, the very men who cut and felled the trees and made home-building possible for the rest of America, were without homes. It was said in the woods that the only things a man needed or wanted came in bottles or corsets, and most of it came in bottles.

From 1871 to 1918 the Great Lakes experienced some of the worst fires in the nation's history—Hinckley, Peshtigo, Marquette, Merrill, Cloquet, Comstock, and Phillips. For fifty years fires, often covering more than a million acres a year, ran unchecked over the country. These conflagrations, with their terrible toll of human lives and the loss of valuable soil cover and wildlife, were accepted as inevitable. Today we have both an enlightened and an informed public and much more adequate fire protection and suppression facilities. In the year 1942, for example, fires in Wisconsin were limited and held to about 3,100 acres. During the past ten years in Wisconsin the average acreage burned over each year amounted to 8,913 acres. The damage or loss in terms of dollars for this ten-year period averaged $28,153 per year.

The soils of the cutovers are podzols—forest soils, generally of low fertility and high acidity associated with abundant rainfall and low temperatures. In general, and with some notable exceptions, their best use is for forest or grass production. Farm development, farm production, and farm income are lower in the cutovers than in the remainder of the three states; and yet in parts of the cutovers are to be found highly productive and profitable specialized potato and dairy farms, the equal of those in any region anywhere in the United States.

Again in contrast, the region witnessed widespread land-settlement and land-colonization enterprises during the early twenties, when a single land-selling organization sold more than one million dollars' worth of land in a single county in one year. Less than ten years later, during the depression, as many as five hundred settlers in one county dropped their land and their holdings and moved out lock, stock, and barrel.

The cutovers, like the Middle West itself, have been called the melting pot of the nations of the earth. Germans, Swedes, Norwegians, Danes, Finns, French Canadians, Poles, Slovaks, French, Irish, Scotch, English, Canadians, Russians, Cornish, Welsh, Bohemians, Dutch, Belgians, Italians, and Swiss—in all, people of twenty-one different nationalities—have joined together around the lakes.

The cutovers have known people from every land and every climate, from city and from countryside—people who have known wealth and poverty, freedom and oppression. Artisan, tradesman, laborer, and farmer, they have come to our land of unhampered advancement and religious freedom.

With each contribution of manpower have come certain human qualities. Inherent in the nationalities that are rebuilding our cutover region are love of freedom, love of home and family, indomitable optimism, the craving for beauty of countryside, frugality, dependability, and the countless characteristics that make us truly a cosmopolitan state.

Why did these people come? They came because of the great opportunity. They came to the Great Lakes cutovers because there were ships to be loaded and sailed, ore to be mined, timber to be cut, roads and railroads to be built, and farms to be cleared and developed and homes to be built.

There is color in the cutover section of the Great Lakes, as in all of the Middle West—color in the songs of the nations that are with us, color in the folk tales and stories, in the folk costumes, in the festivals, in the games and plays, in the crafts and the arts, and in the paintings which reflect the varied backgrounds from whence they came. We are beginning to understand that folk festivals are valuable in combating intolerance, that folk songs and plays win large audiences, and that folk customs and traditions help to explain what we are today. These Old World backgrounds are especially valuable in helping us to understand the different ethnic groups—how they plan and why and how they work together as a group.

That is why George Hill has developed a special map of Wisconsin showing the distribution of the many nationality groups we have in rural Wisconsin. That is why the late John Steuart Curry's paintings of rural peoples and rural scenes of the Middle West, with their vivid strength and character, have met with wide acceptance. That is why John R. Barton has made notable progress with his rural art exhibits, composed entirely of paintings by rural people themselves. That is why, under a Regional Fellowship at the University of Minnesota, some twenty-four authors are at work on American culture. And that is why, in the archives of the Library of Congress in Washington, D.C., there are more than seven thousand separate records of American folk songs collected in the field.

As James Grey has so well put it, "The Upper Midwest contains within itself the memory of everything that America has been and the knowledge of what it may become."

Three great exploitations overran the cutovers. Fur came first. The swamps and sloughs of the cutovers produced some of the best furs in the world. It has been said that the deep snows, the long, cold winters, and even the dark-brown waters of the rivers and streams all combined to produce furs of premium quality.

Fur was the first and only cash crop of the natives. Pelts were traded for kettles, guns, knives, and buttons and for gin, rum, and whiskey. For years, beaver was the "gold standard" in all fur trading. The "take" in the seventeen-eighties was a million dollars' worth of peltry per year. The fight for monopolistic control of this great fur industry involved many men, great companies, and three nations. The Hudson's Bay Company, the Mackinaw Company, and the Northwest Company were the leading groups involved. Although the fur trade reached its peak in the eighteen-twenties, it actually existed for over two hundred years. Fur—not ore, lumber, or grain—was the treasure of the New World longer than any other of its resources.

Logging in the cutovers, unlike trapping, was of short duration; the bulk of the timber was cut, milled, and used in the fifty-year period from 1870 to about 1920. In Michigan the peak of logging was reached in 1880 with a production over four and one-half billion feet of lumber a year. In Wisconsin the peak was a decade later with a production of four billion feet a year. In Minnesota the highest production was reached in 1900. The lumber and allied industries employed tens of thousands of men in the woods and in the mills. They created many sawmill towns, and communities made the change from logging to industry and shipping, or to agriculture or recreation; but many of these settlements—far too many—died out and became known as "ghost towns," rapidly falling into disuse and becoming as empty of life as last year's robin's nest.

In the cutovers, farming followed logging operations. As land was opened up, a few small farms were started. Many of the settlers, however, depended more on the winter work in the forest than on the production of the farm for a livelihood. Logging proceded faster than new farms were developed. In the decade 1910 to 1920, land sales reached their highest peak. People were on the move. Land was what everyone wanted, and in the cutovers there were many millions of acres for sale. Without any detailed soil surveys, without any study of the climate, and without knowledge of what crops to grow or how to grow them—without money, equipment, or livestock—people came and bought land on which to establish a farm. This development had the blessing of the states, the United States Department of Agriculture, and the people themselves. It was a condition of society. We were in a hurry to "get going" in farming. When the demand for agricultural products abroad dropped following World War I, prices of these products also fell. Land values fell; and when the sawmills closed with the disappearance of timber, many struggling settlers lost all hope and left, never to return. This was the beginning of the rural depression in the cutovers. It brought about tax delinquency, farm abandonment, and, finally, idle land and idle men. It also brought about a new interest on the part of local citizens in planning for the future development of their community and for their own security.

The exploitation of these three great resources has taken almost three centuries. The Great Lakes shipping business, it is true, continues; iron ore, grain, and limestone have moved in increasing quantities to the East, and coal and manufactured goods to the West. Again, both Canada and the United States, and their provinces and states, have co-operated in promoting the regulation and development of the fisheries industry. Fortunately, also, we have an intelligent and energetic people, and in this great region we can now see signs of real progress based on sound, permanent development.

The cutover country is rugged country; the people are rugged individualists. In fact, it has been said that if you want to find rugged individualism in its purest form, go to the cutovers of the Great Lakes States.

Our people in this pioneer area have seen both conflict and change. They have seen successes and they have seen failures. They are willing and able to try out new plans and new programs, but such plans and programs must have merit and be reasonably capable of accomplishment. The plans must be developed and discussed with them. They must be in on the planning process from the beginning. The men who hope to work with local groups in the cutovers must first win their confidence and respect. Without such confidence and respect it will never be possible to work side by side with local people in the development of the land.

Since 1927, in every county in the Wisconsin cutover, the University of Wisconsin has had the opportunity to work closely with county committees and county boards in a careful study of their land resources. Beginning in 1925, special land economic studies and surveys were made in Lincoln, Forest, Oneida, Marinette, Taylor, Washburn, Ashland, and Langlade counties. These studies were directed toward finding the significant facts regarding the ownership, use, and development of land—the nature and extent of government services and the possibilities of reducing the cost of local government and of developing new resources on the land.

Resolution No. 3 passed by the Marinette County Board of Supervisors on January 24, 1928, is a typical expression of the interest county boards had in finding the essential facts regarding their county:

BE IT HEREBY RESOLVED, that a committee of three members of the County Board to be appointed by the chairman together with the County Treasurer, County Agricultural Agent and the Director of the County Agricultural School shall be designated as the Farm and Forest Land Survey Committee; that this committee shall cooperate with the College of Agriculture of the University of Wisconsin, and with the county and town officers in the development of an economic survey for Marinette County which will tabulate by townships their trend of agricultural development, local tax expenditures, assessed valuations, roads and school facilities from 1914 to 1928, present maps of soil classification, settlement, crop acreage, forest areas and idle land.

As rapidly as these studies and surveys were prepared and published, a special series of meetings were held in all rural communities in the counties to present the findings and to discuss informally with interested citizens possible new developments.

It was during this period that the Wisconsin legislature, much concerned over the wave of tax delinquency that was spreading like wildfire throughout the northern and central counties, appointed a special Interim Committee on Forestry and Public Lands and assigned to it the task of determining what might be done, through legislation, that would be helpful. The following citation from this report is noteworthy because it contains the first specific reference to rural zoning:

Both the orderly development of northern Wisconsin, and the need for reducing expenditures because of tax delinquency, require that coun-

ties be given the authority to control development. Counties should have
the right to give every possible aid in agricultural zones with the aim of
building up prosperous farming communities. But they should have the
right in sections of isolated farms, with heavy tax delinquency and numerous abandoned farms to set such areas aside as forest and recreation
zones and be empowered to control the construction of more roads and
schools.

As a result of this vigorous presentation of the real needs in the
way of regulatory power, the legislature of 1929 proceeded to amend
the strictly urban zoning law, Section 59.97 of the Wisconsin *Statutes,*
to include the power to "determine the areas within which agriculture, forestry and recreation may be conducted, the location of roads,
schools. . . ." In brief, it was accepted by the legislature that the power
to zone wisely would enable the counties to limit governmental costs
and promote the best land uses.

This amendment gave a new and unprecedented use of the zoning power. Such authority had never before been given over rural
areas. The zoning power had been confined to highly developed urban centers. For this reason, its constitutionality was questioned by
lawyers and landowners.

The Special Legislative Committee on forest fires and delinquent
taxes (1931) requested an official opinion of the attorney general regarding the constitutionality of this law. The attorney general in
reply stated:

The county zoning ordinance is undoubtedly in the public welfare.
The cut-over areas of northern Wisconsin speak as eloquently against
haphazard development as any city condition. The spotting of these
lands with remote or abandoned farms, resulting in sparsely settled districts, with insufficient population or value to support roads and schools,
or to afford the comforts of living that this day should give to all; the
misdirected efforts to farm lands not well suited to agriculture, with resulting personal grief and social loss; the far-reaching economic ill-effects
of stripping the state of timber; the fire hazard of cut-over lands and the
fire hazard of human habitation in their midst, all cry out for planning,
for social direction of individual effort.

. . . I believe the judicial tendency is going to be to recognize more
and more the great social evil of uncorrelated and unrestrained individual
and selfish enterprise, and hence to broaden its views of the power of
government to plan the social and economic conditions of the present
and the future.

Even with the law on the statute books and the clear-cut opinion of the attorney general regarding its constitutionality, some time
elapsed before conditions were ripe for the development of Wisconsin's first zoning law.

Such an opportunity was presented in November, 1932, when
it was proposed to the Oneida County Board of Supervisors at Rhinelander, Wisconsin, that the tax-delinquency problem and the unemployment problem could both be solved in one simple stroke of
the pen. It was proposed that the city of Rhinelander give every un-
employed man a grubstake of one hundred dollars and the county
of Oneida give him forty acres of tax-delinquent land. This simple
solution of the unemployment problem and the land problem
brought home to many of the members of the Oneida County Board
the tremendous need for the establishment of a sound forward-look-
ing policy on land use. The County Board referred this entire matter to its Colonization Committee. The committee, after careful
deliberation, requested assistance from the University, the Attorney
General's Department, and the Wisconsin Conservation Department in the development of a rural zoning ordinance for Oneida
County.

Because rural zoning was new and untried, it was necessary that
a considerable amount of related background material be developed.
This included maps showing (1) the extent and location of tax delinquency by stages of development; (2) the location of farms, both
operating and abandoned, and farm markets; (3) the location of
publicly owned lands—federal, state, county, township, and city
properties; (4) rural schools, school district boundary lines, and
school bus routes; (5) main soil types, topography, and the drainage
system; and (6) recreational lands, both improved and potential recreational properties.

Fortified by this background material and a copy of the proposed
zoning ordinance, the county agricultural agent, with the assistance
of a representative of the University of Wisconsin, proceeded to hold
meetings in every town in the county to present the situation and
to explain the workings of the proposed zoning ordinance. These
informal preliminary educational meetings, held in every county
that considered zoning, while not required by law, have proved to be
of great help in the enactment and administration of a zoning ordi-

nance. The questions and public discussions which followed brought
to light little-understood facts in the operation of state and local
government. This procedure has won the support and respect of
citizens and taxpayers throughout the several zoned counties. Rural
people, especially, were much more concerned with the spirit in
which their elected representatives enacted the ordinance than they
were with the technical aspects of the procedure.

Since the original ordinance in Oneida County was enacted on
May 16, 1933, twenty-four other counties have followed suit. Today,
twenty-five Wisconsin counties are zoned by these self-imposed, demo-
cratically enacted rural zoning ordinances. All of them were born
of stern necessity. They now restrict more than five million acres
of land against future agricultural settlement and legal residence.
Most of them have been in existence for a decade and a half. They
have met the test of time, of judgment, and of experience. They
are bearing fruit beyond the most optimistic expectations of the
men who wrote them. They are here to stay. The same is true in parts
of Michigan and Minnesota. These ordinances will, however, need
to be reviewed regularly and changed as needed, not only to keep
pace with growth and development but to provide a sound basis
for all future development.

In particular, zoning boundaries now need revision in several
counties. New use districts, better to aid a growing recreation industry, should be considered in counties with high potential recreational values. Again, the administration and enforcement of zoning
regulations needs to be strengthened in several counties. With new
members on town and county boards and zoning committees almost
every year, it is important that the basic educational work of giving
these new members the background in zoning objectives and zoning
experience be consistently carried out.

Two important forest laws which came into being during the
same period the rural zoning law was enacted have proved to be
of great value and importance to the north. These are the Forest
Crop Law and the County Forest Law.

The Forest Crop Law and the Forest Crop Program which followed have given real force and meaning to rural zoning. Local citizens who were interested in forestry were willing to accept restric-

tions on the use of land. Forestry, because it can utilize low-cost non-agricultural land, has proved over the years to be an acceptable alternate use of land under zoning.

The expanded Forest Crop Law permits the entry of county-owned land under the provisions of this law. For each acre of county land entered the state contributes ten cents annually. This payment is made to support local government while the forest resources are being restored.

In addition, the state contributes approximately ten cents per acre per year for acquisition and development of the forest. A 50 per cent severance tax is levied on all timber products taken from the county forest crop land.

This partnership between the state and the counties has made possible a rapid advance in public forestry in Wisconsin. To date 2,030,000 acres of land are under this program. The Forest Crop Law, the County Forest Law, and the Rural Zoning Law are companion laws designed to foster the sound development of the northern and central sections of Wisconsin.

More than 10,000,000 acres (net area) is today in organized public forests in the cutovers under capable forest management. The forest, whether to produce timber or pulpwood, to prevent soil erosion, to frame a lake, or to provide the habitat for game and wildlife, will continue to be of vital importance to the future of the north. The forests occupy large areas of low-value lands, and more land in the future can and should go into this productive use. The products of the forest will provide continued and enlarged opportunities for labor and enterprise. The old sawmills have now been replaced by paper mills, plywood plants, excelsior mills, and specialized wood-products plants. Many large private wood-using industries, especially pulp and paper companies, are now well along in their forest-development work.

Many zoned counties have adopted vigorous programs involving the complete demolition of all abandoned buildings and structures on county-owned lands and the salvaging of all usable materials. Bayfield County, during 1935, dismantled upwards of a score of such buildings. Private landowners, with a realization of the social and financial hazard involved in the use of this type of structure, have

likewise adopted a policy of dismantling all unused isolated buildings on their properties. Rural zoning, which prohibits settlement
in restricted districts, followed by a program involving the complete
demolition of all abandoned shacks on isolated lands, has paved the
way for permanent improvement in the health standards of the
region.

Fifteen years ago, in northeastern Wisconsin, a man and wife living in one of these abandoned shacks contracted typhoid fever. The
husband died and the wife left the community. An attempt was made
to persuade local officials to destroy the building, but this was not
done. The next season another family of squatters moved in. In a
short time typhoid fever broke out, resulting in the death of the
father, the mother, and one child. The immediate cost to the county
in this case was six hundred dollars, but this amount represents only
the financial loss to the taxpayers. It gives no indication of the extent and severity of human suffering or of the social loss associated
with families living in dwellings without floors or beds—families
having neither the facilities nor the knowledge to maintain a normal
standard of living, of sanitation, or even of morality.

A year later, in north central Wisconsin, the elderly wife of a
settler living in an isolated area in one of the restricted use districts
died. She had received no medical aid or attention. Her death occurred during one of our most severe snowstorms, when even those
families located on main-traveled highways had difficulty in getting
to town. Three days later a trapper stopped at the cabin of the old
couple and learned of the death of the wife. County officials were
informed, and an expedition including trucks and snowplows was
immediately organized. Finally, for the last several miles, a toboggan
was dragged in by a man on snowshoes to transport the body out
of the cabin for burial. This incident received widespread publicity
in the state press. It served in a dramatic way to illustrate the hazards
of isolation—the expense, the danger, and the futility.

Stranded settlers, upwards of eight hundred families, isolated
from roads, schools, markets, and community centers, on land unfit
and unneeded for farming, have been relocated, on a voluntary basis,
in Wisconsin in the past decade. In all cases, substantial savings in
government costs have resulted from this procedure. More than this

financial saving, relocation has brought new hope and new opportunity to many formerly isolated and destitute families. Careful administration of the zoning ordinances by the county boards of supervisors will prevent a recurrence of the situation which brought about isolated settlement.

County forest ordinances and county land–use and sales ordinances have likewise been adopted in many northern Wisconsin counties. More counties, we hope, will adopt the land–use and sales type of ordinance. This new ordinance came into being to provide for the orderly administration of the land for its highest use, particularly of the land not in any public forest.

Farming practices and farm development have advanced rapidly in the cutovers. We know now that not all land in the cutovers is of agricultural quality. In place of many isolated farms scattered throughout the north, county boards and local committees are now developing compact agricultural communities located on the best lands. These compact communities can be better serviced with roads, snowplowing, schools, markets, rural mail service, rural electric power, and telephones so essential today to profitable farming and the best community life. The agricultural experiment stations and Extension Service in the cutover country are developing for the farming areas in the north new higher-yielding, disease-resistant crops and systems of farming especially adapted to the soils and climate of the area in which they are located. Much of this work is just in its infancy.

The northern sections of the Lake States, during the past twenty years, have developed an impressive resort and recreation industry. This industry, however, sells much more than meals, lodging, and personal services. It sells scenery, forests, clear water, game, and wildlife. Its future is bound closely with the future of conservation. Yet, in the broad fields of conservation we have today too much conflict, too many quick answers, and too little dependence on research. The resort industry needs to be alert and informed on the deer program, the fish program, the game program, and, in fact, all conservation programs. Parts of the commercial recreation industry have grown like Topsy, and there is need for the industry itself to keep its members informed on sound development measures that will directly affect their future welfare and that of their local community.

Some pioneer work has already been done in the development of a special forest architecture for the north. With native materials and an eye for beauty, architects in many parts of the northern region have developed efficient, comfortable, long-lasting structures that blend well into the landscape. In the future the engineer and the architect will have a real opportunity to demonstrate further the possibilities in this fascinating field.

Vilas County, Wisconsin, has redrawn its zoning ordinance to provide a new commercial recreation district. This was done to promote the best use of its recreation resources and to prevent haphazard development. We need more of this kind of careful planning for recreation in other northern counties. We need and we are getting more wayside stops—more beautiful vistas on the highways—less of Coney Island and more of the calmness and quietness that goes with a forest environment and forest atmosphere.

In brief, what this great region and the people in it are accomplishing is the re-establishment of permanent forests, farms, and recreation, and industry based on all three. These new enterprises are in turn supporting permanent homes and permanent communities.

The days of rapid exploitation, of "cut out and get out," are over. Conservation and development for permanent use are now the order of the day in the cutovers, as, in fact, in all America. Much still remains to be learned about the wealth of the cutovers around the Great Lakes. Further exploration is needed for new strategic minerals, in addition to studies now under way in the more complete utilization of lower grade ores. The recent taconite ore development in Minnesota, the proposed Beaver Bay Benefication site northeast of Duluth, and the reported discovery of pitchblende on the north shore of Lake Superior and other radioactive minerals farther north are examples of other types of industrial development that hold great promise for the future.

A great deal of fundamental research is needed in the conservation and wise utilization of our water resources, both underground and surface water, in the Lake States. We need more holding reservoirs, swamps, and ponds, and perhaps even artificly developed reservoirs, to hold surplus water for power development, for fire protection, for irrigation, and for maintaining lake levels.

In this great adventure of planning for the sound, balanced, and permanent development of all land resources, the universities, the state conservation departments, the state planning boards, the state departments of agriculture, and many other public and private organizations in all three states will continue to have a place and a part in shaping the destiny of the cutovers. Someday, someone will bestow on this great "Empire of the North" a new name—a name much more in keeping with the contributions it has already made and will continue to make to the future welfare of all the people of America.

BIBLIOGRAPHY

Rowlands, Walter A. *Relocating the Isolated Settler: The story of relocating isolated settlers—why it is important to follow rural zoning by relocating settlers in restricted forest zones.* National Municipal League, You and Your Government Series XII, Lecture No. 12. December, 1935.

———. "Rural County Zoning in Wisconsin: The story of rural zoning in Wisconsin written to be of help to county and town officials; why zoning is important to northern Wisconsin counties," *Wisconsin Blue Book.* 1937.

———, Fred B. Trenk, and Raymond J. Penn. *Rural Zoning in Wisconsin.* University of Wisconsin *Bulletin No. 479.* Madison, November, 1948.

———, Fred B. Trenk, G. S. Wehrwein, and M. P. Anderson. *Wisconsin's Land Use Program in the Forested Areas: A discussion circular designed to promote discussion among various groups in the country about their land resources.* University of Wisconsin Extension Service, Stencil Circular 203. Madison, August, 1938.

U. S. Department of Agriculture, Bureau of Agricultural Economics. *Rural Zoning and Land Use Planning.* County Planning Series No. 7. Prepared in co-operation with the Extension Service, the Soil Conservation Service, and the Farm Security Administration.

———. *Rural Zoning and Your County.* Washington.

University of Wisconsin. *Making the Most of Marinette County Land: A study of the land resources of Marinette County with recommended steps in the improvement of these resources.* Special Circular. Madison, 1929. Out of print.

———. *The Regional Approach to the Conservation of National Resources: Contains suggestions for co-ordinating through a regional approach the work that is being done toward conserving the resources of a given area.* Serial No. 2341, General Series 2125. Madison, September, 1938.

—— and Wisconsin Conservation Department. *From Public Burden to Public Benefit, the Story of Marinette County's Land and Forestry Program.* Joint publication, University of Wisconsin *Bulletin No. 483* and Wisconsin Conservation Department *Bulletin No. 522.* Madison, April, 1949.

Walker, Herman, Jr. *Some Considerations in Support of the Constitutionality of Rural Zoning as a Police Power Measure.* U. S. Resettlement Administration, Land Use Planning Publication 11. 48 pp. Washington, 1936.

Wilson, A. D. *Progress in Development of a Land and Timber Management Program in Northeastern Minnesota.* Minnesota Agricultural Experiment Station. St. Paul, Minnesota, 1944.

Wisconsin. Committee on Land Use and Forestry. *Forest Land Use in Wisconsin: A very complete study of the land resources of the state with recommendations for their improvement, particularly forests, farms and recreational land resources.* Report. Executive Office, Madison, April, 1932.

——. State Planning Board. *The Cutover Region of Wisconsin, Bulletin No. 7: The report of a special state committee appointed to work out solutions to improve the economy of the "cutovers."* Madison, January, 1939.

Chapter 13

The Great Plains - Missouri Valley Region

Elmer Starch

A LARGE nation's problem is clearly one of bringing together diverse natural interests on the one hand and yet allowing for adaptation of groups of people to a rather definite and specific set of surroundings. The coming of river-basin programs may provide evidence that we are becoming aware of the desirability of having a good balance between a universal national viewpoint and at the same time getting the benefit of the closest possible kinship between people and their immediate surroundings.

Our entire national history gainsays the concept of local adaptation, for as settlement has swept westward there has been a tendency for people to adhere as strictly as possible to the culture which they learned in the area from which they came. We might say that America has overdone the process of amalgamating the cultures of many nations in what is commonly known as the great melting pot. We have stressed the desirability of amalgamation until our philosophy of national sameness has become so sharply imprinted on people's minds that they now feel that they and their area are being held up for ridicule when differences are being analyzed or evaluated.

Many times we have seen resentments arise in the Congress and other national bodies where there have been presented programs designed to alleviate problems which are peculiar to an area. Cotton is king in the South, and we in the Great Plains have been angered when some of our lands were referred to as being marginal for wheat production. I believe it is true that by and large we have shown very great reluctance to recognize differences in climate and soil characteristics. More recently, however, we have become less sensitive about our problems. We have come to recognize some of the areas which might be termed minority areas in the natural-resource and in the

economic-problem sense. We are beginning to use the natural peculiarities of a region as basic in trying to build an efficient national
production and living pattern. I cite as an example of such recognition the report of President Roosevelt's Great Plains Committee.

In a letter dated February 10, 1937, transmitting the committee's report to Congress, President Roosevelt said in part:

I transmit herewith for the information of the Congress the report of
the Great Plains Committee under the title, "The Future of the Great
Plains."

The report indicates clearly that the problem of the Great Plains is
not merely one of relief of a courageous and energetic people who have
been stricken by several years of drought during a period of economic depression. It is much more fundamental than that. Depression and drought
have only accentuated a situation which has been long developing. . . .

The settlers of the Plains brought with them agricultural practices developed in the more humid regions from which they came. . . . The long-
run experience, however, has disclosed that the rainfall of the area hovers
around, and, for considerable periods, falls below the critical point at
which it is possible to grow crops by the agricultural methods common
to humid regions. A new economy must be developed which is based on
the conservation and effective utilization of all the water available, especially that which falls as rain and snow; an economy which represents
generally a more rational adjustment of the organization of agriculture
and cropping plans and methods to natural conditions. . . .

Whatever program is adopted must be cooperative and will require
complementary lines of action by the Federal Government, State Governments, and all the citizens of the region individually. Each has material
interests at stake and can no longer afford to defer constructive action;
each has moral responsibility for unwitting contributions to the causes
of the present situation; and especially each has responsibility for undertaking lines of action essential to effectiveness of action by the others.

The problem is one that can be solved, but the solution will take time.
Therefore a policy should be determined, a long-run program formulated,
and execution begun without undue delay.

We should guard against the retardations of progress which come
from provincialism of thought and from fixity in our way of life, but
I do believe that we should put less premium on the universal habits
and methods—and I use these terms in the broad sense to include
the economic as well as the social aspects of our livelihood. On the
other hand, we are often inclined to confuse enlightened adaptation
with provincialism. It should be the policy of the country to make

the most of our local resources and thereby gain the greatest national benefit at the same time that we assure the greatest happiness and benefit for the people in each of the different areas.

It should not be necessary for localized natural forces to impose repeated failure upon the people who have come to live there before those people have the courage to come forward on their own and set up modifications which will lead to greater comfort and security. Even after people have been battered into submission by natural forces, and after they recognize their own surroundings, it is still extremely difficult to convince the nation as a whole that such adaptations are to the best interest of the entire country.

It is a nice battle between universalism with its standard pattern which runs so strong in our country, and the provincialism which is apt to grow up in a locality. Both are sometimes used as a protective armor to ward off change.

As evidence of the struggle, note the disgust and protest which you experience in a nationwide meeting of technicians when someone rises up and says, "Out our way things are different." True, you can never be sure whether the person who is making the claim of living amid different surroundings has really given serious thought to adjustments in method which will be suited in his area, or whether he is merely saying that the present way of doing things is good enough for him.

Ofttimes the stubbornness with which groups and individuals cling to a local viewpoint is well founded, but it is tragic that just as often they are not prepared to suggest practical and suitable modifications nor are facilities available through which they think out, experiment with, and otherwise crystallize an adapted economy. Until they can make such suggestions, their claim of difference may merely result in a stalemate of progress and a continuing maladjustment in that area. They will be out of step with the larger scheme of things and at the same time be constantly in difficulty in their own surroundings.

A natural counterpart of the region's effort lies in facilities which the nation must have to recognize necessary adaptations. When a region comes forward with a definition of a problem, a sympathetic understanding must be given so that the energies of thought and action can be directed to those problems in a practical manner. Having received a sympathetic hearing from the larger group, the local group may logically be expected to come forward with a clarification of the principles which operate in a given area, and then with specific programs, and finally with a correlation of programs.

The ingredients which go into a satisfactory and successfully adapted pattern are not likely to be different from those which are suitable to the rest of the country, but it is a matter of weighing the quantities which go into the recipe of living and economic endeavor. So as we think of making regional adaptations, let us think of it as using the ingredients in various combinations and quantities and sometimes adding a dash of some special flavoring for a particular area.

Perhaps we should invent a new term or a modified concept which might be named "optimum interdependence." By this term we would express some of the principles which go into a logical adaptation to our varied surroundings. It is essential, of course, that the production of one area fit in with the rest of the country in such a way that it makes good sense in terms of trade and commerce. The pattern must also encompass not only national affairs but world affairs. If the principle of interdependence can be fully realized, we can obtain the best integration of what might be termed economic patches into an economic and social unity.

Throughout recent decades the people of America have made numerous efforts to find means whereby homogeneous areas may be delineated. First of all, they are seeking to break down the economic and social pattern into manageable units. In the second place, they are trying to determine areas that would have a set of common objectives. The search for localized, homogeneous areas has brought a good deal of emphasis to the state as a unit. This avenue has the advantage of localizing both the attempt to determine objectives and the application of activities to attain those objectives. As I shall point out later, the state subdivision is likely to have within it as great a range of natural divisions and as wide a dispersion of interests as the whole nation. In fact, states were often laid out so that they would have a maximum diversity of resources.

The search for homogeneous areas has caused people to turn to the river basin as a means of bounding a composite set of problems. This concept is now in the process of being tested in the Tennessee Valley and the Missouri Valley. As a casual observer one would be likely to say that the Tennessee Valley had a great similarity of interests throughout, with a strong emphasis on power development and flood control. The Missouri River basin, on the other hand, has as widely divergent interests as can be found anywhere, ranging from the water-deficient areas in the upper two-thirds of the basin down to the high-rainfall and flood areas in the lower reaches of the river. It has been necessary for the Congress to bound these conflicting interests by an amendment to the basic law. The amendment says in effect that the development of the river must not jeopardize the irrigation potentialities west of the ninety-eighth meridian.

The people of the country in seeking their media for common interest and purpose have not yet found a boundary which is satisfactory. One of the common errors into which we fall is our tendency to recognize differences in a general way and then to draw arbitrary and sharp lines and try to make every problem within those lines conform to the boundary. I shall have more to say on this point later in the discussion. It is apparent that some reconciliation must be made between the hard and fast geographical lines and the highly variable boundaries for problems.

Some of the elements which may be counted into the similarities of areas may fade with the changes in world demand for certain products. For instance, the wheat acreages may be revised downward in the Plains with the reduction of world food requirements. A change in the demand for wheat will bring on the problems of re-establishing permanent grasses and more extensive farming throughout the entire spring and winter wheat belt. This will mean a major change reaching through farm organization into community organization.

Inventions and new approaches also change the internal social and economic structure even in a local community. I presume I might go back in history and point out that on the Great Plains the bison was a great potential source of food supply for the native Indian. However, because his means of slaughtering buffalo for meat were extremely limited, his entire economy, by and large, was confined to the production of corn, beans, and squash, which were grown in river bottom lands. A vast amount of evidence concerning the early sedentary agriculture on the Great Plains is now being uncovered. With the coming of the horse, the Indian obtained the means for hunting buffalo, and he became the original cowboy and soon overran the farmer. Thus a new element completely changed the original citizen's point of view, his interest, and his means of livelihood.

In the modern day one may say that the invention of the tractor has changed the complexion of the Great Plains part of our nation. The tractor may be an efficient implement for any other part of the country, but it is absolutely the centerpiece of Great Plains agriculture. It would have been impossible to produce 800,000,000 bushels of wheat annually during the war period even with the good weather, without tractors, because it would have been impossible to prepare and plant the 60,000,000 acres on which it was grown.

In agriculture the practices of farming which predominate in some of the major agricultural areas tend to stamp themselves on the entire production pattern of the nation, and people as individuals or through their institutions are likely to look askance at deviations which take place in adjacent areas. They are likely to call these deviations poor farming, or to say that their faraway neighbors are wanting to get rich quick by developing bonanza farming. The farmer who operates in an area where the long-accepted practices work out well is quite likely to be out of patience and say, "If you would farm like I do, you would be successful."

Depending on whether or not the citizen and his institutions can adjust themselves, the Great Plains can be either a poverty area where people come and go according to the climate, or a farming area managed by the most skilled operators in the world. Personally I believe the latter is the trend. The Plains farmer, having extra and unpredictable factors to contend with, may sometime push the orange grower from his pedestal and be recognized himself as the most skilled manager.

Our experience has been that the citizen will take terrific jolts before he will make adaptations. He is hard set in his concept of the right way to do things. Thus the Great Plains farmer has to revise his concept of what is good farming, he has to establish new criteria for good workmanship, and he has to work out a new set of methods.

Our institutions are in process of revision, also. It is often hard to tell which has been the greater handicap—the resistance of the individual or the rules set up institutionally. Take for example the

Homestead Law. In the application of this law, the same rules for size of farm were applied from East to West, regardless of climate or type of production. There is justification for this because the modifying factors were unknown. However, it created a pattern of land ownership which has been extremely difficult to correct.

There may be a tendency to pattern research and education in the same molds which are used on a nationwide basis. I want to use as an example the difference in our interest in soils. In an area with plenty of rainfall the chemical content of soils is all-important, and our research and education revolve largely around this point. In the Great Plains, where moisture is a limiting factor, the soils interest lies as much in the physical capacity to store moisture and yet give it up to the plant at a rate which enables a plant to grow best and to survive climatic factors which may prevail above the surface.

Methods and programs which have only local application are hard to sell to the country at large. A case in point is the shelter-belt program which was instituted in the late nineteen-thirties. It is a specially designed effort to establish tree plantings on what is now a treeless plain. It is one of the important modifications of that area leading to a higher standard of permanence and well-being. It was launched with the greatest possible amount of unfortunate publicity, which made the undertaking look ridiculous in the eyes of the rest of the country. Yet it did prove to be well adapted, and it is a measure which will go far in correcting one of the shortcomings of the Plains. The program has proved its worth and was fully accepted by the people after it passed through its experimental stages. I think it can be truthfully said that no program has more complete backing than this one; yet because it applies only to parts of the nation, it is impossible to create much national interest. Eventually the shelter-belt program will get under way and will add tremendously to the well-being of the local people, and at the same time it will make a great contribution to the national well-being.

Institutionally it is difficult to arrange a grouping wherein the center of interest will coincide with the loci of problems. As I have previously indicated, problems do not bound themselves distinctly, and each problem has its own center of intensity and its own fringe area. The lines which result from the grouping of states or districts may be such that they cut directly through the center of the problem area; and even though the problem may be large in itself and critical, yet when it is sliced up geographically so that a segment falls within each of several regions, the problem may become of secondary interest to any one of several groups even if they assemble regularly to consider the problems. Organizational segmentation of areas of distinct characteristics is as much of a difficulty as is drawing arbitrary lines and saying that all of the differences within this area must conform. In this we disregard the fact which I have just pointed out— that the problems have their own loci, that their center of intensity varies geographically, and that each problem has its own borders.

I quote as an example the problems of wind erosion, which were not considered seriously by any of the policy groups concerned with the main agricultural areas of the country such as the Corn Belt or the Cotton Belt. When wind erosion became an acute problem, however, it brought together a group whose center of interest henceforth was focused directly upon the problem. Thereupon we had a community which centered its thought and activity on a problem rather than upon a more generalized interest based on type of production.

Practical achievements are the things which count. Research, education, and programs can be pointed to alleviation, remedy, and permanent change.

The organization pointed towards practical adjustments must be designed to do two things—first, to establish the setting, isolate the problems, and establish objectives; and second, to provide the means for carrying out the desired measures. Most of these remedial measures are in the hands of farm families themselves, and some of the improvement will come about through the effective workmanship of institutions concerned with research, education, and concerted programs.

Since it is essential to get a large group to work, both professional people and farmers, the function of isolating the problems and establishing objectives is extremely important. The Great Plains is better organized to fulfill this function than it is to provide the means for a unified operations program. The Great Plains organization had its inception in the dark days of dust storms and distress. It was on December 14, 1935, that a group of agricultural leaders who realized the extent of the disaster came together to discuss the methods of combating dust storms which were rolling in huge dark billows over the Plains. A few weeks later, on January 15, 1936, with the marks of disaster imprinted upon them even more strongly, a part of this group met again at Garden City, Kansas. They directed a memorandum to Secretary Wallace saying that it was their unqualified opinion that certain practices as yet untried on a large scale would be effective in diminishing wind erosion. They said that the emergency program should be followed by a permanent program. The resolution brought quick results, and a bill granting the committee's request for two million dollars of emergency funds was passed by the Congress and signed by President Roosevelt on February 29, 1936. By May, forty thousand farmers had covered five and one-half million acres by emergency tillage.

The co-operation of forty thousand farmers is an illustration of the point I have just made—that in each of these undertakings it is necessary to have participation of thousands of people. The recommendations contained in the committee's memo were bold and daring, for never before had any group had the audacity to assert publicly that the problems of the Great Plains were peculiar to its climate. Never before had the opinion been forcefully advanced that even though emergency activities were absolutely essential and fully warranted by the desperate drought situation, yet such emergency measures were not in themselves an adequate treatment of the problem. The committee was convinced that the real answer would be found in a permanent program.

For a time there was little interest in the program in the country as a whole, since the problems of the Plains were regarded as local, isolated, and temporary. Suddenly, however, nationwide attention was focused on the Plains area as a result of dust-clouded skies which left a thin coat of Plains soil on the streets and desks in Washington. Congress enacted conservation laws, administrators became concerned, and the general public gave its support.

In July the President appointed a national committee to make recommendations both for an emergency and for a permanent program in accordance with the suggestion at the Garden City meeting in January. The committee presented its first draft on August 27, 1936, and a revised draft was completed and sent to Congress on February 10, 1937. The committee was extremely foresighted and saw the Plains as an area of common problems for which general objectives could be established. They made a clean break with the idea that the problems were temporary. They made a series of recommendations for a permanent program to be applied over a period of time until the main adjustments had been achieved.

Among their recommendations were development of water resources; establishment of districts for the control of erosion on arable land; management of tax-delinquent lands; adaptations in the public-service pattern; enlargement of operating units; resettlement of stranded families; systematic provision for feed and seed reserves; supplemental irrigation; new irrigation in farm size, small projects, or major developments; conservation of soil moisture; protection of equity; and security of tenure.

To promote the foregoing adjustments, they suggested that a commission or council be formed to encourage as best it might the development and integration of influences and activities in the Plains area. In accordance with this suggestion, the Southern Plains Agricultural Council succeeded its temporary predecessor and took up the functions of establishing a continuing program. In March, 1938, a council was set up for the Northern Plains area. These two groups have joined their functions into a program which applies to all the Plains with their problems of moisture deficiencies, drought periods, variable income, and sparse population. That voluntary group has kept the problems of the area at its fingertips, promoted common interest, suggested measures of correction, and encouraged a concerted action program on the part of all state and federal agencies. It is attacking problems as they arise while at the same time adhering to and evolving a definite policy which is predicated on the premise that the Great Plains are an area in which the practices of other regions have to be modified to suit a particular set of climatic conditions. Throughout its lifetime the council has been dedicated to democratic and co-operative action in securing concerted efforts of research, educational, and action programs. The activities of the voluntary group have been very largely in the field of clarifying situations and establishing objectives. However, the concerted efforts of agencies and farmers have totaled into very impressive results.

Let me turn now to method of operation and state some of the points which such an organization must ascertain if it is going to clear the way for an effective attack on problems.

First, there must be a definition of the area wherein the problem is of significance. It is obvious that if only part of the area is included, the effort becomes segmentized and futile. If too much area is included and the outer fringe is only mildly affected, the interest is lost and the efforts will not be efficient. The size of area ranges from a region down to a single farm. Sometimes it takes in a combination of political units, and sometimes the problem is most acute within a section of a political unit. It is almost certain that the political units and the problem units do not coincide. For example, we find that certain very serious problems which are characteristic of the Great Plains affect one-fifth of the land area of the nation and yet cover only one-fifth to three-fourths of any one of the ten Plains States. We may pick one characteristic—that of sparse population, which reaches from the Canadian border to the High Plains of Texas; yet within each of the states only a part of its farm population is confronted with adjusting a system of schools and roads to the needs of widely spaced farmsteads. So states must have means whereby they can cross the political boundaries and work co-operatively with other states in attacking the problem.

Some states have the complete gamut of conditions. Take as an example the state of South Dakota, where the southeast corner is a part of the most intensive Corn Belt while the northwest corner lies in the great, extensive grasslands. The political unit of South Dakota cannot be characterized altogether as an area of extensive production, for its fourteen southeast counties have everything in common with the Corn Belt and the states of Iowa, Minnesota, and Illinois. Yet some of its most acute and trying problems are shared by Montana and Wyoming. If efforts are made to apply the programs of action, research, or education to South Dakota as a whole, they will not yield full benefit. A group of citizens brought together from all parts of South Dakota are likely to regard some vital problems as incidental, whereas a group drawn from western South Dakota and eastern Montana have almost everything in common. To say it another way, the consideration of a range problem by a group representing all of South Dakota is likely to create only partial interest, whereas a group which is brought together on the basis of the location of the problem may get down to brass tacks in a very short time and may work out a solution.

Problems have different geographical boundaries when general policies are being considered and when specific remedies are to be undertaken. A problem may show similar characteristics over a large area and have sharp local differentiations. When that is the case, the job must be handled in two sections, the first being that of understanding the problem, adapting the local concepts, and getting the sympathetic ear of the nation; and the second being that of directing the energy effectively to the solution of the problem. It may very well be that widely accepted practices have failed over a large area; yet new practices which are substituted may have to be of one type in one area and of a different type in another. The research, education, and programs must be tailored to suit a rather special and limited set of circumstances.

Redefinition of concepts is essential and perhaps a first step. One of the almost inviolate national concepts is that of diversified farming. However, putting the whole concept into a new setting has been a financially costly and mentally painful process. Diversification is fundamentally as good for the Great Plains as it is for the Corn Belt, but the definition must be written differently. So whereas diversification in the Corn Belt means a satisfactory balance between pasture, row crops, and close-grown crops, each of which succeeds the other in regular sequence on several fields of the farm, such a balance cannot be attained by the Great Plains farmer unless he includes some additional features. If a Plains farmer is to have alfalfa, he probably has to provide for irrigation. If he wants to include wheat, he will put that on lands which are suitable for wheat. He finds that wheat yields more than most other crops on these kinds of lands, and if it is good wheat land, its productivity will be a dozen times that of pasture. If he is to have livestock, he needs a large acreage for pasture, and the best pasture is apt to be native grass. So we get a picture of a great gap between the various production enterprises. He cannot successfully grow alfalfa on wheat land, nor does it pay for him to grow wheat under irrigation. Therefore alfalfa land becomes alfalfa land, and wheat land becomes wheat land, and the gap is even greater between the use of land for wheat and the use of it for grazing.

So we get an entirely different operating organization for the well-diversified farm under semiarid climatic conditions than we do under humid conditions. It strengthens the farm organization to have livestock and a good feed base for that livestock, but the fitting together is entirely different from anything that the farm operator experiences in others parts of the nation. It was the insistence of the homesteader that the old methods be maintained which starved out many a family instead of enabling it to look towards a new home in the great new West.

A second illustration of necessary changes in concepts may be that of size of farm. We find that people from areas where more humid conditions prevail feel that the families living under a semiarid climate are trying to build up bonanza farms at the sacrifice of good farm husbandry, when, as a matter of fact, size of farm should be measured in ability to provide a particular level of living. This level may be achieved on a two-hundred-acre farm in the Corn Belt or on a two-thousand-acre farm in the Plains country.

A third illustration of concepts which must be revised is that concerned with public services. The change in farm size establishes a different set of rules for maintaining schools, roads, and rural electrification. These are just illustrations and might be continued through a whole list of concepts.

Now, recognizing the reluctance of the individual to give up familiar interpretations and the pressures he is under from the outside to hold high the banner of long-accepted principles, one finds that the practical processes of adaptation are pretty complicated and require good sense and strategy. Research and education must quickly come to the aid of the baffled individual and must give him the landmarks by which he can shape up his new definition. Otherwise there is a tendency to throw everything to the winds and to damn the country.

Criteria of acceptable workmanship, too, must be revised. Take for example the radical technique of maintaining a stubble mulch on the land surface. This results from a system of surface tillage which keeps the trash on top of the ground. When such persons as M. A. Bell, superintendent of the Havre, Montana, Experiment Station, first uncovered this method through experimentation and asked that the method be tried on a larger scale on one of the Fairway Farms, the managers were tremendously interested in it from the standpoint of lowering the cost of production, inasmuch as the outlay for this method was much below that of the standard plowing methods. However, they were very slow to try the system on a big field because it looked like sloppy farming—and what would the neighbors say? They were finally persuaded, and found that what Bell had said was not only a low-cost method, but resulted in relatively high yields.

It took at least twenty years for the stubble-mulch method to become acceptable to the wheat grower. However, at the end of that time something of a pandemonium broke loose and the whole country began to talk of the plow as being obsolete. There was a period during which the literature was somewhat spectacular and the idea was pointed up in books like *Plowman's Folly*.

In the meantime soil and moisture conservation scientists undertook experimental work which tested the value of the method from the moisture conservation standpoint and showed good possibilities. So what originally had looked doubtful proved to be a method suitable to the climatic conditions of the Plains, and a practice that may eventually become incorporated in the routine of farm operations in other parts of the country.

I use this as an example to show how a farm practice may lie dormant for years even though it is well adapted to an area, but because it is a different system and does not fit the tradition, it is not put into use. It takes a lot of demonstration on the part of experiment stations and a lot of adapted education on the part of educators to get practical results.

The elements within a series of adjustments must be weighed and carefully selected. It will not do to select a secondary or obscure element. It must be possible to isolate the factor to a point where it can be handled as a problem. The factor must be a trouble item which is significant and one which can be solved. Some elements lend themselves to rather quick adjustments, whereas others are age-old chronic ailments which have been stated and restated a thousand times, but for which there is no immediate remedy. The questions must be asked: What are the most essential items? What is causing the greatest confusion and distress? Can this factor be isolated from a dozen other factors in such a way that it can be analyzed and attacked separately? If it can be isolated and if it is evident that the impact of that problem can be alleviated, then it is something which can be taken up. If the problem or factor is obscured by the impact of a dozen others, it will be useless to try to point it up so that a large group of people are willing to devote their energy to it, or so that existing agencies can address part of their program directly to it.

The time must be appropriate even after the several factors can be isolated clearly enough so that they become tangible and manageable. The timing might even be termed opportunistic. Sometimes the acceptance of an idea and the putting it into practice do not coincide. For instance, when the season is dry and the soils are out of control, everyone will accept the idea that certain lands should be returned to permanent cover. However, the reseeding of lands is successful only when there is enough rain so the stand of permanent grass will get started. So what has become an accepted idea in one period must be held over and applied in another period. Ofttimes it requires extraordinarily firm conviction to carry out a program which even though it is effective over a long period of time becomes just the reverse of what you might want to do within a particular climatic cycle. As a case in point, when the ground is wet enough to make the establishment of permanent grass practical, it is also wet enough to grow wheat. The timing must also be worked in stages. Research must be carried on early and even before an exact combination of factors which will solve a problem are known. The educational aspects must be on a long-range basis, must be continuous, and yet must be flexible enough so that they do not run directly counter to the conditions of any one year. Finally, the operations must be initiated during a period when they can be efficiently done.

In these modern times we can mark out in a systematic and scientific manner the reasons for the success or failure of people under various conditions. We can arrange the problems that prevail in a locality, and when we do that we have several outstanding ones for the Plains area: (1) great variation in production due to the shifting to and fro of climate over a critical rainfall level; (2) a generally lower per-acre productivity due to low yields in the dry years which pull down the average for the generous years; (3) tremendous gaps in the intensities of agricultural production, caused by the shifting back and forth between livestock and crop enterprises—a jump which is much greater in the Plains area than in the humid zones; (4) inadequate water supplies; (5) certain insect pests native to the area, for example, the grasshopper, which at times is of as much concern to the Plains farmer as the boll weevil is to the cotton farmer.

These problems bring about a number of features which we now call economic and social characteristics of the area: large acreages and farms, sparse population, single-crop farming, intermittent public ownership, and a costly system of public services.

As I have said, the effort in the Plains is better organized for the process of clarifying objectives than it is for carrying on the work to fulfill them. When it comes to the accomplishment stage, the effort enters a phase wherein the existing programs can be revised to a point where concerted action on the part of each organization as it goes about its segment of the work can be directed towards a single purpose. By common consent the administrators of various activities establish a series of general objectives, which they amend as time and occasion require. The whole undertaking rests upon the process of clear understanding, for it is often hard for each agency or group to see how its activity can contribute to a solution.

Again, some group may see clearly how they may contribute, but become discouraged because they find so many interfering elements. I cite as a case in point the difficulties of establishing conservation practices, because it was found that the making of farm plans was often prohibited by the instability of ownership and by the large numbers of ownership parcels which were included in one operating unit. It was almost impossible for the conservation planner to get agreement between the several owners who carry out the specific programs.

To make clear the point that a good understanding of the problem is necessary in order that all may carry their particular parts of the burden, let me list the agencies as of 1937 which were named by the President's Great Plains Committee as contributors to a program of rehabilitation and improvement.

Department of the Treasury	Office of Indian Affairs
Bureau of Public Health	Office of Education
War Department	Geological Survey
Office of the Chief of Engineers	Bureau of Reclamation
Department of Justice	National Park Service
The Lands Division	Bureau of Mines
Post Office Department	Division of Grazing
Department of the Interior	Department of Agriculture
General Land Office	Office of Experiment Stations

Extension Service
Agricultural Adjustment
    Administration
Bureau of Agricultural
    Economics
Bureau of Agricultural
    Engineering
Bureau of Animal Industry
Bureau of Biological Survey
Bureau of Chemistry and Soils
Bureau of Dairy Industry
Forest Service
Bureau of Plant Industry
Bureau of Public Roads
Soil Conservation Service
Weather Bureau
Interstate Commerce Commission
Federal Reserve System
Federal Housing Administration
Federal Board of Survey and Maps
Reconstruction Finance
    Corporation
Federal Home Loan Bank Board
Electric Home and Farm Authority

Rural Electrification
    Administration
Resettlement Administration
National Youth Administration
Farm Credit Administration
    Land Bank Division
    Intermediate Credit Division
    Production Credit Division
    Co-operative Division
    Regional Agricultural Credit
        Division
    Emergency Crop and Feed Loan
        Section
Federal Farm Mortgage
    Corporation
Federal Emergency Administration
    of Public Works
Federal Surplus Commodities
    Corporation
Works Progress Administration
Emergency Conservation Work
Federal Deposit Insurance
    Corporation
Commodity Credit Corporation
National Resources Committee

Each of these exercises functions of varied importance in relation to the rehabilitation and readjustment of the economy of the Great Plains region. I do not list these for the purpose of showing duplication, for one must not overlook the fact that in a comprehensive program there are many facets of work and many specialties. All of these agencies have made significant contributions and have shown extraordinary patience and willingness in synchronizing their work. They have done well in carrying out the charge given them by President Roosevelt when he said: "I am anxious that we leave no stone unturned in exploring and reporting all the possibilities of this region as one in which reasonable standards of living can be maintained by the largest possible population. We should face the fact that climatic conditions make special safeguards absolutely necessary."

Before I enumerate some of the results, let me repeat the recommendations which were made by the Great Plains Committee in

1936: development of water resources, establishment of districts for the control of erosion on arable lands, management of tax-delinquent land, facilitation of changes in the public-services pattern, enlargement of operating units, resettlement of stranded families, systematic provision for feed and seed reserves, supplemental irrigation, new irrigation in farm-size and small projects and major developments, conservation of soil moisture, protection of equity, and security of tenure. It is a long list, and the interrelations are proving to be complicated, but some of the problems have been resolved in part. I shall discuss some of the practical results.

A problem of first priority and extent was that of soil blowing. In order to reduce the susceptibility of the Plains to wind action, at least a half-dozen agencies directed their energies to it. While those of us who work in the Plains area are not so sanguine as some writers about having achieved control of wind erosion, we do know that we have reduced the susceptibility of many areas to a marked degree, and we have evolved practices of soil management which are effective. The farmers and ranchers of the Plains have incorporated certain tillage practices, strip cropping, and winter cover into their everyday routine. These practices will control the soil under moderate conditions; and should a disastrous, continuing drought strike the area, these farmers all know what emergency practices to apply. An effort is being made to establish local organizations which will be on their guard and which will put into effect every possible preventive measure, and in case of emergency will mobilize an entire community.

A second problem was that a certain portion of the lands which had gone into wheat production as a result of the needs of World War I proved themselves unsuited to cultivation. Having these acres remain under cultivation was an acknowledged hazard. It was determined that about ten million acres of land were especially susceptible, and they were identified as critical lands. A program for returning these ten million acres to the permanent protection of grass cover was inaugurated. The program required action in all phases of work. First of all, additional research and investigation would be needed to give further indication of the marginality of some lands for wheat production. This was followed by an educational program to provide the farmer with information about the yield per acre which would enable him to break even for wheat production. A rule of thumb has now come into universal use which says that wheat lands become marginal when yields run below twelve bushels an acre when the land is summer fallowed and when the price is about one dollar. This rule is based on sound research.

Having gained general acceptance of this concept by the thousands of farmers, a series of programs were pointed towards the reestablishment of permanent grass cover of wheat lands. Even the mechanics of establishing permanent grasses were unknown, and the research departments were called upon to present findings concerning seeding practices. Each of these programs required a thoroughgoing understanding on the part of the farm operator, and it was the responsibility of educational and technical services to make the information available. The next step was an allowance of a few cents an acre to the farmer who would designate his more critical acres as in need of permanent cover. The original approach was not fully effective, in that it made an allowance only for leaving the land untilled, thereby permitting a weed cover to protect the land. It did not adequately encourage farmers to sow permanent grasses such as crested wheat. Later an allowance was made for permanent seedings, and this, together with education and technical guidance, brought a rapid advancement in the program.

The foregoing portions of the program were all well and good for lands which were in the hands of active farm operators. However, large portions of the land had been abandoned because families had been forced out by drought. These lands had reverted to county ownership for being delinquent in taxes, and at one time there were millions of acres of land under the management of county commissioners. Further modification of programs had to be worked out to enable and encourage counties to undertake programs which would restore their lands to a permanent cover.

These efforts, together with making special administrative adaptations in several programs, brought results. Not only was it necessary for county and state groups to appreciate the situation, but national administrators had to see the problem and adapt their programs accordingly. The net result of these efforts is that the original goal was met and exceeded, and about 10,600,000 acres have been restored to permanent cover.

In all parts of the Plains, water is the limiting factor, and in the case of range livestock production, stock water is especially important. The experiences of drought pointed out that lack of water for stock had been one of the most significant elements in the distress of the drought. It was generally agreed that more ways and means of developing stock water should be set in motion. There were no systematic programs in effect to which we might turn for experience needed in the installation of stock-water reservoirs. So special administrative adaptations were asked in order to cover different experiences and localized programs. When the objectives were set up, it was stated that at least 20,000 such reservoirs would be desirable, and that such a program therefore seemed worthy of special consideration. The methods for encouraging stock-water development were untried, and therefore such developments were undertaken experimentally by one or two agencies of government, together with some of the ranchers. Ranchers generally have had some experience over a fifty-year period which could be capitalized on. However, very little was known about the fundamentals of such a program when undertaken on a large scale. The development proved so popular that instead of 20,000 reservoirs, as originally anticipated, over 250,000 were built in twelve years' time.

There was less pressure of emergency back of this program than there was behind the program for reseeding to permanent grasses, for it did not have the threat of dust storms behind it. However, its inauguration proved to be well timed in that people were aware of the difficulties that water shortage had caused during the drought, and they quickly became aware of the advantages of a systematic distribution of water as a part of good range management. Every possible educational channel was used to spread information concerning the benefits which might accrue from an adequate system of watering places.

Irrigation, the fourth problem, has two aspects, one being the small irrigation for one farm or just a few farms, and the other being the larger and more spectacular developments. It was a part of the original objective to develop as far as possible the smaller type of irrigation and to intersperse irrigation lands as widely as possible throughout the agricultural plant. The national irrigation policy rested quite largely on the developments in the arid portions of the

West, and the Great Plains with its intermittent rainy season was not within the generally accepted zone of operation. In irrigation parlance, the Great Plains was subhumid, and the farm operators farmed with one eye on the clouds. This being true, Great Plains people found themselves confronted with making adaptations in irrigation to suit it to the semihumid climate. Their main objective was to use irrigation as a element of stabilization by the means of which they could ride out some of the drought periods. For small farm-to-farm water distributing systems, several agencies combined their efforts by providing technical services, information, and credit. By the combined efforts of all concerned, more than a million acres were brought under one type or another of small irrigation.

For irrigation projects in the next larger size category, it was decided that some tests should be made to determine the degree to which the dispersion of small projects throughout the area would help in stabilizing the communities, and therefore eight small projects were set up with an average of ten or twelve thousand acres. There was no provision in any of the national laws for projects of this size, and consequently a special law was passed which enabled the Reclamation Service to plan and supervise construction work on small projects. During that particular period there were a great many stranded farm operators in the Plains, and so the law carried the further provision that the Public Works Administration be given the responsibility for their part of the construction work. The Department of Agriculture had certain experiences in designing and developing irrigation farms which needed to be incorporated into these particular projects. So provision was made for this department to take the responsibility for the design and development of irrigation farms. Here we have a case of providing special legislation which would enable the work to be done, and three major departments of government were participating agencies.

More than 80,000 acres were developed under this law, and many new concepts were evolved as to efficient preparation of land for farming, the design of farms, the saving of labor in irrigation, and so on through the list. The experience gained in these pilot projects can now be generally applied to the irrigation aspects of the Missouri River development. I might also say in passing that a second special law was passed by the Congress which recognized the needs of developing irrigation and water supply on individual farms. Through this law over ten thousand installations have been made for small irrigation systems and domestic water supplies.

This was done through making a special type of loan, coupled with some technical education. Only 150 of these loans are not paid up or current.

The vast expanse of treeless areas caused this great belt of the country to be named the Great Plains. Its treelessness held back the westward wave of settlement. Many new inventions, including the sod house and barbed wire, were necessary before settlement could be undertaken in a treeless country. The nation undertook to encourage tree-planting by having Congress provide extra grants of land to those who agreed to plant trees. Evidence of that effort is still there, even though most of the trees were overmature when they were overtaken by the great drought and were dried out. In the midst of the drought a considerable interest was centered on tree-plantings, and special projects were set up in addition to those which were already in existence. Under these projects about 275,-000,000 trees have been planted in the last fifteen years, and there is a backlog of requests from farmers for about 50,000,000 more. The actual extent of plantings desired by farmers is shown by a number of spot surveys. It looks as if farmers want about ten times as many trees as have been planted, or a total of about 2,500,000 acres. The program has proved itself, and people are thinking of tree-planting as part of their plan for improving living conditions. Therefore it is incumbent on the agencies of research, education, and action to forward the program through concerted activity.

A sixth need of the Plains was the reorganization of farm units. As a result of the homestead policy, parcels of land were taken up by prospective farmers in sizes which were much too small to provide an adequate living or to prove an economic unit. Through the efforts of several agencies, especially the financial and educational groups, farm units have been consolidated and stabilized in size groups commensurate with the agriculture which is adapted to the Plains. The number of farms in many counties has been decreased by as much as one-third, and it has been the continuing policy of all the agencies of agriculture to lend assistance to a systematic reorganization of farm units.

Many factors have entered into the process of farm reorganization, and it would be impossible to evaluate the net effect of any one of the forces. A combination of farm mechanization and a great demand for personnel in industry has brought about changes in farming beyond those which were anticipated in the early thirties. Observers are not sure even now whether or not a reasonable balance has been struck in the ratio between agricultural resources and the number of farm families. Extensive irrigation may turn the tide towards an increasing number of farm families, whereas the world outlook for wheat requirements may cause some of the present wheat lands to be used more extensively for livestock production. The interested groups did bring some sense out of chaos by providing the means whereby various degrees of farm reorganization could be tested.

The reorganization of public services has not kept pace with the requirements of a sparse population pattern. In fact, the people of the area are in the process of hammering out a satisfactory pattern. The process of reorganization of school facilities and road systems is costly, and to quite a large degree unsystematic. This is one of those fields of work in which it has been very difficult to isolate the problems and provide the research and educational foundations on which adjustments might rest. Sparse population, or greater distances between farmsteads, requires attention also in establishing the new rural electrification. Means need to be developed whereby very few farm families will be left without the benefit of electrical energy. Some adjustments may need to be made in the settlement pattern.

Crop insurance is in effect as a means for maintaining a more uniform series of annual income. The application of the insurance principle is of more direct effect to the Plains than it is to almost any other region of the nation. It is an instrument now being used by thousands of farmers to level off their incomes.

There are numerous phases of the program which are still very much in the thought stage. Among these is a practical means of providing an ever-normal feed supply in an area of great variation in production. Some progress has been made in providing for a more uniform supply of feed which will carry livestock production through the hard winters and partially through years of drought. Amounts of feed vary considerably, community by community, throughout the

Plains; and even though the feed reserves have been improved, yet there is no widespread system of actually insuring against serious livestock losses from feed shortages. Such a system has been discussed in council meetings and elsewhere and will require a thoroughgoing study of the situation and some experimental efforts to work out a practical system which will keep the feed reserves at a high level locality by locality, and do so economically.

Much of the meat production in the Plains depends on a feed supply in terms of forage. The management of forage has made great strides through grazing practices and through distribution of stock water, the diversion of runoffs onto grazing lands, and conscious effort to maintain a scientific ratio between the number of livestock and the available forage. The means for keeping the levels high in each of the three categories—forage, hay, and grain—is a complicated but not impossible problem.

Small rural industries may be mentioned as another element in strengthening the Great Plains economy, and this phase, too, has scarcely gotten to the drawing-board stage. Here again a great deal of research, experience, and education will be brought to bear on the subject.

Most of my discussion up to this point concerns the experience of the people in the Great Plains as it pertains to the working out of a regional program within agriculture itself. However, there has been some participation by agencies from other departments of government. This is especially true of problems of irrigation. The Great Plains is so distinctly agricultural, with only a few industrial centers, that it is quite understandable that the co-operative efforts should be confined so largely to agricultural adaptation and improvement. Since 1944 the Pick-Sloan Plan has been proposed and construction begun which will lead to development of power, navigation, flood control, and additional irrigation. The additional irrigation is the only portion of it which falls partially within the field of agriculture. Developing the additional resources will give more balance to the economy of the Northern Plains.

The influence of the river itself is not so predominant in the Missouri Basin as in some others because of the extent of the land area. When one-sixth of the nation's land area is involved in a single watershed, the stream channels themselves may take their place as one of several factors. I presume that rivers such as the Columbia dominate the whole development much more since the land area is relatively small and the volume of water is very great.

The development of power will provide a new basis for manufacturing plants in what is an almost industry-less area. As I said in a previous paragraph, there are but few large industrial centers in the Missouri Basin. Since there is no concentration of population, it may be that the coming of power will develop many small industries. The Missouri Basin may prove to be the area in which some of the more recent theories of small industry and dispersement of industry will be tried out.

A much discussed portion of the development is irrigation, for it is planned to double the present area of irrigation, which is 4 to 5 per cent of the total cultivated land. When the installations have been made, between 8 and 10 per cent of the cultivated land will be under irrigation.

In applying some of the criteria which I have given for putting boundaries around regions, one finds the Missouri Basin does not readily classify as a homogeneous area. Climatically the area is distinctly bi-zonal.

The upper reaches of the watershed are arid, with an everlasting thirst for water, and the interest of people there is to save as much of that water as is possible and to keep it right on the land where it falls. This is somewhat of a new problem in managing the water of a basin, since most of the watersheds have presented the problem of getting the water off the land in the upper reaches as quickly as possible with a minimum of damage to the land, and then holding the water in the channel until it can go downstream in an orderly fashion so as not to do damage in the lower reaches of the stream. Farmers in the upper portion of the Missouri Basin, however, would like to see very little of the water leave the land, and they are interested in developing new engineering techniques which will help the thirsty soil take up the water. It is clearly evident that not all the water can be absorbed in the land, inasmuch as the land becomes temporarily saturated.

The lower portion of the Missouri Basin is in the humid zone, and drainage problems are considerable. The interest in the lower basin, therefore, is not in absorbing the water on the land, but in leading it off to the watercourses with the least possible damage. In this part of the basin, flood control, navigation, and power are the larger interests.

The two interests seem to be in direct conflict, and yet they can be made complementary one to the other by having the upper areas use every bit of water which the devices of human ingenuity can cause them to absorb. If a goodly quantity of the water can be held in the land of the upper basin, the amounts which will need to be impounded to protect the lower basin will be considerably reduced. If the two conflicting interests can be resolved, the engineering pattern will eventually turn out to be a combination of upstream absorption and mainstream impoundment. The complete success of such a complementary design might even work out so that the use of water would truly become multiple and eventually serve the best interest of agriculture, industry, and navigation.

The area is homogeneous in its need for electric energy, and there is a question as to whether power can be used most effectively in small industries in the upper basin or whether it should be transmitted to the existing industrial centers. The sharp competition for the limited water of the Missouri—and I say limited only in respect to the size of the land area which it drains—has created pressures which have required Congress to take a hand and say in effect that the irrigation potential west of the ninety-eighth meridian should not be jeopardized.

The time schedule will be subject to extraordinary pressure in the Missouri Basin, with a pressure building up for the irrigation phase in drought years. During those times people will become very impatient with the rate at which irrigation facilities are being installed, and they will ask the Congress to step up the rate at which development takes place. On the other hand, during years of heavy rainfall, floods will occur, and pressure for rapid development of the flood-control aspects will develop. There seems to be no question at the present time but that work will go forward at a steady pace regardless of the shifts of the weather cycle, but the pressure for one or the other type of development is sure to become great.

The time schedule between the phases of work would perhaps be classified as an operating problem. The relationship between the rate at which reservoirs and irrigation systems are installed sets the requirement for a greatly accelerated agricultural program. At the present time there is no provision for an agricultural program, but the Budget Bureau has asked the Congress for a beginning appropriation which may eventually be increased to an amount that will enable agriculture to come abreast of the rapid pace set by the construction agencies.

Much is being expected of the river development in the way of strengthening the agricultural economy of the Plains area. The effect of river development on agriculture comes largely through the increase of irrigated land. Since the sum total of the irrigated land is about one-tenth of the crop acreage, or one-thirtieth of the total land area, and since so much dependence is put on this small acreage to help decrease the hazard of drought, the irrigation lands must be fitted into the agricultural plant so that they will go just as far as possible in reducing the hazard. The farmer in a semiarid climate looks upon irrigation as an insurance. He would like to have irrigation assure him of food for his family and feed for a limited number of livestock so that he could pull through the drought years. A large percentage of the farmers in the upper basin would like to have such an insurance for their farms. However, this is entirely unfeasible from the engineering standpoint, and therefore it becomes a matter of striking the most efficient balance between irrigated land and nonirrigated land. All of this is distinctly new in both the agricultural and the engineering field, and consequently much exploratory work is to be desired.

From the organizational standpoint the Missouri Basin development is very similar to the Great Plains Council. In fact, it may be that the organization is patterned after the older council, with its fourteen years' experience. The mechanism for organization is known as the Missouri Basin Inter-Agency Committee and is a voluntary assembly wherein the work programs of each of the agencies which have work under way are explained to the rest of the committee. Each agency or department is required to evolve its own operating program and present its budget estimates to the Budget Bureau. The Congress is the determining body as to what phases of development shall be undertaken and the rate at which it shall be done.

I have said earlier that the Great Plains agricultural group was better equipped for clarifying objectives and isolating problems than it was for carrying out the operations, even though the total result of the operations is very imposing. The Missouri Basin agencies are much stronger on the operating-program side, and so far have fewer facilities for isolating problems and determining over-all objectives.

In conclusion, I would say that the principles of the multiple use of water will be thoroughly tried out in the Missouri Basin. The land area is great and its ratio to the amount of water is wide. Therefore the people of that area will be more critical of the means which are devised for making the best use of water than they are likely to be in areas where water is more abundant. The area has had long experience in development of the voluntary system of integration in one specific phase of its economy, and it is now in the process of testing that voluntary principle in the integration of a more diverse series of enterprises.

Part V

The Limitations and the Promise

of Regionalism

Introduction

Merle Curti

I T IS obvious that some of the difficulties one is faced with in reading these papers result from differences in definitions of region and regionalism. Both Professor Odum and Professor Wirth admit that the terms must be defined. Each goes about it in his own way. Professor Odum rejects some of the connotations that Professor Wirth insists the terms region and regionalism have been associated with in the literature of the subject. Regionalism is not in any sense geographical determinism, nor is it localism or areal homogeneity resting on isolation, Professor Odum insists. Nor is it, as Professor Wirth has it, a "one-way" concept. Again, it is not merely decentralization or planning, though these are involved. Neither is it metropolitan urbanism. Above all, it is not a cult! Proceeding positively, Professor Odum defines regionalism as "essentially a synthesis of differentiation and integration, within the framework of homogeneities and diversities, following the historical process of periodic alternating between the particularist trend of multiplying culture areas and the universalist trend toward consolidation and integration of areas and cultures." As such, Professor Odum thinks, it has served as a highly useful instrument of analysis, understanding, and synthesis in the social sciences. And, further, it promises to be, in the field of policy, a means of achieving a balance between resources and human energies in interrelated areas, whether in peace or in war.

Professor Wirth admits the existence of regions as a fact, and of regionalism as a hypothesis, a practical tool for social engineering, and a state of mind and social movement. He also pays tribute to the seminal character of the contributions of the regionalist social scientists in all these aspects. Thus there is a larger area of agreement between Professor Wirth and Professor Odum than may appear on the surface. But as the papers show, there are also sharp differences between the two. The differences lie not so much in what Professor Odum and Professor Wirth regard as possible and desirable. Each apparently agrees with the other that regionalism however defined or approached has contributed, and can further contribute, to clarification of relationships of social groups with each other and with their "natural" environment and to the promotion of social efficiency through necessary and desirable types of integration. But the major difference between the two lies in the sphere of probabilities. Professor Odum believes that there is a high probability that regionalism may further these desired ends. Professor Wirth is less convinced of that probability. He sees contradictions and limitations in regionalism, whether regarded as a hypothesis, a practical tool for social engineering, a state of mind, or a social movement. Because, as he sees it, regionalism is a less effectively inclusive set of relationships than Professor Odum believes, he is of the opinion that it may lead to a falsification of the facts, to a futile effort to squeeze life into too rigid a mold, or to retard the integration of life on a wider and more inclusive scale. Professor Odum, on the other hand, is convinced that regionalism is the most promising antidote to just these dangers. It cannot be both. Or can it?

It seems that Professor Odum and Professor Wirth are looking at the mountain from a somewhat different point of the compass and at a somewhat different time of day. Thus what one emphasizes is overemphasis to the other. Each indicates, though indirectly and in passing, an awareness that the time factor is pertinent to any discussion of the making and unmaking of regions, to an understanding of intraregional and interregional relationships. Perhaps a sharper focus on the precise bearing of the passing of time on these relationships would resolve some of the differences in the view of regionalism that these social scientists take. The elements in the discussion—those held in common and those disagreed about—have their roots in the past, though they could not be duplicated at any earlier point of time, either as actualities or as interpretations of actualities. We may be sure that some of these emphases each of our social scientists has made will, in varying combinations and modifications, survive into the future. But we may also be fairly sure that some of the present conflicts and questions will then have disappeared and that others will have taken their places. If this is kept in mind, we may not be far wrong in regarding these provocative papers as clarifying, and in some degree catalyzing, contributions to the outcome.

Chapter 14

The Limitations of Regionalism

Louis Wirth

SEMINAL ideas are so rare that when we meet them in the scientific world we tend to embrace them with more than justifiable enthusiasm. Almost inevitably, as a consequence, we are disposed to overextend them and to make them the basis of a cult. To a certain extent this has happened in the case of the regionalism concept. Other papers in this series have emphasized the fruitfulness of the idea. It is my task to call attention to its limitations.

There is a particular reluctance to undertake to deflate the idea of regionalism because it has such a venerable history and has furnished so many fruitful insights into the life of man in society at various periods and because it has done so much to correct and supplement other one-sided perspectives. It should be noted at the outset, therefore, that in undertaking this critical task, there is no intention on the part of the author of this paper to minimize the significant clues for the understanding of the complexities of social life and the many practical suggestions for the solution of social problems which have come from the regional approach.

The regional idea owes its scientific vitality to the fact that it offers a naturalistic and empirically verifiable theory for the interpretation of history. It affords a check on other competing theories in that it keeps the investigator's feet planted on the solid ground of the physical conditions of existence, though it must be admitted that it has not prevented him from letting his imagination soar to the heavens. The view of man in society, however, which singles out the interconnections between the human habitat and the complex fabric of social arrangements, ways of life, ideas and ideals, must be recognized for what it is, namely, a one-factor theory, which taken alone will furnish only a one-sided, and hence distorted, picture of social reality, and which, to be scientifically valuable, must be supplemented by and integrated with other perspectives affording other equally plausible and meaningful interpretations.

From time immemorial, the attention of thinkers in many parts of the world has been directed to the spatial or areal aspects of human existence and to the physical substructure upon which communities and societies rest. Some of these notions have been elaborated into cosmic theories purporting to explain the origin and persistence of certain institutions in certain places on the basis of climate, rainfall, topography, natural resources, and similar factors. The development and the diffusion of civilization and the rise and fall of empires have been traced to such "environmental" conditions. The prevalence of democracy or autocracy, of monotheism or polytheism, of urbanism or agrarianism, and of variant forms of family, community, or national life has been depicted as more or less determined by such physical facts of nature. The influence which such a writer as Montesquieu has exerted upon Western thought is directly traceable to the vigor and persuasiveness with which he documented such a theory.

It would be foolish to deny that through such an approach much light has been thrown on many of the mysteries of cultural uniqueness and similarity; but it would also be naïve to fail to see that such simplistic interpretations of the complexities of social life have obscured other equally significant elements and have led to distorted versions of the complex and seemingly capricious course of human affairs.

There are many and varied conceptions of regions encountered in the rich and rapidly growing literature being produced by scholars and scientists representing a wide range of interests. Geographers, historians, anthropologists, linguists, artists, economists, sociologists, political scientists, administrators, architects, engineers and planners —all have been attracted to the idea and have contributed to its elaboration. The various notions of the region which have emerged from these different sources present many nuances of meaning. To some, the region is an area defined by one or more physical characteristics, such as rainfall, length of growing season, character of soil, vegetation, contours, and similar features. To others, it is an area delimited by the prevalence of one or more cultural characteristics—such as language or dialect, costume, form of social organization, type of architecture, use of given tools, acceptance of a given religion, practice of certain social customs—which distinguish the region from adjacent areas or other regions. This is what the anthropologists have called a culture area.

To be distinguished from such natural and cultural areas defined in terms of homogeneity in respect to one or more traits, is the conception of the region as an area set off from other areas by barriers of various sorts. Mountains, deserts, rivers, lakes, and oceans are the most obvious of these barriers. No less potent, however, may be the artificial, i.e., man-made, barriers such as state and national boundaries and trade, exchange, and customs regulations, which inhibit contact between different areas and which in turn tend to confine the activities of a given area and isolate it from others.

There is a third conception of the region which, in contrast particularly to the first mentioned (which implies homogeneity of characteristics), rests upon interdependence. In a region so conceived the component parts are not necessarily similar or identical but stand in a relationship of significant interdependence or integration of life in one or more respects. Such a region finds difficulty in delineating its boundaries, but is more likely to have a salient or dominant center; whereas the types of regions described above can be more readily defined in terms of their periphery but may not give evidence of the existence of a focal point which dominates the life and activities of the area. An example of this third type of region is the trade area, which is delineated by the network of economic interconnections that holds it together and which can be described in terms of the radii of influence which extend from the center outward. The importance of such regions in historical and contemporary societies may be indicated by pointing to the role of rural trade centers, metropolitan regions, and cultural and political capitals, which extend their tentacles out in all directions and influence the life of their regions in varying degrees.

Such regions cannot usually be set off from adjacent regions by sharply defined lines because, in the first place, the center of dominance may have varying range in respect to the various functions it performs for the region and, secondly, because the periphery may shade off or fade into a no man's land where it meets the influences exerted by a competing center of dominance. The listening areas of radio stations, the circulation areas of newspapers, the ticker services of stock exchanges, the wholesale or retail trade areas of a metropolis, and the drawing area of a medical center, a university, an orchestra, an opera, or a museum may give us indications of how far in its complex functions a center extends in its influence and where it comes into collision with a competing center. Those of us who have labored in the field of metropolitan regions and who are aware of the many and varied functions that tie such regions together are in a position where we must warn others against the naïve acceptance of regional definitions based upon a one-factor criterion, and even more against the disposition to accept the boundaries, when once defined, as permanent. Regions based upon the principle of interdependence and the dominance of a focal center are not only vaguely defined but are subject to infinite flux.

A fourth type of region is an areal unit defined in terms of an *ad hoc* problem. If we would control contagious disease, crime, slums, traffic, or other community problems, we must find suitable areal units of administration corresponding to the areas over which these problems extend and taking account of the factors which underlie these problems. An area which is suited to one purpose may not be adaptable to another purpose. The TVA, which, it should be noted, has multiple objectives—national defense, navigation, and flood control—is such an area; and one of the issues it faces is precisely attributable to the several, and perhaps even mutually conflicting, functions for which it has been established. The New York Port Authority would not seem to be a suitable pattern on which to build other regional services such as the control of railroad or highway traffic, much less the orderly redevelopment of slums or the control of crime in the New York area.

With the development of local, regional, and national planning, it has become increasingly important to search for improved techniques for defining the scope of the strategic functions with which planning agencies must deal. In the course of such efforts, the problems posed by the multifunctional planning area—i.e., one that will reconcile the residential pattern of the community with the industrial, the transportation, the public-service, the cultural, and the political pattern—have become readily apparent. Ideally, a planning region should be one that comprises the territory within which all of the problems of the community can be treated adequately. But the area which affects a central community and the area affected by the central community in one vital way or another encompasses the world. Hence planning regions must of necessity always be based upon compromise and in practice turn out to be more or less unsatisfactory compromises.

What has been said about such *ad hoc* regions as planning areas is, of course, only a particular instance of other single- or multiple-function regions. It suggests that the administrative region, or *ad hoc* region, is a contrast conception which may be put in juxtaposition to the "natural area" as viewed by human ecologists. Nature does not always carve out neatly the lines that set off one area from another, nor does man in his works always obey the dictates of nature. While the natural and the cultural landscape often coincide, they also often clash. Historical factors which have shaped the outlines of cities, counties, states, and nations may impose rather arbitrary patterns upon the features of the human habitat and may themselves in the course of time become as significant as nature herself. Thus, for instance, when some of our states were laid out, rivers were designated in many instances as the boundaries between them. At the same time, rivers were also significant arteries of transportation and thus conditioned the sites of the towns. As a result, we face the problem today of having over twenty of our principal cities located on state boundaries—a situation which, since many of these cities have grown to metropolitan size, creates complicated interstate problems of administration. The planning region is an attempt to overcome the handicaps imposed upon those who have the responsibility of dealing with the actual and emerging problems of today by the rigid and in many instances unsuitable outlines of administrative areas. The planning region represents a recognition of and an answer to the fact that human social life does not always conform to the metes and bounds set by nature; that ongoing life tends to spill over not merely these natural barriers but also the arbitrary or historically conditioned political and administrative units; and that if man is to be a better master over his fate, he must, by all the intelligence he can command, seek to shape the most appropriate units of organization for his collective needs.

This depiction of types of regions has been undertaken here to call attention to the fact that in the concept of region we are not dealing with a single and unambiguous idea, but rather with a variety of notions and approaches. To use the regional concept as if it were one clear and univocal term is to make for misunderstandings and confusion rather than clarity. There now remains the task of drawing some implications from this delineation of the various dimensions of the concept which will indicate its proper uses and limitations.

It seems useful to discuss the fruitfulness and at the same time the limitations of the regional concept by considering the region first as a fact and then in turn as an hypothesis, as a practical tool for social engineering, and as a state of mind and social movement.

All of these conceptions of the region involve a spatial or areal approach to social phenomena. If we do not mean by the term "region" to call attention to the fact that we are looking at life in terms of the space dimension and the interest in location and position which that implies, then the term "region" has no intelligible meaning whatsoever.

It is well to begin this consideration of the spatial aspect of human social life by noting the fact that men and all that they work with and live with and create are located somewhere in space. It is helpful to us in understanding man's relationship to his fellow men to take into account his relationship to his habitat. His habitat is furnished to him, however, only in part by nature. It is in part also molded by himself. Nature sets the stage; but it is man that is the actor. Nature furnishes possibilities and sets limits. It is among these possibilities and within these limits that man can choose.

Climate, topography, resources, and other aspects of nature are not distributed evenly or uniformly around the world. The depiction of the characteristics of the natural landscape furnishes the most elementary factual basis for the delineation of regions.

Just as regions are physical facts of nature, so they are also facts of culture. Peoples, languages, forms of social organization, institutions, customs, and practices are also distributed in space. To point out their location and their movement is to call attention to a no less important fact of regionalism than the regional aspects of nature.

To define the areas on the earth's crust where certain kinds of human beings live in a certain degree of density, making their living through particular sets of activities, building particular kinds of structures, following particular kinds of customs, pursuing certain interests, meeting specific types of problems and seeking to solve them in specific ways, is a legitimate and necessary task which properly engages the scholarly labor of many persons throughout the world. Geographies and histories of specific areas, ethnographies, statistical compilations, linguistic atlases, and economic, political, sociological, and psychological studies are available in abundance, testifying to the fruitfulness of the labor that has gone into this description which is far from finished. While certain local units such as continents, nation-states, cities, and regions have become conventionally established in the course of scientific work for the purposes of collecting, classifying, and presenting this material, there is by no means universal agreement on what the most feasible areal units are for dealing with these data. The basis on which many previous areal units were carved out obviously is no longer suitable for our purposes. We are not collecting population statistics today for the area which once was the Holy Roman Empire; and in our attempt to obtain useful statistics on the population of metropolitan cities, we are attempting desperately to break through the difficulties which have hitherto kept us from getting comparable data on the suburban fringe surrounding central cities.

The fact of regionalism must therefore be recognized in determining the manner in which the student of social life collects the data that will enable him to discern the differences between areas which are worth recording. The determination of the regional units which promise to be most useful for the understanding and control of social life depends not merely upon the facts thus discovered but also upon the purposes for which they shall be used.

Moving from the consideration of regions as fact to the region as hypothesis, we note that scholars and scientists and men of imagination are not usually content with description alone. They also seek interpretation and explanation. The concept of region thus becomes a tool of research, a possible way of explaining the incidence and distributions which have been found to exist. Regionalism in this sense offers a theory accounting for the interrelations between things.

The doctrine that physical conditions of existence influence the character of peoples and their cultures has been so often set forth by notable figures in our intellectual history that it is often taken for granted as an established fact. The general hypothesis that men who live under different physical conditions become and are different sounds plausible enough, as does the more specific hypothesis that men who live differently think differently. In order to turn these rather general aphorisms into useful scientific hypotheses, however, we must ask: What correlations, if any, exist between specific cultural characteristics in a given area and specific conditions of nature, and what factors or processes account for this correlation? Culture, we can say with a good deal of assurance, does not spring directly or automatically from the soil or the atmosphere. It develops, rather, through an intricate process, and the most dissimilar cultural phenomena have been found to exist in the most similar environments, and vice versa. If any relations between natural habitat and social and cultural characteristics exist—and there is high probability that they do—they must be shown to exist in actuality. They cannot be assumed, and, unfortunately, the literature of regionalism has too frequently taken them for granted.

Moreover, while we may have sound reason for inferring interconnections between regional habitat and regional culture in the initial stages of man's conquest over and adjustment to nature, civilizations as they mature tend to emancipate themselves from the soil and the natural context out of which and in which they developed. It is well to remember that things may continue to exist for reasons other than those that brought them into being. The momentum of established institutions and habits is so great that often it requires a cataclysm to uproot them.

Not only must we take account of the impact of past history and practice, which may be quite autonomous of the dictates of nature (for nature, as has been pointed out, merely offers possibilities and sets limits), but we must be particularly alert to the profound influences of communication and movement through which a technology, an institutional form, an idea, or an ideal can be diffused widely throughout the world. Even if regional contexts between natural and cultural facts should become established in a given area, we must always, especially in modern times, reckon with the power of communication and transportation—with the mobility of men and ideas—to undo regions.

There is the third view of regionalism, which envisages it as a tool of administration, of control, and of planning. The region in this sense is a tool in social engineering. The delineation of such regions, to be effective, obviously cannot proceed without taking due account of the region as a fact and the region as a set of interrelations between facts. To do otherwise would be to seek to impose artificial areal patterns of formal control upon human relations, which have a tendency not to be bound by rigid lines. Moreover, as the studies of the National Resources Committee have so convincingly shown, various purposes require different areal scope, and it is difficult to find any single criterion that will satisfy the multiple demands of adequacy. Even if such a criterion or set of criteria could be found, the dynamics of life would soon make it archaic. Short of considering the whole world as a single region, which, of course, would be self-defeating, there is no other regional arrangement, of lesser scope, which will fully satisfy the many interests that clamor for recognition. The best we can do is to make the most reasonable compromises we can invent, which means weighting some functions more heavily than others, and to keep our lines of demarcation flexible enough so that they can be adjusted to changing needs and possibilities. It would be self-deceptive, however, to proceed as if the crude approximations we now make to an adequate regional arrangement were anything more than improvisations.

This is not to deny that, irrespective of their historical origin, the regional units that we construct for purposes of administration, planning, and social engineering may themselves result in the emergence of patterns which have important, and sometimes unforeseen, consequences. If we view such little countries as Luxembourg, Belgium, and Holland in the light of the tribal, dynastic, and historical factors that help account for their present independent position as nation-states, we may, of course, rationalize ex post facto the justification or inevitability of their independent existence. This, however, should not obscure the fact that they have such uniqueness as they possess and are afflicted as they are with problems as small independent nations, in large part, because they have had such a long experience of living under the particular administrative arrangement which separates them from each other by boundaries which in the light of present-day needs are utterly indefensible. If we were planning them anew, with a view to present-day conditions and problems, we probably would not retain them as separate administrative areas and independent political units.

There may have been a time when a better defense could be made for the independent existence of our forty-eight states than can be made today, but it is a fact that their independent existence for so long, with the resulting patterning and differentiation of life that has grown up between them, is today one of the strongest reasons for their continued independent existence. Surely, ideally speaking, a more economical and efficient arrangement of the territory comprising the United States of America could be devised today than that under which we are operating, but it is unnecessary to argue the futility of such a proposal, however practical it may be, in the face of the vested interests and the inertia which stand in the way. A system of law and administration, with its network of functional interrelations, once developed, comes to have great potency for its own self-continuance and for shaping many of the other aspects of the regional complex of life which it embraces.

There are, however, many factors at work which soften the sharp demarcation lines between administrative regions and which may be invoked to transform them into more realistically designed units to meet the conditions and problems of contemporary civilization. The arrival upon the scene of national labor organizations, engaged in collective bargaining on a national scale eventuating in nationwide contracts, tends to wipe out wage, income, and cost differentials that formerly marked one region off from others. The national income tax and national grants-in-aid, which redistribute part of the national income in accordance with regional needs, also national minimum-wage legislation, postal rates, mail-order houses, and many other instances which could be cited, tend to minimize differences in the ways of life of regions and weave the separate regions into a broader national living unit. The fact should, of course, not be overlooked that many vestiges of regional differentials continue to exist. Nor should we minimize the threat—if it be a threat—that a pluralistic pattern of civilization, comprising many unique regional forms of expression, is being gradually transformed into a more standardized national pattern.

Regionalism presents a fourth aspect as a state of mind, as a way of life, as a mode of collective consciousness, as a social movement, and as a cult. The three types of factors considered above do eventually combine to produce a settled way of life and a characteristic consciousness. People who live long enough under similar conditions might be expected to develop some similarity of traits. People who continue to live together under conditions of mutual interdependence and are subjected to the same influences from identical sources might similarly be expected to develop a sense of mutual interdependence and to share a sense of common belonging. Thus regions develop a conception of themselves and acquire a more or less stereotyped conception in the minds of others who think about them or who have relations with them. Out of this common mode of life grow a coalescence of interests and an identification with the symbols expressive of these common interests. This heightened regional sentiment and sense of belonging may be accentuated by conflict or rivalry with other regions. The differences between the South and the rest of the nation on the subject of civil rights tend to strengthen rather than to minimize the regional consciousness of the South, at least for the time being. Regional discriminatory freight rates and similar economic schisms make for regional definition of interests and states of mind which express themselves dramatically in regional political alignments. Regional sentiments may have their constructive uses in mobilizing for region-wide action, but they may also be perverted into regional chauvinism.

Regionalism may thus take the form of a social movement. The cultivation of the arts based upon regional themes or reflecting the regional atmosphere has in some parts of this nation resulted in the crystallization of regional "schools." Whether these regional schools in literature or the arts are the faithful expression of the regional way of life or whether they are an attempt motivated by the tourist trade to manufacture an artificial regional culture, is a question which the present writer is not competent to answer. In France, regionalism is not merely a sociocultural movement, but a strong political force based upon the protest of the provinces against the centralized control and dominant influence of the capital. In its extreme form, regionalism leads to isolation, parochialism, separatism, and secession. As a counterpoise to gigantism, to uniformity, to standardization, and to overcentralization it can have wholesome effects; but these legitimate aspirations can also degenerate into regional cultism and jingoism and lend themselves to exploitation by political and cultural demagogues.

In summary, then, regionalism is not one thing but many things. The failure to discriminate the many distinct factors that underlie the emergence and persistence of regions is a serious fault of present-day scholarship and research. It has led to the failure to distinguish between genuine and spurious regions. Areas of homogeneity have been mistakenly represented as areas of integration. It has been mistakenly assumed that physical regions also inevitably constitute economic, cultural, and political regions.

If the mark of a community is interdependence and the mark of a society is consensus, it follows that many areas which have been conceived as regions are neither communities nor societies, for they show no convincing evidence either of a common basis of existence or of a collective consciousness.

As a tool for the discernment of interrelations between habitat and culture the regional concept has great value, provided we do not assume what needs to be proved, namely that these correlations actually exist, and proceed to analyze the processes that account for these correlations. Regionalism, which is the way of viewing social life in areal terms, is, after all, only one possible perspective of human beings living together. To regard it as the only one leads to distortion of reality. As a one-factor explanation of the complexities of social life it can become a false and dangerous doctrine; but seen as a supplement to and corrective of other one-factor explanations— such as the economic, the sociocultural, and political factors—it can have great value.

Regionalism as a dogma can easily degenerate into a cult. As the basis for a social movement it offers a potent counteragent against the leveling influences of standardization, uniformization, and over-centralization. But it can also become a desperate and futile protest against the tides of progress which, stimulated by the technology of mass communication and mobility, make possible ever wider areas of integration of social life and thus have the potentiality of raising the level of human well-being by a wider sharing in the fruits of civilization. It is well to be aware of the regional aspect of human existence and to cultivate a sensitivity to regional influences.

It is important also to remember that there is no magic in the regional idea. It can lead to the falsification of the facts. It can become a futile effort to squeeze life into a rigid mold, and it can become a vain gesture to retard the integration of life on a wider and more inclusive scale.

BIBLIOGRAPHY

Blache, Paul Vidal de la. "Les Régions françaises," *Revue de Paris,* December, 1910.

Burgess, Ernest W. *The Urban Community.* Chicago, 1926.

Dickinson, Robert E. *City Region and Regionalism: A Geographical Contribution to Human Ecology.* New York, 1947.

Galpin, C. G. *The Social Anatomy of an Agricultural Community.* University of Wisconsin Agricultural Experiment Station *Bulletin 34.* Madison, 1915.

McKenzie, R. D. *The Metropolitan Community.* New York, 1933.

National Resources Committee. *Our Cities: Their Role in the National Economy.* Washington, 1935.

———. *Regional Factors in National Planning and Development.* Washington, 1935.

Park, Robert E., Ernest W. Burgess, and R. D. McKenzie. *The City.* Chicago, 1925.

Thünen, J. H. von. *Der Isolierte Staat in Beziehung auf Landwirtschaft und National-ökonomie.* Jena, 1826 and 1910.

Wirth, Louis. "Human Ecology," *American Journal of Sociology,* Vol. L (May, 1945), 483–88.

———. "Localism, Regionalism and Centralization," *American Journal of Sociology,* Vol. XLII (January, 1937), 493–509.

———. "The Metropolitan Region as a Planning Unit," in *Planning.* Chicago, American Society of Planning Officials, 1942.

———. "The Prospects of Regional Research in Relation to Social Planning," *Publications of the American Sociological Society,* Vol. XXIX (August, 1935), 107–14.

———. "Urbanism as a Way of Life," *American Journal of Sociology,* Vol. XLIV (July, 1938), 1–24.

Chapter 15

The Promise of Regionalism

Howard W. Odum

OUR final tasks in this symposium on American regionalism appear as necessary logical expectations from our previous discussions. To ask "What is the promise of regionalism?" and, by the same token, "What are the limitations of regionalism?" is to ask for a reasonable summary of the total findings, in so far as they can be stated within the framework of American regionalism. Yet our assumptions must go further in that they must comprehend sound theory as it applies to any society and especially as it applies to the regionalism of the Americas. Our assumptions are, further, that regionalism and special aspects of area studies will be increasingly important in the total world society of tomorrow.

More specifically, the promise of regionalism will depend upon the adequacy of our definitions of regionalism; upon the realism with which we define the region in terms of structure and function; upon our success in having these definitions accepted by professional students and leaders; upon the degree to which they can be made articulate in actual situations. That is, our definitions must provide, first, a construct for the conceptualization of regionalism as a multiple approach to the study of total areal-cultural situations, and second, as a tool for both research and planning through the integration of the several social sciences and some of the physical sciences and the action agencies available for practical work.

How important these definitions are may be seen by a glance at the contemporary concepts and practice of regionalism and planning, in contrast to their earlier genesis and meaning. Like other aspects of contemporary society, they have changed greatly. Both planning and regionalism had their beginning in localisms. Planning arose through the stages of concrete, planned communities, then towns, then cities, then planned metropolitan regions. Thus regionalism came to connote the metropolitan region, and for a long time the greater number of titles in any bibliography on regionalism had to do with metropolitan regionalism. The same was true with reference to planning. Now, on the contrary, social planning has become a major concept, symbolizing the best that the social sciences can do and connoting as well policies and philosophies of government. Equally, regionalism now calls for comprehensive definition capable of analyzing the regional structures in a diverse nation or world and serving as structional-functional pattern for both understanding and directing society with its increasing conflicts and needs for retaining cultural autonomies but also resolving differences in a total areal pattern.

How important some agreement on the meaning and function of regionalism is may be seen further from an examination of Louis Wirth's discussion of the limitations of regionalism. For by the very nature of his limited definitions, nearly all of which are now outmoded in the historical process and in the technological changes, regionalism is set back to localism or specialized ideology. Something of this same approach is apparent in some of the other papers, indicating strongly how the promise and limitation of regionalism must depend upon at least a comprehensive and fair examination of the many facets and a synthesis of authentic concepts and practices.

The promise of regionalism in America will depend further upon the extent to which we take advantage of current regional trends; upon the results of our many new efforts toward regional analysis and portraiture and our experiments in regional planning; upon the degree to which the United States maintains her historical heritage of a federation of states and the extent to which regional planning may be utilized to maintain balance in America of resources and people. These in turn will be conditioned by the extent to which decentralization becomes a mandate or a normal structural process, either because of the opportunity for increasing and distributing resources or because of the demands of an atomic age in the setting of threatened war and defense.

There are certain limited promises of regionalism, it is true, that are not primarily conditioned by all these factors. In such instances as the technical administrative aspects of the TVA, where the total situation must necessarily be administered through regional and subregional units, there can be no doubt of the need of regional strategy under any definition. So, too, where areal relations involve differentiation and integration as well as merely area study, to paraphrase Chancellor H. W. Chase, we have, if not regionalism, what would be the same as regionalism. For organic relationships in the space-time-evolution pattern are not much respecters of definitions and semantics. But even here we have to distinguish between that which concerns the area primarily and that which pertains to the area in relation to other areas, or to the place of the area in some total structure. In the United States, both historically and functionally, this is a matter of distinguishing between the old sectionalism, which features homogeneity in isolation and separatism, and the new regionalism, which features differentiation and integration in an ever flexible, complex, and conflicting changing social structure. Justice Brandeis foresaw the need for this distinction in 1936 when he wrote: "Your *Southern Regions* is a great satisfaction. *It is the necessary first step in grappling with our most serious problem!*"

This brings us to our first task in defining regionalism—to emphasize some of the things which regionalism is not, in terms of current popular misconceptions. And the first of these is the fallacy which identifies regionalism with localism or with areal homogeneities due primarily to isolation, either in space through lack of communication and extraregional relationships, or in time as in the case of primitive peoples. Thus in *Twentieth Century Sociology*, published as recently as 1944, and widely used by sociologists, Robert E. L. Faris writes: "The mobility and fluidity of the United States population, the diffusions and standardization of culture, and other influences of the sort, are having the effect of reducing the regional basis of differences in American culture. If this trend continues, as it appears likely to do, the interest in regionalism may become a historical subject." [1] This, however, is a limited interpretation of both regionalism and the facts of contemporary trends.

In contrast, note R. M. MacIver's characterization of modern society in his admirable *The More Perfect Union*. Pointing out the multiplication of conflicting groups, he says:

[1] Georges Gurvitch and Wilbert E. Moore (eds.), *Twentieth Century Sociology* (New York, 1945), 556, 557.

Many historical forces combine to make the relation of group to group the central issue of modern society. . . . Mankind has made great advances toward the solution of many of its ancient problems. But *this* problem is not only unsolved, it has become greatly aggravated. The aggravation has come in the train of technological and social change. The different groups —ethnic groups and culture groups and interest groups—becoming mobile, coming more into contact with one another and at more points, find far more occasion for clashes than in the simpler, more insulated, and more communized life of earlier days. . . . These conditions strengthen the natural tendency to groupbound thinking, the gravest peril in the social orientation of modern man. . . . The tendency itself is as old as human nature. . . . But modern organization has enormously extended its range and intensified its expression.[2]

Consider also the verdict of Robert Cooley Angell's study of contemporary communication processes, in which he points out how the widening range and speed of communication increase, rather than decrease, differences and conflicts. Whereas in earlier time hundreds and thousands of culture areas and their people were not only isolated and unknown to each other but content in their own subjective cultures, they now become an articulate and protesting and differing part of the new "One World." Angell even goes so far as to say "that many believe that the chances of world peace would be greater if we cut off communications between nations altogether."[3]

Or, to take another illustration, compare Northrop's notable *The Meeting of East and West,* in which he points out how each part of the Orient is coming to impress its existence and values upon the Occident. "This coming can be evil and dastardly as well as it can be benign and beneficent," says Northrop, depending upon "each knowing the other's values and interests as well as its own." Again, he says: "It is literally true that . . . what the one people or culture regards as sound economic and political principles the other views as erroneous, and what the one envisages as good and divine the other condemns as evil or illusory. The time has come when these ideological conflicts must be faced and if possible resolved. Otherwise, the social policies, moral ideals, and religious aspirations of men, because of their incompatibility one with another, will continue to

2 R. M. MacIver, *The More Perfect Union* (New York, 1948), 1–2.

3 Louis Wirth and others, *The World Community* (Chicago, 1948), 159.

generate misunderstanding and war instead of mutual understanding and peace." [4]

To take a concrete example notable in the United States, we might cite the oft-quoted assertion that as technology, science, communication, and standardization of fashion and customs increase, the different sections will tend surely to become more and more alike with less and less difference and conflict. But let us look at the situation in three instances. First, modern science, skills, and machinery, making it possible for the South to manufacture its cotton goods on a footing equal and often superior to that of traditional New England, increased competition and conflict. Or again, old New England mills move south; new textile mills and other industries flourish. New freight-rate equalization is protested by the Northeast. The uniformities of machinery and techniques do not make for uniformity in regional culture. Advances in the scientific study of human races, featuring the equality of races, have resulted in multiplied antagonisms, instead of brotherhood; and third, two wars, bringing thousands of Northern soldiers to the South, have resulted in many happy marriages and interregional acquaintances, but also in many conflicts and misunderstandings.

Now, on the usual assumptions, these epochal events ought to have brought New England and the Southeast a greater harmony of likeness and brotherhood. What happened? In 1949, Governor Chester Bowles of Connecticut urged New England manufacturers to raise a large amount of money to unionize Southern labor as a protective device, setting region against region. Governor Dewey of New York protests the equalizing of freight rates for the South on the premise that it would injure the East. What else has happened? The Dixiecrats and a new defense complex have temporarily set the South back fifty years; mass communication agencies have antagonized more than unified. And there is more articulate sectional ideological conflict than there has been since the turn of the century. This has resulted in what national columnists have referred to as "the hatred of the Southern influence in Congress" and in a split in the Democratic party. This is not only sectionalism of pure vintage but an excellent example of the need of modern regionalism.

All this symbolizes a second fallacy, which is that regionalism

[4] F. S. C. Northrop, *The Meeting of the East and West* (New York, 1946), *ix, 3*.

is essentially a movement in favor of priorities for a given region or is a divisive tool. To quote *Twentieth Century Sociology* again: "There is a general reform aspect visible and to some extent political thoughts of altering the administrative aspects of government to fit in with conceptions of regionalism. It is not always clear whether the aim is to *unify* groups of similar states, or to *divide* the nation along regional lines." [5] This is, of course, the sort of sectionalism that Frederick Jackson Turner feared for America, although he did not conceive of its remedy as being realistic regionalism, conceptualized as connoting the interrelationships between the several regions in the total nation, in which not only the nation would be stronger because of the integration of its strong diversified regions, but in which the very processes of interaction would constitute a central theme of the good society. Here it may be that we must frankly face one of the tests of regionalism, namely, whether we can substitute the new regionalism for the old sectionalism which Justice Brandeis designated as "our most serious problem."

Several of Louis Wirth's characterizations appear almost wholly in contradiction to the widely accepted tenets of the new regionalism. One is to identify it with the long-outmoded geographic determinant. Another is to identify it as a cult. A third is to identify it with a "one-factor theory" in contrast to its multiple approach through the integration of all the social sciences, literature, and other tools of study and planning. Regionalism, he writes, "must be recognized for what it is, namely, a one-factor theory, which taken alone will furnish only a one-sided, and hence distorted, picture of social reality." And again, ". . . it would also be naïve to fail to see that such simplistic interpretations of the complexities of social life have obscured other equally significant elements and have led to distorted versions of the complex and seemingly capricious course of human affairs." This is clearly a confusion of regionalism with some of the special concepts of geographic factors in society or with some limited literary picture. It is thus easy for those who do not keep abreast of developments to assume that regionalism is essentially divisive, or is synonymous with separatism, is opposed to centralization, and connotes a doctrine opposed to universalism. Here it must be emphasized that it is not regionalism *or,* but regionalism *and,* since the multiplication of diver-

[5] Gurvitch and Moore, *Twentieth Century Sociology,* 556.

gent groups and interests in the modern world and their discovery through communication render their integration through regional group units an absolute must in any construct of "One World" or "One Nation." It is not regionalism *or* universalism, but regionalism *and* universalism in such a construct as the United Nations, or the more limited construct of the unity of "The Americas," or even of "One America" envisaged in many recent writings about the United States.

We may illustrate this fallacy and approach our general definitions of regionalism by reference to both situations in America and world order that are reflections especially of new arrangements made necessary by the changing structure of contemporary society. Manifestly, the concept of "One World" is not only an abstract construct but a naïve one unless made real by some sort of analysis, classification, and integration of this extraordinary heterogeneous culture-world of situation and conflict. The best volume that has been offered on "One America" begins by emphasizing the fact that the United States is the most heterogeneous society in the world. Manifestly, there must be some sort of strategy for achieving the regional balance of man through organization and order.

This means we must re-examine many of the situations which re-emphasize the importance of the regional equality and balance of man. One is, of course, the world situation of international relations and achievements of science in the modern world. There can no longer be, in the accepted patterns of world order, isolation, separatism, exploitation, and wealth and abundance in some places and poverty and scarcity in others. This is not so simple as the one-way road of those who hold that the only way to peace is to give all peoples bread and shoes. There must be regional and cultural autonomy with financial help.

For, on the other hand, there has never been a time when the individual and group were so important; when the specialized values inherent in humanity were so articulate; and when the distinctive folk personalities of the peoples of the world clamored so much for recognition, appreciation, and participation.

It must be clear that the one undebatable strategy that is needed now is somehow to equalize opportunity and to redistribute resources and the good things of life to the end that we may have a genuine regional equalization and balance of men, instead of the powerful conflict of peoples in nationalistic and economic competition and war. The answers to these situations will be found in some major strategy which provides opportunity for each region to produce wealth and use it wisely within its own domain; yet, at the same time, it provides ample opportunity through technology and communication for the movement of people and resources to and from the region and provides opportunity for achievement outside as well as inside the region.

Involved in the regional balance and equalization of men are all the factors of culture, time, geographic and regional situations, and the carrying capacity of both economic and cultural arrangements. Yet the recognition and statement of the facts of inequality and balance, with the mere philosophical implications of moral obligations to correct the situation, often retard rather than promote enduring adjustment. Regional participation, first in the development of the regions and then in making the regions articulate with the total, becomes the first essential.

It seems clear that a great many, perhaps most, of the tragic situations of maladjustments, disorganization, and pathology, the world over, are due to regional inequalities and imbalance, whether in terms of the lack of natural balance between plant and animal resources or between man and nature, or whether in terms of the "haves" and "have-nots" in advanced civilization. Inherent in the waste and weakness of any region, in the conflict and lack of unity of the people, and in hazards of regional imbalance and pathology are still lurking dangers and dilemmas capable of swelling to flood-tide mass emotion, confusion, and revolution.

By the same token, the main strategy of planning will be found within the framework of regional balance and equality, which must include not only economic opportunity but cultural development and the thing now so much stressed, namely, justice in world organization. Yet, justice, admittedly basic to adequate and enduring arrangements, is not primarily something on the level of abstract morality or moralistic principles, but something on the level of the essential regional equality and balance of opportunity in the places where people live, set in the framework of national or world standards and interrelationships.

The assumptions of balance comprehend a great deal more than the technically defined balanced economy with its factors of balanced agriculture and industry and the other factors defined by the economists. These are assumed as basic to what Buckle a long time ago called order and balance in a country and what administrative authorities have been seeking in balanced parity programs. For the purposes of this syllabus the heart of regional balance is found in the search for equal opportunity for all the people through the conservation, development, and use of their resources in the places where they live, adequately adjusted to the interregional culture and economy of the other regions of the nation or the world. The goal, therefore, is clearly one of balanced culture as well as economy, in which there is equality of opportunity in education, in public health and welfare, in the range of occupational outlook, and in the elimination of handicapping differentials between and among different groups of people and levels of culture.

With reference to the functional definitions of regionalism, it is necessary to re-emphasize the fact that the primary objectives of regionalism are found in the end product of integration of regions more than in the mere study and development of regions themselves. Always, regionalism is a two-way concept. The region, yes, but primarily the region as a composite unit of the whole. The regions are studied and planned to the end that they may be more adequate in all aspects of resources and culture; yet regionalism itself is primarily interested in the total integration and balance of these regions. In American society, it is not so much a question of centralization of authority in conflict with states' rights as it is a problem of developing an adequate federalized central authority capable of achieving realistic decentralization. In other words, it is necessary to have some sort of world order or organization before the regions of the world can be integrated and before they can be co-operatively developed at their best. In American society there must be strong national character and organization before the nation can be made strong through the strength and integration of its diverse regions so that regionalism may supplant the older separatism and isolationism of sectional development.

So, too, the global situation with reference to races, minority peoples, and nationalities has made increasingly clear and vivid the organic significance of this regional quality and balance of the people everywhere. The assumptions of regional balance here are both culturally theoretical and administratively practical in so far as our key tasks must be to rediscover and catalogue all the culture groups; to recognize and give full credit to the folk personality of millions of people; to group geographic and culture areas into regional clusterings of practical administrative proportions; to give them representation; and, finally, to integrate them in the total order. This means that regional balance assumes a healthy diversity; that the way of each region is the way of its culture; and that each culture is inseparably identified with its regional character.

The formula for economic justice follows a similar structural-functional arrangement: first, opportunity for all people wherever they are to have access to resources, and especially to work, in the places where they live; second, opportunity for access to interregional resources and contacts, thus utilizing the modern technology of communication and transportation to equalize opportunity; and third, reasonable opportunity for migration, thus utilizing the universal process of mobility.

This regional quality of culture, behavior, and institutions is, of course, applicable to all regions of world society. The recognition of this regional quality of world society, of its imbalance, and of the need for regional arrangements for world organization and peace, while relatively new, is rapidly becoming the basic consideration in nearly all plans for stabilizing world organization. Symbolic of the swelling tide of regionalism is the conviction of Sumner Welles "that an effective international organization can be constituted only through the creation of regional systems of nations . . . under an over-all international body representative . . . of all regions." But in whatever instance, the point of emphasis is that it is through co-operative arrangement and the integration of diversified cultures that strength and stability are to be found.

Such a functional regionalism thus becomes a tool for attaining balance and equilibrium between people and resources, men and machines, the state and the folk. It is a tool of the democratic process in that it provides for the redistribution of the good things of life and of the opportunity to work within the framework of every people's geography and of their inherent cultural equipment. It is a tool for democratic world reconstruction in the postwar world, because it is through co-operative regionalism rather than economic nationalism that the society of tomorrow can be organized for human welfare instead of for military achievements. It is a tool for social planning, because it takes into consideration the rights, privileges, and resources of people and areas and stresses self-government and self-development as opposed to coercive centralized power, and also because it offers specific technical workable ways of developing and conserving resources for human-use ends. Since regionalism, as the opposite pole of sectionalism, isolation, and separation, is as much a part of international as of national affairs, it wants no self-sufficiency in economy. It wants no isolation and separatism, and it wants no totalitarianistic tragic imbalance between the folk and the state or between power and the people.

There are other assumptions of regionalism which it is not necessary to discuss in relation to our main premises. Assumed are the specifications of administrative regionalism, regional planning, regional mercantilism, and the science of the region which delineates regions, defines its terms, and sets up its adequate methods. There is the final point of emphasis, which is that regional balance is essentially synonymous with the ends of social planning. There are many satisfactory definitions of planning in terms of its attitudes. Two of these I like especially. One is a commonly used one which makes the objectives of planning the attainment of balance and equilibrium between competing factors and the substitution of effectiveness and abundance for inefficiency and scarcity. The other is one utilized by Patrick Geddes which assumes planning to be the bridging of the distance between science and knowledge and practical problems. In both of these, as in all efforts toward world regional balance, there are implied skills, science, and expertness, through which the facts and specifications are provided and through which then the distance is bridged.

There is another fallacy which defines regionalism as primarily a tool for decentralization or as areal arrangements for centers of administrative convenience. This, Hedwig Hintze defines as "a counter movement to any exaggerated or oppressive form of centralization."[6] Regionalism may, of course, serve the cause of decentraliza-

---

[6] "Regionalism," in *Encyclopedia of Social Sciences,* XIII, 208–18.

tion, which is often the incidence for regional arrangements; but in most instances this sort of decentralization serves as a device primarily for effective administration and often strengthens the hand of centralization. It must be clear that the mere establishment of regional centers of what are primarily administrative districts does not constitute regionalism. An illustration of this fallacy may be had in the case of the National Resources Planning Board in the New Deal era. This was an arrangement contrary to the earlier recommendations of the committee *Report* on *Regional Factors in National Planning and Development,* whereby nine cities were designated as field offices directed by personnel from the central offices.[7] The regions were without boundaries or specific service objectives; they had no prime purpose of serving their regions and no organic relation to their economic or political constituency. Thus, vast hinterlands were left as a no man's land. There was little if any regionalism in the field-office services—two in the Northeast, at New York and Baltimore; one in the great Middle States, at Cincinnati; one each in the Southeast and Southwest, at Atlanta and Dallas; two in the Northwest, at Denver and Omaha; and two in the Far West, at Portland and San Francisco.

Another form of this fallacy of administrative regionalism may be observed in the earlier proposed federal organization of National Planning through the administrative units of a total system of river valleys. Under the guise of multiple-purpose planning, which manifestly was a logical necessity for regional development, the system would make possible an almost completely centralized control of resources and economic processes in contradiction to such balanced and regionally related programs as the TVA.

There is, then, to name only one more fallacy, the early widespread usage of the term regionalism as synonymous with metropolitan regionalism, just as, recently, planning was often synonymous with city planning. Up until the late nineteen-thirties perhaps the greater part of the bibliographies of regionalism and planning were catalogued as relating to metropolitan regionalism and urban planning.

The development of regionalism in this respect is similar to that of social planning. That is, each had its genesis in specifications

---

[7] P. 159 of the *Report* published in December, 1935.

relating to the development of the urban areas from which it developed into the wider area involving principles and policies of
organization and control. From concrete specifications of town
planning, social planning came to involve matters of democracy and
freedom of individual endeavor or economic competition. Few
people now make city planning synonymous with social planning;
yet there is still considerable confusion of metropolitan regionalism
with the larger concept of regionalism and its new dynamics of cultural development. This earlier metropolitan regionalism conformed
more nearly to the tenets of sectionalism, since its objectives were
primarily directed toward the development of the city, regardless of
the welfare of surrounding regions.

In the new or metropolitan regionalism, however, often may be
found one of the most promising developments of all regionalism
in America in that its objectives include, not just the development
of cities and metropolitan areas, or not just any haphazard decentralization program, but concentration of certain developments
which utilize and distribute the resources of the region and therefore constitute regionalism in the best sense of the word.

We now come to three more positive aspects of our discussion.
The first two have to do with the definitions of regionalism and the
region. The third has to do with ways in which the promise of regionalism in America may be anticipated. Since previous papers have
already presented a competent catalogue of varied concepts and characterizations of regionalism and the region, and since we have presented full-page catalogues of both in *American Regionalism*,[8] our
task is to undertake here a general definition of regionalism in terms
of a theoretical concept, so well grounded in empirical observations
as to provide both a scientific frame of reference for analysis and a
functional approach to the dynamics of ongoing contemporary so
ciety. With reference to the region, our task is to define the region
in such specific and technical terms as will be adequate for the uniform scientific study and planning of regional and national development. This definition must be twofold. One is in terms of a theoretical construct; the other is in terms of the major composite, multiple-

[8] Howard W. Odum and Harry Estill Moore, *American Regionalism* (New York,
1938), 3, 179.

purpose, areal-cultural unit. This means that we must clearly designate subregions and special administrative areas to fit in with our total areal-cultural situation.

Our general construct must also be adequate for the co-operative efforts of all the social sciences, and our specific definitions of the region must be useful for planning agencies of whatever sort. These assumptions give regionalism a very important role in social research and social planning, so that it appears to be the only adequate device for analyzing the structure of the area-culture society, reflecting the Clark Wissler dictum that "evolution is regional" and the only practical working strategy for the functional dynamics of the new all-world society.

Regionalism is, therefore, an areal-cultural concept on a higher level of generalization than a mere uncritical miscellany of disconnected ideologies. It is essentially a synthesis of differentiation and integration, within the framework of homogeneities and diversities, following the historical process of periodic alternating between the particularist trend of multiplying culture areas and the universalist trend toward consolidation and integration of areas and culture. The spatial and cultural generalizations, therefore, are also correlated with the time element in some such stabilizing processes as are reflected in the ecological adaptation of man to geographical areas. The larger frame of reference for the conceptualization of regionalism is to be found in the construct of the structural-functional reference of total society or the whole, somewhat after the manner of Talcott Parsons' structural-functional theory of relations between the parts and the whole in the total system of society.

If this burdened attempt to define regionalism as the conceptualization of the area-culture structure of society seems to be a sort of theoretical end in itself, its real objective, nevertheless, is to consolidate the efforts toward area study and regionalism and to lay the basis for a realistic science of the region. This must provide concrete regional delineations which take into consideration the organic human-culture regional areas, the geographic factors of spatial relations, the political factors of organization and control, and the more recent technological aspects of communication and atomic potentialities. This appears to be a well-nigh impossible task. The beginnings, however, are available in the testing of certain premises of regionalism as applied to the measurement and development of American society. This test, of course, as in the case of all science, will be an approximation in accordance with the multiple and complex factors already enumerated in the areas of geographic, physical, cultural, political, and historical backgrounds. The first major problem will be the scientific, practical, and flexible delineation of regions and their effective utilization for the greatest number of purposes and with the smallest possible number of conflicts.

The first concrete problem is to be sure that adequate statistical methods applied to a reasonable number of major indices be employed for the delineation of regions within this total framework of cultural, historical, and physical backgrounds already mentioned. For the problem of delineation, recent advances in statistical methods offer more flexible and more objective procedures than have previously been employed for determining areas of maximum homogeneity with respect to any number of indices. The methods proposed for maximizing the homogeneity of states within regions will involve the application at several levels of the factor analysis or principal-component techniques for the combination of series of single indices into composite indices. The steps in such procedures include selection of the major types of information to be synthesized, selection of subgroups within the major groups, selection of the series of measures for each subgroup, combination of series into subgroup indices, combination of subgroup indices into group indices, and combination of the group indices into a final composite index for regional delineation.

In so far as the major tenet of regionalism holds for the United States—that is, that homogeneous major regions do exist—the above methods will delineate them. The methods are not rigid, however, and their reduction of variables provides a simple and convenient end result which may then conveniently be used in combination with nonstatistical criteria, especially in the allocation of border states. Or the composite index may be used with other data in further statistical work. A certain flexibility in choice of groupings according to the index would provide a minimization of regional lines cutting across administrative district lines in a great number of sets of administrative districts already existing.

Keeping in mind the uniformities necessary for scientific analysis and planning and the extraordinary confusion which now exists as the result of haphazard development of the concept of regionalism in America, our first task will be to give accurate definitions and postulates, to limit the number of terms, and to procure the acceptance and use of the same terms for measurement and delineation by all groups of scientists, just as scientists in the fields of mathematics, chemistry, and medicine accept the same symbols, terms, and indices wherever used and for whatever purpose. Such a scientific terminology will enable uniform studies, uniformity and comparableness of data, uniformity in administrative procedures, simplicity and effectiveness in the comprehensive over-all science of the region.

For these purposes it seems possible to utilize no more than five standard terms or measures: the region, the district, the subregion, the state, and the zone.

The "region" in the United States, for purposes of scientific delineation and practical planning, is a major, composite, multiple-purpose, group-of-states societal division of the nation, delineated and characterized by the greatest possible degree of homogeneity, measured by the largest practical number of indices available for the largest practical number of purposes and agencies, and affording the least possible number of contradictions, conflicts, and overlappings. The outer bounds of the major region will always comprehend the total subregions or districts delineated for special purposes.

The "district," for the purpose of scientific delineation and practical planning, is a subdivision of the major region, delimited and characterized by necessary homogeneity for functional, administrative purposes, allowing for flexibility and for as many districts as varied functional, governmental, or administrative agencies may need. The outer bounds of districts in every region must coincide with those of the major region, and the total of all measurements of all districts must add up to the total for the major region. Wirth complains that areas homogeneous in some traits and suitable for administrative purposes in one phase are not suitable for others. This is self-evident but is easily adjusted by uniformities of classification easily defined.

The "subregion" is of two sorts. One of these is primarily what is usually called the "natural" subregion, which is characterized by homogeneity with regard to certain physiographic character or traits. Natural subregions will ordinarily be of three sorts: those determined by geologic factors, those determined by climatic factors, and those determined by topographic factors. In these subregions, as primarily subdivisions of the total nation, overlapping boundaries of states, are found adequate composite measures and tools to overcome the artificiality of states. There is a secondary type of subregion, also overlapping state and district boundaries, which may be delineated according to homogeneity of socioeconomic factors for the purposes of analysis and practical administration and planning. Illustrations are metropolitan regions and rural regions. Woofter, Hagood, and Mangus have presented scientific methods of delineation, which have been utilized by various census studies.

The "state" is one of the forty-eight standard, constitutional, political divisions of the United States. Its definition is fixed and invariable, and it becomes an organic, structural, and functional part of the nation because of its constitutionality and the complex legal, political, and sovereign heritage. It is an essential basic unit also because of its necessity and facility for statistical and other measuring purposes. For the present, the state must remain a technical unit of measurement in the composite region.

The "zone," for the purpose of scientific delineation and planning, is a local area created by legislation primarily for the purposes of utilization and control of natural resources in relation to conservation and human-use ends. The zone is included and defined here primarily to indicate that the term is not to be used indiscriminately as a general area or division, but that it has come to have definite, technical, specific meaning. It is essentially a tool for local planning rather than for regional analysis or planning.

The application of this approach can apparently be best effected by delineating a certain number of major regions in the United States, determined on the above bases and accepted by governmental agencies. There is general agreement that this present chaotic system affords no uniform tools for analysis or planning. It is generally agreed that the number of major regions should be no fewer than six and no more than twelve, eight to ten being the most frequently designated number. The United States Department of Commerce and many minor groups have experimented with the six- to eightfold regional delineation utilized in *American Regionalism* and *Southern Regions*. Conferences with administrative heads in Washington have indicated a desire to set up more uniform and authentic regions so that this approach is not without considerable empirical support.

We may now catalogue briefly some of the ways in which the immediate promise of regionalism, on the evidence of trends other than those already indicated, may be related to the assumptions of this paper. Aspects of these have been discussed and implied in previous papers of this symposium; yet a sort of summary reference is needed to test the validity of most of our assumptions.

With reference to the promise of regionalism in American policy and development of the immediate future, I list a half-dozen specific opportunities—

First in the order of public priority, information and service in the development, utilization, and distribution of knowledge for war and defense. The regional decentralization report of the President's Committee is documentary evidence. There is nowhere any doubt of the necessity for a better regionally balanced economy and strategy of production and defense.

Second, the same sort of research and service for resource development for normal times in the effort to enrich each region, to increase its taxable incomes and contribution to the nation, as well as to augment the wealth and welfare of its own people.

Third, special research and planning with reference to new river-valley regions, and in particular the Missouri River Valley and the Columbia River Valley proposed projects, now imminent.

Fourth, the rearrangement of the national superhighway system to make possible the utilization of resources for both war and peace. The proposed plans provide for more than 50 per cent of the mileage to be in the Southeast and Southwest, making also available the great resources of the Gulf ports.

Fifth, regional representation in the proposed Federal Research Foundation. This, also, is a generally accepted requisite for the full development of resources and personnel.

Sixth, the establishment of new, dynamic national planning agencies in the framework of state and regional structures. The following Work Memorandum of the Institute for Research in Social

Science, University of North Carolina, illustates the fundamentals and specifications involved in a sort of "ideal type."

ADMINISTRATIVE LEVELS OF SOCIAL PLANNING AGENCIES IN AMERICAN DEMOCRACY

CONTINUING THE DEMOCRATIC PROCESS THROUGH NATIONAL, STATE, REGIONAL, AND LOCAL PLANNING AGENCIES AS ORGANIC UNITS OF TOTAL AMERICAN PLANNING

THE UNITED STATES PLANNING AGENCY (the State and Regional Agency inherent in the total)

Constitution. Authorized by Congress as a regular constitutional form of procedure. Appropriations from Congress to include cooperative arrangements with State and regional agencies on the basis of precedents of federal services to agriculture, highways, public health, social security. A major agency implying the highest prestige and most distinguished service. Members nominated by the President and approved by Congress.

Personnel. Nine members whose qualifications correspond to members of the Supreme Court, heads of major commissions, or members of the Cabinet. In general, major parties represented and one member from each of the regions and one or more at large. A central office with a staff of research and planning experts and adequate administrative and secretarial service.

Function. (1) To insure a continuous scientific inventory of the state of the Nation and to provide essential information for the President, the Congress, the Supreme Court, and special needs; to coordinate research and approximate a clearing house; to reduce overlapping and economize on congressional committee investigations.

(2) To act as buffer between the President and the other branches of government and to provide a safeguard against overcentralization and power through government by persons.

(3) To act as buffer between the national government and the States and regions, and provide the necessary federal centralization necessary to effective decentralization.

THE STATE PLANNING AGENCY (the Federal and Regional Agency inherent in the total)

Constitution. Authorized by the State legislature as a regular constitutional form of procedure. State legislation to provide for cooperative arrangements with national, regional, and local planning agencies. A major agency implying the highest standards of public service. Members appointed by the governor.

Personnel. Nine members constituting a board large enough to insure a working quorum and adequate representation of the State; small enough to guard against a promiscuous council. Not more than four to be heads of State departments. A central office with small staff of research experts and planning technicians.

Function. (1) To provide information for the governor and different divisions of State government; to coordinate research and approximate a clearing house; to reduce overlapping and economize on State legislative committee investigations.

(2) To act as buffer between the governor and house of representatives and other branches of government and to provide a safeguard against overcentralization and power through government by persons.

(3) To act as buffer between the governor, counties, cities, and local government; and to cooperate with the regional, national, and local agencies.

THE REGIONAL PLANNING AGENCY (the State and Federal Agency inherent in the total)

Constitution. Authorized by the national and State legislation creating their planning agencies. A major regional agency with membership composed of ex-officio members of each State planning agency in the region.

Personnel. One ex-officio member from each State and planning agency; one ex-officio member from each regional planning or interstate compact group already functioning, such as Tennessee Valley Authority; one member ex-officio from the United States Planning Agency; one member at large. A central office with an executive officer and secretarial and administrative assistance.

Function. (1) To provide a clearing house of conferences and procedures, enabling the States within the region to keep mutually informed and to avoid conflicting procedures.

(2) To act as a buffer between the States, on the one hand, minimizing the trends toward extreme State rights and interstate barriers, but, on the other, also advising and protecting individual States in fundamental matters.

(3) To act as buffer between the federal, centralized government and the individual States; to avoid conflict between States and federal authorities and to create wholesome understanding and relationships between the States and Federal Government.

(4) To cooperate with the United States Planning Agency in special planning and development involved in river valleys, water resources, and other areas overlapping State boundaries.

THE COUNTY PLANNING AGENCY

Constitution. Authorized by the State legislature as a regular constitutional form of procedure. Board created through an enabling act from the State and elected by the County Commissioners, County Board, or other county governing body. A major agency in the public services, implying in personnel and services the highests standards of all departmental divisions.

Personnel. Nine members constituting a board large enough to insure a working quorum and adequate representation of the country; small enough to guard against a promiscuous council. Not more than four should be ex-officia members of the County Board, with the recommendation that the heads of the County Public Health, Public Welfare, and Public Education be members. A central office with secretarial and technical assistance.

Function. (1) To provide essential information for the different county divisions of services; to coordinate research and approximate a clearing house; to reduce overlapping and economize on State legislative committee investigations.

(2) To provide mutual cooperation of the county with State, district, city, or other county planning agencies.

(3) To cooperate with the regional, national, State, and district agencies on problems of intra-State concern.

THE DISTRICT PLANNING AGENCY (where a group of counties elect to combine their planning efforts)

Constitution. Authorized by the State legislature as a regular constitutional form of procedure. Optional appropriation from the State legislature to include cooperative arrangements with county and city planning agencies. A major agency in the public services, implying in personnel and services the highest standards of all departmental divisions.

Personnel. One ex-officio member from each participating county or city (as defined) within the district. A central office with secretarial assistance.

Function. (1) A procedure enabling the counties within the district to cooperate and to avoid conflicting procedures.

(2) To provide mutual cooperation of the district with State, county, city, and other planning agencies.

(3) To cooperate with the regional, national, State, district, county, and city planning agencies on problems of intra-State concern.

THE TOWN OR CITY PLANNING AGENCY

Constitution. Authorized by the City Council, Board of Aldermen, or other local governing board, as a regular legislative form of procedure, in accordance with the constitutional procedure set up by the State legislature. Legislation to include cooperative arrangements with county and state planning boards. A major agency in the public services, implying in personnel and services the highest standards of all departmental divisions.

Personnel. Nine members appointed by the mayor, constituting a board large enough to insure a working quorum and adequate representation of the city. Not more than four members should be heads of city departments, the other members to be drawn from the city leaders at large. A central office with secretarial and technical assistance.

Function. (1) To provide essential information for the mayor and different divisions of the city government; to coordinate research and approximate a clearing house; to reduce overlapping and economize on State and county committee investigations.

(2) To provide mutual cooperation of the city with State, district, county, and other city planning agencies.

(3) To cooperate with the regional, national, State, county, and district agencies on problems of intra-State concern.

Outside the field of governmental efforts, the opportunity for regional and interregional university co-operation in research into the changing structure of American society is almost unlimited. The special regional features include a departure from the usual Social Science Research Council programs in that each university, or universities in the general regions, would pursue the same methodology into the same areas of research analysis, rather than for each to feature different aspects. Implied are the interregional conferences and the testing of co-operative methods. The result would be a body of scientific information on the state of the nation made available and scientific because of this new integration and methodology. Rupert B. Vance has pointed up some of the advantages of the regional approach to research.

Indicative of the American trend toward regional analysis and consciousness of the total picture of composite regionalism is a new and vast literature as source materials. Two of the most significant regional series of books, the "Rivers of America Series" and the "Folkways Series," may well illustrate. The thirty-eighth "River" book has appeared in a series rich in regional portraiture of the total culture. For instance, in the Northeast there are the St. Lawrence, the Delaware, the Brandywine, the Hudson, the Kennebec, the Winooski, and the twin rivers—the Raritan and the Passaic. In the Southeast are the lower Mississippi, the Kentucky, the Tennessee, the Arkansas, the Shenandoah, the Suwannee, and the James. In the Middle States are the Illinois, the Chicago, the upper Mississippi, the Wisconsin, the Sangamon, and the Wabash. In the Southwest is the lower Mississippi. In the Northwest are Powder River, the Red River, the Kaw, the Missouri, and the Colorado. In the Far West are the Sacramento, the Salinas, the Humboldt, and the Columbia.

Through the "Folkways Series" it is possible to map much of the total nation in folk-regional units, shading like culture areas into each other in a fascinating fabric with warp and woof of subregional cultures. Here are some of the quilted patterns: *Golden Gate Country, Town Meeting Country, North Star Country, Deep Delta Country, Far North Country, Mormon Country, Palmetto Country, Desert Country, Piñon Country, Short Grass Country, Ozark Country, Blue Ridge Country,* and *High Border Country.*

In addition to these, there are perhaps no fewer than a baker's dozen other series, including those on lakes and mountains, cities, states, special culture areas, folklore, architecture, and travel. Still other scores of books discuss how the people live, where they live, what they do, what they say, and what they sing.

Finally, the bibliography of regional literature is assuming extraordinary range and proportions. This is illustrated briefly by the appended notes and references and by the count of lists which we have catalogued into the thousands. Reinforcing this bibliography are similar lists on world regions and regionalism which are constantly widening their scope.

We began by saying that the promise of regionalism must depend largely not only upon our definitions and conceptualizations but upon their acceptance. Louis Wirth's paper on the limitations of regionalism has eloquently illustrated this test. Both because such definitions and conceptualization have not been accomplished and because most scholars and planners are afraid to venture too far out, the resulting scepticism and opposition are but logical products. A part of this fear is based upon the thought that such conceptualization as we have called for is too complex and involves too much interdisciplinary co-operation. That is, of course, exactly what is intended, and yet it does demand a wider range of knowledge and a more mature experience than most social scientists are willing to underwrite. The other fear is that we shall get into deep water quickly. This is also a truism, but we ought to learn to swim. Nevertheless, our conclusion at this time must be conservative on any very large immediate promise of regionalism, except in the gradual evolutionary process and in the logical developments made necessary by the changing structure and crises of our civilization.

There is yet one other consideration which may be interpreted either as a hazard or as a promise. It is in the way of the American tradition. One aspect of this goes back to the historic sectionalism with, on the one hand, Frederick Jackson Turner's warning about sectionalism in the United States, and, on the other hand, James Truslow Adams' recording of American tragedy. America sometimes does not seem any more capable of grasping the meaning of regionalism and making out of it a great Americanism than it did in the days just before the Civil War. There are many students who feel that the conception of regionalism is good and effective for general cultural matters, but that in politics and economics it reverts back to sectionalism. It is this hazard which, so far from seeming to negate the over-all conceptualization of regionalism, emphasizes the importance of America's incorporating a genuine regionalism into her structural development.

This theoretical background is immediately important in two ways. One is in the recognition that our federal system gets its power by the consent of the people in its total hinterlands. The needs and problems arise from the people; the financial support and the consent of the governed come from the people; the very education of the leaders to whom the people entrust their government—this comes from the people. Skills and direction come from the top brackets of leadership and from federal and centralized government, thus putting the supreme obligation on a Confederation of States to serve all the people and regions and to integrate them in the total national balance.

Here again, organic regionalism, in the sense of the people and their culture, living close to the soil and their resources, is a supreme measure of the power of the nation. Always and everywhere society has evolved from the folk regional cultures, conditioned fundamentally by the interaction of the folk and nature and then of the folk and their own cultural interrelationships, expanding out and growing from the folk regional group to the larger civilization. Culture has been to the folk what personality has been to the individual; and the conservation and strengthening of character of people and culture in the places where they live, together with opportunity for their freedom in interregional expansion, have constituted a normal process of functional growth. The stubbornness which refuses to recognize this sort of thinking is like the modern technician's insistence that there is no such thing as ecology because he doesn't see it work and doesn't understand it.

Finally, however, there is another part of the American tradition which both gives a mandate for regionalism and reflects a record of great regional development. As indicated in our earlier discussion, modern technology and the world of intercultural relationships accentuate the importance of this aspect of "One America," to be made up of strong differentiated groups, integrated into the total nation.

In some ways, our starting point rather than our closing point might well have been said to be regionalism as reflected in the first principles of Americanism. A part of the American dream of equal opportunity has always been soundly bottomed in the great range and variety of that part of the North American continent which came to be known as the United States of America. It was in the regional quantity and quality of this continent that the first plantings and the later fruits of American democracy set the incidence of the American way of life as distinctive from that which had gone before or that which was European. This regional nature of America was both physical and cultural and set the stage for a nation that was to be strong because of the successful integration of its great diversities. The supreme task in this integration was to be the achieving of a realistic and adequate regional balance of America.

It must be recalled that realistic Americanism was grounded in the physiographic measures of the continent and in the adaptation of the people to the places where they lived. This was true not only because of the extraordinarily wide range and kinds of natural phenomena but because of the sheer size of an America so vast that all Western Europe, so to speak, could be lost in her mountain fastnesses or river valleys or great plains. In this happy convergence of a superabundance of natural wealth and human wealth was to be found the measure of the nation's extraordinary strength and power, as well as her growing pains and sectional conflict.

BIBLIOGRAPHIC NOTE

GENERAL AND SPECIAL BIBLIOGRAPHIES

The primary emphasis of this paper is twofold. One is the emphasis upon regionalism as stated in the subtitle of Odum's and Moore's *American Regionalism:* "A Cultural-historical Approach to Natural Integration." The other is the conceptualization of regionalism as a structural-functional basis for the study and direction of contemporary society. In both of these, the need for general definitions and for specific uniformities in terminology of regions, subregions, states, and districts is essential to scientific work. Our bibliographies, therefore, need to fall into two groupings. The first presents vivid and popular pictures and interpretations of America's flexible regions classified according to a sixfold regional delineation. The second has to do with theoretical concepts, on the one hand, and with practical regional-planning concepts, on the other.

Such a bibliography, intended primarily as an illustration of the range and promise of regionalism, makes no attempt to give adequate representation to four areas of regionalism in which bibliographies are so specialized as to require more than general listing. These are historical references, literary regionalism, economic geography, and world regionalism.

In the case of historical references, it is assumed that history textbooks, in the normal narrative of American development, will follow the westward expansion and sectional developments which are reflected in chronological order. The first "Great Northwest," as told, for instance, in Beverly Bond's *The Civilization of the Old Northwest,* is now more nearly our Middle America or Middle West, while the "Great Southwest," which was Tennessee and Kentucky westward, is now no more than a part of the Southeast. Three volumes by Frederick Jackson Turner are usually considered basic, namely, *The Frontier in American History, The Significance of Sections in American History,* and *The United States, 1830–1850, The Nation and Its Sections.* William E. Dodd's *Woodrow Wilson* presents one of the most vivid accounts of the westward expansion of wealth. There are many "Wests" in historical story, among which Theodore Roosevelt's *Winning of the West,* in four volumes, has been widely utilized. Three standard major texts may be used to illustrate the regional nature of American history in simple routine records. We have already listed the Beards' *Rise of American Civilization.* "The History of American Life" series, especially Vols. VII and VIII by Arthur Schlesinger and Dixon Ryan Fox, are excellent examples. *The Growth of the American Republic,* a two-volume work by S. E. Morrison and H. S. Commager, has a great deal to say about regional development. Chapter 2 of Henry Bamford Parkes' *Recent America: A History of America since 1900* is devoted to "The Regions of the United States." There are many special studies from which regional aspects may be sought, such as W. E. Woodward's *The Way Our People Lived: An Intimate American History,* or

D. E. Crouse's *The Ohio Gateway;* but for the most part the abundance of historical references must be searched out. This note is added primarily to indicate the abundance of material and its logical place in regional study.

In literary regionalism, there is an abundant but specialized source material in regional fiction and biography. Both of these require very specialized and skilled inquiry and arrangement. Anna Green Smith at Chapel Hill has compiled a volume on *Fifty Years of Southern Writing*, and Frank Burtner is undertaking to compare the other regions in these respects through cataloguing and interpreting regional fiction and biography. In the Southeast and the Southwest alone there are more than one thousand regional novels published by national publishing houses.

Below are listed one or two titles in economic geography from each of the two most prolific writers in this field, Russell Smith and Wallace Atwood. More specifically, Smith's *Men and Resources* provides the best subregional arrangement of the United States that I have seen. The popular writings as well as the textbooks of these authors constitute a field in themselves. Also listed are special regional sociogeographical works, but there are also many minor studies to be listed. Carl Sauer's *Man in Nature* is representative of the anthropogeographical, as is Edwin Embree's *The Indians of America*. Many textbooks on economics deal with regional aspects, for example, *Economic Development in the United States*, by C. M. Thompson and Fred M. Jones; but, like the above categories, references must be searched out and arranged for specialized purposes.

Even more difficult is the task of searching out references on world regions. One such book, *European Ideology*, by Feliks Gross, includes a chapter on "Regionalism and Separatism." Sydney Lester at Chapel Hill is compiling and analyzing such a bibliography and finds it necessary to examine several thousand titles.

Books on American Regionalism

Our first series is one of books concerning the general aspects and backgrounds of regionalism. Beginning with Odum's and Moore's *American Regionalism*, other titles that seem to be needed to introduce the subject are R. H. Knapp's *American Regionalism and Social Education*, J. F. Dewhurst's *America's Needs and Resources*, S. G. Branford's *An Introduction to Regional Surveys*, C. C. Fagg's *An Introduction to Regional Surveying*, and Victor Branford's *The Regional Survey as a Method of Social Study*. The list is almost inexhaustible: "Regional Social Study and Research," Chapter 5, pp. 81–89, of *An Introduction to Social Research*, by Howard W. Odum and Katharine Jocher; *Regional Sociology*, by Radhakamal Mukerjee; *Outlines of American Regional Sociology*, by Carle C. Zimmerman; *Divided We Stand*, by W. P. Webb; *Attack on Leviathan: Regionalism and Nationalism in the United States*, by Donald Davidson; *Conference on Regional Phenomena* (1930), Social Science Research Council; *Culture of Cities*, by Lewis Mumford; *Patrick Geddes: Maker of the Future*, by Phillip Boardman; *The New Frontier: An Abstract of American Regionalism,* by W. D. Drake; *Regional Factors in National Planning and Development,* National Resources Committee; *Regional Planning,* Parts I–XI, National Resources Committee (and Planning Board); *Regionalism in France,* by R. K. Gooch; *A Regional Program for Social Studies,* by A. C. Krey; *The New Regionalism in American Literature,* by Carey McWilliams; *Regional United States,* by Hannah Logasa; *T.V.A.; Democracy on the March,* by David Lilienthal; *Studies in Regional Consciousness and Environment,* by I. C. Pate; *In Search of the Regional Balance of America,* by Howard W. Odum and Katharine Jocher; *The Building of Cultures,* by R. B. Dixon; *The Significance of Sections in American History,* by Frederick Jackson Turner; "Middle States Regionalism and American Historiography," Chapter 9 in *Historiography and Urbanization,* by E. F. Goldman; *The Regional Approach to National Social Planning* (Foreign Policy Association), by Howard W. Odum; *Social Ecology,* by M. A. Alihan; *Patterns of Culture,* by Ruth Benedict; *Human Ecology,* by J. W. Bews; *Geography in Relation to the Social Sciences,* by Isaiah Bowman; *Man's Adaptation to Nature,* by P. W. Bryan; *Animal Ecology,* by R. N. Chapman; *The Ecology of Animals,* by Charles Elton; *The Study of Man,* by Ralph Linton; *A New Regional Geography of the World,* by M. I. Newbigin; *The Geographical Pattern of Mankind,* by J. E. Pomphret; *Frontier Folkways,* by James G. Leyburn; *The Folkways of Yucatan,* by Robert Redfield; *The Environmental Basis of Society,* by Franklin Thomas; *The Geographic Factor,* by R. H. Whitbeck and O. J. Thomas; *Man and Culture,* by Clark Wissler; *Man and Weather,* by A. G. McAdie; *Civilization and Climate,* by Ellsworth Huntington; *Men and Resources,* by J. R. Smith; *The Climates of the United States,* by R. deC. Ward; *Soils and Civilization,* by Milton Whitney; *Cultural and Natural Areas of Native North America* and *The Configuration of Culture,* by A. L. Kroeber; *The Great Forest,* by R. G. Lillard; *Geopolitics,* by Robert Strausz-Hupe; *Generals and Geographers: The Twilight of Geo Politics,* by Hans W. Weigert; *The Earth and Man: A Human Geography,* by D. H. Davis; *Geography: An Introduction to Human Ecology,* by George Renner.

The second grouping features "The United States: All Regions" and includes *A Nation of Nations,* by Louis Adamic; *America's Tragedy,* by James Truslow Adams; *The American Spirit,* by Charles and Mary Beard; *Main Currents in American Thought,* by Vernon L. Parrington; *America,* by Stephen Vincent Benét; *Inside U.S.A.,* by John Gunther; *America Moves West,* by Robert E. Riegel; *Leaves of Grass,* by Walt Whitman; *John Brown's Body,* by Stephen Vincent Benét; *Book of the States,* Council of State Governments; *The States* (a separate volume or more for each state, with other special volumes on cities and subregions), Writers' Project, WPA; *Drainage Basin Problems and Programs,* National Resources Committee; *Rocks and Rivers of America,* by E. W. Shuler; and *Songs of the Rivers of America,* by Carl L. Carmer. The *Saturday Review of Literature* has published special regional issues (1942–48) on America. Several publishers have issued series of regional books, individual titles of which are listed according to regions below. Some of these series are: "Rivers of America Series," Farrar and Rinehart; "American Lake Series," Bobbs-

Merrill; "American Mountain Series," Vanguard; and "American Folkways Series," Duell, Sloan and Pearce. Still continues the list of books dealing with all regions: *Regionalism in American Literature,* by Tremaine McDowell; *Literary History of the United States,* by Robert E. Spiller and others; *Guide to America,* edited by Elmer Jenkins; *Rich Land, Poor Land,* by Stuart Chase; *The American Woman,* by Ernest R. Groves; *American Regional Cookery,* by Sheila Hibben; *The American Scene,* by Henry James; *How America Lives,* by J. C. Furnas; *I Sing America,* by C. Lambert; *North, East, South, West,* edited by Charles Lee; *The Physiographic Provinces of North America,* by Wallace W. Atwood; *American Regionalism and Social Education,* by R. H. Knapp; *American Folk Art,* by Jean Lipman; *America in Fiction,* by D. W. Coan and R. G. Lillard; "Nationalism and Regionalism," in *Opinions of Oliver Allston,* by Van Wyck Brooks; "The Drama Regions of the United States," from *Native Roots,* by Felix Sper; *Look at America,* by Editors of *Look; Years of this Land,* by Herman Muelder and David M. Delo; *One Nation,* by Editors of *Look; Names on the Land,* by George Pippey Stewart; *The Significance of Sections in American History* and *The Frontier in American History,* by Frederick Jackson Turner; *The American Land,* by W. R. Van Dersal; *Regional Geography of Anglo-America,* by C. L. White; *Divided We Stand,* by Walter P. Webb; *Migration and Planes of Living,* by C. L. Goodrich; *National Security in Industrial Location,* by the President's Committee.

The third grouping is concerned with the Northeast and includes: Jonathan Daniels' *A Southerner Discovers New England;* A. H. Varrill's *The Heart of Old New England;* James Truslow Adams' *New England's Prospect;* Henry Beston's *The St. Lawrence;* E. W. Bard's *The Port of New York Authority;* Van Wyck Brooks's *The Flowering of New England;* H. S. Canby's *The Brandywine;* Carl Carmer's *The Hudson;* Samuel Chamberlain's *Ever New England;* R. P. T. Coffin's *The Kennebec;* Hulbert Footner's *Rivers of the Eastern Shore;* J. Gould's *New England Town Meeting;* A. F. Harlow's *Steelways of New England;* H. J. Lahne's *The Cotton Mill Worker;* Ferdinand Lundberg's *America's Sixty Families;* L. T. McKenney's *The New England People;* Francis Lichten's *Folk Art of Rural Pennsylvania;* G. C. Korson's *Coal Dust on the Fiddle;* David Marshall's *Grand Central;* Arch Merrill's *The Lakes Country;* C. Weygandt's *Down Jersey;* J. Mussey's *Old New England;* Arthur Pound's *Lake Ontario; The Berkshire Hills,* Writers' Project, WPA; Roderick Peattie's *The Berkshires* and *The Friendly Mountains;* A. B. Tourtellet's *The Charles;* Frederic F. Van de Water's *Lake Champlain and Lake George;* Frederick Way, Jr., *The Allegheny;* C. M. Webster's *Town Meeting Country;* H. E. Wildes's *Twin Rivers: The Raritan and the Passaic; Regional Planning, Part III, New England,* Natural Resources Committee; R. H. Knapp's *American Regionalism and Social Education;* and Lawrence Dame's *New England Comes Back.*

The fourth grouping features the Middle States: L. C. Wimberly's *Mid Country;* B. W. Bond's *The Civilization of the Old Northwest;* E. E. Calkins' *They Broke the Prairie;* St. Clair Drake's and H. R. Cayton's *Black Metropolis;* Howard Fast's *The American;* J. T. Flanagan's *America*

Is West; J. T. Frederick's *Out of the Midwest;* C. Harrison's *Growing up with Chicago;* Arthur Moore's *The Farmer and the Rest of Us;* P. Engle's *Always the Land;* D. B. Hayes's *Chicago: Crossroads of American Enterprise;* J. Graham Hutton's *Midwest at Noon;* James Gray's *Pine, Stream and Prairie;* Florence P. Jaques' *Canoe Country* and *Snowshoe Country;* D. E. Crouse's *Ohio Gateway;* James Gray's *The Illinois;* Harry Hanson's *The Chicago;* H. H. Hatcher's *The Great Lakes;* Walter Havighurst's *Upper Mississippi* and *Land of Promise;* H. C. Hubbart's *The Older Middle West;* L. M. Larson's *The Changing West;* W. A. White's *The Changing West;* M. M. Quaife's *Lake Michigan;* Fred Landon's *Lake Huron;* G. L. Nute's *Lake Superior;* H. H. Hatcher's *Lake Erie;* Edgar Lee Masters' *The Sangamon;* Stan Newton's *Paul Bunyan of the Great Lakes;* W. E. Wilson's *The Wabash;* and D. R. Fox's *Sources of Culture in the Middle West.*

The Southeast is the subject of the fifth group of books: Francis Simkins' *The South, Old and New;* Everett Dick's *Dixie Frontier;* Hodding Carter's *Lower Mississippi;* Thomas Clark's *The Kentucky;* Donald Davidson's *The Tennessee;* C. B. Davis's *The Arkansas;* Julie Davis's *The Shenandoah,* Cecile H. Matschat's *Suwanee River;* B. R. Niles's *The James;* W. J. Cash's *The Mind of the South;* Virginius Dabney's *Below the Potomac* and *Liberalism in the South;* Jonathan Daniels' *A Southerner Discovers the South;* John Dollard's *Caste and Class in a Southern Town;* R. L. Duffus and Charles Krutch's *The Valley and Its People;* John Temple Graves's *The Fighting South;* Charles Johnson's *Growing up in the Black Belt;* H. T. Kane's *Deep Delta Country* and *Lantern on the Levee;* Stetson Kennedy's *Palmetto Country* and *Southern Exposure;* A. G. Mezrick's *Revolt of the South and West;* William Haynes's *Southern Horizons;* H. C. Nixon's *Forty Acres and Steel Mules;* Howard W. Odum's *The Way of the South* and *Race and Rumors of Race;* C. E. Rayburn's *Ozark Country;* J. C. Campbell's *The Southern Highlander and His Homeland;* Jeanette Thomas's *Blue Ridge Country;* Roderick Peattie's *The Great Smokies;* Laura Thornburgh's *The Great Smoky Mountains;* Rupert B. Vance's *All These People* and *Human Geography of the South;* Charles Johnson's *Shadow of the Plantation;* J. Dollard's *The Deep South;* W. J. Robertson's *The Changing South;* Katharine D. Lumpkin's *The Making of a Southerner;* John V. Van Sickle's *Planning for the South;* Ellis Arnall's *The Shore Dimly Seen;* and Thomas J. Wertenbaker's *The Old South.*

The sixth group is about the Southwest: Ramon F. Adams' *Western Words;* C. O. Borg's *The Great Southwest,* R. N. Richardson's and Carl Coke Rister's *The Greater Southwest;* Daniel Long's *Piñon Country;* Howard W. Odum's *Southern Regions of the United States;* N. Otero's *Old Spain in Our Southwest;* E. Corle's *Desert Country;* E. E. Dale's *Cow Country;* J. Frank Dobie's *The Flavor of Texas;* Harvey Ferguson's *Home in the West;* E. Ferguson's *Our Southwest;* A. G. Harper's *Man and Resources in the Middle Rio Grande Valley;* Ladd Haystead's *If the Prospect Pleases;* D. C. Hogner's *Westward, High, Low and Dry;* Will James's *The American Cowboy;* J. A. Lomax's *Cowboy Songs and Other Frontier Ballads;* Winifred Kupper's *The Golden Hoof; The Sante Fe Trail,* Editors of *Look;* M. Major's *Southwest Heritage;* James Marshall's *The Sante Fe;* Hodding Carter's *The Lower Mississippi,* A. G. Mezrick's *Revolt of the South and West;* W. P. Webb's *The Great Plains;* and M. L. Becker's *Golden Tales of the Southwest.*

The seventh grouping is books of the Northwest: O. O. Winther's *The Great Northwest;* W. P. Webb's *The Great Plains;* A. G. Mezrick's *Revolt of the South and West;* Wendell Berge's *Economic Freedom for the West;* W. W. Atwood's *The Rocky Mountains,* J. Blanchard's *Caravans to the Northwest;* H. E. Briggs's *Frontiers of the Northwest;* M. S. Burt's *Powder River;* W. and L. W. Chapman's *Wilderness Wanderers;* E. Dick's *Vanguard of the Frontier;* H. R. Driggs's *Westward America;* J. M. Hanson's *The Conquest of the Missouri;* H. T. Kane's *North Star Country;* B. H. Kizer's *The U. S. Canadian Northwest;* D. M. Larson's *The Changing West;* F. L. Paxson's *The Last American Frontier;* J. P. Prichett's *The Red River Valley;* Wallace Stegner's *Mormon Country;* Nels Anderson's *Desert Saints;* Wallace Stegner's *The Big Rock Candy Mountain;* F. B. Streeter's *The Kaw;* R. A. Summers' *Conquerers of the River* (the Colorado); Eric Thane's *High Border Country;* C. M. Towne's and Edward Wentworth's *Shepherd's Empire;* Stanley Vestal's *Short Grass Country* and *The Missouri;* D. Woodbury's *Colorado Conquest;* E. Dick's *Sod House Frontier;* and *Regional Planning, Part I, Pacific Northwest,* Natural Resources Committee.

The eighth and final grouping features the Far West: Gertrude Atherton's *My San Francisco;* Julia C. Altrocchi's *The Old California Trail;* J. B. Appleton's *Pacific Northwest;* Gertrude Atherton's *Golden Gate Country;* Wendell Berge's *Economic Freedom for the West;* A. G. Mezrick's *Revolt of the South and West;* Archie Binns's *Northwest Gateway* and *The Land Is Bright;* Robert O. and Victoria Case's *Last Mountains;* Elizabeth Coleman's *Chinatown, U. S. A.;* Edwin Corle's *Desert Country;* J. Dana's *The Sacramento;* Anne Fisher's *The Salinas, Upside-Down River;* Otis W. Freeman's and Howard H. Martin's *The Pacific Northwest;* Vincent Ceiger's and Wakeman Bryarly's *Trail to California;* H. E. Maule's *Great Tales of the American West;* Carey McWilliams' *Southern California Country;* D. L. Morgan's *The Humboldt, High Road of the West;* R. L. Newberger's *Our Promised Land;* Roderick Peattie's *The Pacific Coast Ranges;* Lancaster Pollard's *Oregon and the Pacific Northwest;* N. C. Jacobs' *Winning Oregon;* R. A. Summers' *Cavalcade to California;* L. C. Rosten's *Hollywood;* F. Riesenberg, Jr., *Golden Gate;* M. M. Miller's *It Must be the Climate;* C. C. Dobie's *San Francisco's Chinatown;* C. B. Glascock's *Here's Death Valley;* George Putnam's *Death Valley and Its Country;* and Robert E. Riegel's *America Moves West.*